VALUING DIVERSITY

VALUING DIVERSITY

Buddhist Reflection on Realizing a More Equitable Global Future

PETER D. HERSHOCK

Cover art courtesy of Shutterstock.com

Published by
STATE UNIVERSITY OF NEW YORK PRESS
Albany

For information, contact
State University of New York Press
www.sunypress.edu

Production, Diane Ganeles
Marketing, Fran Keneston

Library of Congress Cataloging-in-Publication Data
Hershock, Peter D.
    Valuing diversity : Buddhist reflection on realizing a more equitable global future / Peter D. Hershock.
        pages cm
    Includes bibliographical references and index.
    ISBN 978-1-4384-4459-8 (hardcover : alk. paper)
    ISBN 978-1-4384-4458-1 (paperback : alk. paper)
    1. Buddhist ethics.   2. Difference (Philosophy)   I. Title.
    BJ1289.H47 2012
    294.3'5—dc23   2012000340

10 9 8 7 6 5 4 3 2 1

Contents

Introduction

D iversity matters. Whether it is in the context of talking about ecosystems, educational institutions, corporations, the media, or politics, diversity is now widely recognized as something positive and worthy of being both preserved and actively pursued.

This has not always been the case. Indeed, it is only quite recently that "diversity" came to connote, not just factually manifest differences, but also the *valuable* presence of difference. The first usage in this sense was in connection with the scientific correlation of species diversity with ecosystem vitality and resilience. Roughly a half century ago, this positive conception of diversity began being generalized through a confluence of social, philosophical, and political movements insisting on the productive *salience of difference*: the women's, anticolonial, and civil rights movements; deconstructionism and postmodernism; and the advent of identity politics and multiculturalism.

Over the intervening decades, however, although "diversity" has become an increasingly important part of the critical lexicon, it has remained relatively undertheorized as a synonym for variety. In the contexts of education and politics, for example, diversity has continued to be seen as an essentially quantitative measure of inclusion for those who differ from the majority by reasons of race, culture, religion, age, or gender. In the contexts of biology and ecology, it has likewise remained a basically numerical index of species density. In both cases, while more diversity has come to be affirmed as better than less, the predominant, fundamentally quantitative conception of diversity itself gives no clues as to why this should be so. Notwithstanding the positive aura it has acquired, "diversity" continues to refer simply to the coexistence of many different kinds of things in a given setting.

This book develops a more theoretically robust conception of diversity. At its heart is the recognition that differences are ultimately always *processes* of differentiation, and that significant critical advantages follow if we distinguish between diversification and variation as distinct modes of differentiation, with diversity understood as an *emergent quality and direction of relational dynamics*. More broadly, it is a book that attempts to weave a multilayered historical and philosophical narrative that shows why difference came to be such an important issue and concern in the mid-to-late-twentieth century; why difference can no longer be viewed as just the conceptually vacuous opposite of sameness; and why a richly qualitative conception of diversity affords crucial resources for evaluating and practically engaging our increasing social, economic, cultural, and political interdependence.

The dramatic origins of this narrative, however, are not purely theoretical. They are rooted in deeply troubling questions about the meaning-of and means-to greater equity in a world that is characterized by both fabulous wealth generation and the no less fabulous widening of wealth, income, resource, and opportunity gaps, making our era at once the most developmentally advanced and uneven in human history. The claim that will be advanced here is that diversity is not just valuable. It is a value crucial to working out from within the global dynamics of the twenty-first century to change the way things are changing in a shared commitment to improvising and sustaining ever more equitable modalities of human-with-planetary flourishing.

Among the key features of contemporary global dynamics are their nonlinearity and complexity: their tendency to be recursively structured and prone to *significant* discontinuities. Accounts of how to work out from within these dynamics in pursuit of more equitable futures cannot be expected to take the form of clearly specified plans based on a "blueprint" of the grand architecture of global interdependence. Instead, they are likely also to be complex and nonlinear, more akin to performance notes for a piece of situationally responsive improvised music than a utopian engineer's urban master plan. That, at least, is true of the narrative that follows, in which key distinctions and themes appear and reappear as interactive parts of an emergent, recursively structured whole. Given this, it is perhaps useful here to call attention to some of these distinctions and themes and the global contexts for composing them.

I. CONTEXTS

Getting Things Right and yet Going Ever More Globally Wrong

From a certain point of view, it could be said that humanity is mostly getting things right. Globally, we can produce more than enough food to adequately feed everyone on the planet. We have created living conditions that, along with new medical practices, enable the world's people collectively to enjoy the longest life expectancies in history. Literacy is at an historical high. Communication takes place at the cosmic limit of light speed. The contents of world-class libraries are available anywhere on Earth to anyone with access to an Internet connection. And the range of choices exercised daily in pursuit of lives worth leading by the world's seven billion people is wider and deeper than it has ever been—a pursuit that is now globally recognized as a basic and universal human right.

But in the global systems supporting these positive developments, there is more than just a "devil in the details." Of the world's population, more than eight hundred million are chronically hungry and fully one in five live in what the World Bank terms "absolute poverty"—conditions so degraded and degrading that they do not afford even the *hope* of a dignified life. Today, 1 billion people are without access to clean drinking water and 2.6 billion live without adequate sanitation. Conservative estimates of the effects of human-induced climate change suggest that by 2050 between one and three billion people will lack adequate drinking water of any sort. One out of every seven people in the world is illiterate (two out of every three of these being women or girls). The rate of functional illiteracy in many of even the most highly developed countries is nearly one in four. And for a tragically large number of people, the abstract possession of universal human rights is no compensation for the very concrete effects of being chronically subject to systematic human wrongs.

For those who are hungry and thirsty and who live without even the hope of dignity, the fact that we are mostly getting things right offers scant consolation. The number of people living today in absolute poverty would have been the entire world population in 1865. The number of those who live on less than two dollars per day—figured according to purchasing power parity—is equivalent to every man, woman, and child living in 1965. What must be done to open spaces of hope for these mothers, fathers, sons, and daughters? How do we work out from present conditions, as they have come to be, to realize—at a bare minimum—dignified lives for all?

My own conviction is that truly dignified lives cannot be lived by *any* unless the conditions are realized by means of which dignity is a reality for *all*. I am also convinced that the time has long passed for wishing or waiting for such conditions to materialize. Our dignity is sluicing at an unprecedented and accelerating rate into the chasm of inequality that now separates the 14% of the world's people who use 85% of its resources from the 86% majority compelled to exist on the remaining 15%, or the richest 2% of the world's population who possess 50% of global wealth from the bottom 50% who have less than 1%. Contrary to the central modern myths of increasing equality and universal progress, the depths of such chasms are not decreasing. They are increasing. They are everywhere in our midst. And there is no backstage for the somatic, psychic, and social tragedies they are generating. What can we do in caring response?

Contemporary Globalization: New Scopes, Scales, and Complexity

Any viable answer to this question must take into critical account the dynamics of contemporary globalization processes. The term "globalization" was first employed in something like its current use in the 1960s to capture new sensibilities about the nature and reach of corporate activity. By the 1990s, however, centers studying globalization as a wide array of economic, social, political, and technological processes had become standard fixtures on university campuses as well as in research and policy circles. And at least since the protests of the 1999 ministerial meeting of the World Trade Organization (WTO) in Seattle, globalization has come to connote a fundamentally contested process that constitutes "a leading edge of political conflict" (Robinson 2004, 1). Yet, minimally characterized as a range of processes through which people, goods, and senses of "the good" are placed into global circulation, globalization is hardly an exclusively contemporary (or even modern) phenomenon.[1]

What is new is the scope and scale of exchanges that are now regularly and globally taking place, and the pace and types of change both driving and driven by these exchanges. In brief, the circuits of exchange in goods, services, peoples, and ideas that are primary causes and consequences of globalization have crossed critical thresholds of scale and intensity to begin bringing about truly *complex relational systems* that are both self organizing and novelty generating. This means that present scales and scopes of globalization processes are *not* bringing peoples, countries, economies, and social systems into new patterns of relationship from which they will later be able to extricate themselves, wholly and at will.[2] The relationships into which we are being ushered by contemporary globalizations are not "external" relationships that we will be able to exit without remainder; they are "internal" or constitutive relationships. As is now being recognized, these relationships affect every aspect of our lives, including even the contours of our emotional makeup, significantly altering both who and how we are.[3] Once they are established, breaking these relationships means a breakdown and diminution of who we have come to be, both as persons and as communities. Having crossed crucial scales of scope and complexity, globalization entails deepening both *interdependence* and *interpenetration*.

Globalization and Differentiation as Challenges to Making Sense

To anticipate here how the complexity of contemporary globalization processes will factor into our later discussion of the need for a reconception of difference, two points should be stressed. First, multiplying and magnifying differences are crucial to both the systemic (internally focused) and situational (externally directed) adaptations through which emerging systems of network-organized complex interdependence sustain themselves. This means, in effect, that the differences generated and sustained by globalization ramify *significantly* and *recursively* across scales, sectors, societies, and spheres of interest.[4]

Second, at every scale from the personal to the social, from the local to the global, conditions now obtain for a delamination of the multidimensional "lifeworlds" that allow joint meaning making to occur in everyday circumstances in a taken-for-granted manner. As a foreign traveler quickly discovers, what native and long-term local residents experience as transparently common sense interactions in fact always express dense arrays of distinct—and distinctively overlapping—contexts of relevance that nonnatives experience as a confounding opacity. For the nonnative traveler, even the most mundane patterns of interaction can simply fail to make sense, offering very concrete proof of the existence of deeply uncommon or unshared assumptions about how the world is and should work. When lifeworlds begin coming undone, things stop making complete sense even to lifelong local residents. Under such conditions, it is not just that things can no longer be taken for granted; there is a progressive unraveling of the threads of tacit understanding that normally connect us meaningfully with one another: a comprehension-foiling dislocation of dispositions regarding what and how things *are* and *should be*. This amounts to a disintegration of customary means of constructing meaning and relevance—the growing prevalence of conditions in which the difficulties we face can no longer be framed as problems to be solved because we lack consensus on what would even count as a solution.[5] This is what the anthropologist James Clifford (1988) has called the modern "predicament of culture"—a condition in which distinct meaning systems overlay, interleave, and compete with one another in ways that place the very possibility of making sense in question.

Put somewhat more generally: the multiplication and magnification of differences associated with contemporary globalization processes subject the grammars of daily life to destabilizing arrays of both centripetal and centrifugal forces. Crucially, because this fragmentation and subsequent reconfiguration of lifeworlds amounts to a process of compartmentalizing and recompartmentalizing commitments, it also raises questions about the status and meaning of the self. Lifeworld disruption is correlative with the opening of spaces for reconfiguring priorities and for ongoing deconstructions/reconstructions of identity that can be simultaneously creative and coercive.

Critics of globalization view with great concern the centripetal forces that threaten to sediment effectively coercive grammars favorable to market-aligned power structures and forms of identity that ultimately disenfranchise a global majority. Proponents of globalization view with positive anticipation the individual empowerment resulting from the dissolution of traditional structures and identities, envisioning the centrifugal forces propagating throughout the public sphere in ways fundamentally aligned with increasing autonomy and democracy. What can be said with certainty is that the coevolution of complex systems of global interdependence is now actively reconfiguring global topographies of advantage/disadvantage, and it is doing so in ways consistent with the dominant constellations of values embedded throughout those systems.

II. DISTINCTIONS AND THEMES

From Problem Solution to Predicament Resolution: A Change of Eras

A key element in opening spaces of hope and dignity for all from within existing global dynamics is to recognize that such tragically consequential phenomena as global poverty, hunger, water shortages, and climate change cannot be effectively responded to as problems. They are locally experienced and yet globally constituted predicaments. Problems arise when circumstances change in ways that render existing strategies and techniques ineffective for pursuing our values, aims, and interests. Solving problems involves developing new means to abiding ends. Predicaments occur when we are forced to confront the presence of conflicts among our own values, aims, and interests. For example, while there is global consensus that it would be best to avoid major climate change and instability, the readily apparent technical means of doing so (reduced carbon emissions) runs afoul of prevailing social, economic, and political interests and values. Predicaments cannot be solved or treated with some new technical fix precisely because conflicts among our own values and interests make it impossible to define what would count as a solution. It is the very *meaning* of success that is in question. Predicaments can only be *resolved*. This entails increased *clarity* about how things have come to be as they are, and new and more thoroughly coordinated constellations of *commitments*.

As a combined result of the problem-solving successes of our scientific, technological, social, economic, and political systems, and the difference-generating and risk-amplifying dynamics of reflexive modernization and industrial globalization (Beck 1999; Beck et al. 1994), we are in the midst of a transition from an era dominated by problem solution to one characterized by the centrality of predicament resolution. Among the implications of this, two are crucial for the pursuit of more equitable global interdependence. First, it suggests that we are witnessing the progressive obsolescence of the constellation of values that have informed the social, economic, political, cultural, and epistemic dynamics of global industrial modern-ization for nearly half a millennium—a constellation that includes such hallowed values as universality, equality, autonomy, sovereignty, control, competition, and choice (Toulmin 1990). Second, it implies that the defin-ing challenges of the present moment and the foreseeable future are not centered on the acquisition of practical knowledge (knowing what can be done and how), but rather on the shared consolidation of wisdom (knowing what ought to be done). In other words, we are also in the midst of a transi-tion from predominance of the *technical* to that of the *ethical*.

Yet, in addition, the global historical trajectory that has carried us to the point of the problem-to-predicament transition, combined with the apparent intractability of such issues as global hunger and climate change, makes it clear that in turning critical attention from the technical to the ethical we must be open to turning in the direction of a significantly dif-ferent kind of ethics—one that departs from the modern paradigm of assuming the centrality of individual agents, of identifying freedom with choice, and of forwarding universal definitions of the good life according to which differences are simply contingent attributes attaching to a pur-portedly common human nature.

The Contemporary Aporia of Difference

One way of bringing the imperatives for such an ethical paradigm shift into clearer, critical focus is to see the problem-to-predicament transi-tion and the difference-generating and difference–amplifying attributes of contemporary global dynamics as forcing confrontation with an *aporia*: an impasse or paradox.

Whether within societies or in the context of their interaction, the complex and interdependent dynamics of contemporary social, economic, cultural, and political realities invalidate the assumption that we have common perspectives and purposes. We are now continuously confronted with needs to acknowledge, not only the increasing significance of differ-ences (for example, in terms of gender, ethnicity, religion, and culture), but also the increasing variability of the kinds of difference that are criti-cally significant. At the same time, however, as is powerfully evident in connection with the prospects of global climate change or the threat of a global HIV/AIDS pandemic, these same dynamics also insure that imper-atives for arriving at robustly shared and globally coordinated forms of action are themselves deepening, not lessening.

We thus find ourselves in the troubling position of needing to address two seemingly opposing needs. First is the need to more fully acknowledge differences, going beyond merely tolerating differences from (and among) others to enabling differences to matter more—not less—than ever before.

Second is the need to realize ever more extensively and deeply shared sets of values, subsuming our manifold differences within ever more comprehensively articulated and yet globally coherent patterns of commitment.

One response to this aporia and the fissures opening in the modern world has been to see them as occasions for reinstating some preferred set of premodern ideals and institutions. This is the approach taken by the many fundamentalisms that champion turning back from modern values and restoring (or reinventing) cultural regimes that would subvert secular universalism in favor of a particular religious, social, and political totalism—an approach that would forcibly reinstate conditions in which all difficulties can be framed as problems open to utterly certain solution.[6] Doing so would, of course, dissolve the conditions of possibility for any significant "predicaments of culture." For those involved, there would be but one value system and one set of interpretative assumptions. Fundamentalisms typically involve assumptions of monopoly with respect to truth—a denial of the ultimate significance and dynamism of differences. A global fundamentalist future would bring either a patchwork world of independently governed moral ghettos or the global domination of a single and necessarily coercive vision of right living.

Another response has been accepting the paradoxical or aporia-like character of contemporary life as concomitant with renouncing all claims of absolute truth and common essences; with cultivating skepticism about all metanarratives and rejecting their potentially coercive implications; and with affirming inalienable human rights-to-differ. This is the approach of what can be loosely called postmodern theories and practices that counter modern and premodern emphases on "the same" with contrary emphases on difference and otherness. But accepting the aporia of difference—affirming the particularity and relativity of all forms of life and claims to truth—is also to accept the impossibility of truly global predicament resolution.

The approach provisionally forwarded here is that responding to the aporia of difference in ways that open real prospects for equity-enhancing global predicament resolution requires moving at a "perpendicular" or "oblique" angle to the spectrum of premodern, modern, and postmodern conceptual resources and their contrasting valorizations of moral communion, universalist cosmopolitanism, and free variation—the construction of difference, respectively, as systemically and hierarchically prescribed; as vertically progressive and yet contingently ascribed; and as horizontally proliferating and autonomously subscribed.

Cultural Differences as Critical Resources

It is not easy to envision what it would mean to move in such an oblique fashion. The needs to at once affirm and elide differences are apparently contradictory, and yet the empirical forcefulness with which we are confronted with them suggests that this aporia or impasse is not circumstantial, but rather conceptual—a signal of the inadequacy of our prevailing conception of difference. If so, originating movement of the sort needed will require what might be called a paradigm shift in how we understand difference—a conceptual revision that may be only modest in apparent scope, but that must be utterly *radical* in the sense of reshaping the very *roots* of our experiencing and engaging difference.

Broadly speaking, a paradigm consists in a system of aims, values, assumptions, methods, and institutions that holds together in expression of a distinctive pattern of "family resemblances." A paradigm shift occurs when some element in this system is altered in a way that triggers a reconfiguration of the whole. In the case of the paradigm shift from classical, Newtonian physics to the relativistic physics of Einstein, the radical revision was to see that light was ontologically ambiguous. The experimental evidence confronting Einstein was that light sometimes acted like a stream of particles and at other times like a wave. The prevailing assumption was that light *had* to be either one or the other. Einstein's paradigm-changing insight was to draw the utterly radical inference that this manifestly "contradictory" evidence did not indicate a failure of experimental design (something that could be fixed); it indicated the failure or limited applicability of the either/or logic which had long been considered foundational for rational inquiry. This enabled him to recognize similar limitations in prevailing conceptions of energy, matter, time, and space as supposedly independent dimensions of reality.

Like physicists in the late nineteenth and early twentieth centuries who were confronting evidence of the failure of a scientific paradigm that had generated a broad spectrum of theories about light, matter, energy, gravitation, and motion, we are confronting no less confounding evidence of the failure of a critical paradigm that has generated the current global spectrum of competing ethical, economic, and political theories. The analogy suggests that the "contradictory" needs of enabling differences to matter more than ever before while at the same time subsuming these differences within globally shared commitments indicate our arrival at the limits of our prevailing conception of difference. Breaking through the aporia entails breaking with prevailing assumptions—logical and metaphysical—about what difference is and is not.

Such a conceptually radical break is not likely to be accomplished in either cognitive or cultural isolation. A key finding in the cognitive sciences over the last quarter century is that such apparently simple or elemental concepts as identity, sameness, difference, and change are in fact among the most difficult to model. What this means is that, in spite (or because) of informing virtually all of our sentient activity, such concepts

are very difficult to make "visible" in the way needed to formally define
them or translate them into another language, precisely because they are
constitutive of the very conditions of "visibility." Directing critical attention to such concepts on our own is like trying to see our own eyes: an
effort doomed to failure in the absence of an appropriately placed reflective medium. Much as mirrors enable us to see our own eyes, intercultural
encounters enable us to see that we have *uncommon assumptions* about the
basic constituents of human experience. They make visible what is usu-
ally invisible in ways capable of spurring quite radical revisions of how we
understand the world and ourselves. The paradigmatic conceptual revision needed to break through the aporia of difference is most likely to be
accomplished *interculturally*.

The French philosopher and sinologist Francois Jullien (2000) has
argued well and at length on behalf of intercultural investigations of basic
concepts, demonstrating the surprising degree to which cultural "detours"
can grant new and critically incisive "access" to our own experience. But
to press his language, it is not always easy to discern what will prove to be
a revelatory detour; what will turn into a progressive immersion in being
lost; and what will amount only to a circuitous and wearying course back
to where we began. It is not easy to distance ourselves from the familiar in
the resolutely open ways necessary to revise something as rudimentary as
our conception of difference.

What is certain is that intercultural encounters of the kind needed
will not result from booking a "cultural tour" to some far-flung part of the
world or inviting home guests from afar. While physical relocation and
"cultural immersion" can play important roles in bringing uncommon
assumptions to light, paradigm-challenging cultural detours cannot be
primarily geographical or motivated by simple curiosity. They are acutely
conceptual and intentional, where concepts are understood as distillations
of lived experiences and practices, and where intentionality implies recursively dynamic and values-generated commitment. Detours of this type
are not abstract; they are existential.

The detours that will be invoked here in pursuit of clear passage
through the aporia of difference will thus be at once personal and provisional. They are personal in the sense of being detours that I have taken
in the course of my study and practice of Buddhism (and to a lesser extent,
Confucianism and Daoism) and in the sense of having been undertaken
in hopes of revising the meaning of personhood. They are provisional in
the sense of being edited "reports from the field," rather than exhaustively
detailed accounts of journeys completed, and in the sense of being locally
coherent expressions of insights rather than purportedly absolute truths.[7]

For those who (I think, too narrowly) regard Buddhism as a system
of meditative practices for individually attaining spiritual liberation,

the merits of undertaking Buddhist detours for insight into contemporary global dynamics are likely not immediately evident. But, the central insight of Buddhist practice is that all things occur interdependently. And as I hope to make evident, the conceptual resources that have been developed over the last 2,500 years in support of realizing this insight are extraordinarily useful in challenging foundational assumptions about identity and difference, in critically engaging the emergent dynamics of complex systems, and in resolving conflicts by means that eschew both force and compromise.[8]

Confucian and Daoist traditions emerged (in China) at roughly the time as Buddhism (in India), and from about the third century enjoyed considerable interaction with it. All three traditions have sought distinctively to discern how best and most appropriately to sustain appreciative (that is, value-according and value-generating) continuity in a world wherein relationality (not things-related) and change (not the unchanging or eternal) are ontologically primordial. As such, they afford distinctive resources for rethinking difference; for challenging the assumption that the individual is the natural and proper unit of ethical, economic, and political analysis; and for developing an ethics of interdependence and relational equity.

Ontology Matters: The Primacy of Relationality

There is now considerable evidence and increasing recognition that contemporary realities are best understood in terms of relational concepts like "interdependence, conjoint construction of meaning, mutually interacting entities, and systemic process" (Gergen 2000, 211). More strongly stated, the patterns of interdependence and interpenetration that are emerging with globalization at contemporary scales, scopes, and complexity cannot be adequately or accurately engaged as long as we remain critically wedded to the ontological primacy of individual and independent existents that only contingently enter into relationships. Attempting to do so is like trying to eat soup with a fork—an effort that will inevitably leave behind what is most distinctive about contemporary realities. What these realities invite us to see is that relationality is not contingent; it is constitutive. Rather than continuing to take individual existents to be the basic "building blocks" of reality, we should understand them as abstractions from more rudimentary relational dynamics. Again, it is relationality—and not things-related—that is ontologically primordial.[9]

It is, of course, one thing to recommend such a change of ontological paradigms and quite another to carry through with it. It is not merely that we are being compelled to trade in one set of world-constructing building blocks for another; we are being compelled to abandon the very idea of a "building block world" and to relinquish our commonsense notions of what it *means to be*, and thus also what it *means to change*.

To return to the analogy suggested earlier, we are not unlike those who witnessed the circumscription of classical physics by then emerging relativity and quantum paradigms based on empirical demonstrations that Newtonian concepts of time, space, energy, and the independence of the observer and the observed were useful only in a middle range of physical phenomena and only as approximations. In the realms of the very small and the very large—the microscopic and the cosmic—time and space, matter and energy, observer and observed are revealed to be related in ways not unlike the "two sides" of a möbius strip: a three-dimensional object that strangely has only one edge and one side.[10] Likewise, from the perspective of a relational ontology, separately existing things—any given "this" and "that"—occur only as aspects or abstractions of relational dynamics: opposing "aspects," "edges," or "sides" of a situational whole that are ultimately continuous.

If this is so, then such modern dichotomies as those of "mind" and "body," "free will" and "determinism," the "individual" and the "collective," "self" and "other," "progress" and "stasis," "order" and "chaos," or "facts" and "values" can have only conventional or heuristic utility. To use a phrase from the philosophy of science, they do not "cut the world at its joints" because, as it turns out, the world is not originally jointed. Seeing relationality as more primordial than things-related is, in other words, to see that difference cannot be a simple *fact* of discrepancy or an essentially static "relation." Difference is a complex, historically realized and value-laden function of qualitatively charged, implication-generating, and recursion-rich relational dynamics. Put more simply: differences never simply *are*, they always *mean*.

From this ontological perspective, the kinds and degrees of differences being generated by contemporary globalization processes and network-structured industrial modernization can be seen as indices of changes in what we mean to and for one another, and it is critically important to ask: changes that are benefiting whom? in consonance with what values? in favor of which and whose grammars of life? in support of or antipathy with what structures of feelings, what kinds of communities, and what kinds of politics?

III. NARRATIVE CURRENTS

The ten chapters of this book offer a recursively structured approach to answering these questions, oscillating at different registers between historical and philosophical vantages from which it becomes evident how and why the dynamics of global interdependence have been biased overwhelmingly toward variation, how this is connected to global inequalities being at historical highs, and why the pursuit of greater environmental, social, economic, cultural, political, and cognitive diversity is crucial to realizing and sustaining conditions for greater equity. Brief descriptions of the main narrative currents are offered here to provide a synoptic—albeit partial—overview of the whole.

The Nonduality of Sameness and Difference

Modern conceptions of difference arguably began acquiring important new philosophical depth with Hegel's use of the dialectic. But it was not until the late twentieth-century advent of what can broadly be called postmodern thought that a paradigmatically new approach to understanding difference began being articulated. As is discussed in Chapter 1, postmodern thinking offers important correctives to the coercive potentials that attend modern essentialism and universalism, explicitly rejecting the foundational nature of sameness—either ontologically or ethically—and asserting instead the primacy of difference. Postmodern thought, however, does not so much break with as it inverts the values constellation that defines modernity. And its emphases on the relative, the particular, and the local work against its effectiveness in addressing the kinds of equity-eroding differentiation processes that have been so manifestly apparent in the last two centuries of market-driven industrial modernization and globalization.

Buddhist thought offers an alternative to both the modern subordination of difference to sameness and its postmodern inversion. The core Buddhist insight that all things arise and abide interdependently entails seeing that there are no ontological gaps between things and hence no metaphysically ultimate boundary between what something "is" and what it "is not." As Buddhist logicians were quick to point out, this means that one of the foundation blocks of propositional logic—that there is nothing "between" identity and difference—must be seen as a conventional truth, not an absolute one.[11] The logical assertion of the so-called "excluded middle" affirms that things are either the same, or they are different. This implies that while sameness or identity has potentially limitless content or meaning, since difference consists only in the absence of identity, it can have only minimal (and at that, ultimately parasitic) significance. Seeing all things as interdependent disallows understanding the relationship between sameness and difference as an asymmetrical disjunction of this sort and challenges the notion that either identity or difference should be understood as primary or foundational.

As is affirmed in a very early canonical text, the *Sutta Nipāta*, conflict and suffering are unavoidable whenever we divide the world up in terms of conceptual opposites. Rather than granting priority to either identity or difference—or to either universality or particularity—it is more appropriate to regard them *nondualistically*. Elaborating on the work of the seventh-to-eighth-century Chinese Buddhist thinker Fazang, Chapter 1 closes with a nondualistic reading of sameness and difference. Concisely stated, all things are the same, precisely insofar as they differ significantly from one another. That is, all things *are* what they *mean* for one another.

Diversity as Value

From such a nondualistic perspective, difference is not ultimately a static absence of identity; it is the dynamic presence of conditions for mutual contribution. In Chapter 2, this insight is used as a point of departure for exploring the merits of undertaking a conceptual bifurcation, using "variety" and "diversity" to point to two distinct qualities and directions of differentiation processes, with variety indicating only the minimal relationship of coexistence, and diversity the realization of a certain quality of interdependence or mutual contribution.

This distinction enables a novel critical approach to examining the multiplication and magnification of differences that characterizes contemporary modernization, marketization, industrialization, and globalization processes. Specifically, since this distinction specifies the conditions in which differentiation processes will be relationally enriching, it has considerable explanatory and evaluative potential, especially in clarifying the means-to and meanings-of equity. Moreover, Buddhist nondualism implies that, notwithstanding the conventional utility of the fact/value and means/ends distinctions, they are without any ultimate metaphysical or ethical warrant. A nondualist affirmation of the ontological primacy of relationality enables developing a relational theory of values that is used in the second half of Chapter 2 to explore the merits of seeing diversity as a *value*—a modality of appreciating relational resolution and refinement that has critical relevance across a broad range of domains from the environmental to the political.

Changing the Meaning of Change

A core Buddhist teaching is that if we aim to dissolve the conditions of conflict, trouble, and suffering, we should see all things as changing. While the conventional logic of the excluded middle depicts differences as static and instantaneous matters of fact, the Buddhist perspective is that, like all things, differences should be seen as aspects of dynamic relationality and hence as irreducibly temporal phenomena. Being different is, in actuality, always a function of *differing*. Or more simply stated: difference entails change.

It could also be said, however, that change is a primordial expression of difference, and this implies that our conceptions of change may be as much in need of paradigmatic revision as prevailing conceptions of difference, especially if we are intent on changing the *way* things are changing. With this in mind, Chapter 3 undertakes an intercultural consideration of "uncommon assumptions" about time and change. As with difference, non-Western conceptual resources are used to open possibilities for seeing change as qualitatively differentiated. This enables introducing two sets of polarities—control and contribution; choice and commitment— that exemplify contrasting modalities of change associated with variation and diversification, and that direct attention to links between the meaning of change and the meaning of freedom that become critically important in evaluating the dynamics of contemporary globalization processes.

Histories and Possibilities: Reorienting the Dynamics of Change

Another, related Buddhist teaching is that positively and sustainably addressing conflict, trouble. and suffering can only be done on the basis of critical clarity about how things have come to be as they are. That is, histories make a difference. And so, while asking and answering philosophical questions about the meaning of change is crucial, responding to these questions fully cannot be undertaken usefully in either a cultural or a historical vacuum. On the contrary, critical engagement with the meaning of change is inseparable from engaging cultural differences in the meanings and uses of history.

A common popular assumption is that history is a study of the past with the aim of developing a complete and accurate view of all that has transpired. Contemporary historiography rejects this simplistic view, but is itself divided as to how best to understand the proper scope and aims of history. The first part of Chapter 4 considers tensions between modern "histories from above" and postmodern "histories from below," and in response forwards a Buddhist-inspired historiography according to which an important function of history writing is discerning resources for normatively reorienting, rather than simply explaining, current change trajectories.

The second part of the chapter initiates such a recursively structured reading of changes in the political, economic, social, cultural, and technological spheres that are correlated with the global spread of modernity and the progressive dominance of industrially powered market economies. The purpose is to develop a broad understanding of how the merger of modern and market values served to accelerate differentiation processes, especially in the social sphere, ironically bringing about conditions for both the problem-to-predicament transition and the intensification of paradoxical imperatives to at once accept, accentuate, and sublimate differences in identity and values both within and among societies.

More tightly focused readings of roughly the same period of time are presented in Chapter 5 and Chapter 7. In Chapter 5, the focus is on how modernity- and market-driven changes in mass media have been correlated with changing conceptions and practices of personhood and community; with the emergence of a global attention economy and the progressive colonization of consciousness; with the increasing identification of the optimal with the optional; and with a progressive normalization of both multiple identities and elective communities. Chapter 7 concentrates on the period from the stock market collapse of 1929 to the present, offering an account of the rise of the military-industrial-communications complex; its relationship both to the spread of rational choice theory into public policy making and the development of postmodern ethics; the dissolution of the modern agenda of global unification and the building of *"cosmopolis"*; and its replacement by a postmodern agenda of free variation and utopian constructions of *"netropolis."*

Toward an Ethics of Interdependence

As with globalization, differences in conduct, values, and personal and cultural identities are nothing new. What is new are the scales, scopes, and complexity of differentiation, including the production of differences in who enjoys which outcomes and opportunities associated with economic growth and industrial modernization. Morality, law, and ethics can be seen as distinctive responses to perceived needs to manage or constrain "deviance" and promote congruent conduct through, respectively, strategic exercises of communal pressure and persuasion, objectively prosecuted punishment, and rationally constructed proof. In premodern and modern contexts, all three can be argued to have had the primary aim of subordinating difference to sameness.

Late modern patterns of social differentiation and intensifying tensions between competing political and economic universalisms considerably complicate this focus on the same. While the contexts of morality and law remain communally or state focused, the context of ethical discourse has undergone remarkable expansion. Although always oriented toward determining what all reasoning persons should do to secure the conditions of the good life, there has been a marked expansion of both who is considered capable of ethical deliberation, and who and what is to be granted ethical consideration.

Chapter 6 opens with reflections on how modern constructions of the private and public as separate "spheres" of life affected the conception and conduct of morality, law, and ethics; how the globalization and social differentiation processes spurred by industrialization and marketization combined with philosophical and political valorizations of universality, autonomy, and equality to produce conditions for an ethical tension between competing universalisms; and how liberally framed values pluralism emerged as an attempt to make space for differing conceptions of the good in a world recovering from the horrific effects and implications of the Second World War and grappling with the prospects of a nuclear winter ending of the Cold War. But while pluralism of this sort was a reasonable response to tensions between competing universalisms, it was wedded to the idea that rational deliberation was capable of establishing a single, hierarchically ordered set of values valid for all. And in the context of the historical conditions that led to deepening cynicism about claims made for one or another route to global unification, this struck many as being neither tenable nor desirable.

One response was the gradual articulation of a postmodern, particularist (or relativist) ethics of difference. Yet, in spite of their otherwise stark opposition, an ironic kinship obtains between universalist and particularist ethics. Both express commitments to the value of equality that—however disparate their scopes of application—eventuate in the denial of critical relevance to difference. That is, although with irreconcilable reasons and objectives, universalist and particularist ethics have in common a de facto strategy of *disarming difference*. Because of this, neither approach is suited to responding to the variation-amplifying inflection of contemporary global dynamics—a world in which equality remains a fiction (however powerful), and in which equity (understood as equality of opportunity) remains an attractive, but ever distant goal.

Chapter 6 concludes by anticipating the need for an alternative to modern universalism and postmodern particularism—an ethics of interdependence and diversity that would neither work against nor simply accept the presence of uncommon assumptions about the meaning of the good life, and that would instead work out from within those differences in the direction of a shared conception of human-with-planetary flourishing.

For reasons developed more fully in Chapter 8, the failure of efforts to realize truly equitable patterns of global interdependence can be seen as reflecting the inadequacies of current models of collective action and the basic incongruity of modern ethical tensions (and dichotomies) in an "other-than-modern" world characterized by the problem-to-predicament transition and the emergence of complex patterns of global interdependence and interpenetration. To reprise an earlier metaphor, while the divisions within modern ethics purport to cut the world at its "ethical joints," they in fact constitute a consistent pattern of imposition upon it. And while the many merits of this imposition are historically evident, no less evident now is that these tensions—between agents and actions, free will and determinism, virtue and duty, individual rights and collective responsibilities, egoism and altruism, principles and consequences, discovered and constructed conceptions of the good, and the universal and the particular—reflect modern sensibilities that divide the world up in terms of categories that obscure rather than clarify concrete possibilities for effective commitment to greater equity.

Relational Equity: Beyond Equality of Opportunity

The concept of equity has historical roots in classical Greece where it was invoked in legal contexts to avert unfair rulings that would result from the universal application of law. That is, equity was invoked in cases where, in the interest of justice, differences should *not* be ignored. Over the course of the modern era, however, equity underwent significant conceptual revision in the historical context of a split between economics and ethics that occurred in the late eighteenth and early nineteenth centuries. This revision culminated in the twentieth century with the identification of equity with equality of opportunity.

Chapter 8 begins by tracing the historical development of the concept of equity, the gradual migration of its focus from legal matters to considerations that are economic, political, and ethical in nature, and its eventual presence at the center of debates between liberal theorists and their communitarian, feminist, and postcolonial critics about the meaning-of and means-to justice. Consistent with this complex history, practical considerations of equity over the past quarter century have come to focus predominantly on calibrating *how much* wealth, power, access, and opportunity various individuals or groups have—an objectively measurable state of affairs—and are essentially agnostic with respect to *how well* these individuals and groups relate. Inequity is taken to consist in the persistent *absence* of sameness or equality in some specified and measurable senses, and equity in the lessening of those differences. This is true even for those who insist on recognizing and respecting differences as crucial to the achievement of justice.

Placed in the context of the dynamics of differentiation-accelerating and advantage-skewing reflexive modernization and world risk society (Beck 1999; Beck, Giddens, and Lash 1994), however, recognizing and respecting differences is clearly not enough, and the identification of equity with quantitatively indexed comparisons of equality of opportunity has the critical liability of directing attention to absolute changes in, for example, wealth, income, and educational access, rather than relative changes that manifest concretely as relational transformations consistent with values, aims, and interests that are embedded within and embodied by existing power hierarchies and their institutional infrastructures.

Addressing issues of justice in a world of complex interdependence and interpenetration requires a fully *relational* conception of equity that does not resist differentiation processes, but rather focuses on evaluating and reorienting them as needed to realize the conditions for systematically enhancing relational quality. According to such a conception, inequity consists in the *presence* of debilitating or degrading relational patterns: the differential atrophy of interactive strengths, often in the context of deepening power asymmetries. Equity is not a comparative state of affairs, but rather a process of inflecting differentiation processes in ways conducive to strengthening relational dynamics and fostering increasingly mutual contribution to sustainably shared flourishing—an open-ended process of relational appreciation. Greater relational equity does not mean greater equality, but rather greater diversity.

Rethinking Global Commons, Global Public Goods, and Collective Action

Over the last quarter century, equity—that is, equality of opportunity—has come to be seen as a global public good that is crucial for realizing social, economic, and political justice. Would this hold true after delinking equity from equality and developing relational conceptions of both equity and justice? And if so, what would this imply more generally about needs to expand or revise our conceptions of resource commons, public goods, and the kind of collective action needed to ensure that their protection and provision are actually conducive to sustained human-with-planetary flourishing?

The development of contemporary discourses on global public goods and global commons can be seen as a response to needs for new kinds of analytical and practical traction in efforts to address justice issues in the context of increasing global interdependence and industrially powered global market economies (Buck 1998; Kaul et al. 1999; Keohane and Ostrom 1995). Chapter 9 investigates what it would mean to see diversity as a global relational commons crucial to realizing greater global equity.

The difficulties associated with the protection and provision of resource commons and public goods are often referred to as problems of collective action,[12] as those associated with addressing issues like global climate change, poverty, and hunger might be. In this context, the "problem" of collective action refers to the necessity of generating individual choices and actions that may not be optimal in terms of every individual's self-interest, but that will maximize collective benefits or those benefits shared among all the individuals involved. Seeing these difficulties as *predicaments* suggests that addressing them effectively will not be a finite and primarily technical endeavor, but rather an ongoing and explicitly ethical one in which diversity and equity would function as *coordinative values*.

The most widely prevalent models for understanding and addressing the difficulties of collective action—the "prisoner's dilemma" being
far and away the most influential—are wedded to an ontology of autonomous, rationally self-interested individuals acting independently in the
context of relatively fixed external constraints on the basis of constant and
coherent interests. Whatever their utility in sharpening theoretical issues
related to the exercise of choice, these models greatly oversimplify the
situational dynamics that are foregrounding issues of collective action,
imposing on them a gamelike structure in which benefits accrue (or fail
to accrue) to individual players who entertain essentially similar and yet
practically incompatible sets of outcome priorities.

In the context of the problem-to-predicament transition, however,
assumptions built into predominant game theoretic models of collective
action—that actors already know what outcomes are desired, that they
agree on what "winning the game" means, and that they know and will
follow a common set of rules for play—become a serious liability. To use a
helpful distinction drawn by James Carse (1986), predicament resolution is
not a "finite game" played in accordance with the assumptions just noted,
but rather an "infinite game" in which the point is not winning, but rather
sustaining and enhancing the *quality* of ongoing "play" for all involved.

It is characteristic of finite games that winning them results in increased
power for the winner(s)—that is, increased capacities for determining situational *outcomes* or "how things turn out." By contrast, well-played infinite
games characteristically advance the *strengths* of all players—foregrounding their capacities for generating *opportunities* to keep playing and to
enhance the value of doing so. As I will draw the contrast: skill in playing
finite games leads to increasing freedoms-of-choice; skill in playing infinite
games leads to steadily appreciating capacities for relating-freely. Importantly, while the benefits of finite play consist of individual "gains" of some
sort, the benefits of infinite play are fundamentally relational in nature.

Seeing the pursuit of collective action as a finite game has some merit
so long as the action needed is, in fact, problem solution. But if the requisite action is to engender globally shared commitments in ways that will
yield sustainable courses of predicament resolution, thinking in terms of
strength-oriented infinite play has marked advantages over the power-
oriented pursuit of calculable gains. In Buddhist terms, these reflect the
disparate karma or patterns of experienced outcome and opportunity that
are associated with a bias, respectively, toward the valorization of control
(power) and contribution (strength).

In the context of the problem-to-predicament transition, the central
difficulty of collective action is not overcoming our individual differences
to act in our common interests, but rather activating and sustainably coordinating the relational strengths made manifest as a function of *how well*

we differ not just *from* but also *for* one another in contribution to conserving and creatively expanding our capacities-for and commitments-to shared flourishing. This is a necessarily "infinite" endeavor in which valuing diversity—environmentally, socially, culturally, economically, politically, epistemologically, and technologically—actively constitutes a resource commons for expressing new meanings-of and means-to equity and just interdependence.

From Power to Strength: Toward Political Diversity

In a complex world of "multiplying and volatile geographical differentiations operating at scalars which are themselves rapidly changing," significant liabilities attach to ways of thinking and systems of values that operate or are relevant only at one scale or that are formulated from within a single disciplinary framework (Harvey 2000, 30). This suggests that ours is a world that demands not only an ethics founded on the "dignity of difference" and the realization that "universalism is the first, not the last, phase in the growth of the moral imagination" (Sacks 2002, 51), but also a politics founded on the productive activation of differences—a diversity-enriching politics capable of responsibly coordinating local, national, regional, and global responses to an unpredictably expanding and predicament-rich array of challenges.

Modern democracies arguably evolved to take significant political account of the facts of plurality endemic to nation-states that were constructed as multiethnic, multireligious, and multicultural polities. As such, democratic government might reasonably be deemed appropriate for meeting the political challenges of a predicament-rich world. But given the ways that political legitimacy is now increasingly tied to economic vitality; given that economic growth is now complexly linked to the production of unpredictable threats, risks, and hazards; and given evidence that the costs and benefits of growth are being disproportionately distributed in favor of an increasing narrow elite, it is not clear that governmental politics of any sort is likely to play a positive role in realizing enhanced diversity and equity. Chapter 10 addresses the possibility that coordinating collective action of the kind and depth needed to respond effectively to global predicaments and the aporia of difference may be the work of a yet-to-be and other-than-governmental politics.

Much as ethical systems can be situated along a spectrum from universalist to particularist, democratic governments can be situated along a spectrum from liberal to illiberal systems that differ according to whether the primary bearer of rights to autonomy and equality is the individual citizen or the sovereign state. Although democratic governments across this entire spectrum are committed to conserving rights to differ and rights of participation, they have done so to date in ways that index commitment only to conserving relationally thin *political variety*, not to fostering the emergence of relationally thick *political diversity*. That is, they have focused on insuring conditions within which citizens and states can *differ-from* each other while remaining agnostic in both procedure and principle as to whether and how well they *differ-for* one another.

If ours is, indeed, a world in which we must develop shared responses to unpredictable and predicament-generating challenges, it would seem that the familiar *politics of power* will need to yield to a *politics of strength*—a politics of contributory virtuosity rather than ideologically driven exercises of control. Envisioned through Buddhist conceptual resources, this shift appears to be less a matter of crafting new institutions than it is about fostering the emergence of a new "structure of feeling." Extrapolating on the Mahayana Buddhist ideal of the bodhisattva who demonstrates unlimited relational virtuosity (*upaya*), this structure of feeling might be characterized by expressing superlative (*kusala*) capacities-for and commitments-to relating-freely—a structure of caring improvisation in which differences from others are realized as openings for making beneficial differences for them.

What this might mean in concrete practice will itself be a matter of improvisation. But theories of deliberative democracy make a step in the right direction by procedurally recognizing that differences can serve as sources of critically distinctive contribution to policy development and decision making. Placed into sufficiently broad and deep practice, deliberative democracy would bring about a politics focused on consensually balancing rights to vary from others and imperatives for acting in unison with them—a politics capable of practically merging the postmodern agenda of netropolis and the modern agenda of cosmopolis. Such a politics could be instrumental in reconciling the globalization- and network-driven multiplication and magnification of differences with our manifestly increasing needs for globally integrated collective action.

This said, however, processes of deliberation are not open-ended. And while the conditions for deliberation do include attention to issues of relational quality (including respect for others and discursive civility), they are by definition finite and task oriented. That is, they are problem-identifying and problem-solving processes that acknowledge needs to consider alternative conceptions of what "good" means in relation to particular issues, but that remain focused on determining which policies and courses of action to empower and which goals to establish. In short, democratic deliberation is instrumental—a political means, not a political end in itself. To make use of a key Buddhist conceptual distinction: it is an unequivocally good thing, but it is not yet a *kusala* or superlative one.

The politics of diversity—like the politics of recognition, respect, and democratic deliberation—will at once result from and result in responses to difference that are capable of acknowledging and resolving conflicts. Buddhist teachings on conflict resolution suggest that while recognition, respect and deliberation are well suited to establishing and extending the practical reach of political *cooperation*, this is not enough in a world of complex interdependence and interpenetration. The politics of diversity will emerge as we align ourselves with the relational value of *coordination*—the simultaneously structural and aesthetic expression of means-to and meanings-of relational transformation in the direction of enhanced resilience, fluency, and responsive virtuosity. In sum, political diversity is not a destination; it is a direction that will emerge as we demonstrate nondualistic readiness to interrupt conflict from within by improvising movement oblique to the relationally compromising opposition of variety and unity.

———

Of course, it is perhaps inspiring to envision conditions that are conducive to a new structure of feeling expressing our readiness to demonstrate the meaning of relating-freely in shared improvisation of enhanced diversity and equity. But if the complex narrative just rehearsed does not result in recommending real and effective steps for addressing the kinds of global predicaments in which we already find ourselves immersed, then so what? How do we know that the "spaces of hope" it purports to open are anything more than imaginary?

In the Epilogue, these questions are raised and reflected upon in light of the Arab Spring and the Occupy Wall Street movements that, as I write, are still opening up as pathways to what many hope will be greater political, economic, and social justice. Perhaps appropriately and perhaps unavoidably, these reflections do not culminate in a checklist of principles and practices for moving forward more quickly on these or other more familiar pathways. Instead, they result in the offer of yet another detour—not an ideally finite one intending arrival at a distant and much anticipated utopian future, but rather a practically infinite one of improvising together, facing the world as we have come to know it, and arcing out crosswise to it in devotion to ever more superlatively shared relational appreciation.

CHAPTER ONE

Toward a New Paradigm of Difference

As it happens, we no longer have the relative luxury of indifference with respect to difference. Even a casual survey of news and entertainment media, on any given day, anywhere on the planet, leaves little doubt that present day scales and depths of globalization processes are serving as multipliers and, frequently, magnifiers of difference, both within and among societies.

Perhaps the most high-profile examples of contemporary increases in the prominence and power of difference are those differences underpinning the emergence of global terrorism, the elusiveness of global resolve in addressing the causes and likely impacts of climate change, and the global fair trade—not "free trade"—movement. These represent the effects of especially deep differences in what, for convenience, we can refer to as "values and interests." But as important as are such powerful and often tragic manifestations of the increasing gravity of differences, they represent a tiny fraction of the ways in which difference is now being felt, fomented, protested, and praised.

Whether locally, nationally, regionally, or globally, in evaluating and responding to the processes that constitute and shape our day-to-day lives and the dynamics of the public sphere, we are now compelled to consider not only state-centered political differences, class-based socio-economic differences, and the possibility of underlying differences in explicitly held values and claimed interests, but also patterns of difference reverberating within and across such complex and densely interwoven domains as morality, gender, ethnicity, culture, religion, and historical experience. In domains like these, differences—especially among both real and ideal identities—often factor concretely (and yet nearly invisibly) into institutions and practices. Some of the affected institutions and practices, like marriage, are traditional; others, like legal same-sex domestic partnerships, are still in their formative stages. Either way, they are relatively stable features of the societal landscape that shape our daily interactions in consistent (though seldom holistically coherent) ways. Changes to such institutions and practices, especially if rapid or sudden, will often fundamentally challenge not only *how* we live, but also *why* we live as we do.

The longevity of institutions and practices in traditional societies can be seen, then, as an index of stable patterns of difference and identity: for example, relatively constant ways of distinguishing male and female roles and responsibilities. By contrast, it is a hallmark of modern and postmodern societies that both the private and public spheres are continuously undergoing differentiation, characterized by new or intensified constellations of differences that are often of a magnitude capable of transforming even the most basic and time-honored institutions and practices. Beyond certain thresholds of scale and scope, such transformations entail a basic restructuring of our lifeworlds—a substantial revision of the meaning of common sense and a reorganizing of those shared contexts of relevance that Jurgen Habermas has termed "the grammar of forms of life."[1] Such restructurings cannot but alter our possibilities for (and approaches to) both self-making and making sense to and with one another. Consider again the ways in which emerging differences with respect to gender construction and sexuality over the past quarter century have destabilized and/or transformed the institution of marriage and the practice of adoption; altered the legal landscapes of benefit sharing and inheritance; forced into existence new medical and public health protocols regarding such issues as contraception, abortion, and the treatment of sexually transmitted diseases; and significantly reframed the roles of parenting and the meaning of family.

Undoubtedly, there is much to recommend celebrating the conditions that are accelerating change and fostering the advent of enhanced experiences of and sensitivities to difference. Confronting the range of differences with respect to gender construction, for instance, has opened concrete possibilities for challenging and developing alternatives to institutions and customs that have long denied women either equality or equity, either in public or in the home. Within the global political sphere, the voices of nonstate actors—for example, those of civil society groups and nongovernmental organizations (NGOs)—are being raised in ever-greater numbers and to ever-greater effect, significantly extending the scope of democratic processes. And, at a more pedestrian level, market-driven innovations in goods and services are continuously expanding not only choices with respect to meeting basic needs, but also the horizons of desire, opening freedoms of choice with respect to an ever more variegated range of lifestyles and experiential possibilities.

Yet, globally broadening and deepening economic interdependence is at the same time bringing about markedly uneven geographies of development, accentuating (rather than alleviating) disparities in the distribution of the benefits and costs of industrialization and globalization. For instance, while the wealth and income gap between the richest 20% of countries in the world and the poorest 20% stood at a ratio of three to one in 1820, after a century of industrialization and globalization in 1913 that ratio had increased to eleven to one. In 1950, it was thirty-five to one; in 1973, forty-four to one; and in 1998, eighty-six to one (1999 Human Development Report, UNDP). These disparities are not simply numbers in statistical arrays. The new global standard of fragmented and spatially dispersed production systems are bringing about equivalently fragmented patterns of labor needs, with the effect in many locales of shifting or truncating opportunities for long-term skills development. The global explosion of educational opportunities and a burgeoning internet-mediated "marketplace of ideas," while arguably positive developments in their own lights, have not proven synonymous with education for all and seem likely to presage a widening rift between the qualities of education and knowledge available to the global majority and those available to a contracting and disproportionately wealthy global elite. For many, postmodern multiplications of difference are inseparable from threats of endlessly magnifying spirals into relative—and perhaps also absolute—disadvantage.[2]

To give a single concrete example of the unevenness of development and the profound association of difference with disadvantage, consider the geography of health in the national capital of the world's wealthiest nation, Washington, D.C. There, the life expectancy of an African American male living in the city center is a mere fifty-seven years—compared to the fifty-five years expected in Sudan or the forty-seven years expected in Uganda, countries deeply ravaged by war, famine, and disease. But by stepping onto a commuter train traveling into the city's suburbs, it is possible for an African American man to "add" a year to his life expectancy with every passing minute. Twenty miles out of the city center, African American male life expectancy is seventy-seven years.[3]

Facts like these notwithstanding, it must be acknowledged that new kinds and degrees of difference also open possibilities for forming new commonalities. These can take the form of support groups for those bound together by a disease like HIV/AIDS; interest groups aligned with emerging lifestyles; or international organizations like the World Social Forum, constituted in acknowledgement of links among residents of the "global South." But they can also take the form of transnational capitalist classes, the members of which have more in common with elites scattered on the "commanding heights" of the global economy around the world than they do with the local populations immediately surrounding them. The dark side of difference acquiring (or being laden with) normative force as something that *should* be attended and perhaps celebrated is that, at some level, recognizing differences is also a projecting or attributing of identities—a process that becomes troubling when emerging differences so often signal emerging power differentials, new hierarchies of advantage, and new categories or classes of disadvantage.

DIFFERENCE AS RELATIONAL DYNAMIC

The general point here is that the multiplications and magnifications of difference being brought about by contemporary industrialization and globalization processes are inseparable from accelerating and significantly reorienting *patterns* of change. The more specific truth is that difference is never just a state of affairs or a particular status attaching to individual persons, societies, or cultures. Neither is it simply an artifact of comparison—a "gap" measured along some dimension of relevance between what are taken to be self-identical events, things, or beings. Difference is a relational process that *occurs* or "carries forward" in a particular direction. Far from being a generic and conceptually vacuous category of contrast, difference marks the occurrence of relational potentials—an opening of specific directions for relational change and creativity.[4] In short, differences are ontologically ambiguous—at once emerging as generic *means* (for making a difference) and as specific *meanings* (of differentiation). Put another way, difference is a function of differentiation: a situationally focused and recursive process.

This truth that differences are always dynamic and meaning-laden is often overlooked in contemporary discussions, where difference has become a politically charged category that is conceptually grounded in assumptions about relatively fixed personal, sexual, cultural, social, ethnic, and political identities. Seeing difference as a process of meaningfully inflected differentiation disallows reducing it to a simple fact about the absence of identity or sameness. Differences mark the opening of new relational dynamics and possibilities.

But if difference is *not* the content-less and static opposite of sameness, then it is important to question—as we will here and in subsequent chapters—what kind of differences are being generated, to what end, in whose favor, and with what wider ramifications? If differentiation processes are inevitably directed, and hence significant, what patterns of meaning (if any) are being promulgated by the difference-generating workings of contemporary industrialization and globalization regimes, and how do these affect our prospects of realizing increasingly equitable systems of social, economic, political, cultural, and technological interdependence?

A second imperative that follows upon this way of seeing differences is to recognize that they are seldom ethically neutral. The chasm opening between the poorest fifth of all humans and the wealthiest ultimately must be seen as a key *meaning* of the differentiation processes generated and sustained by global markets as conditions for their own growth. As I will be arguing, changing what the world's poorest and wealthiest *mean* for and to one another will finally involve changing what global markets have come to *be*: engines for profitably translating one form of difference (diversity) into another (variety), with inequity as a key by-product. Seeing differences as expressions of changing relational dynamics calls into question both modern and postmodern tendencies to construct differences as occasions for exercising tolerance rather than as openings for mutual appreciation and the shared cultivation of contributory virtuosity.

This is not currently a "common" or "natural" way of thinking about difference. The dominant presupposition—and it is, indeed, a *pre*supposition because it is almost never consciously entertained *as* an assumption—is that things *are* different because, or to the precise extent that, they *are not* the same. The existence of difference, in short, is taken to be parasitic on the prior existence of things, situations, events, or beings that in some relevant respect are independent and incommensurable. First there are things, and then there are differences among them. To the extent that current common sense accords difference some form of existence, it is strictly prepositional: difference obtains only as a fundamentally insignificant "between" or "among." According to such a view, differences are essentially contingent.

Conceiving of differences as contingent—especially those differences that derive from linguistic, ethnic, cultural, religious, and social practices—has been key to many of the most important successes of the global project of modernity, including that of institutionally recognizing equality as a central, modern political value. But, such an understanding of difference is not without shortcomings. The logical and metaphysical biases embodied in our predominant conceptions of identity and difference are now so powerfully at odds with contemporary realities that they are major obstructions to any effort that would orient global interdependence toward greater equity. To achieve such an orientation, we must reconceive difference.

POSTMODERN PRIVILEGING(S) OF DIFFERENCE: A PREVIEW

The need to reconceive difference is one that has been recognized by many of the most incisive critics of modernity, and at various points we will engage their views in some detail. Here, however, I want in a preliminary way to consider whether the trajectory of ongoing changes in the conception of

difference in Western philosophical traditions is carrying us in the direction of developing the critical resources needed to realize greater equity, or
whether we are likely to do so only if we seek outside the Western tradition
for an alternative or at least complementary set of perspectives on both
what differences ultimately *are* and what they do or might *mean*.

As early as the nineteenth-century works of G. W. F. Hegel and Friedrich Nietzsche, modern emphases on sameness, identity, universality, and
the nondynamic character of truth and being were being called into question. Hegel's dialectic, for example, stressed the productive nature of difference, albeit as a means to an all-encompassing "absolute idea." Roughly
a half century later, Nietzsche railed with great vigor and acuity against
all previously hallowed conceptions of the good because of their common
failure to assert the importance of distinctiveness as a function of actively
willed self-overcoming and creativity. And, Darwin's theory of evolution
posed a profound scientific challenge to the idea that species were essentially determinate forms of life with a fixed point of origin (divine creation), offering instead a vision of the biosphere as a self-regulating system
shaped by ongoing processes of adaptive differentiation.

But it was only with mid- to late twentieth-century poststructuralist/
postmodern theorists like Emmanuel Levinas, Jean-Francois Lyotard,
Michel Foucault, Jacques Derrida, and Gilles Deleuze that the primacy of
such core concepts as universality, sameness, certainty, identity, presence,
being, and the univocity of truth were not only called into question, but
actively (and some would say, aggressively) subordinated to particularity,
relativity, difference, ambiguity, absence, and multivocity. Philosophical
postmodernity announces a sharp break both from the universalism of
systematic philosophies like those of Plato, Aristotle, Descartes, Kant, and
Hegel, and from the constructions of modernity informed by them—an
intellectual stance that Lyotard famously described as "incredulity toward
metanarratives" and the totalisms they imply (Lyotard 1984).

One way of reading this break from modern idealizations of the univocity of truth and the goal of certain knowledge—especially in thinkers like Lyotard, Foucault, and Derrida—is as a critical extension of late
nineteenth- and early twentieth-century work of linguists like Ferdinand
de Saussure who understood languages as formal systems in which the
basic units were signs, each composed of a signifier and signified. Much as
those linguists traced language to a combination of differential elements,
early articulators of postmodern thought traced the origins of all things,
not to inviolable identities, but to ambiguously configured regions of contingency, erasure, dissension, and disparity (Foucault 1977, 142)—what
Derrida would refer to as *différance*.

For many in this generation of postmodern thinkers, a deconstruction
of the foundations of knowledge was of crucial concern—a deconstruction

of purportedly unified origins, subjects/selves, narratives, and coherences. For others, however, the turn toward difference was motivated by recognition of its ethical primacy. Levinas, for example, explicitly located the very possibility of ethics in the confrontation with an "other" that was incapable of being assimilated within the ambit of "the same"—the intrusion of an infinity that manifests as an experiential lacuna or hiatus eluding all attempts at being fully grasped or comprehended.

It was with a second generation of postmodern thinkers epitomized by Gilles Deleuze that emphasis shifted from the epistemic and ethical centrality of difference to its ontological function. For Deleuze (1995), difference is not simply the negation or superseding of identity; it is the very source of all genesis, the root of all material production. With this shift, difference is fully freed from its presumptive modern determination as a purely negative or parasitic concept or factor, and understood instead as the precondition of all being and beings. Importantly, Deleuze rejects the temptation to depict this relationship in such a way as to cast difference into the (expected) metaphorical role of the "root" of being and identity. Arguing against the foundationalism and verticality implied in the "root" metaphor, he forwards instead the metaphor of the "rhizome"—depicting difference and differentiation as a center-less, "horizontal" process of proliferation. The moral relativism often associated with postmodern thinkers expresses a resolute unwillingness to engage in hierarchic orderings of difference—a refusal to establish any sort of privileged position from which a ranking of perspectives, identities, and moralities might be undertaken.[5] This would seem to be the point of departure for Deleuze's positive invocation of schizophrenia as both a descriptor of capitalist processes and a metaphor of potential for resistance to capitalism as a deterritorialized regime of desiring-production (Deleuze and Guattari 1983, 1987)—a resistance that takes the disruptive, nomadic form of unpredictable eruptions or uprisings.

The work of Deleuze—like that of other postmodern theorists—has been subject to wide countercriticism. Yet, it is hard to deny an unsettling parallelism between postmodern thinking and postmodern realities of the sort that led Fredric Jameson (1991) to see postmodernism as the "cultural logic" of late capitalism. That is, contemporary realities are coming to be characterized by something like global process of perpetually decentering regimes of production—regimes that do not so much resituate us as consumers as they free us to take up any one of virtually limitless positions of desire. The result is a rhizomatic proliferation both of different goods and services, and of ever-fluctuating populations of consumers experiencing needs and desires for them—a virtual realization of what Deleuze and Guattari have anticipated as the freeing of desire from all beliefs.

It has become utterly commonplace (at least in global urban settings), for example, to eat at "food courts" serving, side by side, edibles from three or four continents prepared with reference to any number of disparate cuisines; to jump instantaneously among ninety or one hundred channels of cable television entertainment, sports, news, and infomercials; or to establish "friendships" with hundreds of people around the world through social media that allow making contact with anyone, anywhere, at any time of day or night. In all such cases, there is a celebration of being different and of differentiation as a response to ever-changing desires and imaginations of the worthwhile. This all happens with an apparent absence of hierarchy or priority, without even the imposition of necessary temporal sequence.

Indeed, the commercial Internet is a particularly apt metaphor for the condition of rhizomatically proliferating differences—a domain characterized by simultaneity and coexistence without any experienced spatial separation, and yet also structured so as to stimulate and maximize the exercise of choice. The physical shopping mall happily juxtaposes a bookstore and a lingerie shop, a fast-food eatery and a health food and vitamin outlet. And within any of these shops will be found a reiteration of a resolutely relativist organization of space—a space in which every item available for choice and purchase equivalently constitutes a means to the fulfillment of need and desire. Prices will vary, as will the personal and display services by means of which consumption is encouraged, but each and every item in a mall presents an *equally valid* appeal for attention. The Internet amplifies the possibilities of the mall to infinity, and in doing so frees consumers from any identities other than those articulated by the exercise of their unmediated desires—the sites they visit, the purchases they make, the personal information they make accessible to an ever more readily individualized global public.

To put matters rather provocatively, there is a sense in which the "schizophrenic" rise of postmodernity both as a condition of late capitalist contemporary life and as an anti-ideology of radically nomadic individuation is the result of an incestuous historical relationship between modern and market values and institutions—a union to which we will later turn our direct attention in search of alternative historical resources for more equitably and fairly orienting the dynamics of global interdependence. The point here is that while the history of Western thought has, indeed, come to include a turn toward the epistemic, ethical, and ontological significance of difference, this turn has occurred under conditions that do not seem to promise the resources needed for mounting shared responses of the sort needed to address the predicaments being posed by contemporary realities. As critics like Jameson (1991) and Habermas (1987) have argued, it is a turn that is conducive to allowing the paradoxically paired needs to recognize differences and to engage in increasingly profound common cause to remain a defining paradox or *aporia* of contemporary life—a paradox in respect of which we choose only our demeanor and degree of good humor.

This is not to deny that postmodern thinkers—including Derrida, Deleuze, and Guattari—do not concern themselves with issues of social justice and abuses of structurally enacted power. But to the extent that we embrace the postmodern ideal of free variation, affirming the absence of unified subjects and the ontological primacy of difference as such, it is difficult to imagine the basis for sustaining critical engagement with questions about "difference, or differing, to what end?" In fact, the postmodern metaphor of the rhizome would seem to deny this question intelligibility, affording no profoundly shared position from which to effectively critique, for example, the differences of wealth, resource use, risk, and power that are being systematically generated by the engines of global capitalism: relational by-products of their proliferation of commodified goods, services, and consumers in desirous need of them. An ethics of difference in which individuals remain the unit of analysis (however bereft of unified subjectivity and self-identity) is not yet an ethics of interdependence.

DIFFERENCE AND THE MEANING OF NONDUALITY: A BUDDHIST DETOUR

One of the liabilities of taking difference to be ontologically primary is that it is easy to interpret this as equivalent to accepting that differences ultimately do not *mean*; they simply *are*. That, I think, is a grievous liability in a world where interdependencies have emerged that relegate fully one-fifth of the world's people to lives of such absolute poverty that they do not have even the hope of a dignified life. There are means-to and meanings-of difference that should not, under any circumstances, simply be tolerated. And so, while postmodern thought may be quite useful in the deconstructive work of dissolving hegemonic, totalizing, and finally unilateral claims to power, it is much less suited to the further task of consolidating and strengthening responses to the inequities resulting from the manifestly nonrandom and value-laden circulations of goods, services, populations, ideas, and ideals that are characteristic of complex contemporary industrialization and globalization processes. For this, we need a carefully and resolutely *oriented* understanding of difference.

Buddhist teachings and concepts afford open and yet critical access to such a constructive understanding of difference. And while other traditions of thought and practice that have had origins outside the dominant conceptual genealogies informing the global West may provide further alternative approaches, I will make primary use here of Buddhist resources in working out from present global historical circumstances toward a global ethics of interdependence. Buddhism has a 2,500-year history of focused investigation of the means-to and meanings-of realizing liberating patterns of interdependence, based on the insights that relationality is ontologically primary and that relational dynamics are always open to significant improvisation. Especially in Mahayana traditions, these insights have been understood as entailing, not (as in postmodern thought) the subordination or erasure of identity in favor of difference, but rather the realization of their nonduality.

Buddhism's stress on realizing the absence of any fixed or abiding self (*anatta*), impermanence, the interdependent origination of all things, and the origins of much conflict in univocal claims to truth can be seen as conceptual kin to postmodern philosophy's antifoundationalism, its emphases on contingency and the ambiguity of origins, and denials of the unified subject. That is, they can be seen as functionally related responses to similar concerns. But they are quite distinctive in their ultimate orientations. Postmodern thought deploys these concepts as part of an explicitly unsystematic (rhizome-like) pursuit of unrestricted freedoms to *differ-from* each other—freedoms from all externally imposed values, identities, ideologies, and institutions. Buddhist practice—especially in its Mahayana manifestations—is systematically oriented toward realizing our own emptiness (*śūnyatā*) of fixed identities for the purpose of reorienting the dynamics of interdependence that constitute us as persons-in-community with others.

Thus, while postmodernism and Buddhism have in common efforts to dispel any and all myths of the given, Buddhist practice is not ultimately a process of deconstruction, but rather one of what might be called reconstruction—an always improvised process of resolving trouble and suffering. As we will see in connection with the Buddhist teaching of karma, experienced differences never just *happen*. They *occur* as workings out from and toward particular patterns of meaning or significance, patterns in which we are implicated and which we are thus always in a position to alter. Differing-from others is inseparable from the possibility of differing-for them in ways conducive to realizing the conditions for *relating-freely*.

In sum, Buddhism ultimately enjoins an explicitly constructive, normative stance toward difference. It establishes, in effect, a set of imperatives to realize that perceiving difference always entails opening both potentials and responsibilities for *making a difference*. That is, there is no ultimate warrant for assuming neutrality with respect to differentiation processes, either in the sense of "taking neutrality for granted" or that of consciously adopting "an attitude of neutrality." The occurrence of difference is always ethically charged and morally implicating. The perception of difference is never just enacted *from* a particular perspective or position; it is a function of having *taken* a position that expresses specific values and intentions. In other words, perceived differences are always meaning-laden.

Western discourses on meaning have tended to be of two broad types.[6] On one hand are those that would claim transcendental meanings for things, where meaning is somehow "given from above" as an essential and objective feature accessible to all of sufficiently keen insight and intellect. On the other hand are those that would claim that nothing has intrinsic meaning (whether transcendentally determined or immanent); meaning is attributed by interpreting subjects. Between these two perspectives, it has been taken as axiomatic that there is no "middle ground," just as it has been logically insisted that there is none between identity and difference or between being and not-being.

In sharp contrast, Buddhist discourses have been unwavering in regarding such dichotomies as conventions that may have a certain utility (like the geometric convention that parallel lines never meet), but should not be taken to be inviolable truths. In fact, questioning such conventions is often necessary to develop apt responses to new conditions or concerns (allowing parallel lines to meet in a nonlinear geometry that more accurately maps objects and events in relativistic space-time). In a world in which relationality—not preexistent "things" that come into relationship—is ontologically basic, the object-subject dichotomy can have only conventional value. The same is true for the opposing, subsidiary conceptions of meaning as either an intrinsic *attribute-of* things or something extrinsically *attributed-to* them. Ultimately, from a Buddhist perspective, meaning—including the meaning of difference—should be understood nondualistically.

To begin fleshing this out, let me refer to the work of the influential second-to-third-century Indian Buddhist philosopher, Nagarjuna. Working in the philosophically plural world of early classical India, Nagarjuna discursively linked a nondualistic concept of interdependence or emptiness (*śūnyatā*) with a tetralemma or fourfold denial of the adequacy of conceiving identity and difference in dichotomous terms. In brief, he claimed that with respect to what some "thing" *is* and what "it" *is not*, none of the following claims can be sustained: they are identical; they are different; they are both identical and different; they are neither identical nor different.[7] In keeping with the early Buddhist claim that "is" and "is not" are the "twin barbs" on which all humankind is impaled, Nagarjuna links conventional (*samvritti*) conceptions of identity and difference to the occurrence of errant patterns of interdependence. Logically emptying these conceptions of their claims to being true in any ultimate (*paramārtha*) sense is, for him, not simply a matter of intellectual rigor; it has soteriological significance as a cognitive means-to begin healing the "wound of existence" by gesturing toward the meaning-of nonduality.

Nagarjuna's denial of an ontological gap between what a thing "is" and "is not," along with his demonstration of the ultimate unintelligibility of conventional conceptions of "identity" and "difference," direct us toward engagement with the ontological primacy of relationality as such. For him, understanding the emptiness (*śūnyatā*) of all things is to realize that all things are mutually engaged or relevant for one another (*Mūlamadhyamakakārikā* 24:14). To *occur* is already to *mean*. Meaning is not something imposed on or derived from relational dynamics, but rather the recursively articulated expression of their orientation and quality.

The Inseparability of Interdependence and Interpenetration

This is a rather abstract way of explaining the nonduality of difference and meaning. For help in doing so more concretely, we can turn to the distinctive interweaving of the concepts of difference, meaning, and nonduality that was forwarded by the seventh-to-eighth-century Chinese Buddhist thinker, Fazang. Like many of his contemporaries, Fazang had a considerably wide and deep understanding of Indian Buddhist teachings and commentaries, including those of Nagarjuna. But his application—or perhaps better, activation—of key concepts like that of emptiness (*śūnyatā*) and interdependent origination (*pratītya-samutpāda*) belie a decidedly Chinese propensity for seeing the nature (*xing*) of things in dispositional rather than essential or substantial terms. This is well reflected in what we might term his philosophical merger of meaning and presence—a merger undertaken in response to questions and concerns about the means-to and meanings-of enlightenment, framed around the Chinese conviction that all beings have/are buddha nature (*fo-xing*).

For Fazang, it was clear that if all things are truly empty (*śūnya*) of any independent and abiding self, nature, or essence, then interdependence must be understood as entailing interpenetration. That is, interdependence is not a contingent, external relationship; it is constitutive or internal. Ultimately, all things are irreducibly relational in nature. Understood in this way, seeing all things as interdependent is to see that they share in the same true nature—the same relational dispositions—that the Buddha expressed through his own practice and teaching. That is, all things must have buddha nature—a propensity for realizing and sustaining enlightening relational dynamics.

The obvious, conventional response to this claimed nondualism of all things is to point out that there are quite clearly both sinners and saints in the world, or in more typical Chinese terms, both commoners and sages. Some people are evidently going good with good motivations, others conduct themselves in ways that result in considerable suffering for others and often for themselves as well. Given these apparent differences, what possible truth can there be to explicitly nondualistic conceptions of the world?

Simply stated, Fazang's response was that all things can be seen as the *same*, precisely insofar as they *differ meaningfully* from and for one another. That is, realizing the nonduality of all things was tantamount to realizing that things *are* what they *mean* for one another.[8] In keeping with Nagarjuna's claim that ultimate truth can be taught or expressed only through use of conventional language and concepts (*Mūlamadhyamakakārikā*, 24:10), Fazang makes metaphorical use of the familiar process of assembling a traditional Chinese timber-framed building in the final section of his *Huayan Essay on the Five Teachings* (T. 45, no. 1866).

Traditional Chinese buildings like Buddhist temples were constructed by erecting an array of large poles on stone foundation blocks and linking these together into a stable unit by bracketed tiers of beams and rafters which are jointed to a central ridge beam. Atop this array of major timbers is a latticework of purlins onto which are layered clay roofing tiles. These tiles protect the structure from the elements. But more importantly, since no nails or screws were used in this type of building, the immense weight of the roof tiles served the structural function of compressing all the joints and stabilizing the entire construction.

For Fazang, the complex relationship among the components of such a building is analogous to that which obtains among all things. Insofar as the removal of rafters would cause the entire building to collapse, the rafters can be said to be the cause of the totality of the building. Simultaneously, it is true that it is only when they are bracketed into the beams that join the vertical poles that individual timbers become "rafters." Prior to that, each is simply a length of planed and shaped wood. And, the same can be said of all the beams, purlins, and roofing tiles used in the construction—each also is a focus of the same, nondualistic relationship of the mutual causation of part and whole. More generally stated, each particular in the world (*shi*) consists at once in causing and being caused by the totality, and ultimately *is* precisely what it contributes functionally to the patterning articulation (*li*) of that totality.

This metaphor dynamically recalls one used by the historical Buddha—that of individual sheaves of just-harvested grain placed in such a way that each stands leaning against another to form a stable and upright conical stack. Crucially, none of the individual sheaves is able to stand alone; and, in fact, removing or knocking down any one of the sheaves will cause all the others to fall. This common agrarian image was invoked specifically to illustrate how each one of us is a conditionally arisen expression of interdependence among the five elemental factors or constituents (*khandha*)—bodily form, feelings, perceptions, impulses, and consciousness—each of which is individually empty (*śūnya*) of any abiding essence and thus lacking in any capacity for standing alone in independent existence. Each of us is intrinsically plural—an expression of a specific play of differences. Whether our life experiences are troubling or liberating is a function of the quality of plurality we attain—the precise kinds and directions of relational dynamics constituting us as persons.

Both metaphors are intended to guide practitioners toward realizing the ontological priority of relationality as such. But Fazang's building metaphor goes an important step further than the agrarian figure of stacks of bundled grain. What we call poles, beams, rafters, and ridges are not just lengths of wood. They are carefully shaped pieces of lumber, prepared for complex jointing. Trees with relatively straight trunks are felled, trimmed, and stacked for drying. Once properly dried, these logs are milled into planks and beams of various dimensions that are then dried further before ultimately coming under the hands of skilled carpenters who cut them to fit and function as needed. In the absence of this temporal process—which could be extended back indefinitely into the growth of the trees through their incorporation of soil, water, and sunlight within forests that are themselves part of self-sustaining and ever-evolving ecosystems—and in the absence of construction-related knowledge traditions, there would be nothing to call poles, beams, rafters, and ridges. But even after appropriately sized and shaped pieces of lumber have been crafted, it still cannot be said that there are "beams" or "rafters." Beams and rafters occur only in a framed building, when all of the hundreds of pieces of lumber incorporated within it are in proper relationship with one another.

To the degree that Fazang was intent to deny the intelligibility of independent existents and to affirm the ontological primacy of relationality as such, he can be seen as anticipating postmodern reflections on difference like those of Derrida and Deleuze. But distinctively, Fazang did not regard things as existing or standing out and apart from one another in a rhizomatic flux that has no intrinsic meaning or dynamic tendency. All things arise, like "rafters" and "ridge beams," in mutual realization of particular relational patterns—relational dynamics in which they not only differ distinctively *from* one another, but also *for* one another. Difference, for Fazang, is the expression of *reciprocal contribution*. Or in more traditional Buddhist terminology, difference consists in the *specific activation* of interdependence/emptiness. Every difference signals a distinctive appreciation of the irreducibly mutual relevance obtaining among all things, and each is thus a direct demonstration of the meaning of nonduality.[9]

It is easy to imagine Fazang leading an isolated and mystically aloof monastic existence on one of China's many "sacred mountains," far in both time and materiality from a life anything like our own. In doing so, it is easy to question what relevance his nondualistic approach to understanding difference and meaning might have for us today. But in fact,

Fazang lived and worked in the early Tang dynasty when China was a geographically extensive, highly urbanized, and both ethnically and linguistically diverse polity of some fifty-five million people—roughly the size of contemporary France. The capital city of Chang'an supported a population of more than one million within its urban core—roughly the size of the cities of San Francisco and Oakland combined—and another million in the immediately surrounding suburbs. Situated at the terminus of the famed silk roads that linked imperial China with the cultures and societies of Central and South Asia, the Middle East and even Europe, Chang'an was the wealthiest and most cosmopolitan city in the world— one of the earliest centers of truly global commerce.

Living in the Tang capital, Fazang wrote in a context of intercontinental economic networks, continental-scale infrastructure, sociocultural and political imperatives to confront issues of identity and difference, and very apparent needs to govern rapid and qualitatively intense change. He was also living, however, in a place and time in which natural, socioeconomic, political, and spiritual orders were assumed to be intimately interwoven through relationally constituted patterns of sympathetic resonance (*gan-ying*).[10] Far from being of a purely philosophical and personal import, Fazang's writings would have been understood by his contemporaries as having social and political, as well as religious or spiritual, ramifications. And this no doubt had much to do with his patronage by the Empress Wu (r. 690–705 CE). The only woman to ever officially sit on the dragon throne of the Chinese empire, Wu Zetian was a ruler profoundly concerned with integrating complexly variegated regional interests into a functionally harmonious economic and political whole.

In short, Fazang's conception of difference was not developed in anything like a social, economic, or political vacuum. From a Buddhist perspective, it is one intended to inspire and support efforts to resolve the suffering of all sentient beings, and it demonstrates—within present circumstances—the meaning of liberating relationality. It is a conception of difference that requires *appreciating*—that is, both valuing and adding value to—difference in a way that precludes seeing the contemporary multiplication and magnification of differences as simple matters of fact. Not unlike postmodern thinkers like Deleuze, Fazang understood difference as ontologically productive—a process resulting in the advent of new beings and things in relationship. But going further, Fazang also understood that for differentiation to be directed toward the resolution of suffering—like the suffering imposed by inequitable and dignity-denying distributions of global wealth—it is necessary to realize that it is impossible to separate being *different-from* one another from making some kind of a *difference-for* one another. To be different in ways that are insignificant and irrelevant are ultimately *not* options.

In the Buddhist context within which Fazang worked, the nondualistic affirmation that all things are the same precisely insofar as they differ meaningfully from and for one another would have triggered a host of specific resonances, perhaps the most important of these being with the concept of karma.

Karma: The Inseparability of Reality and Responsibility

Unlike the concept of interdependence, which has become relatively well accepted in the global West, especially after the emergence of ecological and environmental discourses, karma has not fared well in the transmission of Buddhism outside of Asia. In part, this is a function of the quite varied appropriations of the term "karma" within Hindu, Jain, Tantric, popular religious, and new age discourses. In these cases, "karma" is generally invoked as a kind of shorthand for the roles of predestination and the operation of a cosmic moral economy in shaping past, present, and future experience, often in association with beliefs in the literal reincarnation of eternally abiding souls or personalities. Such roles and beliefs are in substantial tension with modern celebrations of free will and scientific rigor, and are considered by many to be theoretically and practically vacuous insofar as they represent claims that can neither be proven to be true nor falsified.

In sharp contrast, the Buddhist concept of karma centers on the experience-modulating force of intentional conduct—that is, conduct that expresses capacities for freedom regarding the *dynamics* and *direction* of experience.[11] The Buddhist concept of karma, in short, aims to *qualify* human freedom rather than invoke the ineluctable workings of destiny or fate. Hence the historical Buddha's claim that it is only on the basis of karma that practices for realizing liberation from trouble and suffering are possible. But even in its most elemental formulation, the Buddhist concept of karma does not fall neatly within dominant Western categories of knowledge and causality. And, indeed, precisely because it is so significantly at odds with the ontological commitments informing current, globally dominant constructions of knowledge and causation, karma may be of particular critical value.[12]

For present purposes, let me simply gloss karma as a horizonless correlativity that becomes evident when one pays sufficiently sustained and detailed attention to the relational dynamics or dramatic topography of one's life, as it unfolds moment by moment. That is, karma consists in the meticulous consonances that obtain between abiding patterns of *values-intentions-actions* and the patterns of *outcomes and opportunities* we experience. To discern the operation of karma is thus to discern the irreducible co-implication of experienced realities and responsibility. And, it is to realize that ethical disengagement is simply not an option. Since nothing is absolutely destined or fated to be, we have no ultimate warrant for claiming any situation in which we find ourselves to be intractable. Changing our values, intentions, and actions is always possible, and thus so is revising the meaning—the direction and quality—of the relational dynamics that constitute us as persons and communities.

A signal implication of the Buddhist teaching of karma is that realizing untroubled and untroubling patterns of interdependence necessarily entails both a *critique of self* and a *critique of culture*. While critical evaluation of our personal complexions of values, intentions, and actions may have practical primacy, many of our most deeply held and powerful values have historically framed, familial, cultural, social, economic, and political origins. These values are embedded within social, economic, political, cultural, and technological institutions, in the structures of intentionality that they embody and facilitate, and in the patterns of practice that they encourage and regulate, and profoundly affect our lives as persons-in-community, shaping the relational topography of the public sphere. Seen through the lens of karma, far from implying any kind of ethical or cultural relativism, Buddhist nonduality obliges engagement in *diversity-enhancing* processes of ethical and cultural *coordination*—terms that will be more fully fleshed out as our discussion unfolds.

In terms of our present concerns, the Buddhist teaching of karma enjoins us to become critically engaged with discerning how the experienced consolidation of particular patterns of difference and interdependence evidences the presence of abiding sets of values and intentionally sustained practices. Changing the dynamics of interdependence and interpenetration is to change the dynamics of differentiation by *means of* which each thing expresses its *meaning for* others.

One of the key implications of the Buddhist concept of karma—and a factor in its problematic integration into contemporary Western discourses—is that it entails recognizing not only the ultimate nonduality of means and ends, facts and values, and theories and praxis, but also the nonduality of experiencing subjects and experienced objects or situations. Changing the way things are changing is inseparable from changing the relational dynamics that at once constitute who we *are* and what we *mean* for one another. In a karmic cosmos, change is always recursive: a möbius-like process of mutual implication/explication.

In a world characterized by increasingly complex patterns of interdependence and change, then, there is much to recommend following Fazang's lead in thinking through the implications of a full-fledged relational ontology for understanding and engaging difference. According to such an ontology, relationality is to be seen as more basic than "things related"—an inversion of more typical propensities to insist on the primacy of things over relations and of facts over values. Minimally, this entails seeing that no things exist or stand apart from one another in primitive independence, and that all things arise, instead, through ongoing processes of interdependence. But more strictly speaking, it involves realizing that all "things" are abstractions from patterns of relationality that are ultimately horizonless, spatially as well as temporally.

Common sense, of course, insists to the contrary that things exist prior to the relationships into which they enter. According to common sense, atoms exist independently before they combine to form molecules; molecules exist independently before combining to form cells, which then join to form organisms of various sorts. You and I exist, independently and originally entirely apart, and are brought into relation only by words that I am now typing in what will be your past when you read them in what is now my future. Even at the philosophically developed level at which everyday claims about things and beings can be called explicitly into question, common sense has customarily reasserted itself, insisting that there must at any rate be some substance that primordially exists in order for things that differ in relation to one another to have come into being in the first place—even if this preexisting "something" is, to use John Locke's famous phrase, we "know not what." The bias toward seeing things or substances as more basic than relationality runs very deep.

But consider the parent-child relationship. Although it is typically assumed that parents come before (and indeed "have") children, in actuality parents and children "give birth" to one another, enjoying an irreducibly common advent. "Parent" and "child" emerge together as specific routes of differentiation within the overall dynamics of familial relations. And as any parent knows, becoming a "mother" or a "father" is not an instantaneous event, but rather something learned over time—from one's own parents and grandparents, from friends and other relatives, but primarily and most crucially from one's own children. Children, too, learn to be "children" (and more specifically "sons" and "daughters") in the context of ever-evolving family dynamics, which themselves develop in complex interdependence with a virtually limitless range of socioeconomic, political, technological, and cultural conditions. Alternatively, it is clear that apart from the relational dynamics of economic exchange, there are no "buyers" or "sellers," no "students" or "teachers" apart from their co-constitution in educational encounters; one cannot "have a friend" without also "being a friend." There is no being—and there are no beings—prior to or apart from relationality.

Affirming the relationality of all things is tantamount to denying the presence—and, indeed, even the possibility—of ontological gaps. In the absence of such gaps, there is no ultimate warrant for speaking of independently existing things or beings, or for seeing difference as a function of their contrast or comparison. Parents and children are not self-identical entities linked through the "relationship" that they "have" with one another, where their "relationship" is conceived as some sort of invisible and fundamentally contingent bridge joining what each of them *is* within the totality of all that each *is not*. "Parent" and "child" do not refer to independently existing entities, but rather reflect definition-generating points of view. It is only through the adoption of particular stances or positions, within specific horizons of relevance, that we can *identify* anything at all. Identities are a function of restricted attention— a limited prospect on the ultimately uncircumscribed totality of ongoing relational dynamics.

Put somewhat differently, identifying specific things—for example, parents, children, forests, and trees—brings into focus particular currents of relationality. As explicitly affirmed in a great many traditions of indigenous knowledge, there is tremendous power in the phenomenological focusing associated with naming. Through learning the "names" of things, a walk through a wooded terrain is transformed from an experience of amorphously variegated plants and trees into a coursing through distinct *relational potentials*—for carving or canoe-building, for decorating the body or adding comfort to the home, for gathering sustenance, or for altering consciousness and enhancing capacities for healing. At the most basic level of experience, this does not involve overlaying plants and trees with a veneer of usefulness, but instead finding specific relational potentials arising in the environment through a process of mutual elucidation. Differentiating among various kinds of flora is a compositional endeavor that for many indigenous peoples has led to affirming their genealogical roots as people-of-the-land. Naming brings into focus precisely how people and land *are* what they *mean* for one another.

Fazang's insistence that all things are marked by the twin characteristics of interdependence and interpenetration is a way of inciting realization that *all presence is mutual elucidation*. But he does so in the Buddhist context of full awareness that interdependence can, and very often does, go awry. Mutual elucidation can, in other words, make plain our own ignorance, attachments, emotional blockages, and relational resistances— the ways in which our own patterns of values-intentions-actions are conducive to suffering and trouble. As a result of such a troubling karma, it is possible, as Jared Diamond (2006) has demonstrated through comparative historical analysis, for culture, climate, and resource use to be spun into such a disastrous feedback loop that it brings about the collapse of an entire society or civilization. Or to choose a more immediate example, a plant like tobacco can be converted from being a distinctive element in the sacramental activation and affirmation of human-with-human and human-with-nature communion to being the catalyst for addictive habits and social practices that open tremendous opportunities for corporate profit while severely damaging both personal and public health.

Importantly, while Fazang was acutely aware of the degree to which conventional constructions of difference—especially as reflected in personal and social patterns of likes and dislikes, attraction and aversion—can result in troubling outcomes, he did not advocate a blank-faced nonduality of "all frozen sameness." Instead, he advocated realizing nonduality as the presence, in any and all outcomes, of opportunities for differing meaningfully, in ways conducive to liberation rather than trouble. Or more actively stated, realizing nonduality is a function of taking the meanings-of prior patterns of differentiation as offering relational potentials or means-to reorienting interdependence in ways conducive to relating-freely in resolving trouble and suffering, when and as they arise. In short, *re-conceiving difference can be both the means-to and meaning-of dissolving the conditions of errant interdependence and interpenetration.*

LOOKING AHEAD

What has this detour accomplished? To what new avenues for understanding difference has it afforded us access? Let me mention three that we will be taking, sometimes "simultaneously," over the next several chapters. The first involves following through on Fazang's invitation to see that difference is not a simple and content-less opposite of sameness or identity, but rather an expression—and, under some circumstances, suppression—of means-to specific relational potentials. While this honors the important insights of postmodern conceptions of difference, it also opens prospects for enhancing resolution with respect to contemporary imperatives for going beyond them.

The second avenue leads to new possibilities for critically linking history and complexity by extending the karmic insight that abiding configurations of values-intentions-actions play crucial roles in shaping situational outcomes/opportunities. Seen through the conceptual lens of karma, the recursive structural dynamics and emergent propensities of complex systems of global interdependence can be brought into sharper, predicament-resolving focus. The advent of complexity theory, while it can be seen as an outcome of modern epistemic biases and their scientific and technological expression, is also an opportunity to recursively challenge those biases and open spaces for restoring value and meaning to positions of ontological centrality.

Finally, our Buddhist detour has opened possibilities for seeing that the pluralizing and homogenizing effects of contemporary globalization and industrialization processes are not "two sides" of a single coin, but rather only apparently opposite surfaces of the "single-sided" (möbius strip–like) interplay of interdependence and interpenetration—an interplay that can as well be directed toward enhancing and sustaining equity as it can toward inequity. Yet it also invites seeing that passage through the aporia of difference hinges on practically realizing that the means-to greater equity are inseparable from articulating new meanings-of equity. In a world of increasingly rapid and profound differentiation, conceiving of equity in terms of individually focused pursuit of equality of opportunity is good, but not good enough. Equity is not ultimately achievable through guaranteeing some minimal degree of equality (sameness), but rather through establishing conditions for the emergence of virtuosic differentiation.

Karma (2)

Buddhism vs ... (3)

Religion - priests
Transmission

CHAPTER TWO

Variety and Diversity

Two Qualities and Directions of Difference

The historically evident trend of especially the last century has been toward both global integration and fragmentation, both homogenization and the multiplication and magnification of differences. If, indeed, differences are always occurrences or *propensity-expressing processes of differentiation*, this trend should not be assumed to be value neutral. Yet, the dualistic opposition of sameness and difference, even when refracted through postmodern lenses, is simply not conducive to realizing the kind of conceptual resolution needed to discern precisely what qualities and directions of relational dynamics are opportune for the sustained and deepening realization of equity. The sought-after route to breaking through the contemporary aporia of difference can only be accessed by relinquishing the view that difference is an axiomatic relationship that may vary in degree as it manifests in lived experience and in the structures of our lifeworlds, but not in kind. We are in need of a concept of difference that is itself differentiated, not only quantitatively, but qualitatively.

If we follow Buddhist traditions and those streams of contemporary thought that affirm the ontological primacy of relationality (and not individual things that are or are not in relationship with each other), this means that we are in need of a concept of difference that is irreducibly relational. This should *not* be confused with taking difference to be a specific kind of relationship—akin to relationships like identity, greater, smaller, older, and younger. A relational ontology is not equivalent to an ontology of (logical/functional) relations. If we consider how "difference" is used in everyday discourse, it's possible to intimate what moving in the direction of a truly *relational* concept of difference might mean.

It is, of course, common practice to categorize differences depending on the domains in which they manifest. We talk, for example, about "political differences," "cultural differences," "gender differences," and "differences in taste." But in fact, the concept of difference remains essentially unchanged across these domains, and differences within them are customarily ranked along a spectrum of measured intensity. And so, we speak of "great" and "small" differences, and differences that are "sharp," "acute," "extensive," "slight," "major," and "minor." People can be passionate about their differences, but difference itself signals nothing more than some quantum of dissimilarity, some expressed magnitude of mismatch. Likewise, current conceptions of change or differences over time are mathematically biased. Change is "rapid" or "slow"; it is "accelerating" or "outstripping" us in our efforts to "keep up."

These conventional ways of talking about difference focus concern on the "things" that "are different." To note a difference is, fundamentally, to make a comparison. A nondualist conception of difference focuses attention on differing itself as a relational dynamic. To play with the common locutions of "major" and "minor" differences and changes, what we are talking about is not a numerically expressible comparison, with major differences or changes being, for instance, something we would rank as more than seven on a ten-point scale in a questionnaire. Instead, we are talking about an expressed quality. To speak of a "major" or "minor" change or difference in relational terms is to direct attention toward something (metaphorically) like the total harmonic or tonal character of a piece of music played in a major or minor key—an immediately appreciable and unique pattern of relational dynamics among the notes being voiced in the piece. Differences *occur* as qualitatively distinct relational modulations.[1]

MODULATIONS OF DIFFERENCE: RELATIONAL SCOPE AND QUALITY

To begin the qualitative rehabilitation of difference, I would like to distinguish between two ways in which differentiation occurs: as means-to (with the meaning-of) increasing *variety*, and as means-to (with the meaning-of) enhanced *diversity*. Here, variety and diversity can be seen as denoting distinct *modulations* of differentiation processes—a bifurcation or branching out of the *meanings* of difference. Variety is a function of relational dynamics that are conducive to the production and sustained presence of multiple things, beings, or processes: a pattern of random, simple, or complicated *coexistence*. Variation is a means-to and has the meaning-of generating novel incidents of nonidentity—a process of increasing the quantity of individual things present. Diversity is a function of relational dynamics that are conducive to the production and sustained presence of a particular quality of interaction: a distinctive *complexion of interdependence*. Diversification is a means-to and has the meaning-of generating creatively enriching patterns of mutual contribution to sustainably shared welfare. It marks the advent of a distinctive qualitative shift in *how* things are present.

Variety can be noted at a glance. One can walk into an unfamiliar situation—for example, a university classroom or a cosmopolitan street bazaar—and see immediately whether there are a variety of people or goods present. In a university classroom, variety may be evident among the students present in terms of their body types, ethnic heritages, styles of dress, and choices of personal decoration (jewelry, piercings, tattoos, and the like). To the keener eye, these latter features may also announce a range of class affiliations and subculture identifications. But the variety of the students present says nothing, and presumes nothing, about the kinds of interaction that they presently enjoy or that they may develop over the course of the school semester. Student variety is simply a function of institutionally imposed curricular requirements and individual registration choices.

Diversity is *not* a surface feature. It cannot be seen at a glance. To determine whether a situation is diversity rich, it is necessary to observe the relational dynamics playing out within it over a substantial enough period of time to discern their qualitative inflection. Put another way, diversity is not a formal characteristic of a situation, but an historical one. Indeed, it could be said that diversity is not manifest at any given point *in time*, but only *over time*. Whereas the variety present in a university classroom can be exhaustively expressed as a function of the number of students who have come to *be* together, the diversity of these students would indicate the emergence of particular ways of *belonging* together. Diversity signals a distinctive and achieved quality of interaction.

Granted this way of describing their contrast, it might be assumed that variety is a necessary, but not a sufficient, condition for diversity. Factual multiplicity, in other words, might be claimed to be the minimal condition for the emergence of complex interdependencies that foster mutual contribution to sustainably shared welfare. But this would be to confuse, not to clarify, matters, suggesting that variety is in some sense a "state of affairs" that is ontologically prior to diversity. Indeed, it is with the aim of forestalling such a ranking of variety and diversity that I have described them as limbs of a *bifurcation* in the expressed meaning of difference. In much the same way that both melody and harmony are equally possible processes of sonic modulation, neither *variation* nor *diversification* can be seen as primordial. In any given situation, it is a matter of historical conditions whether one apparently "comes first" or whether they appear as equally primordial (and typically mutually conditioning) possibilities for differentiation.

A Metaphorical Contrast: Zoos and Ecosystems

A useful metaphor for further clarifying the variety-diversity distinction is to contrast the relational dynamics and patterns of differentiation constitutive of an ideal zoo and of a naturally occurring ecosystem. Although an ideal zoo might contain all of the plants and animals that make up a particular ecosystem, it will not function like an ecosystem. First and foremost, zoos are not self-organizing and novelty-generating complex systems. This is because the various species representatives in a zoo—although themselves complex organisms—are not in complex interaction with one another. Zoo animals and plants live in carefully segregated environments that are functionally closed to one another, even though these environments are open to external inputs like sunlight, food, and water, and the zoo as a whole depends on external inputs like electricity, nutritional products, medicines, and (especially) funding. Also, although the species in a zoo are in limited adaptive relations with their own (segregated) environments, they are not substantially able to adapt those environments to their own needs. Neither are they able to engage other species in patterns of mutual adaptation. If the food, water, waste removal, and medical care organized by the zookeepers were to cease, the animals in a zoo would not be able to contribute to one another's survival, certainly not in any sustainable fashion. The causalities associated with the "life" of a zoo are, finally, highly centralized and linear.

An ecosystem—for example, a rainforest or near-shore environment—exhibits very different relational dynamics. Ecosystems are self organizing, self sustaining, and capable of quite remarkable creative transformations. Natural ecosystems are functionally open at all scales, with individual species in unrestricted, complex interdependence. The causalities associated with the dynamics of an ecosystem are network-like or decentralized, with influences and innovations propagating both upward and downward among nested systems and subsystems. Although it is possible to see species within an ecosystem as in competition with one another over scarce environmental resources, it is more accurately reflective of evolutionary dynamics to see species as distinctively freeing up environmental resources and placing them into effective circulation. Evolutionary niches are not constrained spaces in which species take refuge, but rather resource frontiers opened through creatively expanding the scope of relationalities activated and maintained within a given environment. That is, in an ecosystem, while individual members of species certainly compete for resources, and while competition among similarly constituted species does occur, the fundamental relational dynamic is one of complex coordination.

Zoos exhibit high species variety. In zoos, differentiation takes place primarily with the opening of new exhibits and the introduction of new species of plants and animals to their overall collections. But the overall pattern of relationality obtaining among the species held in a zoo remains essentially one of complicated but secure coexistence. *Ecosystems express high species diversity.* Species dwelling together in ecosystems are in complex interdependence with one another, contributing both directly and indirectly to one another's welfare. In an ecosystem, differentiation involves generating new patterns of both species-environment and interspecies relationality— a change in the overall quality and complexion of interdependence that enhances the value derived from presence in a given environment.

In sum, then, variety is an index of simple multiplicity; diversity is an index of self-sustaining and difference-enriching patterns of mutual contribution to meaningfully shared welfare. Enhancing diversity in any given situation thus involves heightening sensitivities-to and sensibilities-for *differing distinctively* in ways that bring about an appreciation—an increasing valuing—both of the situation as a whole and of being positioned anywhere at all within it. As a direction of differentiation, diversity implies a *significant* lack of sameness—a lack without which the dynamics of mutual contribution would be effectively short-circuited.

Beyond the Metaphors of Cultural "Melting Pots" and "Salads"

The variety-diversity distinction is, of course, not just a means of depicting contrasting manifestations of difference in artificial and naturally occurring environments. To return to an example given earlier, the food items for sale in an international food court afford the hungry customer a wide variety of options for taste, texture, and price, but do not demonstrate culinary diversity. A cuisine like that of Thailand, however, can be fairly described as a manifestation of culinary diversity: it has married foreign foods and preparation techniques from India and China with an array of local foods and techniques to create a distinctive set of self-sustaining and continuously evolving sensitivities-to and sensibilities-for taste, smell, texture, presentation, hospitality, and conviviality. Thai cuisine is not only different from other Southeast Asian cuisines into which similar foreign influences have been imported, it is also internally differentiated and differentiating. Thai cuisine is a living part of Thai culture—an always-evolving expression of distinctive practices and values.

Likewise, although it is possible that a university seminar will contain students from a dozen countries, representing at least an equal number of cultural traditions (and perhaps more, given the multicultural nature of many contemporary societies), this is not a guarantee that the seminar will evidence anything other than a variety of cultural and national identities. In such an artificial or "constructed" environment as the university classroom, diversity is never a given: it is an achievement that, when it occurs, signals a distinctive shift in the relational dynamics of inquiry and learning. Again, cultural variety implies nothing more than factual coexistence. Cultural diversity in the classroom—a much rarer achievement—occurs with the emergence of a self-sustaining relational dynamic wherein cultural differences make meaningful differences in the overall creativity and adaptability of the seminar group as a whole. Cultural diversity, when fully realized, is a means-to and has the meaning-of both *valuing* and *adding value* to a shared situation *through enhancing the significance of cultural difference.*

Whatever their ostensive rationale, the most common metaphors for valorizing what (inappropriately) has been termed the cultural diversity of the plural societies resulting from nineteenth- and twentieth-century patterns of global emigration—the "melting pot" and the "salad bowl"—are quite revealing legacies of modern approaches to politically disarming difference. Each metaphor draws attention to the presence of a variety of ingredients, without making clear whether or how the combination of these distinct ingredients makes a significant difference. A "garden" salad less cucumbers or tomatoes is still a "garden" salad. And while it may be that cucumbers and tomatoes complement one another nicely in the presence of a suitable infusion of herbs, oils, and vinegars, their complementarity occurs through a strictly external relationship. The cucumbers and tomatoes that are placed into a salad are not altered meaningfully by their inclusion therein; they remain essentially unchanged. In the "melting pot," differences undergo at least partial (and often almost total) erasure. The distinctive colors, textures, and flavors of various ingredients are cooked out of evidence to produce a "stew" in which each ingredient's contribution is equally generic and indistinct.

What these metaphors suggest is a bias toward recognizing (and perhaps institutionally promoting) cultural variety, not diversity. In fact, to the extent that peoples and cultures are viewed as "ingredients" in the making of modern nations, their capacities for creativity and meaningful contribution are functionally denied. Ingredients are used (or not used); they are subject to, but do not participate in, the creative act. There is thus an assumption of top-down, linear causality in these metaphors that recalls the centrally determined dynamics of change in a zoo, not the nonlinear patterns of change that emerge in the context of complex and diversity-rich ecological interdependence. Finally, as in such alternative metaphors as the "rainbow," there is no acknowledgement or anticipation of appreciation occurring *within* cultural differences. Salads, stews, and rainbows are enjoyed *only* from the outside.

DIVERSITY AS A DIFFERENTIAL VALUE

Contrasting zoos and ecosystems serves the metaphorical purpose of building a bridge from a somewhat familiar set of engagements with difference into the unknown. Like all metaphorical constructions, to the extent that this contrast works, it intimates possibilities for encompassing and exceeding our horizons of engagement with difference. That is, insofar as it is successful, the zoo-ecosystem contrast directs us out of our current conceptual circumstances, but does not specify our destination. This openness, however, is not incidental to the concept of diversity—a function only of the choice to approach the concept metaphorically—it is crucial. Although diversity does manifest in concrete patterns of relationality—e.g., in ecosystems, within and among cultures, and even in connection with economic modes of production—it does so in a manner that, more than anything else, resembles what we have come to refer to as "values."

The Modern Concept of Values

This statement requires some unpacking and, to that end, a bit of history. In current usage, a distinction is commonly allowed between "value" as the actually determinable *worth* of something, and "values" as verbally encapsulated expressions of what is *worthwhile*. Although it now seems quite natural, this distinction is actually relatively recent. It was only in the early part of the twentieth century that a transition began taking place from exclusively associating "value" with worth to an opening of discourses on "values" as bundles of personal and social attitudes expressing relatively abiding patterns of desire and/or judgment. This was not a shift that was undertaken in a systematic fashion. On the contrary, it seems to have proceeded by way of metaphorical leaps induced by cumulative developments in economic theory that infused the notion of value with greatly expanded relational considerations.

The origins of the concept of value are undoubtedly as ancient as those of barter. English-language uses of "value" in relation to material goods as a term for measurable worth are well documented in some of the earliest of premodern texts, and an extension of this use to cover persons and situations deemed to "have value" was established by the fourteenth century. But it was not until the work of economists like Adam Smith, David Ricardo, and Karl Marx—beginning in the late eighteenth century and gathering momentum throughout the nineteenth century—that the concept of value began to be opened up critically. In the context of attempting to understand, explain, and rationally improve or redirect the functioning of markets, distinctions were drawn among patterns of use, exchange, and labor as variously articulated dimensions included within the broad economic concept of value. In Marx's critique of capitalism, value came to be seen as a complex function of material inputs; the costs of infrastructure required to produce and market commodities; the time and quality of labor incorporated into the commodity through the process of its production; the institutional dynamics in the political, social, and economic spheres that frame and sustain specific patterns of consumption and use; and so on. That is, value arises as a function of the total field of relationships brought into specific focus by any given commodity.

The arc of change undergone by the concept of value from Smith through Ricardo and Marx was broadly oriented toward greater internal articulation, but also toward becoming increasingly imbued with considerations of fairness or justice, at once bringing to light and reflecting a mounting tension between the economic and the ethical. As the narrowly economic concept of value was thus expanded as a means of grappling with new realities that highlighted the (for some troubling) interplay among the economic, social, cultural, and political spheres, considerations of value leapt disciplinary boundaries.

Alongside this economic expansion of the conceptual scope of value, the historical effects of modernity and of rapidly consolidating global market economies also impelled expanded study of the dynamics of social cohesion and identity formation, particularly in relation to explaining and countering evident and anticipated patterns of exploitation and social disintegration. The study of the societal interplay of difference and identity in historical context was initially undertaken with the aim of developing a comprehensive science of the human that was christened "sociology" by August Comte in 1838. But by the third quarter of the nineteenth century, this vision of a comprehensive science gave way to convictions that a formal division was merited between natural and human sciences. With the accumulation of social and anthropological research, it became clear that the general laws and patterns of objective causal necessity that defined the study of natural systems fell far short of what apparently was needed to understand the dynamics of human systems, whether psychological, social, economic, cultural, or political.

A key reason for this, influentially posited by Wilhelm Dilthey in the late nineteenth century, was that the dynamics of the human sphere reflect acts of interpretation and meaning making which establish hierarchies of concern and senses of what is good. As such, they can be reduced only imperfectly—and often misleadingly—to functions of material or mechanical operations. In other words, human societies, as well as their institutions and processes of change, cannot be understood apart from considerations of such factors as felt significance, cognitive coherence, and symbolic resonance. Working at the turn of the twentieth century, Georg Simmel joined this insight with earlier economic expositions of the nature of value to set what can be seen retrospectively as the central pilings for a bridge between value as economic worth and values as clusters of dispositions informing what is understood as worthwhile. In his monumental *Philosophy of Money*, published in 1900, Simmel argued that value is rooted ultimately in social relations as a complex function of subjective and intersubjective desirability. While money serves as a generic medium for exchange that allows a full rationalization of exchange processes, it also can be seen as symbolizing interests in ways that disengage them from their natural settings, greatly facilitating social differentiation and providing practical support for the modern rhetoric of choice and voluntary association.

However, the first systematic exposition of values in the contemporary sense emphasizing both social origins and psychological attitudes was published just after World War I as a methodological aside in a work on Polish peasants (Thomas and Znaniecki 1918–1920). This usage was fully mainstreamed by the 1930s, and was especially central in social psychology—a field of study based on a recognition of commonalties in the dynamics of individual and group behaviors. George Herbert Mead was particularly forceful in drawing out the implications of these commonalities for identity formation. Developing a relational conception of the self and anticipating by a half century the now increasingly well-recognized need to frame social realities in terms of a fundamentally relational ontology, Mead explicitly located values in processes of interaction conjoining the subjective and objective, the personal and the social, and the private and the public.[2]

In the aftermath of the Second World War, the concept of values crossed a crucial threshold of projection to become a key element in postwar political discourse, and expanded relatively quickly into something very close to its present scope. In a 1950 *Foreign Affairs* article, Isaiah Berlin argued that the atrocities of the war could be traced to "crumbling values" and a collapse of civilizational standards. At about the same time, the reconstruction of Germany came to be widely described in terms of a reassertion of "democratic values." As Cold War rhetoric about diametrically opposed value systems approached feverish intensity by mid-decade, Berlin cautioned against all thinking in terms of universal solutions. In a move that would become crucial in shaping late twentieth- and twenty-first-century social and political thought, he proposed instead the embrace of value pluralism as a necessary antidote to the twin ills of moral relativism and moral absolutism—a move that set the stage for an eventual wedding of values discourse with the discourse on difference.

Today, the distinction between value (worth) and values (the worthwhile) is taken completely for granted. The historical detour just taken serves in part to highlight the recent mintage of the concept of values and of a discourse on values that spans the social, economic, political, and cultural spheres. This is instructive, I think, to counteract a stubborn human tendency to reify our own concepts, assuming that they denote naturally occurring features of a purportedly objective and independent reality. But I would hope that the detour would also serve to problematize seeing the construction of the concept of values as complete. It is only at great risk that we view anything that has arisen historically as having arisen completely—unless, of course, it has already met its demise.

That clearly is not the case with values. Although "values" are regularly invoked to explain patterns of concern and decision making, the ease and regularity with which we do so is not apparently correlated with great clarity about their nature, scope, and origins. Like emotions, values have the curious property of seeming to be commonplace and well-understood phenomena until we are asked to define them precisely or explain their formation and the power of their effects on how and why we live as we do. Then we suddenly find ourselves at a significant loss.

The term "values" is now commonly used in reference to a remarkably wide and disparate range of phenomena, including social norms, cultural ideals, action assessments, subjective beliefs, objects, value orientations, behavioral probabilities, and generalized attitudes (Hutcheon 1972). This lack of conceptual precision or resolution is partly due to the fact that the transit from "value" to "values" remains incomplete and one navigated by means of metaphorical leaps. But perhaps more importantly, the elusiveness of a fully convincing definition of values reflects the degree to which values—like emotions—cannot be easily or satisfactorily mapped onto the ontological and epistemological dichotomy of experiencing subjects and experienced objects.

Emotions and values confound our attempts to define and categorize precisely because they occur in between or across the presumably natural divides between subject and object, mind and body, the conceptual and the concrete, the ideal and the real. Our inability to place them clearly and firmly is not due to their ontological amorphousness, but to the limitations imposed by the dichotomously framed concepts of "subject," "object," "mind," and "body"—concepts that presume that external relations are ontologically fundamental. Regarding diversity as a value—rather than as a simple matter of fact—is to anticipate that it will be only inadequately and ineffectively understood as a particular "state of affairs" obtaining among otherwise independent existents.

Conceiving Values Relationally

Reflecting a methodological commitment to examine the geography of difference through the lens of a relational ontology, David Harvey (1996,

11) has argued for a shift of emphasis from fixed ideas of "values" to concerns for "processes of valuation"—for example, the processes of establishing priority rankings, degrees of relevance, and levels of importance and desirability. What we commonly take to be permanent values—like those inscribed within social institutions or actively subscribed to by individuals and communities in a sustained fashion—are in fact historically dynamic phenomena subject to considerable change and eventual dissolution. And, because social, political, economic, cultural, and technological processes are intimately informed by values, emancipatory efforts aimed at addressing these processes will, at some level, require articulating and *fostering alternative* values or *processes of valuation*. As Harvey argues (1996, 12), since values inhere within the full range of socio-spatial processes, "the struggle to change the former is simultaneously a struggle to change the latter (and vice versa)."

Harvey's insistence on the simultaneity or interdependence of changing values and changing socio-spatial processes points explicitly toward recognizing the centrality of values in reorienting global interdependence. But while his recommended shift from thinking in terms of fixed "values" to "processes of valuation" aptly stresses the dynamic nature of values, it does not seem to go quite far enough in drawing critical attention to their ontological peculiarity. As a further step in that direction, I would suggest seeing values as ongoing relational expressions of distinctive means-to and meanings-for differentiation. Or, in more descriptive phrasing: values express particular *modalities of appreciation*. Value terms like "equity" and "diversity" do not refer to free-floating ideas or ideals—immaterial epiphenomena that are ontologically disparate from the material/factual dimensions of our lives and lifeworlds—but rather to the *tenor* of their recursively evolving dynamics.

Prevailing conventions for describing and categorizing values have the unfortunate tendency of falling explicitly on one side or the other of the ontological divides noted above, most especially those between the subjective and objective and between the ideal and the real. The concepts of "modality" and "appreciation" anticipate values discourses that might bridge and eventually close these divides in ways compatible with a nondualist interpretation of difference.

In the Chinese Confucian classic attributed to Mengzi (or Mencius), the master is asked what the difference is between the human and the animal. His answer was that it is "infinitesimal." For Mengzi, as for Fazang, all natures are processual and dispositional. To be a "human" or to be a "horse" is not to have some specific intrinsic *essence*; it is to manifest a distinctive pattern of relational *propensities*. Thus, from a classical Chinese perspective, to be a horse is not simply or even fundamentally to possess a particular genetic makeup or bodily structure. Being a horse means having tendencies to graze on certain grains, to trot or gallop in ways suited to specific kinds of terrain, to travel in herds, to be amenable to domestication and emotional bonding, and so on. Simplistically stated, the Chinese conception of human or horse nature does not focus on what humans and horses *are* in isolation from their lived circumstances, but rather what they *do* under various circumstances or, more accurately perhaps, how they distinctively inflect processes of interaction.

In claiming that the difference between the human and animal is infinitesimal, Mengzi is simply stating what should be obvious: humans and animals *do* many of the same things. For example, both take in nourishment from their environments, communicate with others of their kind in some way, demonstrate particular patterns of association, and engage in acts of procreation. As the Confucian scholar Roger T. Ames frequently notes in discussing this passage, what distinguishes human from animal nature is that human beings are disposed to enchant the ordinary, turning eating into cuisine; transforming warning cries and howls of pain into poetry and song; deepening and expanding uterine groupings into the growing of families, communities, and nations; and transmuting procreative sex into romantic love and spiritual merger. Humans differ distinctively from other animals in respect of their capacities-for and apparent commitments-to qualitatively transforming the everyday. From the Confucian perspective, our distinctively *human* nature is to express remarkably strong propensities for appreciating—that is, progressively enriching and being enriched by—our constitutive relational dynamics.

The patterns of relationality through which we nourish ourselves, through which we nurture personal and communal growth and our capacities of self-expression, and through which we develop expanded structures of feeling are each a distinct *domain* or *dimension of appreciation*. Human nature is not an intrinsic essence possessed by each human being, but rather a dynamic expression of the complex and emergent totality of all such relationally manifest dimensions or domains. Or more accurately stated, the structuring and articulation of this ongoing relational totality are a function of the situation-specific interplay among distinct modalities of appreciation or "values." We are, in a sense always only *becoming* human through our distinctive—and both historically and materially conditioned—approaches to sustained and qualitatively progressive differentiation.

To the extent that values continue to be conceived in ways that allow them to be assigned to one side or the other of such divides as those stipulated between so-called subjects and objects or between the private and public spheres, we continue paying allegiance to an ontology of discrete existents. Values will be taken to be either something like coded expressions of empirically determinable norms or structures of priorities, or something like Platonic forms that hover always just out of reach as mental, spiritual, or otherwise ethereal focuses of personal, cultural, social, or political aspiration. Values will, in short, be apportioned either to the "real" or to the "ideal," rather than being seen as given in the *relational arcs of change* from which the so-called real and ideal are ultimately equivalent abstractions.

Let me attempt to make this somewhat less abstract. Although sense perception can be talked about generally as a particular dimension or domain of experience, in contrast, for example, with imagination or cognition, we do not directly engage in generic sense perception. Rather, our experience is a function of coordinated interplay among a distinct set of sensory modalities—at a minimum, the visual, auditory, gustatory, olfactory, kinesthetic, and tactile—that shape and are shaped by our ongoing relationships in and with our environments. Other species have other sets of sensory modalities, reflecting specific relational possibilities. Bats and cetaceans like dolphins and whales, for example, are capable of echolocation or a capacity for determining their orientation to other objects through interpreting reflected sound waves (much as in the mechanical system of sonar used in submarines). Many fish and sharks are able to sense electric fields. Many insects can directly sense humidity levels. And narwhals are capable—through their tusks—of directly sensing temperature, particle gradients, and air/water pressure.

As everyone who has raised (or helped raise) a child from infancy, or who has trained extensively in either fine or martial arts, knows quite well, sensory abilities are subject to considerable refinement. Although everyone can hear the sounds produced by a jazz pianist, for example, a trained musician is able to hear (and, if need be, write out in detailed musical notation) the various melodies and harmonies that the pianist is rhythmically layering over the course of a given performance. Sense modalities—and interactions among them—do not predetermine what is sensed or perceived. Rather, they open specific approaches to experiential resolution and refinement—not just *more*, but rather different *kinds* and *qualities* of detail and interactive potential. Likewise, values *occur* as openings of distinctive approaches to qualitatively progressive relational resolution and refinement.

DIVERSITY AS RELATIONAL RESOLUTION AND REFINEMENT

As a value, diversity should not be taken to be a generically applicable effect—like **bold** or *italic*—that can be added to or removed from a situation, altering its appearance, but not its presumed essence. Analogously to the way in which so-called family values or the more specific value of loyalty consist in opening and structuring new domains of care and concern regarding personal affiliation, diversity emerges and deepens recursively as the differences among those present in a specific situation are activated as means-to differing for one another by amplifying the meaning-of difference.

Variety signals the presence of differences that do not alter the meaning of being present. Diversity signals the emergence of new arcs of differentiation—newly emerging meanings of presence. Glossing "variety" and "diversity" in this way contravenes current usage. Most dictionaries define these words in terms of each other as synonyms for heterogeneity or the factual presence of difference, and in everyday speech no attempt is made to distinguish them. Celebrating "diversity" thus involves little more than stating approval of plurality as such. This is true even in environmental circles, where biodiversity is championed as key to ecological health, but remains conceptually grounded in fundamentally quantitative measures.

In pressing for a more robust conception of diversity and contravening the habits of day-to-day language use, I have chosen the path of rehabilitating an existing vocabulary rather than one of inventing neologisms. One reason for doing so is to take advantage of emerging tendencies in the science of ecology and in environmental policy to amplify the concept of diversity to index issues of interrelatedness, adaptivity, and resilience. And this broadened and more qualitatively inflected understanding of diversity can readily be seen as applicable to other kinds of complex systems—economic and political, for example. As such, "diversity" is a good candidate for being drafted into service for addressing global issues related to the quality and direction of our deepening interdependence and interpenetration—a conception of difference that promises critical traction across scales and domains.

Seeing diversity as a relational value, however, forces recognition that diversity is not a goal to be arrived at, but rather a distinctive modality of difference-enriching change. One implication of this is that diversity is not everywhere possible. Indeed, in contrast with the conditions for coexistence, which can be established in a linear, deterministic fashion, diversity occurs only as an emergent (hence never necessary) and recursive (hence continuously revised) function of complex interdependence. Unlike variety, diversity cannot be imposed. Indeed, diversification inevitably expresses and enfolds both creative and destructive relational dynamics, and as such is less likely to occur in the context of abiding situational equilibrium than in destabilizing conditions of the sort that would frustrate efforts at explicit control.

A second implication is that since diversity does not arise as a function of simple (or even quite complicated) aggregation, but rather as an emergent property of complexly sustained interdependencies, diversity is not everywhere the same. Unlike variety, diversity is acutely *site* and *scale* sensitive. Where the systems under consideration are relatively small in

scale and limited in scopes of interaction, diversity will be relatively modest. That is, the traction of diversity as a relationally embodied value will
be relatively slight. This is true whether or not the system in question
is, for example, ecological, educational, socioeconomic, political, or cultural. Stated otherwise, diversity tends to be locally "thin" and globally
"thick," and tends to be thickest or deepest where the scale and scope of
interactions are greatest—that is, where the scale and scope of sustainably coordinated mutual contributions are potentially greatest. Thus, the
greatest natural diversity does not occur in the core region of a given ecosystem. Instead, diversity is greatest in the *ecotone* or zone of interaction
between distinctive ecosystems. That is, ecological diversity is greatest
where the relational currents constitutive of adjacent ecosystems converge
and interpenetrate.

The ecotone is a complex and fluctuation-prone borderland where
species must adapt to distinctly different, at times quite contrary, and
unpredictably shifting environmental forces and realities, and within
which they must be valuably enough situated to survive and then flourish. In an ecotone, species must be capable of valuing distinctly different
relational complexes, drawing sustenance from them; but they must also
adapt to those complexes in ways that allow them to be continuously valued therein. In a sense that will be clarified shortly, it can be said that the
survival and flourishing of species living in ecotones depends on their
capacity not only for problem solving, but also for predicament resolution.

More generally stated, diversity tends to emerge most readily in
sites or zones where different, complex "ecologies" interact and interpenetrate—self-organizing and innovation-generating systems of values
and practices that are in constant feedback and feedforward relationships
with their environments. These "ecologies" can be biological, social, economic, political, technological, or cultural in nature, and interactions taking place among them are inseparable from the interpenetration of their
constitutive values, practices, and histories of adaptive innovation. Diversity is thus most likely to be heightened or enhanced where: 1) *confluences*
among distinct systems of values, interests, and practices are *most intense*;
2) where the probability of *conflicts* among them is correspondingly *highest*;
and 3) where the *scale and scope of coordination* and situational appreciation
(but also manifest inequity) are *potentially greatest*.

These are conditions into which we collectively have been ushered by
contemporary globalization processes. As noted in the Introduction, as a
function of the increasingly complex interdependencies developing both
within and among societies, we are now in the midst of an epochal shift
in the *kind* of difficulties, trouble, and suffering associated with increased
globalization: a shift from *problems* to *predicaments*.[3] To reiterate: problems develop when changing circumstances render existing practices

ineffective for meeting continuing needs and interests—a failure of specific means for arriving at ends we intend to keep pursuing; predicaments
arise with conflict-generating confluences of values, interests, and patterns
of development or meaning. Problem solving involves removing blockages or disruptions in a particular and still-desirable pattern of situational
development or meaning. That is, solutions consist of new or improved
means for arriving at abiding ends. Predicaments mark the occurrence
of impasses regarding the direction and quality of interdependence and
thus cannot be solved. Predicaments can only be resolved, where resolution jointly implies sustaining detailed attention to factual dynamics and
realizing clarity with respect to coordinating situationally complex flows
of meaning and valuation. The conditions that are conducive to a global
shift from an era of problems to one of predicaments are also conducive to
expanded and enhanced diversity.

Of course, predicaments are not always resolved and do not always
result in heightened diversity. Both individual species and the ecosystems
comprising them can fail to adapt effectively when placed into direct confluence with distinctly differing others. Likewise, social, economic, political, technological, and cultural "ecologies" and the values, practices, and
institutions comprised within them can dissolve or considerably contract
in terms of scale and scope when situational potentials for coordination
go unrealized and when competition proves disadvantageous. But achieving expanded and enhanced diversity is always, at some scale and in terms
of some scope of interaction, a function of predicament resolution. Succinctly stated, *diversity is most likely to increase* (be required) in zones of
(value) system convergence *where the occurrence of predicaments is highest*—
locales where conflicts of interests are most apparent and the imperatives
for mutual accommodation most acute.

The third implication of seeing diversity as a value is that, while ecological discourse provides very useful examples for explaining the bifurcation of variety and diversity as distinct modalities of difference, ecological
diversity should not be seen as exemplary. This is perhaps counterintuitive, especially since it was the study of complex ecological systems that
brought to light the possibility of differences among the elements in a
system being qualitatively significant. The concept of biodiversity can be
seen, that is, as ancestral for diversity as a globally relevant value. But, the
biological expression of diversity is, in fact, a fairly "local" phenomenon
in the sense that the domains of coordination associated with biodiversity
are relatively limited. Natural ecosystems, although they have undergone
tremendous qualitative development over the past billion years, are not the
most complexly recursive systems of interdependence. The diversity that
they express is, likewise, not the most expansive or situationally enriching.

The advent, for example, of fully reflexive cultures—cultures based on the active and adaptive transmission of values and practices and the recursive amplification of specific kinds of virtuosity—marks the emergence of entirely new dimensions for the expression of diversity. Generally stated, the more expansive the scope of interdependence and interpenetration, the greater the compass of differentiation processes and relational dynamics, and the greater the potential for the emergence of distinctively new expressions of diversity. The historically unprecedented complexity of contemporary social, economic, political, technological, and cultural "ecologies" signals—at the very least—vastly expanded opportunities for diversity.

That said, predicaments are not always resolved and potentials for diversity are not always realized. Indeed, because the conditions for heightened diversity are also conducive to heightened occurrences of predicaments, the expansion of opportunities for diversity almost invariably involves an intensification of challenges to it. Given this correlation, it should not be surprising that while the development of contemporary patterns of market-driven global economic interdependence have opened vastly expanded scales of opportunity for diversification, they have also come to pose profound and systematic threats to diversity, converting local production ecologies into global production monocultures and institutionalizing conditions under which accelerating wealth accumulation for some occurs at the intensifying expense of harrowing poverty and inequity for vastly greater numbers of others.

A second caution is that the "evolution" of conditions for diversity is itself complex—a function of recursion-rich emergence. In complex evolution, adaptations-to a given environment are inseparable from adaptations-of that environment. Contrary to simplistic readings of Darwinian thought, evolution—whether biological or cultural—is neither teleological nor dialectical in the sense of progressing toward a point of consummate perfection. Diversity is a good. But present expressions of diversity cannot be read as ideal or as approaching some specific ideal. As a function of complex interdependence that occurs most readily under nonequilibrium conditions, diversification is necessarily improvisation. Its results cannot be either fully predicted or prescribed. Valuing diversity ultimately means valuing creativity, where creativity implies *significant* innovation: relational transformation in the direction of unprecedented and yet meaningfully enacted capacities-for and commitments-to appreciative coordination. And, granted that equity obtains to the extent that all present in a given situation are positioned to contribute to furthering their own interests, in ways that are situationally deemed valuable—a claim to be taken up more thoroughly in Chapter 8—it follows that enhancing equity is ultimately rooted in valuing diversity.

As modalities of appreciation, values express particular qualities and directions of relational dynamics, generating situationally specific arcs of change. As a value, then, diversity consists in the realization and appreciation of sustained histories of mutually beneficial co-implication. In this sense, diversity functions ultimately as a kind of metavalue recursively coordinating patterns of ongoing differentiation in the means and meanings of differentiation. Diversity changes not only the way things are changing, but why.

CHAPTER THREE

Time Differences

The Changing Nature of Change

I n distinguishing between variety and diversity as two qualities and directions of differentiation, I have stressed the irreducibly temporal nature of difference. In terms introduced earlier, differences *are* only insofar as they *mean*. Every difference signals the presence of a situationally specific arc of change, and the multiplication and magnification of differences that are associated with intensifying global interdependence are thus also a multiplication and magnification of the scale and scope of change. For this reason, passing through or resolving the contemporary aporia of difference can never be a matter of just getting things *right*, once and for all. It depends on coordinating how best to keep *righting* things as they go awry and this requires a certain kind of attention to change.

Attending to change is, of course, central to Buddhist practice. One of the core teachings of the Buddha was that for the purpose of alleviating trouble and suffering, one should see all things as impermanent (*anicca*). But attending to change is not as simple as it sounds. Like difference, change is a concept. It is not a pure matter of fact. Our concepts of time and change derive from a filtering of natural cycles through culturally specific sensitivities and sensibilities (Aveni 2002). Far from being universal and a priori forms for the possibility of experience as Kant maintained in an effort to ground the possibility of epistemic certainty and consensus, our concepts of time, change, and causality are themselves relationally and historically constituted. Or, as David Harvey (1996, 218–31) more pointedly argues, our concepts of space and time are keyed to prevailing social, economic, political, cultural, and technological practices that both express specific values and patterns of self-other relations and establish the horizons of candidacy for immediate relevance and concern. And so, while the contemporary transformations of these practices commend (and perhaps even command) rethinking the means and meaning of change, resistance is natural. Changing how we think about change is ultimately to change how we think about our own being and becoming.

The Buddhist teaching of impermanence is at one level simply an injunction to recognize that all situations are changing: stasis, the absence of change, is relative to attentive scale and scope. Change is always already occurring, and so the critical question is not *whether* things can change, but *whither* they are changing—along what heading? As noted earlier, in the context of Buddhist practice, answering this question involves realizing precisely what karma—what configurations of values, intentions, and actions—are implicated in how things are presently changing. This requires extraordinarily high-resolution holistic attention to change as a continual and qualitatively inflected relational unfolding on which we can take an "objective" perspective only by imagining ourselves to be independent and abiding "subjects"—an act of ignoring our own constitutive implication in this relational unfolding.[1]

As a legacy of modernization, industrialization, and globalization processes, most of the world's people now attend otherwise to time and change. In spite of the revolutions that have occurred in physics (especially with the theory of general relativity and quantum mechanics) and the sciences of organization (with general systems, chaos, and complexity theories), our everyday engagements with change—and with time more generally—remain largely quantitative and objective in character. Our concerns about change tend to cluster around its pace (is it fast enough? too fast?), its predictability (can we tell what will happen? will it bring us what we want? what we fear?), and its purpose (why is it happening? by whom or what is it being caused?). That is, we have come to evaluate change primarily in terms of its rapidity and results; to assume that change must be either random or determined, a function of either the operation of natural laws, chance, or some form of agency; and to experience change either as something that happens to/around us (something imposed) or as a consequence of our own willpower and choice (something intended).

This way of conceiving change is now so transparently a matter of common sense that it is difficult—as it is with difference—to imagine doing otherwise. The advent of postmodern thinking is in part a function of our coming to grips with the deepening obsolescence of modern stances with respect to time, history, and change, and with the need for paradigmatically revising what we mean by them. Yet if as suggested in the Introduction, postmodernity does not so much forward an alternative to modernity as invert its central values, postmodern skepticism about metahistories, metanarratives, and universally convergent change may be useful in stalling further movement along current courses, but not sufficient for opening distinctly different ways forward.

What would it mean to shift away from our biases toward a "vertically" cumulative, quantitative, objectifying, and outcome-oriented understanding of change, while also refraining from an opposing bias toward reading change as a "horizontally" proliferating, subjectively qualified correlate of intentionality? What would it mean, in short, to engage difference-generating historical processes nondualistically?

MODERN PROGRESS AS PURIFICATION

Questions about origins—and hence about time and change—are common to virtually all the world's mythic traditions. Rites of passage, divinatory rituals, and both ceremonial and conceptual stances toward birth, aging, and death have crucially informed cultural and, more specifically, religious practices since prehistory. And, as indicated by the many ancient monumental sites that have calendrical functions, charting the course of time within and across monthly and yearly cycles from very early times has been powerfully associated with wielding cultural and political authority and state formation.

Expectedly, the oldest strata of recorded philosophical thought—in the Mediterranean world, Indian South Asia, and Chinese East Asia—include explicit concerns about the nature of time and change. And in fact, worries have abounded "perennially" regarding the ontological status of the past, the present, and the future; the reality or illusory nature of change and motion; whether time is an absolute medium or a relative function of relationships between events; the finite or infinite extent and/or divisibility of time; the independence, dependence, or interdependence of time and space; the relationship between the (at least apparently) changing and the (at least supposedly) unchanging or eternal; and whether the natures of time and change are linear, cyclic, or (as more recently considered) in some other way nonlinear.[2]

As with difference, what is striking is the degree to which concerns about temporal *quality* have not been integral to modern formulations and responses to these philosophical worries, and the degree to which temporality came to be modeled in linear terms. In effect, modernity has sedimented a view of time as a kind of featureless or neutral terrain, and of change as an incremental function of its traversal.[3] Much like space, time came to be seen as a conquerable factor in the expression of human freedom. This attitude is most explicit in the quintessentially modern notion of progress and its bold assertion of a vectorial understanding of change that assimilates human to divine temporality, claiming for humanity the rights of intervention and initiation once reserved solely for an absolutely transcendent Being or beings.

It is not possible here to lay out in any significant detail the dynamics of the modern conquest of time and change, or the intimately related dynamics by means of which difference was first submerged within various modern universalisms only to reemerge as a key value and concern over the past half century. Nevertheless, it is important to have at least a general sense of the broader social, economic, political, cultural, and technological shifts that informed and were informed by these dynamics. To that end, I would like to follow Stephen Toulmin's masterful lead in his book, *Cosmopolis*, by characterizing the birth of the modern era as a protracted labor occurring from roughly the late sixteenth through the mid-seventeenth century, as Western Europe came to grips with a range of crises reverberating throughout the public sphere.

In contrast with Renaissance humanism and skepticism, which emphasized epistemic humility and both tolerance for and interest in differences of culture, social organization, political sensibilities, and aesthetic sensitivities, the advent of modernity involved a contrary coalescence around rationalism and the search for certainty, emphasizing such values as universalism, equality, progress, control, and autonomy.[4] This led to a systematic biasing of concern and priority away from the oral to the written, from the particular to the universal, from the local to the general, from the timely to the timeless, and from rhetoric to logic. Along with these shifts of interest and emphasis came a "canonizing" of such dichotomies as reason/emotion, mind/body, and spirit/matter, and a powerful tendency to regard differences (especially of religion, ethnicity, language, and culture) as contingent matters of fact properly accorded only minimal relevance in considering how best to frame and realize social, economic, political, and moral good.

This shift from premodern to modern sensibilities and sensitivities regarding time, change, and difference did not occur in a vacuum. A signal characteristic of the early modern period was the purposeful consolidation of nation-states that were multiethnic, multicultural, and religiously plural. This was, on some readings at least, a simple necessity. Throughout the first half of the seventeenth century, Western Europe was wracked by virulent interreligious wars, a fracturing of medieval structures of authority, bloody confrontations over rights to rule and the meaning of right rule, as well as catastrophic interruptions of trade and commerce. Estimates are that, in combination, these effects of profoundly felt differences between Roman Catholic and Protestant Christians resulted, just over the course of the Thirty Years War (1618–1648), in the deaths of some six to eight million people. It was against this background of ongoing crisis that modernity consolidated in response to tragically evident needs for unity (order) and uniform (not chaotic) change.

Distinctively, modern values came to be understood as having comprehensive practical, and not merely theoretical, relevance: values that enjoyed traction in every dimension of life, both throughout and among societies. And while the long-term impacts of these values can be debated, there is little doubt that with the full flowering of modernity, history forever ceased being a mere recollection and recording of things past. History was also something to be made. The Hegelian and Marxist views of history, however much they are otherwise opposed, each epitomizes the modern construction of history as an artifact marked heavily by human agency—not a simply "natural" sequence of events playing out over time, but a creative appropriation of time. Importantly, while this reconstruction of "history" was actively projecting human aims and interests into the central role of making historic differences, science promised progressive access to a unifying and universally valid vision of the structures of being and becoming—insight into the causal orders shaping human experience and, eventually, complete control over them.

The modern disposition toward seeing history as something to be made, and change as something to be consciously initiated and accelerated, is in many ways nicely summarized in the assertion made by the American philosopher George Santayana that those who fail to know their histories are doomed to repeat them. This innocuous sounding statement has come to epitomize what amounts to global common sense regarding time, change, and history: it is only by dispelling ignorance of our pasts (as well as rooting out past forms of ignorance) that we can free ourselves for personal advance and social progress. Modernity, as a key project and expression of the European Enlightenment, involves breaking out of the cyclic temporality that has characterized daily life for most of humanity, for most of human history.

In part, this conceptual break from the repetitive spirals of nature can be seen as a function of real industrial capacities of control that began developing in earnest over the eighteenth century. But it also represents the consolidation of universal ideals for human conduct and capability. Dominance over the natural world connotes dominance over its manifestly spiral rhythms—a capacity to straighten out nature's tendency toward recursion or folding back on itself, and to establish instead a clear trajectory into a future that, in *significant* degree, will be something both new and never to be repeated. To press the metaphor, the European Enlightenment was as much about pushing back the darkness of night and of winter as it was about evaporating the provincialities of blood, vision, and interest that purportedly characterized the premodern mind.

Modernity and its distinctively proliferating families of technologies brought—or perhaps more accurately, bought, at costs still being calculated—freedom from the diurnal cycle, from the rhythm of the four seasons, and at least a mitigation of the humiliations of a life cycle that hoists

us from birth out of cellular dust through maturation and mid-life mag-
nificence only to drop us into the galling depredations of aging and death.
Modernity in this sense has always been "perfumed" by a somewhat utopian metanarrative. Whatever excesses of creative destruction have been
undertaken in making room for progress—aimed, in a quite common
modern vision, at the eventual elimination of want and need—modernity
(particularly from the nineteenth century onward) has enjoyed a strenuously heroic self-understanding.

Considered in this light, the modern emphases on cleanliness and
hygiene, not only as medical necessities, but as social ideals and as merits
of accelerating industrial advance, suggest broad commitment to sanitiz-
ing space and time—divesting them of earth-bound cultural attributes
derived from seasonally defined toils, and generating forms of learning
and knowledge applicable to and applied by all. This cleansing convergence of modern and industrial values is beautifully symbolized by the
historical process by means of which the vernacular practice of making
soap by adding lye to home-rendered animal fat came to be commercialized, commodified, freed from dependence on "unclean" waste products,
and then spun off into the sparkling efficacies of industrial-scale chemical
engineering—a process charted in wondrous and sobering detail in Richard Powers' novel *Gain*.

We can detect in Santayana's affirmation of historical consciousness,
then, a resolute valorization of linear over cyclical temporality, a championing of time and change informed and ordered by intentionality, a freeing of time and change from material and cultural contaminations. The
process of cleansing bodies, homes, livelihoods, and daily rhythms of their
earthly and celestial origins cannot be divorced, however, from the intellectual cleansing also sought by the Enlightenment and epitomized by the
Cartesian goal of knowledge derived a priori or before the soiling of reason by experience. Modern science and philosophy were distinctive, not in
their concerns, but rather in the force of their pursuits of universality and
certainty—their searching for inviolable (and so eternally and everywhere
applicable) laws and truths.

The broader, value-laden convergences that constitute modernity as a
complex of historical phenomena will occupy us more directly in Chapter
4. But it bears stressing here that the Enlightenment learning to which we
can trace contemporary scholarly institutions, practices, and norms—and
thus the core concepts within our critical toolbox—was itself profoundly
value laden and biased ontologically toward the study of individual existents (whether things or events) taking place against a background of
universal and objectively divisible space and time. The Indo-European
root of the English "learn" (*leis*) expresses metaphorically an association of learning with transforming relationships, referring to a furrow

or furrowing—a purposeful opening of the earth to create a well-tended space hosting the cycle of seeding, germination, growth, and maturation or ripening. In sharp contrast, the modern notion of learning idealized its dissociation from culturally specific forms of relationality and its association, instead, with optimizing powers of analysis, choice, and control.

If its root connotations are any indication, the premodern association of learning with farming and with building a body of lore (also a derivate of *leis*) points toward a cultural ethos in which learning embodies the real remembrances of an enduring community: the distinctive practices and meanings of being human in relation to a particular locale or place, over a shared span of time. Modern learning, by contrast, opened opportunities for breaking with any history that would repeat itself in however complicated a fugue. Peter Ramus captured this sense of learning beautifully, if somewhat ironically, toward the end of the late sixteenth century by envisioning and advocating curriculum-based education, claiming that the then-prevailing *studio* method of learning was outmoded. Studio learning took place in the context of sustained and potentially lifelong improvised dialogues between a master of a particular knowledge domain and individual apprentices. Against this model of relationally embedded transmission, Ramus claimed that knowledge could be mapped and that its dissemination could be logically and universally ordered or methodized. Education not only could, but *should* follow a particular and explicitly terminal course. His invocation of the term *curriculum* captured his innovative vision perfectly—a Latin word referring to a circular course of standard length that was used to order the competitive movement of charioteers.

With the notion of a curriculum, Ramus forwarded an understanding of knowledge as a quantifiable good most efficiently and effectively delivered via logically ordered sequences of individually simple knowledge units and building progressively to a fixed end. As those passing through preestablished curricula, pupils in modern educational institutions came to be conceived as generic and yet individually competing travelers instructed by methods expressing and transferring the deep structure of various, independent (and typically church- and state-authorized) bodies of knowledge and competence. Modern education effectively translated learning practices from relationally focused modes of self-cultivation into instructional regimens for individually expressed self-transformation: a decisive *rendering* of the dynamics of change.

LATE MODERN TEMPORALITIES

By the middle of the nineteenth century, however, visions of modernization as purification and of learning as a universal key to freedom and gain for all were becoming ever more difficult to sustain. The stark contrast and widening gap, for example, between the opulent lives of the capitalist class and the gritty squalor of the working class in industrialized countries like Great Britain and the United States spoke volumes about biases intrinsic to modern market universalism. This contrast spurred Marx and Engels to reconstruct history in pursuit of an alternative (albeit no less universalistic) route of modernization—one aimed at fundamentally changing the global complexion of change. But at a more personal level, there began to consolidate a sense that modern values and ways of knowing might themselves be basically flawed, that they might constitute an impediment to the full realization of our individual human potential, a herding of sensibilities toward one brand or another of conformity. The ever-accelerating pace of change, much remarked upon by nineteenth-century social commentators, seemed to have taken on a life of its own, transmitting into daily life a troubling aura of relentlessness.

Nietzsche's announcement of the "death of God" in *Thus Spake Zarathustra* (1885) can, at least in retrospect, be seen as a disintegrative turning point in the project of modernity—a turning point to which the various genealogies of the postmodern can plausibly and yet ironically be traced. Less an iconoclastic statement of presumed fact than a rhetorical scission aimed at stripping away every vestige of egalitarianism from modernity's heroic individualism and celebration of choice, Nietzsche's "death of God" signaled an irreversible unraveling of all transcendent orders and a blanket denial of authenticity to all universalistic perspectives.

This said, by valorizing the "will to power"—and hence our human capacities for demonstrating creativity and control of a depth that warrants taking full responsibility for the shape and meaning of change—Nietzsche did not so much reject the modern celebration of breaking heroically free of nature's mandates as he reframed it in dramatically individualist terms. And although his imagination of "eternal recurrence" can be interpreted as a challenge to personally express unlimited confidence in our present creative power—as befits those who would hold in virulent contempt any kind of herd mentality—it is a curiously premodern rebuttal to modern champions of linear change.[5]

Nietzsche's iconoclastic hammering of both tradition and modern universalist transformation did not have its desired shattering effect. But by the beginning of the twentieth century, reservations about the modern notion of progress and its essentially quantitative and vectorial understanding of change had massed sufficiently to begin threatening modernity's social, economic, and political foundations. Giddy enthusiasms for the promises of technologically secured progress gave way to sobering admissions of mounting alienation and evidence of history having gone awry. Philosophically, the results were explicit and widespread assertions of a deepening crisis of meaning—a loss of global purpose as well as personal attunement that was articulated with particular force by such heirs of Nietzsche's radical conception of human freedom as Martin Heidegger and Jean-Paul Sartre, for whom the way forward came through a confrontation with human limits, especially the ultimate limit of death itself.

As expressed in Heidegger's monumental *Being and Time*, originally published in 1927, the possibility of deriving meaning from a relation to the eternal and universal—the progressive realization of modern ideals—could be sustained only in ignorance of the acute temporality of our engagements with others, our shared world, and our very own selves. The conviction, endemic to modernity, that meaning, universality, equality, freedom, and the certainty of *being* human could be seen as *given* was, in light of our actual temporality, nothing more than a conceit. The freedom of being human, as Heidegger and others navigating in the wake of modernity would insist, cannot be separated from our uncertainty—especially our uncertainty before death.

The centrality of uncertainty to the human experience and the possibility that modern achievements in the pursuit of universality and control might have a restrictive, if not coercive, shadow were by no means exclusively philosophical concerns. Alongside the philosophical crisis in modernity, convictions that something was deeply amiss in the way things were changing found broad expression in the arts, most powerfully and complexly perhaps in dystopian literature and films like E. M. Forster's *The Machine Stops* (1909), Fritz Lang's *Metropolis* (1927), and Aldous Huxley's *Brave New World* (1932), all of which called attention to potentially dehumanizing effects of technologically enabled control. Modern means to freedom and individualism seemed frighteningly liable to become enslaving.

Shared by these philosophical and artistic confrontations with the dystopian potentials of modernity was a concern that the individual might become the prey of the collective, of a faceless system, an order of compelling efficiency. As we shall later see, these concerns would remain crucial to the coalescence of the condition of postmodernity over the second half of the century in the aftermath of the violent exclusivism and totalitarianism of Nazi "final solutions" to the problems of modernity. There were, however, also more hopeful expressions of these concerns—most influential and popular prior to the Second World War and much less so thereafter, but no less conceptually rich than their dystopian kin.

A more comprehensive and hopefully healing criticism of modern constructions of time and change was, for example, forwarded by the Nobel laureate, Henri Bergson. Against modern certainty, mechanism, and control, and nascent existentialist stress on confrontations with death, Bergson placed emphasis on *élan vital* or the "life impulse," articulating a world thoroughly infused with enduring, purposive, and yet nonteleological change—a world of self-organizing, creative evolution. Writing in the late nineteenth and early twentieth centuries, Bergson's criticism of the modern bias toward seeing change predominantly through the lenses of questions about pace and predictability grew out of his conviction that sufficient attention to daily experience reveals what the science of his day—grappling both with evidence of biological evolution and the relativity and quantum revolutions in physics—was beginning to make clear: ours is not a world of myriad distinct *beings*, perhaps composed of more basic elements, but rather a world of distinctive and ceaselessly creative *becomings*.[6]

Bergson identified the modern disposition toward seeing change and time in overwhelmingly quantitative terms with a "cinematographic" bias in the intellect—a bias toward taking things and forms as "elements" of becoming and duration rather than as "views" or "snapshots" thereof. In doing so, he joined the company of William James and other pragmatists who, at roughly the same time, were intent on refuting the so-called "ontological fallacy" of assuming that our conceptual units of analysis denote real features of the world around us. But whereas the pragmatists remained largely wedded to applying differently what remained a fairly mainstream modern understanding of rationality, Bergson asserted a need to complement and complete the perspective offered by modern rationalism. This he referred to as "intuition"—a capacity for seeing change in qualitative terms and as always and necessarily implying growth and creativity. Time, as he put it, is not a neutral medium; it "is invention or it is nothing at all" (Bergson 1944, 371). Change cannot be reduced to a series of instantaneous juxtapositions in space that disallow meaningful differentiation because difference itself is taken to be only an empty expression of nonidentity. Rather, change should be understood as a "continuity in interpenetration," a qualitative multiplicity that cannot but be falsified by being filtered through reason's cinematographic prejudice. More systematically than those inclined toward a dystopian reading of the human condition, Bergson sought to express a relational alternative to the modern ontology of individually existing—and so mutually limiting—things, beings, and events.

Nevertheless, like Nietzsche and Heidegger, Bergson was a thoroughly Western philosopher at once working against the grain of his own inherited tradition and constrained by it. Although his emphasis on change and creativity, combined with his denial that the lived world can be best explained or engaged by appeal to teleological or deterministic mechanisms, can be seen as anticipating contemporary theories of complex emergence, his celebrations of change and evolutionary advance remain perfumed with modern progressivism and a stress on agent-centered freedoms of choice. Bergson's critique of modern constructions of time and change, like those of Heidegger and, more recently, Derrida and Deleuze, remains an essentially *internal* critique.

From our own early twenty-first century perspective, what is interesting is how Heidegger's emphasis on the projective temporality of human nature might be combined with Bergson's emphasis on the intrinsically enduring creativity of time to evoke a sense of temporality for which inexorability is a less apt qualifier than terms like exploratory and explanatory. Such a merger has, I think, been forwarded by Gilles Deleuze. In calling for a revival of Bergsonian thought in spite of all the late modern and postmodern animosities directed at it—particularly by those affronted by Bergson's intuitionist skepticism about language—Deleuze (1991) has usefully stressed both Bergson's celebration of multiplicity or differentiation as an ontological basic and the exploratory dimension of his invocations of creativity and invention.[7]

But to be seen as suggesting a conceptual arc oriented obliquely to the tension between the monolithic "verticality" of modern universalisms and the rhizomatic "horizontality" of postmodern relativisms, the exploratory dimension of differentiation must be seen as penetrating and penetrated by the explanatory. The "internal" critiques offered by Bergson's and Heidegger's hermeneutically inclined heirs become effective to the extent that they are held together as complementary resources for rejecting the modern bias toward dualism.

Bergson's claim that we do not live in a world of juxtaposed beings and moments but rather one of inherently inventive and interpenetrating becomings, combined with a Heideggerian emphasis on the intentional nature of human temporality, suggests that we live in a world of irreducibly shared meaning making. Every becoming is a distinctive kind of explaining or mutual elucidation. Or, to recall Fazang's expression of nondualism: all things *are* what they *mean* for one another. Seeing change nondually is to see change, not as a process of moving along strings of individually existing and ever-varying moments, but rather as a process of relational resolution in which both senses of "resolve" are necessarily implied: change expresses and brings into focus distinctive means-to significantly differing meanings-of presence. Change-from does not simply imply change-to, but also change-for. Or in terms introduced earlier in respect of difference: change is no more primarily a function of things *happening* than it is of things *occurring*. Variation is no more basic than diversification. Linear changes are no more rudimentary than changes that are nonlinear.

Importantly, to the degree that change processes *are* biased away from diversification toward variation, from nonlinearity toward linearity, change becomes at once increasingly predictable and empty of value, increasingly unlikely to express the dynamics of complex emergence. In fact, variation represents an apparent interruption or opening of gaps within change processes: the production of functionally discrete coexistents through the consolidation of restricted scopes of interdependence. That is, variation means a diminution or deactivation of the meaning-generating, elucidative function of differentiation, reducing creativity to the mere production of novelty. In thermodynamic terms, variation is ultimately an entropic modality of change—a process of decreasing potentials for meaningful interaction in qualitatively appreciating patterns of relationality.[8] Or, accepting de Saussure's claim that language is only difference, variation expresses nonsensical differentiation—an unoriented (and perhaps disorienting) expression of difference: a speaking that says nothing.

Importantly, to the degree that we experience and engage change as a function of relational transformations that are less aptly described as happening from-this-*to*-that than as occurring from-this-*for*-that, we move away from assuming that change is or should be basically law bound. A defining presupposition of modernity has been that change happens in accordance with an abiding infrastructure of natural laws that, while they do not initiate change in the sense of providing its originative impetus, nevertheless sustain and constrain it. Modernity presumes, in other words, the basic predictability of change processes. Given sufficient information about initial conditions, change patterns can be as well and accurately projected into the future as accounted for causally in examination of the past. But as we will see over succeeding chapters, the actual changes brought about by modernization ironically led to confrontation with the fact that the basically lawlike nature of change finally cannot be derived from experience, but rather only presumed of it.

It was, in other words, modernity's very real successes that set the stage for late nineteenth- and early twentieth-century nihilism and crises of meaning. Evidence of the absence of an essentially regular and regulative infrastructure within change processes—whether in science, economics, politics, or society as a whole—began mounting precisely as the integrative processes of global modernization became complex enough to begin exhibiting the self-organizing and novelty-generating dynamics of emergence. By technologically and conceptually expanding the reach of certainty and control beyond the threshold of their own utility, modernization processes themselves began generating ironically destabilizing and constraining effects, setting up conditions under which further "progress" in pursuit of modern ideals would exacerbate the sense of being immersed in patterns of ever-intensifying predicament.[9]

DISENTANGLING CHANGE, CHANGELESSNESS, AND CHANCE

Underlying the modern notion of progress with its conceptual reliance on natural, universally valid laws of change is a fundamental bias toward the changeless, the eternal: an ideal beyond all vicissitude. Modernity's dynamism, however "evolutionary" in formulation, is an expression of abiding and all-encompassing principles that are taken to be realized in varying *degrees of completeness* economically, socially, politically, scientifically, and technologically, at any given point in time and space. The project of modernity—the realization of "cosmopolis"—ultimately was one of aligning the temporal with the eternal, constructing knowledge as completing our grasp on things (comprehension) and progress as a function of result-oriented change. Nothing was more devastating for this project than scientifically compelling evidence that completion was a false ideal, and in this sense the death of modernity can be traced symbolically to Kurt Gödel's 1931 proof of the incompleteness of all formal systems. By denying certainty and completeness even in the realm of mathematics, Gödel effectively proved as well the untenable nature of modernity as an historical project, dissolving the cornerstone of the foundations of modernity that Nietzsche had begun dismantling half a century earlier.

Of course, the quest for certainty and the view that change is opposed to (or appears only against the background of) the changeless are not uniquely modern. What is distinctive is the extent to which the modern expression of this quest and perspective on change was realized materially and yet ironically culminated in a vision of the world as resting on chaotic foundations. The lesson driven home by modern science in the opening decades of the twentieth century was that a focus on certainty and predictability might well prove restrictive rather than revelatory. The indeterminacy that quantum mechanics located at the most fundamental strata of material organization demonstrated that even if (as Einstein would protest) god did not play dice with the universe as a whole, the most fundamental processes of change informing the workings of the cosmos were in fact akin to the rolling of dice: uncertainty was ontologically most basic, not certainty.

The responses of Heidegger and Bergson to this indeterminacy—oppositely affirming the authenticating power of death and the creative power of life—can be seen as attempts to retrieve meaning from the chasm opening between necessity and chance. On very different bases, each can be seen as working to conceive human freedom in a way that did not depend on the exercise of fully determinate control: freedom located in the situated act rather than the situational outcome. Whereas Nietzsche's trope of the "eternal return" at least ostensibly articulated freedom in terms of *choosing* the inevitable, the streams of nineteenth- and twentieth-century thought epitomized by Bergson and Heidegger locate freedom in the gap between the absolute and the arbitrary. For Bergson, this is the topos or place of the naturally occurring, the *élan vital*; for Heidegger it is the topos of intentionality exercised subjectively in spite of

objective constraints and determinations. In each case, the driving intuition is that time must be freed from the metaphor of "passing." Modernity's essentially calculative treatments of time and change—its focus on
issues of pace, prediction, and purpose—can only deliver false promises.

Granted the disparity of their influences in the second half of the
twentieth century, with Heidegger's thought vastly eclipsing that of Bergson, it is interesting that it is Bergson's views on time and change that
afford the most ready resources for articulating an ethics of equitable relationality. For Heidegger, being human is to be *thrown* into circumstances
not of one's own making, positioned accidentally in specific historical and
cultural circumstances. And it is the world into which we are thrown that
is the site of our activity. Our being thrown sets the horizons within which
we carry out the work of realizing our aims, making use of those resources
we find ready-to-hand. As Heidegger's later work makes clear, the site
of our being with others in an attitude of care is not an abstract *space* in
which we find "humanity," but a real *place* in which we find ourselves part
of a people, with a language, a distinctive set of customs and concerns. In
many ways, Heidegger's route around the modern focus on universality,
certainty, and control is by way of the premodern, a returning "home."[10]

For Bergson, especially as interpreted by Deleuze, this structure of
being-in the world is challenged. Bergson discerns two kinds of time and
multiplicity: a time of simultaneities, of passing moments; and a time of
duration, of continuity and penetration. The first correlates with a multiplicity of juxtaposition that is essentially a numerical construct; the second, with a multiplicity of interpenetration that is essentially qualitative.
As Bergson makes clear in *Creative Evolution*, these multiplicities differ
typologically, and are not to be understood as opposed to oneness or unity.
The choice is not between the one and the multiple, but rather between
distinct kinds of multiplicity or difference. In thus framing multiplicity,
Bergson comes very close to expressing the variation-diversification distinction. But by opposing intellect and the abstract time of moments to
intuition and the concrete time of *la durée*, claiming that the former presents a false view of the world and the latter a true one, Bergson presents us
with a very modern set of dualisms between the false and true, the static
and dynamic, and the abstract and concrete, remaining firmly wedded to
the metaphor of time as a flow.

SWITCHING METAPHORS:
FROM RIVERS OF TIME TO TEMPORAL ECOLOGIES

In the end, neither Heidegger nor Bergson offers a consistently nondualist understanding of time and change. By insisting on the ontological gap
between the discontinuous images accessible by the intellect and the fluid

continuity available in intuition, Bergson belies his effort to disable the one/many distinction. Heidegger's insistence on the thrown nature of being human introduces an ethically significant gap between reality and responsibility that is not closed so much as addressed by intentionality and care. As a means to pressing forward with Bergson's distinction between juxtaposition and penetration as types of multiplicity and modalities of change, and with Heidegger's stress on intentionality, in ways that will break more completely away from modern biases and respond to the contemporary aporia of difference, let me set us forth on a metaphorical detour.

Among the most widely cited metaphors for time in the history of Western thought is one attributed to the pre-Socratic philosopher Heraclitus. According to Plato, whose rendering of Heraclitus becomes canonical for Western thought, Heraclitus espoused a doctrine of universal flux according to which all things are continuously changing, comparing existents to the flowing waters of a river into which it is impossible to step twice (*Cratylus* 402a).[11] By assimilating the process of change to an inexorable flow, the metaphor depicts time as a unidirectional and internally undifferentiated motion that is generally thought of as an irreversible current proceeding from future into present and then to past. This is a metaphor to which Bergson remains attracted, if not entirely attached.

The river metaphor encourages thinking of time as a relatively neutral medium, like water, that is well suited to quantitative measure. It is a metaphor that fits rather nicely with the modern disposition toward temporal concerns focused on issues of rate or rapidity, as well as with the plausibility of predicting the course of change by peering "upstream." It informs common idioms about how quickly "time passes" when we are having a good time, about the quaintness of those places that "time has left behind" like eddies in the stream, and about the ceaselessly oncoming rush of "current events." Not incidentally, through a set of connections that we will look at more closely later, it is a source metaphor for the modern (also metaphorical) assertion that "time is money" and the association of money—a medium of economic exchange—with currency.

Like all metaphors, seeing time as something that flows in a river-like manner brings into focus some dimensions of the complex relational dynamics that are distilled into our ever-evolving conception of temporality. At the same time, it draws attention away from and even blocks awareness of others. For the sake of sharp contrast, I would like to consider the metaphorical complex that deeply informed traditional Chinese conceptions of time and change at least through the early twentieth century, when China sought to bootstrap itself into modernity, and that arguably remains widely prevalent in the present.

The earliest evidence of how Chinese understood time and change can be gleaned from animal scapulae and tortoise shells that were used in oracular rituals during the Shang dynasty (approximately 1600–1000 BCE). After an "oracle bone" had been polished and had pits or hollows carved or drilled into its surface, it was inscribed with a question—typically formulated in such a way as to be "answered" in a yes or no fashion—and then subjected to heat in order to produce a cracking pattern that the diviner (often a Shang king) would interpret to decide how the dilemmas posed were to be understood. Like many of the world's peoples, the Shang apparently believed that the future—through the intervention of the heavenly or celestial realm—could in some ways be made to reveal itself. Time, in short, was understood as a procession of events that could be known, not only after the fact but also, in some degree at least, before it.

Subsequent to the demise of the Shang in 1027 BCE, the Chinese developed a very different kind of divinatory practice and conception of time. These new practices and conceptions came into full flower from the Zhou through the Han dynasties—an historical span coinciding roughly with the development of Hellenic culture from the time of Homer (ninth c. BCE) to that of the skeptic Sextus Empiricus (third c. CE). In sharp contrast with what emerged as the mainstream of Hellenic thought, the Chinese did not move in the direction of contrasting time with eternity or the timeless, or of seeing change as either subordinate to the changeless, as preordained or teleological, or as ultimately a function of (finally transcendental) agency.[12] Instead, as evidenced both in ritual and textual traditions, the Chinese came to see change itself as ontologically basic and took the most fundamental philosophical questions not to rest on discerning Being or the true nature of the Good, but rather on how best to accord with and harmonize always ongoing patterns of becoming.

Superficially, the Chinese stress on the basic reality of change recalls Heraclitus' affirmation of flux and his denial of permanence. But the dominant Chinese metaphor for time and change was not at all that of a river flowing relentlessly past, like water under the bridge of the present, a single substance that taken on its own is colorless, tasteless, and shapeless. Rather, as made evident in the *Yijing* or Classic of Change—a central text in the Chinese cultural canon for nearly 2,500 years—the dominant metaphor is ecological. The oracular practices undertaken by the peoples of the Shang centered on concerns about whether and when to act and the likelihood of achieving desirable outcomes—concerns like those that dominate in modern constructions of temporality. In sharp contrast, the *Yijing* is a heuristic for discerning and altering the quality and meaning of change. In it, concerns center on the tenor, complexion, or character of time and change. And, although the metaphors for time and change in the *Yijing* are, like that of Heraclitus, basically natural, they are metaphors of complex interrelatedness.

The root structure of change in the *Yijing* is one of qualitative diversification, founded on a polar (or bifurcating, rather than dichotomous) contrast of *yin* and *yang*. These terms originally referred to the shaded and sunny sides of a valley, and came to refer generically to any pattern of qualitatively complementary contrast. Rather than being fixed characteristics or basic energy types/elements, *yin* and *yang* designate explicitly and irreducibly correlated *directions* of relational dynamics. In the *Yijing*, *yin* and *yang* factors (represented as solid or broken lines) combine to form sixty-four hexagrams (six-line figures) representing all possible configurations of *yin* and *yang* propensities, with each hexagram describing a particular situational quality and set of possibilities for relational transformation. Traditionally, each hexagram is understood as comprising two trigrams (three-line figures) representing a set of directional contrasts affecting change dynamics—inner and outer, upper and lower, social and personal, and so on. Importantly, each of the eight possible trigrams was associated with a guiding metaphor, a specific emotion, a center of bodily functioning, a cardinal direction, season, and so on. In total, they constitute the basic "vocabulary" of change.

For the Chinese, at least from the Zhou period onward, divination was not centered on discerning what would or would not happen and when, but rather on how best to appreciate existing trajectories of change dynamics to realize the most productive and sincerely creative harmonization among the greatest possible number of situational elements. As represented by the metaphors associated with each of the eight trigrams, change was not only understood as ontologically basic, it was understood as qualitatively diverse: as celestial, earthy, lakelike, watery, fiery, windlike, thunderous, and mountainous. Each of the sixty-four hexagrams represents, in turn, an archetype of situational or complex relational development—a particular axis of affiliations and propensities within an encompassing ecology of change.

These glances sideways and back toward ancient Greek and Chinese notions of time and change hopefully make the point that, even in terms of a concept as seemingly rudimentary as that of change, great disparities can obtain, not just across, but within cultures. Further, the longevity of the contrasting "Greek" and "Chinese" conceptions of change and the metaphors through which we have access to them indicates the extent to which such basic concepts are often so deeply embedded in the contours of daily life that they elude direct critical attention. It may be the case, in fact, that the most effective ways toward the revision or elision of such basic concepts will be initiated metaphorically.

This, perhaps, is not at all surprising. As is argued persuasively George Lakoff and Mark Johnson (1980), there is a sense in which we all "live by metaphors." Not only do metaphors structure our most basic understandings of the world, but *significantly* new knowledge is at first almost invariably approached metaphorically, on imagistic bridges cantilevered out from the familiar into the hitherto unknown. In attempting to develop new conceptions of time, change, history, and difference, we are in need of new—or at least previously neglected or underutilized—metaphors. The ecological metaphors for change that have traditionally informed Chinese sensibilities encourage sensitivities to interdependence that, in spite of their origins in antiquity, afford surprisingly apt points of embarkation for nurturing an understanding of complex, nonlinear change that is conducive to elucidating diversity as a distinctive modality or means-to and meaning-of differentiation processes.

MEASURE, MEANING, AND THE HETEROGENEITY OF TIME

At the same time, all metaphors have specific limitations and liabilities. The ecological metaphors embedded in the *Yijing* serve to radically displace issues of measure, shifting them to the periphery of temporal concerns and foregrounding, instead, issues of relational quality and meaning. Efforts to determine when, for how long, and how quickly to act or enact change then yield to efforts to discern how best to accord with naturally ongoing patterns of change. As understood in both the classical Confucian and Daoist traditions, the most appropriate stance in engaging change is one of according with the already unfolding *dao* or way of things—a stance that in the Confucian case had the liability of resulting in a socially, culturally, and politically conservative valorization of the status quo, and in the Daoist case a tendency to valorize the "natural" or "spontaneous" (*ziran*) and the wisdom of noninterference. In both cases, the ecological metaphor—especially in combination with the correlative yin/yang cosmology informing it—was conducive to understanding change as a kind of homeostatic process, a continual returning to equilibrium. Heidegger's focus on intentionality and Bergson's on creativity can be seen as counters to this premodern stress on homeostasis—a valorization of sustained patterns—even as they offer individualizing and naturalizing rejoinders to modern emphases on the universality and inevitability of progress. They do not, however, entail a full-fledged ethicization of time and change.

One contemporary effort to foreground the relational and nonhomogenous nature of time in a way that attempts to circumvent a bias toward homeostasis while also being highly sensitive to the need for a resolutely qualitative construction of spatiotemporality is that of David Harvey. Synthesizing a unique array of modern and postmodern intellectual streams, Harvey (2006) forwards a tripartite heuristic for investigating space-time, distinguishing among: 1) *absolute and universal* space and time (the independently existing domains of objective measure invoked by, for example, Newton and Descartes); 2) *relative* space and time that exist only as a function of external relations between existing objects, including observing subjects (the interdependent and flexible domains invoked so powerfully by Einstein and such non-Euclidean geometers as Janos Bolyai and Hermann Minkowski); and 3) *relational* space-time (a domain of internal relations implied by Leibniz's monadology, by Whitehead's process philosophy, and now invoked by many at the cutting edge of cybernetic science).[13] Harvey is careful to avoid ranking these hierarchically, but admits that the more closely we conceive and engage space-time relationally, the more problematic measurement becomes and the closer we come to a point where mathematics, poetry, and music—measure and meaning—converge and perhaps merge (p. 124).

As I interpret it, Harvey's attempt to understand spatial and temporal dynamics in terms of a relational ontology leads him to insist on the spatiotemporal as basic; to argue for a balanced recognition of measurability and meaning as intrinsic dimensions of time and change; and to do so in a way that nevertheless undermines the starkly diametric contrasts which characterize modern conceptions of the relationship between the spatial and the temporal. This is, for me, the point of his advocating a tripartite heuristic: an insistence on understanding time and change as intrinsically heterogeneous or differentiated. Time, from such a perspective, is not of a single essence.

The importance of this insight and approach can be made quite evident by taking a concrete example. Harvey himself considers for this purpose the spatiotemporal considerations involved in redesigning the site now known as "Ground Zero" (the site of the terrorist flight of a commercial jet into the World Trade Towers on September 11, 2001). What immediately strikes anyone embarking on such considerations is the utter centrality of relational issues. Ground Zero is so terrifically fraught with such deep and often quite contrary patterns of meaning that it defies being understood in any reasonable semblance of "adequacy" by appeal to its absolute measures—its size in square meters, the tonnage of the wreckage removed, the amount of money that will be needed to clear and build anew on the site. Ground Zero is a site that brings into remarkably sharp focus the intrinsic relationship between what a place *is* and what it *means*.

The differences among the absolute, relative, and relational dimensions of any spatiotemporal focus can be brought into greater (and less tragic) resolution through considering the distinction drawn between "house" and "home." This common and quite comfortable distinction can be traced to the meanings that come to be imbued directly within the spaces defined objectively or absolutely by adjacent walls and opposing floors and ceilings, in the textures of the materials out of which they have been crafted, in the plays of light and shadow that are orchestrated by each window over the course of a day or through the procession of the seasons. The first night spent in a newly purchased house does not transpire in accord with the distinctive structure of feeling that will accompany a similar night five or ten years hence, after every surface has taken on a patina of memory and meaning, and after both materials and spaces have come to resonate so deeply with familiarity that one can walk half-asleep or in complete darkness from bed to bath to baby's room. A house is experienced initially in terms of almost exclusively external relations—one is concerned about the measurements of the rooms, the size and acuteness of the triangle of working surfaces and appliances in the kitchen, the distance to shopping, schools, and work, and the relative value it has by virtue of where it is situated and precisely when in the real estate history of the neighborhood. "Home" develops as a function of emerging internal relations that shift focus from issues of measure to those of meaning.

Harvey's point, of course, is to recognize and respond to the interdependence and interpenetration of measure and meaning. Remodeling the kitchen in your house will affect its homely qualities; the value of one's home will appreciate or depreciate depending on the frequency and prices of sales of other houses in the neighborhood; a bitter argument can make an otherwise spacious home seem intolerably cramped. The absolute, relative, and relational dimensions of space and time are finally inseparable even if it is only from the perspective of the relational that this inseparability really matters. Every place and every arc of change has both a measurable extent and a meaningful depth. And, because every place and arc of change consists finally of dynamic relational ensembles, there are no grounds for assuming useful purchase to be afforded by any fixed perspectives on either measure or meaning. Spatiotemporal differentiation occurs both all the way "up" and all the way "down."

CHANGE AS PROBLEM; CHANGE AS PREDICAMENT

The tripartite heuristic offered by Harvey resonates well with the qualitatively rich ecological sense of change expressed in the *Yijing*, and is very useful in directing attention to the relational complexity of time and change. But insofar as Harvey is himself deeply concerned with understanding and addressing the measure and meaning of geographically uneven development, his heuristic is designed as well to direct attention to possibilities and perhaps imperatives for significantly and sustainably altering the direction of change. More specifically, it enables discerning both imperatives and concrete possibilities for addressing the lack of convergence on well-being and the social inequalities that are currently being exacerbated, rather than alleviated, by industrially wrought rates, scales, and directions of change.

Working out as he does from a relational ontology, Harvey is led to see change processes as being affected by how we understand or theorize them, as well as by practices aimed explicitly at their initiation, modification, or redirection. Constitutive internal relations—not merely accidental, external ones—obtain between theory and practice, and also between all situationally activated meanings-of and means-to change. Seeing this, however, is to see that there is no avoiding intimate implication in the qualities and direction of the change processes with which we find ourselves being confronted. It is to realize that our fundamental mode of presence—itself a function of bringing into focus certain relational ensembles—is always one of simultaneously posing and answering questions about how and why things are changing as they are. In Buddhist terms, we live in karmically informed circumstances that offer no grounds for severing reality from responsibility. Inquiry into how best to change the way things are changing is inseparable from inquiry into how best to change both who we are and what we mean.

As a heuristic, it is possible to speak about two broad modalities for initiating changes in the way things are changing. One is to exert some measure of direct *control* over change dynamics, altering existing conditions, institutions, and practices (or developing new ones) in order to achieve determinate outcomes. We can change an aging appearance and sense of self by engaging in new exercise and dietary regimes or cosmetic surgeries; we can redistribute wealth by instituting nonregressive tax codes. The other is to *contribute* to the emergence of new change dynamics by appreciating present possibilities for opening new and self-sustaining patterns of opportunity, constituting new configurations of values and domains of appreciation. We can counter the physical and psychic effects of aging by enrolling in a dance class, not in order to turn back the biological clock or lose weight, but to deepen youthful engagement with gracefully and joyfully coordinated movement in the company of others; we can redistribute wealth by promoting a culture of prestige based, not on accumulations of material wealth, but on attentive capacity, commitments to offering, and skill in hospitality. The former approach addresses the issue of change as a problem to be solved; the latter, as a predicament calling for astutely reconfigured values and resolve.

Problem solution and predicament resolution each have merits and are by no means mutually exclusive. In fact, it can be argued that insofar as responsive problem solving (crying in order to receive care or food) in the process of human maturation clearly precedes responsible predicament resolution (sharing toys in an expression of friendship rather than keeping them all to oneself), problem solution is the more basic or default mode. It may well be that it is through experiencing the ironic consequences of ill-coordinated problem solutions that we first begin to be seriously aware that, both personally and communally, *we* are always intrinsically differentiated, living in complex interdependence with others and with our environments. The experience of predicament can be seen, then, as coeval with the dawning realization that the shift from surviving to thriving depends on taking plural interests—our own and others—as deeply into account as possible. That is, predicaments draw critically recursive attention to our own values-intentions-actions, opening concrete opportunities for explicitly and resolutely harmonizing arcs of change. To enter into a predicament-rich environment of change is, in other words, to enter conditions suited to the complex emergence of diversity.

If our relations with one another and our environments were strictly external in nature—that is, if we lived in a world adequately and accurately mapped in terms of an ontology of fundamentally independent existents—then it would be easy enough to imagine treating our decreasing convergence on well-being in a world of increasingly acute inequalities as symptoms of objective problems awaiting some form of technical fix. We could imagine, in other words, changing circumstances in such a way that we arrive at desirable outcomes without needing to significantly revise or reconfigure our values. And, under the sway of such imaginations, it would be quite natural to assume that the most fundamental element in changing the way things are changing is simply to choose now which future—which ends—we want to realize among the myriad possible.

Such a view accords well with the "progressive" modern dream of determining the course of history. And, as we will see in the next chapter, it is a dream that has remained as seductively attractive as it has at least in part because of the way globally expanding market economies have extended real freedoms-of-choice, and the ways in which market growth has been sustained by successfully valorizing consumption as a primary mode of agency. So profound is the modern and postmodern bias to identify positive change with increasing the ambit of choice that it has become politically plausible to argue that expanding freedoms-of-choice alone is sufficient to guarantee "progress." This presumed identity underlies the ironically persuasive claims made by the current generation of neoliberal market fundamentalists that competition-generated choices will eventually and most efficiently bring about greater well-being and equity, guided by the market's beneficent "invisible hand." And it underlies, as well, the ascent of rational choice theory to near canonical status in public policy circles—a theory that explicitly denies that to achieve greater social good it is necessary to question inclinations to pursue individual self-interest. Over time, the theory maintains, autonomously subordinating cooperation to competition will result in things sorting out as well for all as is compatible with the best interests of each. Positively changing the way things are changing need not require differing-for others in any significant degree. Under these conditions, advocating for change is advocating for a multiplication of externally related perspectives on coexistence. In short, the rhetoric of equity through expansions of individual choice evidences powerful biases toward variation.

The presupposition that we can change our circumstances, our relations with it, and our relations with one another *without* changing ourselves is axiomatic for modern and postmodern constructions of agency. In Harvey's terms, it is an axiom that critically merges absolute and relative approaches to time and change. Developing a capacity for seeing all things as interdependent and every situation as a complex ensemble of internal relations exposes this presupposition as implausible and potentially detrimental. Given the co-implication or mutual enfolding of each and all, of theory and practice, of values and facts, and of the meaning-of and means-to change, we cannot avoid confrontation with the disturbing realization that our ability to remain "the same" while "making things happen" is only a reflection of our own restricted scope of attention.

One of the key insights of Mahayana Buddhism is that working to alleviate the troubles and suffering of all sentient beings—conducting oneself as a bodhisattva or enlightening being—is not a matter of acquiring paranormal abilities for control. It is a function of realizing unlimited responsive capabilities or improvisational genius (*upāya*). In a world wherein all things consist in distinctive patterns of irreducibly internal relations, changing the way things are changing is accomplished recursively and nondually, in the absence of ontologically segregated agents and things acted upon. It is only within narrowed horizons of relevance that we can even imagine fully controlling what happens. Ultimately, we can only contribute, as skillfully and aptly as possible, to how things are occurring.

From Controlling to Contributing

This is a humbling realization. But at the same time, it should be heartening. In a world of horizonless interdependence and interpenetration, it is not possible to be situated in such a way as to be blocked from contributing to our own and others' welfare. It is always possible, in some degree, at some scale, to make a difference that has (at least) the potential of ramifying globally. At the same time, not being blocked from possibilities for critically engaging our situation and reorienting its dynamics is no guarantee of doing so. It is a familiar fact, for example, that providing legal rights and practical access to education for all is no guarantee that all children will be educated. In many societies where education has traditionally been a male privilege, equality of opportunity across genders has yet to result in equality of outcomes. But if it is not control that is needed to effectively and sustainably activate our potentials for equitably changing the way things are changing, what is? How do we best contribute to the occurrence of greater equity?

The short answers are to better differentiate among distinct ways of making a difference; to deepen our capacities-for and commitments-to predicament resolution; and to foster the advent of ever more extensive and intensive expressions of diversity. As just noted, the shared modern and postmodern inclination is to insist that the most basic requirement for changing the way things are changing is a capacity for acting autonomously or exercising freedoms of choice in a way that demonstrates a fundamental independence with respect to our context. But rooting change in autonomy, whatever its other merits, is in considerable tension with fostering equity as a qualitative index of capacities-for and commitments-to contributing to one's own well-being *in ways that are deemed valuable by others*. Autonomously chosen courses of action are in consequence also ill-suited to resolving the contemporary aporia of needing at once both to recognize and respect differences more fully, and to subsume differences within shared and deepening commitments. Indeed, granted that the tenor and direction of situational dynamics at any given moment is a function of interacting complexes of internal relations, separating means and ends is ultimately arbitrary and counterproductive. In a world of complex interdependence, the means-to and the meaning-of change are recursively related. Some ways of making a difference are intrinsically self-defeating.

This is almost invariably true of approaches to initiating and sustaining change that fail to take account of—or actively obscure—the predicament-laden structure of the conditions presently inviting or compelling change. Responding to such conditions as if they pose a problem to be solved, whatever new means are deployed in the process, will only intensify schisms among the sets of values shaping their dynamics. Identifying something as a problem entails identifying with a particular perspective and a critically closed set of considerations and priorities since the failure to do so is tantamount to a failure to define what could count as a solution. Especially in terms of dealing with global issues like anthropogenic climate change, a problem-solving approach works *against* engaging differences as the productive basis of mutual contribution, effectively imposing conditions for the further segregation of stakeholders as each attempts to define the terms of solution in individually favorable ways. This may enable open conflict to be deferred, but at the cost of continued climate disruption and deepening climate change impacts.

From Choice to Commitment

Also self-defeating are approaches to making a difference that focus on discrete moments of completion rather than continuous arcs of change.

The change dynamics occurring in relational—not absolute or relative—space-time are always analogue, not digital. This is easy to overlook to the degree that *choice* is taken to have precedence over *commitment*.

The metaphysics of choice is grounded on the ontological priority of external relations. It expresses a world of fundamentally distinct agents, actions, and situations or things acted in or upon. In such a world, choices are made between virtually present, essentially independent, and mutually exclusive eventualities. The freedom to choose is a freedom to leap suddenly from one state of affairs to another—from one job or one globalization regime to another, for example—as if the present moment is always something like an air or train terminal from which it is possible to depart for any one of a potentially unlimited number of destinations. We choose between alternative futures as if time were structured as a linear sequence of moments like beads on a string—a string that can always be broken to splice an already experienced past and present to a future preferable to the one toward which we otherwise seem to be moving.

Choosing between alternative futures digitalizes the dynamics of change. The alternative is to contribute to change as a process of continuous or analogically structured modulation that disallows any neat compartmentalization of actors, actions, and things acted upon. What is crucial here is not the presence of alternatives among which to choose, but rather the strengths needed to express differing depths of commitment *to* specific arcs of affinity or alignment. The metaphysics of commitment is not grounded on the supposition of a present that exists or stands apart from all other moments and opposes other "presents" that either no longer or do not yet exist. The arcs of affinity and alignment expressing a given commitment are never decisive in the literal sense of "cutting off" connections with how things have come to be in order to get what we want in the dual sense of what we desire and what we lack. Commitments signal continuously renewed processes of investing and entrusting that have the function of converting external relations or patterns of coexistence into internal relations characterized by increasingly complex interdependence. Commitment generates a nondual space-time of mutually enhancing and continuously interfusing realities and idealities. Consummate contributors—the bodhisattvas of Buddhist tradition—are not architects of change; they are improvisational collaborators in it.

This said, however, a distinct feature of commitment-inflected change is that it involves working out from present circumstances precisely as they have come to be. This is a subtler point than might at first be appreciated. There is a strong modern bias for stressing aims and goals and keeping attention focused on our targeted future. If the general premodern bias was to emphasize personal and collective *destinies*, the bias of modernity has been to emphasize personally and collectively chosen *destinations*. In each case, however, the present is depreciated as a means to an ontologically and normatively distinct end. In contrast, working *out from* present circumstances is to focus on the *direction* of situational dynamics as a whole, and as a function of the continuous and recursive interplay of means and ends.

At the very least, resolutely working out from within current relational dynamics requires subordinating concerns about quantifiable outcome achievement to qualitatively assessed opportunity enrichment. That is, primary attention must be shifted away from unit tasks of measuring stages of completion to continuously enhancing relational significance along specific arcs of appreciation. Granted such a shift, instrumental attitudes toward our circumstances as repositories of resources for making headway toward our chosen ends give way to appreciating—valuing and enhancing the value of—situational resources in such a way as to activate sustained patterns of creative emergence.

CHANGING: A FUNCTION OF BEING-FREE OR RELATING-FREELY?

Change of this resolutely analogue sort marks the opening of what can be thought of as a dimension of freedom "perpendicular" or "oblique" to that of exercising choices among a virtual array of mutually exclusive destinies or destinations. It is a quality of change that can only be sustained on the basis of strengthening and coordinating situationally apt values—modalities of appreciation suited to enhancing resolution (clarity) and resolve (commitment). This is not an agent-centered freedom-from (for example, oppression or the constraints imposed by custom) or freedom-to (for example, do whatever one wants, when and more or less as one wants). It is, instead, a distinctive relational quality to which we can point with the adverbial expression "relating-freely."

More fully characterizing the meaning of relating-freely and the allied concepts of virtuosity and improvisation will be undertaken in different contexts over the remainder of our conversation. But to begin countering the rather abstract characterization offered thus far, let me return to a claim made in the Introduction that predicament resolution is best understood as an "infinite game" in which the point is not winning, but rather enhancing the ongoing quality of play experienced by everyone involved.

Predicament-resolving change cannot be engineered through win-lose competition of the sort that is definitive for finite play. Finite games are not played for merits internal to the process of play; they are played to win, to arrive at specific and desired outcomes. As noted by James Carse in his discussion of finite and infinite play (1986, 10–14), the determination of clearly distinct winners and losers requires playing under agreed upon and objectively fixed time constraints and rules.

In an Association of Surfing Professionals (ASP) contest, four-person, thirty-minute heats are conducted in accord with a clearly and objectively stipulated set of rules and point-scoring system. Each surfer works within these constraints, jockeying for strategic advantage and making use of both physical and psychological tactics to compromise the attentive and performance quality of his or her competitors. Only winners advance. A session of "free surfing" engaged in by the same group of four surfers will not result in clear winners and losers. Although individual surfers will certainly do their best to catch the best waves possible, the overall attitude is one of sharing the waves. In sharp contrast with a contest session, free surfing is typically peppered with hoots of appreciation and encouragement as each surfer does his or her best to increase the overall quality of surfing taking place, even to the point of sharing "expert knowledge" about the peculiarities of the location or conditions to maximize their collective enjoyment of the waves. There are no rules for doing so. It's just what makes for the highest quality surfing experience for all involved. The point is not to win; it's to get better at doing what each surfer is already doing best. Infinite play brings about conditions in which the qualitative changes realized are greater than the sum of individual efforts.

Choice- and control-oriented approaches to change have the character of finite play. It is only in the context of terminable scopes of engagement and impact—that is, within limited horizons of relevance, space, and time—that it is possible to definitively identify "good" and "bad" choices or courses of action. As forms of finite play, change processes grounded on the primacy of autonomously exercised choices can be expected to result in and further define the means-to and meanings-of *power*. They will amplify capacities for determining situational outcomes in factual terms, but also capacities for redefining what is meant by winning, workability, or utility. Because of this, amplified power implies amplified conditions for conflict.[14]

Contribution- and commitment-oriented change processes are "infinite" endeavors that consolidate new and resolutely shared relational headings. They do so by conserving and yet differentially activating the creative potential of significant differences, fostering both means-to and expanded meanings-of *strength*, where strength is what is needed to engage situations in ways conducive to enhancing qualities of engagement and relational opportunities for all. Strength is realized together. It is not an individual possession, but rather a distinctive capacity that is drawn from participating in current situational dynamics as needed for the emergence of new, more comprehensive, and situationally responsive values or modalities of appreciation.

Habituated to problem solution, it is easy to think of collective action as a matter of getting on "the same page" and establishing a common agenda, reducing the process of ongoing value coordination to a relative-absolute process of conclusively distinguishing good values and practices from bad, right from wrong, the desirable from the undesirable. Whatever its conventional justification, this eventually becomes a process of zeroing in on the *correct* hierarchies of needs, practices, and values, rather than one of opening up situationally responsive, *corrective* constellations thereof.

The point of such hierarchies, of course, is to get everyone to take the same perspective—a precondition for any finite game of problem solution. These hierarchies can take more universalist or more relativist forms, but solving problems and making "the right choices" requires that they be organized around a single set of rules for determining what is or is not good, useful, workable, and so on. And, crucially, whether these rules are modern or postmodern in their formulation, they will tend to disarm differences by being externally binding on all.

The difficulty of bringing about change equitably—at least as we have defined equity in terms of conditions that foster acting in our own self-interests in ways deemed valuable by others—is that it means resisting the temptation to establish fixed and correct orders of values that achieve unity of purpose through disarming rather than aptly activating differences. The constellations of ideals and values that must be consolidated in responding to the often very deep predicaments that characterize contemporary realities must be shared constructions in which differences are articulated in ways suited to enabling each to distinctively contribute to all. This is not a task to complete—an incremental step in the journey to success, however that is defined. Predicament resolution is ultimately a form of infinite play that emerges when sufficient commitment—and, hence, mutual trust and interconnectedness—is realized to let go of the dichotomous inclinations/desires to either "get things right" once and for all, or to "go it alone" for better or worse. Sharing is in this sense a relational quality that occurs as choice yields to commitment, competition to coordination, and control to contribution.

THE ETHICIZATION OF TIME AND CHANGE

It should be noted that contrasting the "correct" (a state) and the "corrective" (a quality) is itself a nondichotomous approach to differentiating among ways of making a difference—expressing both a means-to and meaning-of changes realized nondualistically. This approach is characteristic of many early Buddhist discourses aimed at fostering understanding of how best to respond to troubling, karmically-configured patterns of interdependence. For example, instead of dichotomously contrasting truth with nontruth, the Buddha used an oblique, three-way distinction among truth (*sacca*), confusion (*musā*), and bad luck (*kali*, literally, an unfortunately cast die). Such oblique contrasts have the effect of framing distinctions in ways that do not support directly oppositional dynamics, practically expressing the Buddha's observation that negatively charged relational dynamics arise "when things are set in pairs as opposites."[15]

This logic of oblique engagement becomes a signature emphasis within Chan and other Buddhist traditions that valorized direct demonstrations of the meaning of eschewing views or stances about "right" and "wrong," "good" and "bad," "pure" and "impure." Especially in Chan, Buddhist practice itself came to be conceived explicitly as the means-to and meaning-of fully realized nondualism or resolutely liberating patterns of relationality. As illustrated in the many "encounter dialogues" that record exemplary interactions of Chan masters and their students, the practice of desisting from dichotomous thinking—and explicitly from any indulgence in "seeking" attainments or acts of "picking and choosing"—comes to ultimate fruition in distinctively virtuosic capabilities for *relating-freely*, even in the absence of any options for exercising freedoms-of-choice. In Chan, the epitome of realization was simply "according with situations, responding as needed" (*sui-shi-ying-yong*): demonstrating, not blind acceptance of whatever is happening in an attitude of critical disengagement, but rather active commitment to changing the way things are changing by *elucidating* the liberating nature or disposition (*xing*) of present circumstances, as they have come to be.

This emphasis on qualitatively revising the meaning of relational dynamics was perhaps most clearly articulated in Chan. But in ways relevant to our present discussion, a crucial part of Buddhist advocacy in China was to focus on the importance of Buddhist insights into how best to activate an ecological, but nevertheless critically directed, understanding of time and change. As Buddhism took sufficiently deep root in China for processes of mutual accommodation with Confucian and Daoist sensibilities to be alloyed with outright advocacy for Buddhist preeminence, one of the most pointed critiques of traditional Chinese culture was its failure to generate a karmic understanding of time and change.[16] As we have seen, the dominant Chinese understanding of time and change expressed in the *Yijing* supported a moral inclination toward adaptive, harmonizing engagement with continuously changing circumstances. It was not, however, an understanding of time and change that encouraged stimulating a holistic "evolution" of the dynamics of change. The Buddhist emphasis on karma—that is, discerning the recursive interdependence among experienced outcomes/opportunities and patterns of values-intentions-actions—entailed a more basic and yet also more encompassing ethicization of time.

Whereas Confucianism and Daoism respectively advocated according with situational dynamics as a means to sustaining cultural and natural patterns and continuities,[17] Buddhist critics saw this as ethically static—a failure to fuse *responsive* genius with *responsibility* for the direction or meaning of change. Buddhist teachings about karma articulated an irreducibly dramatic or narrative temporal order in which conservative and creative dynamics are finally inseparable. From a Buddhist perspective, the ultimate function of according with the present situation, as it has come to be, is to enable responding as needed to activate the relational potentials therein for establishing resolutely liberating arcs of change—a process that Chan master Linji described as "facing the world and going crosswise."

It should be clear that while "going crosswise" implies differentiation, in the context of Buddhist practice, with its emphasis on realizing nondualism, the process advocated by Linji cannot be one of opposition or contrariety. Instead, "going crosswise" refers to a situationally specific process of oblique differentiation through which change dynamics become aligned with an appreciation of what each thing in that situation is and means for all others. In less Buddhist-inflected terms: "going crosswise" implies differentiation oriented toward enhancing and ever more deeply coordinating patterns of mutual contribution—the ongoing and situationally specific appreciation of diversity.

The widespread early Buddhist image of *samsara*, or suffering- and trouble-laden sentient existence as an ever-spinning wheel of life and death, and *nirvana*, or liberation from trouble and suffering (*dukkha*) as the dissolution of that wheel, graphically depicts Buddhist practice as directed toward breaking free of cyclic/habitual temporal dynamics. Buddhist liberation involves dissolving the premodern disposition to regard time through metaphors derived from daily, monthly, seasonal, and annual cycles, and to project these cycles generically into the moral domain through the concept of destiny.

This said, however, the Buddhist conception of liberating change is not progressive in the modern sense that would structure time normatively along an axis of linear accumulation, universally specifying the meaning of the good and quantifying its own validity in terms of anticipated and achieved outcomes. Neither is it a nonlinear conception of change in the postmodern sense that would promote the rhizome-like proliferation of options and perspectives, and that would insist on the ultimate relativity (and, finally, mutual irrelevance) of all expressions of the good. "Facing the world and going crosswise" means actively revising the historically deep complexion of values-intentions-actions that has resulted in present patterns of outcome and opportunity to open liberating alternatives to premodern, modern, and postmodern arcs of spatiotemporal dynamics, realizing conditions for the sustained resolution of conflict, trouble, and suffering.

The crucial question, of course, is: how is this done? Or, more specifically, what arc or arcs of change will result in predicament resolutions compatible with realizing ever-greater equity and diversity? How do we undermine the conditions for conflict or for the persistence of gallingly uneven geographies of development?

These are questions that will occupy us at length over succeeding chapters. As a way of anticipating the discussions to follow and of drawing together (and to a close) the reflections on change already presented, let me sketch—however provisionally—a response in terms that emerged in early Buddhist responses to comparable questions about reconfiguring the patterns of outcome and opportunity associated with our karma.

As already noted, efforts to significantly change the way things are changing must be undertaken on the basis of understanding things *yathabhutam* or as they have come to be. It is not, in other words, enough to know things as they *are* and *are not* at present, or to know the present as what has simply *resulted* from the past. From a karmic perspective, the present moment is a *phala* or fruit of prior patterns of value-intention-action, where *phala* literally means "fruit that is ripe to the point of bursting." Unlike an "effect" or "result" that is ontologically distinct from its antecedent causal conditions—for example, the flame that "results" from rubbing sticks together as "cause"—a fruit bears within itself the seeds of its own regeneration. As a karmic "fruit," the present is a concentrated expression of complexly related conditions that—like a mango—incorporates and brings into specific and recursive focus both conservative and creative propensities. The present is a dynamic blending of "feedback" and "feedforward" processes that are a means-to the future from the past—from seed to second-generation tree—but that also express a unique and continuously evolving meaning-of the three times (past-present-future) as a relationally dramatic whole. Responding to things as they have come to be is necessarily to engage in a process of "genetic" *revision*.

Importantly, the fruit metaphor also draws attention to the role of situational or environmental factors in the realized quality of karmic outcomes/opportunities, and ultimately calls into question the apparent independence or ontological (rather than heuristic) distinctness of actors, actions, situations, and experienced consequences. That is, the fruit metaphor draws attention to a peculiarity in the metaphysics of karma: purposeful activity and its dramatic consequences ultimately are best seen as phases of an ongoing, self-generating, and self-modifying process. Just as in posing the cliché conundrum—"which came first, the chicken or the egg?"—a basic error is committed if we ask which among purposeful beings, their actions, their situations, and experienced consequences are ontologically more or most basic. In a sense—a point insisted upon especially in Mahayana teachings regarding the emptiness (*śūnyatā*) or interdependence and interpenetration of all things—actors, actions, and situations acted upon are equally primordial aspects of a dramatic whole. What is most "basic" is value-shaped and value-shaping change: the dramatic or narrative reality of relational maturation and transformation.

Given this, changing the way things are changing can be seen as a process of opening, within present realities, new and mutually enriching courses of meaning making. Here, the early Buddhist contrast between aims, attitudes, endeavors, and eventualities that are *kusala* and those that are *akusala* is quite useful. *Kusala* and *akusala* are normally translated as "wholesome" and "unwholesome," but *kusala* actually functions as a superlative. *Kusala* does not refer to something that is good as opposed to bad, skilled as opposed to unskilled, wholesome as opposed to unwholesome, or to something that is just "good enough." Indeed, the entire spectrum from the bad to the good qualifies as *akusala*. Instead, *kusala* connotes manifestly heading in the direction of excellence or virtuosity.

Conducting ourselves in a *kusala* manner is the Buddhist meaning of going "beyond good and evil." Dichotomous distinctions like those between "good" and "evil," the "true" and "not true," the "real" and the "ideal" set the terms (both the boundaries and the rules) of a kind of finite play that is counterproductive to relating-freely and to realizing superlatively corrective turns of events. Conducting ourselves in a *kusala* manner is to express resolutely appreciative karma: intentions and conduct that continuously eventuate in adding value to or enriching our situation, but also in our becoming ever more valuably situated. Ultimately it is only by going beyond dichotomous thinking that we can dissolve the conditions of conflict. Or, in Buddhist terms: it is only by both decreasing the *akusala* and increasing the *kusala* that we stop proliferating impediments to liberation (*papañca*), dissolving the root conditions of trouble and suffering.[18]

To break through the aporia of difference with which we now find ourselves confronted, we must go beyond constructing differences as a function of fundamental incommensurabilities. But we must also go beyond purportedly nonjudgmental avowals of our essential sameness and equality. These approaches to difference may perhaps help decrease the *akusala* effects of dichotomous thinking; but they will not generate *kusala* patterns of outcome and opportunity. For that, we must conserve our differences rather than disarming them, working our way resolutely out of the opposition of the same and the different. This requires opening new modalities of appreciation, initiating oblique arcs of change that ever more skillfully fuse differing-from each other to differing-for one another, shifting relational dynamics in the direction of ever-greater and deeper diversity. For this, however, it will be necessary to "rewrite" history.

CHAPTER FOUR

Writing Histories, Making Differences

I t was famously announced by Winston Churchill that "history is written by the victors." If so, we have every reason to believe that histories have been "rewritten" for as long as there have been conflicts resulting in broken winning streaks. And, as made clear, for example, by the new histories drafted with the inauguration of each Chinese imperial dynasty, histories are not written and rewritten only to shed light on how things have come to be as they have. Histories are also written to set and legitimate new courses forward. Rewriting history is, from this perspective, a privilege of those accorded the power to affirm or alter the rules of the game in which they have proved victorious, and, at least in principle, to alter the very means-to and meaning-of victory.[1]

Whatever the merits and shortcomings of such a view of history, it usefully brings into focus some important considerations regarding the task we have set for ourselves: to understand why difference has come to be a signal late modern and early postmodern issue and concern, and then to discern how to collaborate in most equitably directing that global arc of change.

First, it draws attention to the other than descriptive, value-laden nature of the endeavor. The primary function of memory, no less than those of the other sense faculties, is to better orient ourselves toward and attune ourselves with the ongoing dynamics of the here and now. The remembering of history—whether through writing or oral recitation— is no different. We may smile at the Queen's remark in Lewis Carroll's *Through the Looking Glass* that "It's a poor sort of memory that only works backward." But while the statement illogically implies the possibility of remembering the future, that does not keep it from truing or correcting a common narrowness of prospect on the meanings or purposes of history and memory.

Second, histories not only embody certain propensities, they also instill them. The fruit (*phala*) metaphor used in Buddhist constructions of temporal dynamics implies that the present moment holds within it the seeds for differentially regenerating its own past. If so, there is no rewriting of history that is not also a recursive reauthoring of current propensities. Rewriting history is not just cosmetic surgery; it is genetic revision. It is a process of intervention that opens nonlinear possibilities for change— possibilities for new arcs of affinity and new value alignments—even as it apparently depicts a determinate linear sequence of events resulting in the present. At the very least, rewriting history has the political potency to alter the range and depths of our "imagined communities"—altering the scope and scale of our identities as persons and as peoples.

These may seem like considerations most happily left to professional historians and historiographers. But, one of the points that the previous and present chapters hope to make is that the contemporary aporia of difference is not just something taking place in history, or more accurately perhaps, at this particular point in time; it is a function or product of history. The rising prominence and increasing eminence of contrasting *issues* of difference reveals, in other words, a specific genetic trait in the means-to and meaning-of making/writing history—traits emerging not only *in* history, but also *through* it. The writing of history and the aporia of difference are profoundly co-implicated. Responding to or resolving this aporia, as it has come to be, cannot be undertaken in the absence of an explicit—and critically recursive—stance in and engagement with history.

With this in mind, it is useful to rehearse briefly some key shifts in thinking about history that have occurred over the last century in parallel with the gradual migration from strongly modern to ever more postmodern lifeworlds and (to use Raymond Williams' evocative term) "structures of feeling."

DIFFERENTIATED HISTORIES

As we have already seen, over roughly the same period that economists and social theorists were formulating needs to reconceive value in more profoundly relational terms and eventually began crafting perspectives on values in the wider senses now familiar, philosophers were calling deeply into question basic assumptions about being, time, and change, opening spaces within which postmodern emphases on difference would eventually germinate and flower. Historians were similarly engaged in rethinking the fundaments of their discipline, grappling with parallel concerns about pluralities of perspective and interpretation, calling into question assumptions that there is (or should be) a single history for all, or that there is an ideal method for arriving at valid historical insight.

In reflecting on the history of the discipline of history, the sociologist Randall Collins (1999) usefully identifies two main trends in twentieth-century historiography. One attempts, on the basis of several centuries of accumulated and detailed historical data generated by thousands of individual historians, to construct a comprehensive macrohistory of the world—a composite picture of global dynamics, formed by bringing together many interconnected histories of modest scale but extremely high resolution to reveal otherwise invisible structures. The conviction driving this approach to history is that "whatever is large and widely connected can be brought into focus within no perspective but one larger still." The opposing approach has been to object vehemently to the hubris (and often hegemonic implications) of adopting a global perspective that aims to organize our myriad pasts in the hope of showing that history reveals something other and "more than ourselves hopelessly contextualized in patternlessness" (Collins 1999, 1). Yet, as Collins astutely points out, the relationship between these two approaches to understanding the nature and value of history (one quintessentially "modern," the other "postmodern") is best seen as a false opposition. They are, in fact, not mutually exclusive but rather mutually constituting approaches. Neither could have come into existence or continue existing in isolation from the other.

In reading Collins' description of the contrariety that came into sharpened focus within the discipline of history over the course of the twentieth century, it is hard not to be struck by the familiarity of the contrast. It resonates, of course, with the contradictoriness of Hegelian and Marxist philosophies of change rooted respectively in "spirit" and "matter," but also with that of universalist and relativist ethics, essentialist/orientalist and particularist/postcolonial perspectives on culture, idealist and realist metaphysics, and the distinctive emphases placed on the global and the local in various approaches to the study of globalization. Plausibly, this familiarity might be attributed simply to the structure of dichotomy itself. In short: what is familiar is the tendency to split the world by means of an ontologically construed either/or—to deny the existence of any intimately connective middle ground. But in the context of our present conversation, what is most striking is how historiographical dynamics reiterate the aporetic structure of the needs both to subsume differences within common courses of action and to deepen recognition of and respect for difference. It would seem that history and historiography alike present us with the inevitability of a recursive turn toward difference.

The universalism that informed teleologically hued, global histories of the sort championed by Hegel did not survive intact the historical crisis of the Second World War. Nazi globalism and its predatory relationship with difference brought harshly to light the short step from universalist to absolutist and totalitarian visions of world history, making impossible any simple reversion to metahistorical aspirations of the sort common from the mid-nineteenth through the first third of the twentieth century. The predominant paradigm of history writing in the final two-thirds of the twentieth century has been one that insists on eschewing "history from above" in favor of "history from below," and on abandoning the aim of narratives that embody objective consensus in favor of presenting opposing viewpoints that reveal the cultural construction of all presumed permanences and points of fixed reference.

Especially over the last half century, the discipline of history has undergone astonishing differentiation, with histories, for example, of women, the body, the senses, emotion, popular cultures, consumer goods, and fashions decisively displacing traditional emphases on political history, great events, and great personages. The "new history," in short, is one intent on overthrowing all singular voices of history in pursuit of an ever more variegated heteroglossia—a "total history" that is anything but totalistic.[2] And yet, at the same time, the increasingly broad and deep patterns of interdependence that have emerged as a key characteristic of the postwar era have directly compelled the rise of globalization studies and indirectly compelled what might be called a reglobalization of history (Dorfman 2005).

No matter how locally construed, the contemporary dynamics of the everyday and hence the writing of histories "from below" cannot be dissociated, except at great risk, from consideration of global dynamics and the effects of what James Rosenau (2003) has called "distant proximities." While it may be possible, as Walter Benjamin demonstrated in his *Passegenwerk* or *Arcades Project*, to gain deep insight into the global phenomenon of modernity through the particularities of a few dozen nineteenth-century Parisian structures of iron and glass—a micro-detailed, street level view of modern values and practices—it remains true that these same structures cannot be fully understood except within truly global horizons of historical relevance. Neither can the German Nazism from which Benjamin was fleeing at the time of his death (perhaps by suicide) in 1940 be fully understood simply as a tragically consequential peculiarity of German national history. It is only in light, for example, of worldwide and world-dividing mergers of nationalism and imperialism, the global economic paroxysms of the Great Depression, and the industrialization of competing ideologies that became possible with nineteenth- and twentieth-century communication technologies that a phenomenon like "German" Nazism can be effectively understood. Similar observations hold for Maoist communism or capitalist neoliberalism. It is not that the local/particular produces the global/universal or the reverse. The relationship is not a linear, causal one. Rather, each *directs* or refers us to the other. The shortcomings and dangers of resolutely particularist "bottom-up" approaches to history are not less grave than those associated with the assertion of unitary "top-down" global narratives.

As Ernst Breisach (1994) has emphasized in reflecting on the interpretative role of history writing and rewriting, while an intricate interrelationship obtains among theories of history, historical narratives or schema, and the lives of societies, it is often theoretical approaches to history that serve as correctives for the understandings of change dynamics that are embedded in social practices and institutions. This jibes well with the now widespread affirmation of the constructed (and ontologically ambiguous) nature of social realities. But Breisach goes further to aver that a careful survey of more than two thousand years of written and other evidence strongly suggests that "whenever the interchange between historiographical theory and collective praxis has been severed, life made even harsher correction" (Breisach 1994, 408). Granted that this is not just an expression of the vanity of historiography, what does it mean that the discipline of history has come to be structured as an ongoing, corrective dialectic between, let us say, an emphasis on the universal and the particular, the globally same and the locally different?

I take Breisach to be making a crucial point: the interrelationships among histories, historiographical trends, and the lives of societies are mutually corrective, complex, and ongoing, and almost necessarily reveal shifting patterns of consonance and dissonance. Although there has been a longstanding bias in (at least Western) historiography for mimicking the objectivity of science and the rigor of its method, histories emerge in and contribute to the lives of societies in ways that necessarily amplify certain circuits of attention, knowledge, and practice rather than others. The depths of resonance generated by these feedback and feedforward relationships will differ as a function of the entirety of situational dynamics playing out, and of the absolute, relative, and relational space-times both constituting and brought into (and out of) focus by them.

Granted this, the changing and yet persistent interplay of the contrary streams of historiography identified by Collins is likely to be sounding out abiding tensions that obtain within the complex relational fabric of contemporary society, with each stream responding to distinct and yet internally related arcs of change and arenas of correction. Together, these streams articulate/demonstrate what might be called either a "history of predicament" or the current "predicament of history." That is, whatever their conventional references, they ultimately direct attention to the extent and depth of the unreconciled values, interests, and patterns of meaning suffusing our lifeworlds and the structures of feeling characteristic of them. The contrary streams of contemporary historiography reveal the aporia of needing to at once celebrate and subsume our differences, but they do not provide passage through it.

The question we must grapple with is how to move obliquely to the spectrum defined by universalist and particularist historiographical streams, the social, economic, political, cultural, and technological practices and institutions with which they resonate, and the tensions they evidence but fail to resolve. What kind of history writing and rewriting will shed *kusala* light on prospects for more equitably orienting our ever-deepening and expanding interdependence?

THE COMPLEX EMPTINESS OF THINGS PAST

I would like to begin thinking through how to answer these questions by expanding on Harvey's affirmation of the heterogeneity of time and reflecting on the historiographical implications of complexity.

Conceived as a "humanistic science," history should be written from a position of neutrality, demonstrating thoroughness, accuracy, and objectivity. This seems a plausible ideal for histories written in the context of Harvey's absolute and relative dimensions of space-time—histories that we might for the sake of clarity refer to as "records" of things past. But the dimension of relational space-time would not seem to support such an ideal since it is hard to imagine how histories focused on it could ever purport to be either comprehensive or purely descriptive. In fact, it is hard to see how such histories could even pretend to be composed in a disinterested fashion since they must at some level be expressly self-implicating. They are not *records* of things past, but rather live *rehearsals* of meanings still in the process of being composed. Histories which address the dynamics of relational space-time are written (and rewritten) to establish (or disestablish) specific affinities between desired relational headings and evidence of the past.

In some ways, this is true of all histories. No matter how ambitiously thorough in its underlying research, history writing is an unavoidably editorial practice that will always manifest (even when it does not explicitly express) certain norms or horizons of relevance while eschewing others. Although the ideal of a complete and accurate record of things past persists, realizing this ideal would require not just an infinitely detailed recording of the past, but its ongoing reproduction. And were this possible, we would be forced in the end to confront and honor the insight informing Jorge Luis Borges' story "The Library of Babel," which describes a library that contains not just every book ever written, but all possible books: a truly "total" history would be at once useless and meaningless.

A complete record of things past would lack both utility and meaning precisely because it would be impossible either to navigate within or exit. To use Borges' imagery: the text of each page, chapter, book, or encyclopedia would compose a line of indeterminate length through a sphere, the center of which could be (or is) anywhere, and the circumference of which is inaccessible. Such a line might or might not cross scales or dimensions or domains. It might provide indefinitely rich detail about the quantum fluctuations in a particular locale or skim over the highlights of stellar birth, maturation, and death. Or it might combine the two in the thought trains of a physicist bicycling home to husband and children, and soon to collide with an unanticipated pedestrian whose arms are full of other texts which fall open to pages of arguments concerning freedoms of the will and choice. A complete record of things past would not support an infinite number of interpretations or orientations toward significance; it would support none.

Contrary to the English metaphor of knowing as "comprehending"— a metaphor stretched to its breaking point by Borges—making sense of the world is not a function of grasping things totally, but rather of discerning how best to move among them. This is a process much more closely imagined through the Chinese metaphor of knowing as a function of *tong* (通) or "penetrating" the situations in which we find ourselves. Histories are not—and neither can nor should be—neutral and ideally comprehensive records of the total coursing of time past, but rather compositions of caringly and carefully identified currents of change. As such, histories are invariably value laden, and consciousness of history can never be very far removed from issues of conscience.

This raises methodological (and moral) concerns, of course, about selective bias or partiality. These concerns, however, seem to presuppose a simply existent past composed of linear patterns of change. Yet, one of the implications of the *complexity* of change is that the singularity of the past— our conviction that there is such a thing as *the* past—is ultimately hypothetical. It is not only that our pasts are not dimensionally homogenous; their relational potentials with respect to present and future are irreducibly open. Accepting this is to accept that the responsive nature of history writing cannot be disentangled from the responsibilities of making history.

Among the distinctive features of complex systems is that they are both *autopoetic* (self-organizing) and *novogenous* (novelty generating). In effect, this means that complex systems are dynamically and recursively structured. That is, they are ceaselessly incorporating and reincorporating their own relational histories, doing so in such a way that their own structures and developmental dynamics are continually being recontextualized and altered by feedback and feedforward processes attuned both to heightening their own resilience and fostering adaptive mutuality. Complex systems, then, are continuously producing the conditions of what might be called systemic-and-environmental coevolution. Histories of complex systems are histories of expanding and deepening interdependence and interpenetration.

Given that complex systems occur at and across scales from at least the molecular to ecological, their histories are, of course, not generally *written*. Nevertheless the histories of complex systems invariably *express* consistent patterns of adaptive interplay between a given system's semiotic and material elements—that is, its constitutive values/interests and its distinctive structuring of matter and energy—and the specific environments within which they occur and with which they are functionally interdependent (Lemke 1994). The histories of complex systems are, then, expressions of distinctively responsive arcs of meaning making, and complex systems are for this reason often referred to as "learning systems."

Importantly, while complex systems and their histories evince continuous development, they do not do so in an exclusively linear fashion. In the language of evolutionary theorist Stephen Jay Gould, the histories of complex systems are histories of "punctuated equilibrium"—histories that evince causal relations and developmental dynamics that are nonlinear, network-like, and prone to sudden and in principle unanticipatable reconfiguration. The histories of complex systems, in other words, are characterized by *significant discontinuities* or patterns of *emergence* that violate the logical order expressed in the "if this, then that" pattern of conditional entailment. Instead, they express what might be termed a "narrative order" of interweaving "first this, then that" patterns of change that, while persistently meaningful, are nevertheless irreducibly underdetermined, open, and subject to revision.

In a world of complex interdependence, then, it is not possible to read back from present states of affairs making use solely of reason and knowledge of natural laws to reconstruct how things came to be as they are. On the sole basis of a factual "snapshot" of the present, scientific knowledge and reason can provide modestly reliable hindcasts and forecasts, identifying what has likely just happened and what will likely soon happen. But beyond a relatively narrow set of temporal horizons, the indeterminacy of both past and future becomes strikingly evident.[3]

The indeterminacy or nonlinearity that lies "ahead" of us in the future is generally only mildly disconcerting. We are used to the future being uncertain, and have even developed institutions like stock market exchanges to enable that uncertainty to be rendered economically productive. Much more disconcerting, however, is that this indeterminacy also characterizes time past. We are accustomed to thinking of things past as fixed and given, their secrets ready and waiting to be disclosed with sufficiently acute knowledge of the laws of nature, sufficiently diligent investigation, and sufficiently thorough and valid reasoning. In actuality, however, a nonlinear past is no more readily accessed, based on present conditions, than the future is anticipated. While a plausible route from past to present can always be determined from where we are now, *there is no one route that is ever fully predetermined in respect of future moments.* There is a sense in which the emergent dynamics of nonlinear change involve significant alterations in the topography of our pasts—the appearance of new and unexpected "peaks," "ridges," "valleys," and ""channels" of significance in an otherwise stable surface array of "moments" past.[4]

The point here is not to question the asymmetry of temporal relations, to suggest that changes can propagate "backward" in time, or to claim that the complexity of relational space-time renders moot any questions about the impossibility of certain turns of events. These may be philosophically valid pursuits, but here I want only to stress that in a complex world, what we might call *causal magnitudes*—the capacity of specific events to generate major turns in the course of time—are only poorly anticipated or modeled on the basis of existing precedents. What we currently refer to as "*the* past" cannot be expected to do any more than provisionally and partially warrant the efficacy of any given approach to changing the way things are changing now. Increasing uncertainty about the future mirrors increasing uncertainty about the past. Granted this, the benefits of acting in accord with previously successful change strategies finally have less to do with zeroing in on the bedrock of reality (and hence on means to greater temporal leverage) than on expressly refining the meaning of present commitments. And, since higher orders of complexity in the formal sense sketched here are correlated with increasing degrees of freedom—or decreasing constraints on behavioral possibilities—the importance of commitment will be progressively pronounced as the systems and interdependencies within which changes are to be made exhibit greater complexity.

The centrality of commitment rather than control in initiating and sustaining meaningful change in a complexly interdependent world is, of course, implied in the fact that while emergent events are in principle unexpected, they are not anomalous. Emergent events occur as consolidations of unanticipated patterns of meaning within present circumstances—the realization of distinctively differing relational (and, at some level of analysis, causal) gestalts. In this, they express ontologically something deeply akin to the workings of metaphor. Moreover, because complex systems are not static, but irreducibly dynamic, they do not occur *in* time, but only *over* time, and the process of inducing change in them cannot be momentary, even if its effects are apparently sudden. Indeed, using Lemke's (1994) distinction between semiotic and material processes within complex systems, it could be said that even in instances of very substantial material discontinuity, there must be a significant degree of semiotic continuity since, otherwise, the system would simply disintegrate into component subsystems, falling below the threshold of complex self-organization. Changing the way things are changing in a world of complex interdependencies is, in other words, likely to be less about exercising power than about improvising aptly strengthening sets of values and interests in pursuit of new gestalts—or, perhaps, new genealogies—of affinity and significance.

In sum, complex change fundamentally challenges any historiography aimed at representing *the* past, whether global or local, total or partial. Because complex systems are continuously informed by their own histories, writing the histories of complex systems and their interdependence necessarily affects those systems and their ongoing interactions. There is—as implied in Breisach's remarks on the interplay of history, historiography, and social change—an irreducible reflexivity even in the most cautious effort to engage and explain complex change. In Buddhist terms, complex interdependence compels seeing that there is an important, nontrivial sense in which past, present, and future do not exist at all, but arise interdependently, ultimately empty of any abiding self-nature. And, because of this, history writing cannot avoid being both ethically and karmically charged.

Revising the Complexion of the Three Times

To my mind, these reflections on the nature of history in relation to complex change recall Fazang's nondualistic insight that things ultimately *are* what they *mean* for one another. This insight suggests that, especially in a complexly interdependent world, engaging in purportedly objective—or we might say, dispassionate—forms of historiography may serve to constrict or interrupt the critical recursion by means of which history and social change are held in mutually corrective relationship, biasing change dynamics in ways favorable to the continued exercise of power and the growing force of creativity-constraining common values. But at the very least, it is an insight that compels confrontation with the fact that if complex global interdependencies now *are* resulting in ever greater social, economic, political, technological, and cultural inequities, this tells us something very important about the inadequacies characteristic of what we have come to *mean* by and through history.

In a thoughtful piece aimed at challenging the perpetuation of violence in and through history, Timothy Brook (2005) has usefully described the primary work of the historian as articulating both the contexts in which experienced events took place and those through which experiences come to be indexed to certain meanings. Stressing how thinking of time as "a linear channel of causes and effects" has proven conducive to seeing history as a function of chain reactions through which "violence successfully reproduces itself," Brook appeals (as I have done) to Huayan Buddhist resources for turning "ninety degrees" off axis to see time, "not as a line of flow but as something more like a simultaneous array of reference and connection." (Brook 2005, 2) Granted that the web of mutual causalities reflected in any given event is practically infinite, Brook charges the historian with responsibly establishing contexts of meaning that will index possibilities for breaking the cycles of physical and structural violence that continue to characterize humanity's planetary presence.

The crucial work to which Brook would direct contemporary historians requires them to establish new contexts of values—new modalities of appreciation—in relation to the rich resources of all that is past. Brook himself lobbies for the inclusion of compassion as a key value in the context of which historical meaning can be indexed away from violence and the reproduction of conditions conducive to it. Our own discussion thus far would seem to point us in a similar direction, especially if compassion is understood in the broad sense of "feeling with" others—the realization of shared and harmonizing "structures of feeling."

But while compassion as a caring-for and caring-about others is crucial to redirecting history (and historiography) toward positive nonviolence, it would seem necessary to wed it to increasing clarity about how most appropriately to engage the complexly recursive processes of value- and meaning-generation that are presently consolidating ever-deepening patterns of inequity. Shared passions, by themselves, provide no guarantee of more equitably orienting the interdependencies that are emerging across ever-differentiating scales and domains—a fact driven home by the common (and tragically consequential) structures of feeling that Nazi German propagandists were capable of generating through modern media and communications theory.

Given the complexion of today's historical dynamics—including the multiplication and magnification of differences—I would argue that the process of infusing history and historiography with compassion should be informed by commitment to discerning, in the complexion of things past, resources useful in elucidating the means-to and meaning-of enhancing diversity in the context of increasing global interdependence. To configure the dynamics of our deepening social, economic, political, technological, and cultural interdependence in a more equitable and sustainable manner, we are in need of a history of difference—and in particular, a history that will shed critical light on how modern (as well as postmodern) values and institutions have been conducive to empowering variation, but also to generating both imperatives and possibilities for strengthening diversity. Any history of difference that does not take responsibility for making a difference—breaking through the aporia of difference—will either be drafted into servicing further social, economic, political, technological, and cultural variation, or simply spun off into irrelevance.

THE GREAT TRANSFORMATION:
MODERNITY, MARKETS, AND THE VALUE OF VARIATION

A history—or better, a lineage of histories—of the sort needed will not be written by a single set of hands from a single perspective. Rather, it will emerge as a function of complex interactions among distinctively differing perspectives, each offered in a spirit of contributing to the *kusala* realization of sustainably shared welfare. Moreover, it will not be first and foremost a history of persons and events, but a history of values playing out at and linking different scalars and domains. Here I want to explore one axis of contribution to such a history of difference—one centered on critically linking the values of modernity and those of market economics with an eye to discerning opportunities for redirecting the dynamics of contemporary globalization processes.

In discussing the advent of modernity, I earlier followed the lead of Stephen Toulmin and his identification of a distinctive set of values governing its "hidden agenda"—the realization of change dynamics capable of universalizing and rationalizing every aspect of human endeavor from the social to the scientific: the engineering of "cosmopolis." In drawing out the implications of that "agenda," I emphasized how the emergence of a discourse on values (the worthwhile) out of economic ruminations on value (worth) can be seen as revealing deep tensions within the "project" of modernity and its rendering of time as a uniform medium of universal progress. As a step in the direction of composing an equity-enhancing history of difference, I would like to draw out a parallel set of implications of the fact, mentioned earlier in passing, that the complex conditions that led to the birth of modernity led also to the birth of truly global market economies. The universal principles of governance to be realized in cosmopolis are intimately related to those shaping global commerce—a pattern of co-implication ironically favorable to a progressive alloying of unification and variation. If history is to be aligned with a turn toward greater equity and diversity, what are we to make of the *twin* birth of modernity and global markets?

In his classic of economic history, *The Great Transformation*, Karl Polanyi traced the apparent demise of nineteenth-century (European) civilization and the global plethora of social, economic, and political crises that afflicted the first four decades of the twentieth century, to eighteenth- and nineteenth-century efforts to orchestrate the realization of a market utopia—an effort to disembed economic processes from broader social and political contexts and achieve market operations utterly freed from external constraints.[5] This modern utopian project of "purifying" markets of state adulterations is, of course, the ancestor of today's neo-liberalism, the foundational architect of which, Friedrich Hayek, was a contemporary and lifelong opponent of Polanyi's construal of economic history and the imperatives he derived from it. And, given the dominance of neoliberal views in shaping current globalization processes and the strikingly uneven geographies of wealth and development correlated with them, it is perhaps useful to revisit Polanyi, however briefly, as a means of opening historical possibilities for a significant and equity-enhancing realignment of contemporary dynamics.

Among the key theoretical insights informing Polanyi's work were: 1) that the disembedding of markets was based on the "fictitious" com-modification of land, labor, and money; 2) that free markets will progres-sively compromise social welfare to the point that they produce distinct movements of resistance; and 3) that truly democratizing economic processes or orienting them toward greater social well-being requires challenging the naturalness and superiority of the (neoliberal) "dogma of the necessary conformity of domestic regimes within the orbit of the world economy" (Polanyi 2001, 253). Taken together, these insights sug-gest that orienting globalization processes toward greater equity implies a diversification of interests and institutions rather than a quest for greater uniformity. The irony of this implication (at least from a modern perspective) is compounded by Polanyi's conviction that it is precisely the free play of markets that will produce conditions ripe for resistance aimed at promoting equity and social welfare: the differentiation pro-cesses stimulated by market activity—at least in Polanyi's view—are ulti-mately self-limiting.

Writing in the second and third quarters of the twentieth century, when global markets were (in comparison with those prevailing today) still relatively immature, Polanyi was not in a position to see or (given the complexity of the processes involved) forecast the advent and profound impacts of new information technologies and media on market-society interactions. In hindsight, we can see what he could not and have an opportunity to expand and deepen his insights in a way that significantly reconfigures or inflects the twin histories of modernity and global market economies, and explains the remarkable resilience of neoliberal orthodox-ies and orthopraxy.

First, Polanyi did not take into account the degree to which the imperatives to expand market reach and density would constitute eco-nomic drivers for expanding consumer freedoms-of-choice in ways highly compatible with rewarding nonconformity, although this phenomenon is consistent with his general reading of the interplay of market dynamics and social well-being. That is, Polanyi did not foresee the degree to which the "resistance" movements generated by market excesses would be co-opted by markets through the commodification of freedom as a means-to and meaning-of exerting individual control over experiential outcomes.[6] In effect, the rapid development and spread of information and communications technologies over the second half of the twentieth century facilitated the emergence of a complex set of internal relations between market structures and processes and those of both personal and communal consciousness—relations that are powerfully biased toward intensifying variation and toward what amounts to a progressive "colonization of consciousness" (Hershock 1999, 2006).

As already noted, Polanyi saw market utopianism as an ideology that depended for its plausibility on telling a persuasive "fiction" about the commodification of land, labor, and money—a fiction that he believed would be revealed as such as free markets generated manifest social and economic shortfalls and instabilities. Market ideals would run aground on social and economic realities. And, in fact, the decades immediately following the Second World War do offer evidence of the predicted expressions of opposition to socially and politically disembedded market activities, nationally as well as internationally. In the United States, for example, by the mid- to late 1950s a groundswell of resistances began breaking against the political conformism and socioeconomic injustices characterizing the market-assisted leap of the United States into a position of global economic dominance. First was the late-50s poetic howl of the Beat generation and jazz's aggrieved rending of modern harmonies. In the early 60s came the civil rights march into Selma and the Berkeley Free Speech movement, and in the mid- to late 60s the explosion of psychedelically informed antiwar and anticorporate countercultures, burgeoning assertions of Black Power, and the movement for women's liberation. These successive and increasingly intense waves of nonconformity and asserted freedoms-of-choice epitomize open confrontation with the fictions of American market utopianism and political egalitarianism.

By the late 70s, however, nonconformity had become significantly commercialized. Countercultures had been commercially co-opted almost wholesale, and market-designed and -delivered freedoms-of-choice had softened the shock of losing, not only the Vietnam War (or, from the Vietnamese perspective, the "American War"), but also the Great Society's "wars" against poverty and racial injustice. By means telegraphed in the transition from a "we generation" to the so-called "me generation," wide-ranging commitments to "making a difference" had been effectively translated by technologically evolving market magic into no less wide-ranging and increasingly profound concerns about, and eventually celebrations of, "being different." The intrinsic *solidarities* of a diverse "we" consciousness and conscience were transmuted into the multiplex *solitariness* of interleaving—but not interfusing—consciousnesses and consciences belonging to an ever more internally variegated "me."

From the perspective of Polanyi's analysis of society-market inter-actions, the process by means of which this transition or transmutation was accomplished is perhaps best seen as an ironic reembedding—but not subordination—of markets within social, political, and cultural dynamics. More usefully, however, I think it can be seen as marking their complex integration—an emergent, distinctive, and arguably consummate fusion of market and modern values. From the perspective of the present, it is tempting to see this fusion as a simple accident of technological change, dating it perhaps to the advent of the Internet—the opening up of cyber-space and the dawning of the Information Age. For all that would other-wise recommend it, however, the liability of such a perspective is that it directs attention to the proximate means-to this fusion rather than to the meanings-of its advent. In Brook's terms, this would *not* provide a con-text suited to indexing this signal pattern of occurrences to meanings and values helpful in challenging the bias—characteristic of current global-ization, modernization, and industrialization processes—toward translat-ing diversity into variation, both within and across multiple domains and scales. Doing so requires widening our historical aperture with an eye to value-specific pattern recognition.

Polanyi's analysis of the origins of the global crises characteristic of the late nineteenth through mid-twentieth centuries turns on a utopian disembedding or freeing of market activities from the kinds of social, political, and cultural governors and constraints (both informal and for-mal) that he saw operating in premodern societies. The current global triumphs of neoliberal doctrines and institutions, and the quite real (as opposed to merely fictional) commodification of land, people, and money can be seen as evidence that his anticipated reembedding of markets will not occur without significant challenge to the mutual entrainment of modern and market values, practices, and institutions. Crucial to the process, especially from the eighteenth century onward, has been a con-fluence of scientific and technological advances centered on the value of control. The result has been a powerful interlocking of change modalities oriented toward universality, precision, progress, sovereignty, autonomy, tolerance, and equality with those oriented toward competition, conve-nience, and choice.[7]

Contemporary historiographic skepticism about periodization not-withstanding, the mutual entrainment of modern and market values, practices, and institutions can—for heuristic purposes—be seen as having four distinct phases or eras: the classical colonial era; the era of modern industrial development; the postmodern era of reflexive modernization and global information capitalism; and a still emerging era in which consciousness itself is systematically colonized.[8] Each era has been characterized by a distinctive complexion of empowerment and commodification processes.

The first of these eras occurred from roughly the early seventeenth through the early to mid-nineteenth century as newly consolidating European nation-states entered into global political and economic competition, carving out exclusive rights of access and ownership with respect to material resources. The second phase began taking shape in the early eighteenth century, but became predominant only in the nineteenth century as national power and prestige were wedded to rapidly expanding trade regimes and industrialization in strenuous pursuit of modern, progress-oriented development—a fusion of economic, political, and technological futures that would be almost religiously idealized through most of the twentieth century. By the final third of the twentieth century, the scale and scope of globalization and industrialization processes crossed crucial complexity thresholds to link further growth with increasing risk and volatility, and to foster the emergence of systems of power and prestige accumulation based on the commodification of information and communication. Finally, over the past ten to fifteen years, we have begun witnessing the emergence of a global economy in which the technologically enabled extraction and circulation of attention itself is a primary means of fueling economic growth—an economy in which the most basic resource for making a difference in our own lives is so thoroughly commodified that even meaning making and belonging are subject to marketization.

Functionally, these four eras can be seen as describing an arc of change marked by a profound (albeit geographically uneven) "dematerialization" of core economic processes and the achievement of technologically generated efficiencies that have almost completely dissolved spatial and temporal constraints on the expansion of market scale and content. In combination, this has made possible the permeation of virtually every dimension of human endeavor by *market-produced* and *market-producing* goods and services. In consequence, it has become possible to extract economic value even from the expression of personal values and the complex processes of identity construction. It is an arc of change along which a realm of sociocultural, political, and spiritual values is opened in explicit contrast with economic value, only to be exploited for no less explicit economic purposes.

More schematically stated, this arc of change has meant: 1) the successive *commodification* of first natural resources, then labor, information, and attention; 2) the progressive extension of *power* over the production and flow of goods, patterns of consumption, the generation of knowledge/human capital, and finally over even the most intimate constructions of identity and significance; 3) the steadily lessening *strength* and resilience of natural ecologies, traditional societies, self-sustaining (rather than fashion-driven) cultures, and familial/personal relations; and 4) the continual expansion and amplification of experiential freedoms, including the freedom to warrant the ultimate contingency of differences though crafting almost entirely elective identities and communities.

An important turning point in this process occurred in the late nineteenth century. Spurred and sustained by the industrial revolution, markets of truly global reach were by this time rapidly maturing. But the rapidity of market expansion was threatening to result, as well, in mounting disparity between the actual velocity of consumption and the rates needed to insure continuing economic growth. Theorists like Thorstein Veblen were, by the end of the century, noting that expanding markets mandate expanding consumer bases, and that limits exist as to how far this expansion can be driven by the lowering prices associated with efficiencies in production and transportation. Sustaining growth requires continuously increasing the absolute quantities of goods and services placed into global circulation. But, beyond a certain scale threshold, it also requires increasing the ranges of goods and services marketed, and accelerating overall rates of consumption. In short, maximally extended market *reach* produces powerful imperatives to maximize market *density*, incorporating entirely new populations (e.g., children) and new commodities (e.g., news and entertainment) within the scope of market exchanges.

In effect, increasing the density of market activities involved generating needs and problems that might be addressed by new market-designed and market-delivered goods and services. As Jeremy Rifkin has noted in his discussion of the early twentieth-century "gospel of mass consumption," in an era of technologically achieved production efficiencies and associated job losses, continued economic growth depended on "a metamorphosis of consumption from vice to virtue" (Rifkin 1995, 19).

Under the aegis of added convenience and expanded freedoms-of-choice, market growth came to be sustained by systematically finding fault with the familiar and traditional. In the words of General Motors executive Charles Kettering, written somewhat ironically in January 1929, some nine months before the onset of the Great Depression in the United States, the "key to economic prosperity is the organized creation of dissatisfaction."[9] As already noted, homemade soap was faulted for being "unhygienic"—produced by rendering animal fat wastes—and far inferior to the scientifically engineered and "pure" cleaning agents produced by the burgeoning chemical industry. Homemade soups were faulted for being excessively time consuming in a world in which the commodification of labor firmly equated time with money. Homemade stories and music were faulted for being old-fashioned and of lesser quality than those made available commercially. Over the first half of the twentieth century, first convenience and then also novelty itself were aggressively elevated to the status of key selling points. And, particularly in the United States, accelerated consumption was successfully sold to the public as a means of both bringing "the future" into every home and neighborhood and effectively saving (both the time and money needed) for it. Keeping current in one's consumption practices came to be conceived as a familial and civic responsibility, and as necessary for the ceaseless and accelerating flow of currency that insured continued social and political progress.

By midcentury, the seminal liberal economist John Kenneth Galbraith was confidently able to assert that the modern mission of business was not to simply meet public needs for goods and services, but to "create the wants it seeks to satisfy" (Galbraith 1984, 127). The marriage of modern commitments to universalism, progress, order, and autonomy with market commitments to competition, convenience, and choice had matured sufficiently—along with technological advances in production and communication—to set into motion a global and perhaps irreversible commodification of the full range of human subsistence needs and the value domains they establish, including those for food (cuisine), clothing (fashion), shelter (domestic order), medical care (health), education (knowledge), sensory stimulation (entertainment and the exercise of attention), and a sense of belonging (meaning making). Far from being an autonomous or anomalous phenomenon, the creative heroism associated with modernity as a sociopolitical phenomenon has, throughout, been inseparable from commodification and commercialization processes that affected even aesthetic sensibilities, cultural production, and, ultimately, the construction of identity.[10]

With globally achieved mass literacy, the early- to mid-twentieth century explosion of electronic mass media suited for consumption by nonliterate and preliterate populations, and the eventual dawning of the Internet-mediated Information Age, it became possible for market reach to encompass all phases of the human life cycle and to extend into all basic value domains, from the most material to the spiritual. In effect, modernization and marketization have infiltrated all of the qualitative dimensions along which humanity expresses its own distinctive differences as a part of the planetary ecology—those modalities of appreciation along which humanity has extended the meaning of flourishing.

The commodification of subsistence has both driven and been driven by the sustained expansion of market reach and density. It has also been a primary factor in the emergence of what I have termed the contemporary aporia of difference. In this, the role of control-biased technologies has been, and remains, crucial.

The Distinctive Difference of the Modern West?

Much historical ink has been committed to explaining the "great divergence" that occurred between Western Europe and other global societies—especially those in South and East Asia—during the first century of the modern era. Until fairly recently, it had been assumed that the causes for Europe's clear global dominance in political, economic, and military terms by the middle of the nineteenth century could be traced back to the distinctive cultural efflorescence of classical Greek and Roman antiquity, and their modifications in keeping with Christian values. According to such a view, the "rise of the West" was practically inevitable. This long-standing thesis of European exceptionalism is now widely criticized, if not discredited.

Empirical evidence gathered from other than European sources clearly documents the vibrancy of South and East Asian societies well into the modern era—levels of political stability and economic vitality that, for example, afforded the Chinese populace average life expectancies, standards of living, and levels of productivity that were equal to or greater than those prevalent in Europe until the eighteenth century (Pomeranz 2000). It has been persuasively argued that the burst of economic globalization that took place over the seventeenth and eighteenth centuries was instigated, not by European hunger for trading partners, but rather by the Chinese appetite for silver bullion (Flynn 1996), and that Europeans controlled only a small fraction of the massive Indian Ocean trade in agricultural and manufactured goods until well into the eighteenth century (Gupta 1994). Yet, in spite of the presence in Asia of effective indigenous, large-scale production and trading networks and capitalist institutions, a sharp divergence did occur between Asian and European trajectories of development—one that both greatly expanded then prevailing "limits to growth" and established conditions for the rise of egalitarianism as a social and political ideal.

Among the approaches to accounting for this divergence of developmental trajectories, a particularly succinct and rich one for our present purposes is that of world historian Jack Goldstone (2001). In distinction from those histories that identify a single, key factor, Goldstone suggests that the global economic and political ascendance of the West must be understood as the result of a *chance confluence* in England of a unique configuration of political, social, scientific, and ecological forces. This confluence, he argues, produced conditions favorable to a series of technological breakthroughs that eventually enabled the highly controlled conversion of heat to rotary motion—the basis of what we aptly designate the "industrial *revolution*." The specifics are interesting for the degree to which they clarify the decisively modern roots of this accidental—or, more accurately, emergent—phenomenon.

Against a trend toward cultural conservatism and religious orthodoxy that prevailed across Eurasia in the seventeenth century and that resulted generally in the consolidation of politically stable states, conditions obtained in England that linked possibilities for internal security and political stability to a de facto tolerance of religious plurality and dissent. In addition, in contrast with much of mainland Europe, Protestantism assumed predominance in England, and the Anglican Church in particular demonstrated a decisive openness to Newtonian science and a willingness to hold in high esteem both the expression of engineering genius and technological innovation. Newton's demonstration that the same basic laws governed both the heavens and the earth had the dual effect of subverting classical Greek and Christian cosmologies and inspiring confidence in human capacities for reordering and, indeed, reauthoring the natural world.

Importantly, at this same time—the late seventeenth and early eighteenth centuries—England was beginning to experience a natural resource crisis. In contrast with Japan, where forest conservation practices were institutionalized under imperial mandate during medieval times, England's naturally modest forest cover had by early modern times already been largely decimated by population pressures. Distinctively, the use of wood as the primary fuel for cooking, heating, and manufacturing was, in England, replaced by the use of coal—an abundant and easily accessible local resource. By the beginning of the eighteenth century, however, England's ever-deeper mines—for both coal and metal ores—were increasingly subject to groundwater intrusion and flooding. This presented a site-specific technical problem that was solved by Robert Newcomen's steam-powered pump—albeit with such great inefficiency as to have been feasible only where fuel (in this case, coal) was extremely cheap. Subsequent refinements, especially those of James Watt and Matthew Boulton, enabled geometric increases in both mechanical efficiency and control in converting the energy sequestered in coal—ironically, the compressed remains of finite and nonrenewable fossilized forests—into consistent rotary motion. Far from being "inevitable," the European—that is, English—origins of the industrial revolution can be traced to an apparent historical happenstance.

A crucial context for the spread of mechanical engineering in England from the early eighteenth century onward, and for the eventual shift of global trade in its favor, was the unique combination in England of particularly high wages and particularly low costs of energy. Due to a unique set of conditions, while the costs of labor in, for example, Beijing, Delhi, Vienna, and Florence remained relatively static from 1575 to 1775, those costs increased nearly fourfold in England. This had the effect of producing a general population earning three to four times what was needed to support basic subsistence, thus opening a large local market for wider ranges of consumer goods and luxury items like those arriving in England via global trade—particularly from India and China. But it also provided great incentives for English entrepreneurs intent on increasing profits to seek out ways of substituting readily available capital (one result of increasing global trade) and energy (in the form of coal) for labor. The mechanization of cotton milling and cloth manufacture enabled England first to profitably substitute local cloth for Indian and Chinese imports, and then to drop production costs to levels that significantly undercut global competition—a process of technologically reshaping the dynamics of global trade that was very quickly adopted in other industries.[11] From this perspective, the industrial revolution was engineered to insure a decisive shift in the global topography of commercial advantage.

Whether seen as originating as an accident, as engineered, or as an instance of complex emergence, the industrial revolution undeniably marked a shift in the dynamics of global manufacturing, trade, and consumption. Along with this came profound revisions of local, national, regional, and global structures of political and economic power—all with deep and far-reaching impacts on social and cultural relations, not the least of which was rural-to-urban migration of an historically unprecedented scale, and an associated shrinking and increased mobility of the domestic sphere. The ability to translate the energy released from breaking down fossil fuels into various kinds of precisely controlled work opened entirely new possibilities for both mass production and bulk transportation, but also for new kinds of human capital.[12] Steam locomotion made transcontinental and transoceanic shipping of both raw materials and manufactured goods not only exponentially more rapid, but also more reliable, making possible in turn the commodification and marketization of perishable goods, time-sensitive information or "news," and indeed traveling itself.

TIME-SPACE COMPRESSION AND THE ACCELERATION OF SOCIETAL DIFFERENTIATION

Among theorists of contemporary globalization processes, it has become commonplace to draw critical attention to the technologically driven alteration of space and time through, for example, the "shrinking" of distances due to vastly reduced transportation times; the elimination of inventory spaces through just-in-time production regimes; the conversion of information/value that is physically embodied, and thus transmitted against inertia and friction, to electronically encoded and almost instantaneously transmitted forms; and a relentless acceleration of capital turnover. As dramatic as these facts of accelerating change and contracting distances are, however, they are often looked at in essentially quantitative terms. While the phenomenon of "time-space compression" has been remarked since at least the mid-nineteenth century, and while philosophical attention has long been drawn to the fact that the technological "shrinking" of distances has brought about a paradoxical loss of nearness (Heidegger 1971, 165), it is only relatively recently that the full impact of time-space compression on identity construction, the prospects of social action, and the biasing of differentiation processes has begun to be appreciated (Harvey 1996, 242ff).

Prior to the era of fossil-fuel powered machinery and mass industrialization, the provision of basic subsistence needs—particularly food, clothing, and shelter—was a fundamentally local process and a primary context for the emergence of sustained patterns of mutual contribution to shared welfare. For example, even in such large cities as London, Paris, and New York, quite significant food production—and not merely processing—took place within city limits well into the nineteenth century.[13] Prior to steam-powered transportation and refrigeration technology, highly perishable dairy products, meats, vegetables, and fruits were generally provided in a highly localized manner, with supply chains typically only a few, comparatively short "links" in length. As these new technologies became increasingly widespread and efficient, supply chains lengthened dramatically, leading to a profound qualitative shift in the dynamics of trade: a conversion of personally mediated local-to-local patterns of trade to anonymously mediated and monetized local-global-local patterns of exchange. Especially from the second half of the nineteenth century through the early part of the twentieth, this resulted in a mass disruption of high-diversity local production/consumption ecologies and their replacement by interlocking regimes of global production monocultures. Importantly, this shift proved to be highly compatible with increasing market density through heightening needs for market-designed and market-delivered goods and services.

Meeting our basic human needs is a primary context for generating and sustaining patterns of mutual contribution and shared welfare—that is, a primary context for realizing intra- and intercommunity diversity. To the degree that meeting basic subsistence needs—eventually including health care, education, sensory stimulation, and a sense of belonging—becomes market aligned, the relational dynamics involved are significantly transformed by such key market values as competition, convenience, and choice. In effect, producing and making use of the goods and services by means of which daily life is sustained come to be entrained with change dynamics that are conducive to increasing both market reach and market density. That is, a key meaning of the commodification and marketization of subsistence is the production of both new kinds of wants and new kinds of populations in want. To sustain market growth, it is not enough to produce more goods and services for market-mediated consumption; it is necessary to produce populations that, in practical terms, cannot live without them. At a certain scale, this process begins affecting the root conditions of personal, social, and cultural flourishing—a subordination of values (modalities of appreciation, the worthwhile) to value (unit measures of worth).

The causalities involved in this process are complex or network-like. It is not the case, for example, that transportation efficiencies and the commodification of subsistence goods and services have directly broken apart the extended family and normalized first the so-called nuclear family and then the single-parent household. But viewed at appropriate spatial and temporal scales, clear correlations become evident among ease of transportation, labor mobility, commodification processes, and the erosion of both traditional familial institutions and the values associated with their flourishing. Further correlations become apparent among the erosion of familial institutions, the commodification of entertainment, market-encouraged associations of identity with choice, and intensifying felt needs for belonging. Similarly, to anticipate later discussions, it is possible to meaningfully track the global expansion of market reach and density over the eighteenth to twentieth centuries alongside policies regarding such "subsistence" services as education. Traditionally met by familial and religious institutions, the need for education increasingly came to be seen as crucial to political and economic vitality from the eighteenth century onward. Initially provided as *a* public good for the purpose of enhancing national economic performance, and later provided publicly for the expressed purpose of enhancing *the* public good in response to issues of rising inequality and inequity, education subsequently underwent marked commodification and neoliberal reprivatization over especially the final decades of the twentieth century. That is, as market reach and density crossed critical scale thresholds to begin laying the foundations of the so-called information society, education began to be subjected to the market logic of rapid differentiation: the creation of new education niches as well as new populations in need of the goods and services associated with them. Education expanded well beyond the boundaries of the school, becoming ever more finely responsive to ever more varied needs, opening up in education the same kinds of quality and cost differentials found in other markets.

It was a presupposition in Marxist theory that industrialization and the mechanization of labor would release human creativity from the drudgery of meeting basic needs. And, if the maximum scope of commodification had left the needs for health care, education, sensory stimulation, and meaning making in the hands and hearts of local communities, this might indeed have come to pass. But the complex recursions that came to obtain between markets and the populations served by—and eventually, dependent on or laboring in service to—them worked very much against this hopeful vision of a technologically attained, humanistic utopia.[14] If the continued growth of economies structured around the dynamics of global markets depended (and still depends) on the massive translation of energy latent in fossil fuels into work directed toward an accelerating profusion of goods, services, and populations in need of them, the growth of modern and now postmodern societies has depended on an analogous breakdown of social and cultural bonds—the productive and profitable release of relational energy from farms, families, and communities, and an associated proliferation of elective identities and lifestyle choices, but also of classes of advantage and disadvantage (Hornborg 2001). And in the most densely marketized societies today, attention itself has been drawn into the ambit of commodification processes as the self has come to be primarily constructed and presented in terms of consumption relations keyed to ever-changing product characteristics (Lowe 1995, 67).

CHAPTER FIVE

The Commodification of Difference

M ass media have played so profound a role in embedding modern and market values throughout the contemporary lifeworld that they merit direct critical attention. In addition to being a primary connective tissue between the public and private spheres, mass media have been instrumental in bringing about the commodification and commercialization of the most intimate and social dimensions of human need: sensory stimulation, shared meaning making, identity construction and reinforcement, and a sustained sense of belonging. Mass mediation has not only been crucial to the colonization of consciousness, it has also been globally crucial to the progressive biasing of differentiation processes away from sustaining and enhancing diversity toward ever-proliferating regimes of variety.

To an extraordinary degree, media history exemplifies both the value-laden nature of all technologies and the modern bias toward the values of autonomy and control. To date, however, mass media have most often been considered to be "communication tools" that are neutral with respect to the content and values that they are used to transmit or disseminate. For this reason, mass media and their technological infrastructure have tended to be engaged critically in terms of engineering or technical evaluation, rather than those of ethics.[1] That is, mass mediation as such—apart from its deliverable contents—has been exempted from systematic ethical evaluation. Correcting that tendency is crucial to any history of industrial globalization that would open possibilities for challenging its contemporary correlation with increasing social, economic, political, and cultural inequity.

SEEING MASS MEDIATION AS TECHNOLOGY, NOT AS TOOL

Contrary to popularly received opinion, I want to insist on seeing mass media as technological phenomena which, unlike tools, *cannot* be assessed directly in terms of their task-specific utility or how well they meet our individual needs as users. It is a crucial feature of tools that we enjoy practical and readily exercised "exit rights" from them. That is, we can always opt out of the unique ways in which specific tools quantitatively extend our capabilities for meeting our individual needs and interests. We can elect *not* to use such tools as televisions, computers, wireless Internet connections, and so on. But we are affected by technologies even if we do not make use of tools produced through them. Technologies emerge as a function of complex systems of material and conceptual practices, embodying and deploying particular strategic values. That is, technologies are immaterial, relational looms through which certain kinds of worlds and lived experiences are woven, qualitatively transforming *how* we are interdependent. As such, technologies can only be accurately and adequately assessed in terms of changes brought about within and among societal systems and values—the specific arcs of change and modalities of appreciation they establish.

As technological phenomena, mass media cannot be effectively and critically engaged solely in terms of the information content they transmit. Mass media and information and communications technologies (ICT) more broadly also encompass the extraction of raw materials needed to manufacture ever-changing arrays of communication tools; the marketing and servicing of these tools; the "worlds" to which they provide access; the needs they help to instill; the changes they foster in communication practices and legal institutions; shifting patterns of global capital investment and exchange; and increasingly dense capacities for controlling the content and velocity of lived experience.

And so, while a critical history of mass mediation cannot avoid the technical, even less so can it avoid the ethical. In an era of global ICT, critically engaging the means and meaning of mass mediation is to make evident mounting needs for a resolutely global and relational ethics. More specifically stated, and for reasons that I hope emerge from the following discussion of the historical arc of mass mediation: we are in need of an ethics of interdependence in which agency-regulating moralities of choice are subordinated to an attention-enriching ethics of appreciative and contributory virtuosity—an ethics in which commonality is understood as an effect or correlate of community, not its cause. According to such an ethics, community emerges and flourishes, not on the basis of converging patterns of choice and custom, but rather through sustained diversification. If contemporary patterns of industrial globalization and mass mediation are placing community at risk, it is not because of their real (but relatively limited) homogenizing effects, but rather because of how they shape practices and purposes of differentiation. With this in mind, let me briefly rehearse the historical development of mass media.

MEDIA AND THE MARKETING OF
MODERN SENSES AND SENSIBILITIES

While hand-distributed newssheets began being printed in Europe in the 1620s, and ads began appearing in English newspapers in 1622, the first daily newspaper did not appear until 1650 in Leipzig. Five years later, the term "advertising" was coined, and along with it the commercial support of news distribution was formally inaugurated. Yet, it was not until the fully mechanized mass production of newspapers in the nineteenth century that news could be effectively mass marketed.

The same technological advances that made possible the mass production of cloth and the global distribution of perishable goods also made available vastly greater powers for the mass duplication of communications content, and for both its geographically expanded distribution and heightened frequency. The leap of printed daily and weekly newspapers from local to regional and national scales of distribution, for example, required both greatly increased unit production and greatly expanded means of reliable and rapid transportation. The first truly mass market news daily, the *New York Sun*, hit the streets selling for a penny in 1833 by taking full advantage of the scale efficiencies afforded by steam-powered industrial production and transportation. Less than ten years later, the first fully dedicated sales agent for newspaper advertising was hired, and by the 1880s advertising spread to magazines, fully cementing the relationship among not only news media, commercialization, and commodification, but also other print media aimed at mass entertainment and non-news information sharing.[2] By 1905, when the U.S. population stood at 83 million, the leading serial publication, the *Ladies Home Journal*, boasted a circulation of over 1 million, and the top 20 magazines a combined circulation of nearly 6 million.[3]

Print media would remain authoritative for nearly a century, but the cutting edge of mass mediation began shifting toward electronic media from the beginning of the twentieth century. Radio, for example, made possible both a "dematerialization" of news and entertainment commodities, and vastly amplified, simultaneous audiences. The early, premonopoly years of radio were vibrantly local in character, and featured both scripted and improvised news and dramatic entertainment, but also live public commentary and music performances. As transmission and reception technologies improved, increasingly large numbers of geographically disparate listeners were enabled by radio to participate in a joint experience—a "miracle" with potentials for shaping mass opinion that was not lost on either corporate or political powers. In 1928, the Dodge Victory Hour, featuring Al Jolson and his band, reached 35 million listeners over 47 stations broadcasting nationwide under the auspices of the National

Broadcasting Company (NBC), and until eclipsed by television in the 1950s, the most popular syndicated radio programs regularly attracted audiences of 40 million—this at a time when the total U.S. population grew from 125 to 150 million.

Phonographic music reproduction was first made commercially available in 1887, but was confined to "phonograph parlors" in which patrons paid to listen to recordings. The industry underwent exponential growth with the mass production of cylinder and disc recordings in the first decades of the twentieth century, spurred on in part by radio audiences afforded the opportunity to listen to favorite performers and performances as a matter of choice, whenever and wherever they desired. This early iteration of entertainment "on demand" was so well received that by 1918, over 100 million records were sold annually and top "hits" could sell upwards of a million copies. Today, annual sales of music in CD, DVD, and digital download formats total in the neighborhood of $130 billion globally, with 15% of sales taking place through downloading services, including more than 1.7 billion single-track downloads in 2007. It is estimated by the International Federation of the Phonograph Industry that the global ratio of illegal to legal music sales may approach 20 to 1.[4]

Film, too, caught on as a mass entertainment medium in the first part of the twentieth century, with 40 million tickets sold for movie screenings in the United States in 1922, when the total U.S. population was 110 million. Annual per capita ticket purchases began skyrocketing after the first "talkie," *The Jazz Singer*, was released in 1927. Per capita sales in the United States rose to 16.86 by 1929, jumped to 29.76 the following year, and peaked at 34.29 in 1946.[5] Total admissions for the most popular film ever shown in the United States, *Gone with the Wind*, total over 200 million, with blockbuster films today regularly reaching 50–95 million in U.S. theater ticket sales. To give a sense of the global scale of the film industry, while theater admissions in 2005 totaled over 7 billion,[6] admissions in most global markets were between 10% and 85% lower than ten years previously—primarily as a function of both authorized and (increasingly) pirated DVD, videocassette, and download distribution. Actual film viewings globally are much higher, especially since home viewers of films often watch individual films more than once. Significantly, although global admissions or viewing statistics for individual films are not available, global box office earnings demonstrate Hollywood's continued dominance over cinematic space and imagination in spite of growing national film industries around the world: the top 20 box office draws in 2005 were *all* produced by either American film companies (12) or by American-British (4), American-New Zealand (2), American-Canadian (1), American-German (1), or American-German-British-Estonian teams (1).[7]

Television, which like radio brought mass mediated information and entertainment into the home, was commercially available from the late

1930s, but did not become a mass media phenomenon until after the Second World War , with just 9% of American households owning a TV in 1950, 87% in 1960, and 95% in 1970.[8] According to the Nielsen Media Research company, in 2006, the average American devoted 4.5 hours daily to television viewing, with an average of 8.2 hours total viewing taking place per day in each media household.[9] Globally, the average time spent watching television is 3 hours and 39 minutes, with events like the 2008 Olympics attracting some 4 billion viewers devoting an estimated 40 billion hours to watching its coverage over the course of sixteen days.[10]

Taking into account traditional print and broadcast (television/radio) media as well as new media like the Internet, video games, DVDs, and mobile device music and video services, total media consumption in the United States now averages over 9 hours per day.[11] American school-aged children (8 to 18 years) are using multiple media roughly one-third of the time they spend in media consumption, for an average total exposure of 8.5 hours a day. Approximately 25% of all school-aged children report more than 9 hours of media use per day, with 12% reporting more than 13 hours of media use (approximately 17 hours of media exposure).[12] This degree of media consumption among youth is fast becoming a global norm, and it is estimated that by using multiple media simultaneously some youth are logging as many as 44 hours of media exposure per day.[13]

We will presently consider some of the wider implications of such statistics. But it is important, first, to stress that the *quantitative* expansion of mass media audiences that we have briefly documented has been inseparable from a technologically achieved expansion of the *qualitative*, sensory reach of mass media and a radical extension of their content and effects. As noted above, the history of mass mediation begins with print media—a highly abstract means of communication that, prior to the modern institutionalization of mass public education, was practically limited to a relatively small, literate proportion of the population. But once nominally visual mass media like newspapers were augmented, first by lithographic illustrations and then by still photography, previously excluded populations were brought into the margins of mass mediation. Moreover, the presentation of relevant visual information/images and not just linguistic representations of them established means to commercializing the sense of sight and the rich imaginaries associated with it. Visual content not only augmented information coded in print, it opened a sensual domain for access by advertising and—more importantly in the long run—for shaping and commodifying visual sensibilities.

The advent of audio recording and broadcast radio likewise opened the sense of hearing to mass mediation and commercial influence. Through the end of the nineteenth century, the "music industry" was centered on the reproduction and distribution of sheet music. Although there was certainly a mass, commercial aspect to music culture, printed music could only be read and played by the musically literate, and performances inevitably varied widely in skill and character. "Playing music" required, at the very least, acquiring an intimate understanding of one or more instruments—an embodied understanding earned only through dedicated practice—and music listening was necessarily a social experience. Mechanically reproduced music made it possible both to "play music" without any prior training and to consume aural commodities in private and for purposes of mood and ambience regulation. With radio and phonograph recordings, playing music ceased being associated primarily with personally fashioning meaning in sound and came to be increasingly subject to private preference and public fashion.

With motion pictures it became possible to incorporate gestures and other forms of dynamic nonverbal communication like physical humor within the arsenal of mass mediation. Motion pictures made it feasible to mass produce the experience of live dramatic performances and to significantly program (if not dictate) shared emotional experiences, quite literally crafting mass mediated sympathies between actors and audiences. The births of cinema and television thus inaugurated an era of unprecedentedly specific and large scale commodifications of feeling. And, as the processes of shooting and editing film for cinema and television became increasingly sophisticated, it became possible to present audiences with settings and actions that could never have been produced in live theater, but that nevertheless engulf them in highly realistic—and ultimately hyperreal—joint experiences.

At the same time, the history of cinema and television describes a trajectory of increasingly radical transformations of visual, kinetic, and dramatic grammars. After nearly a century of commercial film, audiences in most markets have become so accustomed to the editorial parsing of experience that the experience of rapidly changing point of view—the absence of a sustained angle of attention—has become fully normalized. Contemporary audiences now hungrily submit to filmic techniques that amount to a regime of "temporal dictatorship" leaving no time or reflective space for personalizing the dramatic experience or for drawing out within it unique configurations of meaning. Exercising control over what programs to view and thus over the contours of one's experience has almost entirely eclipsed the value of cultivating more broadly appreciative ways of engaging dramatic experience to insure and deepen its participative nature.

Examining the effects of postmodern scales and depths of mass mediation, anthropologist Thomas de Zengotita (2005) draws critical attention to the emergence of the "flattered self" as experiential sovereign and to the displacement of reality, not by the false or virtual, but by the *optional*. Social networking sites like MySpace, Facebook, Friendster, Hi5, and Orkut are a key component in the flattering of self that de

Zengotita sees as a distinctively postmodern sense of public narcissism—a narcissism based on exercising near absolute authority over what is experienced, but also on being a center of global attention. In 2008, it was estimated that there were 530 million users of social networking sites in the world, with visits at the top 7 sites running at about 70 million per day, and total monthly accesses from home or work (but not Internet cafes or libraries, for example) by unique visitors running at nearly 1 billion per month. Sites that allowed users to download videos were even more popular, with more than 10 billion videos downloaded per month in many American, European, and Asian countries, and with sites like YouTube attracting more than 250 million visitors per month.[14] These numbers are now dramatically higher, of course, with social networking, games, and media content now continuously accessible through the new generations of mobile devices. For the flattered self, mass media and integrated telecommunications devices like new generation mobile phones and handheld computers make it possible to exercise such continuous control over what is experienced and with whom that the presence of options at any given moment—the freedom to opt in or out of a shifting array of social and sensory opportunities—is now taken by many to be a basic right.

However, the shift away from the real to the optional is clearest, perhaps, at the cutting edge of mass mediated entertainment in interactive computer-based gaming. This new media merges visual, audio, kinesthetic, and dramatic content in ways that make possible an almost horizonless exercise of choice. The video-game industry cut its teeth in gaming arcades in which individuals or pairs of players would use game-specific machines, but very quickly moved to selling both dedicated hardware and computer software for both home and mobile game playing. The top-selling noninteractive game genres are action-adventure, first-person shooting, racing, fighting, stealth, puzzles, traditional sports, and simulation, and as indicated by this list, a key attraction of video-game play is the biochemical rush that accompanies the presence of danger or high degrees of risk—a hypersensitivity to changes in our environment and acutely compressed response and learning curves. To this, the advent of massively multiplayer online role-playing games (MMOs) adds capacities for and mediums within which players can assume and continuously articulate personas or characters in virtual worlds that operate according to rules and with goals that are often emergently structured or dependent on player input.

The multiplayer, interactive game format has progressed to the point that there are now fully operating virtual or optional economies (that nevertheless link to real world costs and profits), and an extraordinarily wide range of "realms" within which players may choose what amount to wholly elective identities. Globally, some 60 million people now regularly play online MMOs, with leading games like *World of Warcraft* attracting 7 to 8 million players—roughly 1 out of every 1,000 people on the planet. According to a recent study, gamers globally average nearly 23 hours of online play per week, with more than half of all players assuming characters of the opposite sex, and nearly half choosing to discuss difficult life issues with online, rather than real-world, family members and friends (Cole and Griffiths 2007). We have reached a point—not only in the wealthiest nations, but in countries like China and Vietnam that have significant populations subsisting on less than $2 per day—where friendship is being effectively mass mediated, and in ways that are commercially viable.[15]

In sum, what we have witnessed over the course of the expansion of media from printed broadsides through the Internet is a gradual commodification of the experiential nexus at which sensation and meaning making take place. But if relationality is understood as ontologically prior to things-related, the commodification of sensation and meaning making is a commodification primarily of relational dynamics, not of putatively internal or subjective events. *Meaning making* is rooted in *relational appreciation* or what can be characterized as *becoming more significantly present*. Meaning making is, in other words, not a fundamentally reflective or cognitive process, but rather a *contributory* one. The developmental arc of commercially viable, electronic mass communication from the mid-twentieth century onwards clearly has linked the maximization of market reach and density with quantitatively and qualitatively expanding freedoms of experiential choice. But in doing so, it has also fostered the systematic erosion of those locally vibrant patterns of direct mutual contribution crucial to both personally and communally realizing and enhancing diversity.

PROMOTING DIFFERENCE

As a transition to more explicitly linking this developmental arc to issues of difference, let me rehearse four key aspects of the marketization of sensation and meaning. First, as ICT opened new possibilities for mass producing and mass marketing experiential commodities, mass media were enabled to circumvent the literacy hurdle presented by print media and, in some degree, to perforate the language barriers that had hitherto segmented and/or segregated media markets. Second, this then made possible the deep and pervasive penetration of mass media into the lives of children—a huge and previously untapped market. Third, the mutual entrainment of market dynamics and the coevolution of media and technology over the twentieth century fostered the convergence of production and consumption on maximally ephemeral experiential goods, greatly accelerating space-time compression and radically collapsing the consumption-to-waste cycle. Fourth, the individualization, mobilization, and spatiotemporal saturation of media consumption through increasingly user-friendly, inexpensive, and highly portable media tools opened a readily and almost seamlessly accessible realm of sensory distraction, with media portals serving a crucial "capillary" function in the circulatory dynamics of the global attention economy.

Whatever aspirations may have been associated with specific print, broadcast, or Internet media in terms of their delivered content, the historical reality is that true mass media became commercially viable only through their intimate relationship to advertising and its aims—the systematic promotion of economically useful needs, fears, and desires (O'Shaughnessy and O'Shaughnessy 2003). To reprise Toulmin's invocation of a "hidden agenda" in modernity, modern mass media have been dynamically adapted for the purpose of supporting continued economic growth through generating powerful and effective links between realizing ever greater *market reach and density* and ever more *compellingly varied senses of belonging and identity*: a "hidden" agenda of promoting the commodification and commercialization of values.

The tendency for advertising and mass mediation to become increasingly targeted over time closely parallels the broader market history of first expanding the geographic reach of consumption and then heightening its spatial and temporal density. As noted earlier, once market-mediated economic activity had attained global geographic scope in the nineteenth century, the dynamics of growth shifted toward an infusion of market processes into the widest possible spectrum of lifeworld dimensions and the eventual commodification, over the second half of the twentieth century, of the full range of material subsistence needs as well as health care and education. With electronic mass media, this process of infusing contemporary lifeworlds with market forces crossed over into the commodification of such immaterial subsistence needs as sensory stimulation and the experience of shared identities and significance.

Here it should be stressed that the commodification of subsistence needs has involved much more than the spread of market forces into the social, cultural, and political domains. It has enabled an ever more profound rooting therein of the core market values of control, convenience, competition, and choice. Considering, then, the fact that markets produce not only goods and services, but populations in need of them, it is not surprising that the explosion of increasingly differentiated media products in the 1960s and 1970s was correlated with increasingly differentiated populations of media consumers—a proliferation of lifestyle and identity choices, and a remarkable valorization of "being different." And, given this, it should also not be surprising that as mass mediation becomes globally ubiquitous, contemporary structures of feeling come to be characterized by crises of meaning and identity. Populations primed for continuous consumption of media products offering an array of life-style and identity options are, necessarily, populations that are not only hungry for something different, but also fearfully in need of it. In this light, it is not surprising that the literature and arts of the final half of the twentieth century—and especially of the crucial decade of the 1960s, when difference begins appearing in bold on the critical map—are awash with a sense of seemingly unlimited choices, a plenitude of possibilities, but also a sense of fathomless dislocation, a stunning evacuation of significance both personal and public.

Again, the point here is not to suggest this be seen as evidence of linear causality—media change causing social change. It is, instead, to direct attention to the twentieth-century emergence of a recursive network of feedback and feedforward processes that have vastly amplified the dynamics of social, economic, political, cultural, and technological differentiation. This network has most commonly and positively been seen as promoting "innovation"—a term that implies renewal and creativity. But if creativity implies not just change, but significant change, and if renewal entails both revitalization and conservation, the use of "innovation" is not particularly apt. The change dynamics in question have tended to render significance problematic and to foster a shift from furthering traditions to forfeiting them in pursuit of ever-proliferating freedoms of choice.

To make matters more complex, the feedback and feedforward processes associated with the co-implication of market growth, mass mediation, and technological change have also tended to increase—rather than decrease—differences among populations in terms of their relational opportunities and potentials for experiential enrichment. Of course, technologically advanced and market-integrating mass mediation do not directly cause an accelerating magnification and multiplication of differences in wealth and opportunity. The causes of deepening inequity are manifold, network-like, and complex. But there is a case to be made for seeing mass mediation as crucial to the globally dominant biasing of differentiation processes toward variation rather than diversification.

INTERPERSONAL DIVIDES:
AN IRONIC CONSEQUENCE OF MASS MEDIATION

In the context of unwavering modern appeals to the trinity of nation-state, science, and the market as sources of progressive order, it is difficult to raise questions about the possibility of troubling consequences associated with the deepening symbiosis of markets, media, and technology, however ironic these consequences may be (Busch 2000). The emancipatory, if not salvific, merits of unlimited, competitively structured, and technologically driven economic growth have come to form a key article of modernist faith. Yet, the imperatives for opening new "markets" and modes of mass mediation clearly exemplify the broader modern commitments to "creative destruction," and it is not unwarranted to ask questions about what is lost in the process, especially in light of the empirical evidence for mounting inequity both within and among societies under the global regime of market economics and ubiquitous mass mediation.

One way of describing the modern processes of opening new markets and expanding the ambit of mass mediation is as an expansion of options for making choices suited to pursuing lives worth living (Sen 1999). The greater the range of goods and services supplied by the market, the greater the range of options for fine-tuning the means-to and meaning-of acting in our own self-interest. But it is also possible, and critically useful, to focus not only on the supply-side flows toward consumers, but rather on the circulatory dynamics in which markets and media can be seen as intimately involved in generating demand-side change. At the most obvious level, the interdependence of media and advertising followed a developmental trajectory of aggressive demographic differentiation. This began as early as the late nineteenth century, with both advertising and media (first magazines and newspapers, and then broadcast programming) that targeted specific populations—for example, women, children, and ethnic/racial groups. Over the intervening century, there has been an accelerating proliferation of target audiences, with, for instance, the "children's market" becoming highly gender and age stratified.

At the microlevel of the individual consumer, the creation of ever-finer categories of market-designed and -delivered goods and services has typically been experienced as entirely welcome. Some choice is undoubtedly better than none, and more choices are—in the minds of many—better still. But more broadly, the process of generating an ever more differentiated consuming public can usefully be seen as one of "splitting communities" as a means to releasing their latent economic energy.

The modern world and the industrial globalization processes undergirding it owe their scale to the historic transition from muscle power to mechanical power—a transition made possible by burning or chemically splitting coal and oil to release energy stored therein. The still more powerful process of releasing energy by splitting heavy atoms like uranium and plutonium carries on this modern legacy, but is not the culmination of the developmental trajectory. That honor goes to the postmodern, market- and media-facilitated splitting of community through which attention—the most basic form of human energy—is systematically "mined" and "released" (or more accurately, distracted) into global circulation.

As might be expected, this logic of community splitting has twin technological and social expressions. The individualization and miniaturization of media tools and their steadily lowering relative costs, for example, have made it possible and apparently desirable for most American homes to have multiple televisions, music players, video-game consoles, and Internet-connected devices including desktop computers, wireless-ready notebook computers, and mobile phones. It is now possible not only to remain continuously mediated from waking to sleep, but to engage in the uninterrupted weaving of multiple streams of mass media. In combination, the proliferation of corporate mass media, Internet websites, and social networking portals is resulting in a staggering acceleration of opportunities for nearly immediate access to information and moment-to-moment control over the contents of experience.

Optimistic visions of an increasingly mediated future are, of course, in no short supply. But every opportunity array is also a structure of outcomes. And in spite of being conditionally realized on the basis of a common genealogy of values, intentions, and practices, the pattern of opportunities and outcomes occurring in any given situation is by no means necessarily biased in one direction or another. Change and differentiation processes are always playing out live. Optimistic visions of the mediated future are born with pessimistic twins and a full spectrum of visions in between.[16] Leaning somewhat in the direction of the pessimistic, it is possible to see the splitting of community that is part of the means-to and meaning-of maximizing the reach and density of both markets and mass media as a very real and very troubling "digital divide."

Reflecting on the ways in which mass mediation affects both consciousness and conscience, Michael Bugeja observes an ever-widening "interpersonal divide" that has worrying implications for the quality, depth, and ethical vitality of community (Bugeja 2005). To be sure, there is no denying that mass media and telecommunications technologies more broadly have also resulted in opportunities for maintaining social and cultural relations at a distance, and for realizing new patterns of association—if not community—based on electively shared interests and needs. But as de Zengotita stresses, even these putatively positive effects of high-tech mediation must be seen as embedded within relational regimes biased toward subordinating the actual to the optional. And in this context, it is useful to recall Rosenau's notion of "distant proximities"—the intensifying propensity under current scales and scopes of globalization for the constituent elements of our personal, social, economic, political, and cultural identities to be not only highly plural, but widely distributed in spatial terms. Contemporary mass media and the communication tools through which they are being accessed grant nearly miraculous capacities for choosing and controlling what to experience, when, and with whom. In doing so, however, they promote an understanding and practice of community in which belonging is interpreted as essentially a function of choice, not commitment.

Among the strongest concerns of critics like Bugeja is the likelihood that seeing identity and community as fundamentally elective and spatially distributed will work against emotional and relational maturation. The digitization of identity and community—their subjection to an on/off, binary logic of liking/disliking, wanting/not wanting—is not only conducive to fragmentary dynamics of the sort that can result in increasingly virulent fundamentalisms, but also to a radical attenuation of what we might call relational bandwidth. The broadening of the sensory dimensions of electronically enabled mediation associated with fiber-optic and wireless data transmission is not resulting in a parallel broadening of the bases of virtual communities, but rather an ironic a narrowing of their foundations. To the degree that we can opt out of dealing with difficult issues of value differences, for instance—a key factor in the wholly elective nature of digitally mediated patterns of belonging—we can opt out of the conditions within which we are most likely to be compelled to grow in terms of both sensitivity and sensibility.

It can be argued, of course, that the tools of mass mediation do not predetermine their uses. Whether and exactly how we use mass media and the web to address our needs for sensory stimulation and entertainment, or for learning, a sense of belonging, and the experience of meaningfulness in the course of daily life are also elective—a function of choices that we make as fully embodied and socially embedded persons-in-community. But a certain amount of critical slippage occurs when we elide the tool/technology distinction. We find ourselves powerfully inclined toward a comforting stratification of choice into those that are incidental (pertaining to the means to belonging) and those that are essential (pertaining to the meaning of belonging). Below certain thresholds of scale and complexity, this compartmentalization might not prove at all problematic. But just as events in the realms of the very small and very large made evident the limited applicability of classical Newtonian mechanics and the inseparability of matter and energy or space and time, events taking place at the most private and the most public scales of mediation compel insistence on the inseparability of the means and meaning of belonging.

If mass media are understood as technological phenomena or strategically structured relational flows, then it is entirely possible that the sum of all individual stories about *media use* will still not tell us much—at least, not much that is critically relevant—about overall *media effects*. Something that is good for each and every one of us, considered individually, may *not* be good for all of us. For example, engaging in modern-style mass industrialization was arguably good for all the nations who took the global leading edge on that mode of social and economic development, and even for all of their citizens; but as we are now becoming painfully aware, when a sufficient portion of humanity began securing the goods afforded by modern industrialization and identifying with the meaning of the good life promoted by it, the conditions were established for potentially devastating climate change and variability.[17] Critically engaging mass media requires keeping the bigger relational pattern in mind. To this end, I want to look at attention itself as a form of energy or *capital* that is not only crucial for realizing diverse and caring communities, but that is also circulated by and essential to the "health" of the global market economy.

THE ADVENT OF THE ATTENTION ECONOMY

Over the past decade, in spite of both popular and widespread political endorsements, there has been growing discomfort with the notion of a postindustrial "information economy." As aptly noted by Richard Lanham (2006) in his book *The Economics of Attention*, if economics is the discipline which studies the allocation of scarce resources, there is a certain irony, if not obfuscation, in referring to current global economic dynamics as evidence of an "information economy." If there is anything that is *not* scarce today, it is information (Lanham 2006, xi). In fact, the dynamics of the global economy over the past several decades suggest that what is actually quite distinctive about the present era is the emergence of complex interdependencies that make possible what Georg Franck (1999a) has in a seminal article called the "capitalization of attention."

Claims for the economic centrality of attention have been expressed from a variety of independent theoretical perspectives (Goldhaber 1997; Franck 1999a, 1999b; Hershock 1999, 2006) and business strategists (Davenport and Beck 2002). The roots of this interest can be traced with some justification to the Nobel Prize–winning political economist Herbert Simon, who can be credited with the first clear articulation of the basic insights regarding the relationship among economic activity, information, and attention. In a prescient 1971 article, Simon argued that an increasingly information-rich world produces conditions in which attention necessarily becomes scarce. That is, the production and dissemination of information "consumes the attention of its recipients" and "a wealth of information creates a poverty of attention and a need to allocate that attention efficiently among the overabundance of information sources that might consume it" (Simon 1971, 40–41).

Simon did not develop this insight further. But its implication that attention can usefully be seen as a kind of currency or commodity has been taken up especially by Franck, who argues that attention income is a primary driver, not only of the mass media, entertainment, and sports industries, but even of scientific research (Franck 1999b). For Franck, the primary function of receiving attention is to generate prominence, which now is best seen, not as the result of success, but rather its precondition.

In his view, mass media supply information in order to gather attention from consumers who offer such payment in order find out what they like, serving as exchanges through which the value of capital denominated in attention currency is assessed. Media must do so, of course, in competition with information gleaned directly from unmediated engagements with reality, and so must present information—that is, program content and experiential dynamics—that consumers will deem preferable to their actual, immediate situation.

Franck considers the attention economy to have always been a functional element in the social and economic organization of human societies, but one that has rapidly grown in centrality and overall importance from the era of modern industrialization onward. This growth has resulted partly because of the advent of mass media and their technological achievement of truly global reach, but also because of a progressive dematerialization of the global economy that (like the crisis that triggered the industrial revolution in Great Britain) responds to a powerful confluence of labor, environmental, scientific, and technological forces, the upshot being a shift of economic innovation (and profitability) from resource extraction and production to the tertiary or service sector—a shift from material to "mental capitalism."

Analogous to linkages of the sort identified by Jeremy Rifkin among mechanically achieved gains in productivity, eroding blue-collar employment opportunities, and increasingly aggressive cultivation of consumer markets, critical linkages have begun emerging over the past quarter century among the computerization of mechanical production, a shift of human labor to design, planning, administration, and supervision activities, and the proliferation of both technological means and social needs for increasingly dense media consumption. Economic growth, in short, has come to be predicated crucially on accelerating *attention turnover*. And as this means to sustaining economic growth matures, media naturally are drifting toward what Franck refers to as "the colonization of virtual space" and toward providing increasingly differentiated kinds of content and access—producing, over time, ever more variegated consuming publics.

Rethinking the Ontology of Economics

The epochal shift from industrial capitalism to mental capitalism and from a material economy to an attention economy mandates rethinking the logic and ontology of economic processes. Popular terms like "information economy," "knowledge economy," "risk economy," and "casino economy" quite rightly point toward a significant dematerialization or virtualization of economic processes—a transition Lanham describes as a shift from the economic centrality of "substance" to that of "style."

Working from a different angle, Scott Lash (2002) highlights the logical transition from an economic "logic of accumulation" to the "logic of circulatory flows," and from the primacy of the factory, products, and real property to the design studio, prototypes, and intellectual property. To these perspectives, I would add that understanding the dynamics of the new economy will entail focusing explicitly on the ontological priority, not of independently existing things, beings, and processes, but of relational qualities and directions.

We have already outlined the broad rationale and significances of such an ontological shift, making use in particular of the Buddhist teaching of nonduality, which directs us toward seeing that all things are the same precisely insofar as they differ meaningfully from one another. In the phrasing introduced earlier: things *are* what they *mean* for one another. In the present context, however, we might usefully characterize the first step in the direction of such a relational turn as a shift from economic realism to economic constructivism.

Realists assert the ultimately independent existence of experiencing subjects and experienced objects. Constructivists assert the complex interdependence of the subjective and objective, holding that reality is never a neutral, prereflective ground of experience, but rather an always value- or meaning-infused emergent thereof. In economic terms, moving from a realist to a constructivist perspective involves a refusal to reify, for example, "natural resources," "manufactured products," and "consumers" as transparently objective elements of social reality. From a constructivist perspective, all are ultimately functions of social interaction and have no existence independent of it. Thinking of trees, coal, oil, minerals, and flowing water as "natural resources" that can be conserved or exploited expresses the predominance of particular sets of values, intentions, and relational dynamics. "Resources" are not givens in the natural world; they are a particular way of configuring our relationships with/within "the natural world" that is itself socially defined as what is not a matter of human artifice.

In their pathbreaking 1966 book *The Social Construction of Reality*, Peter Berger and Thomas Luckmann explored the recursive implications of challenging the ontological assumption that there are things that exist or stand fundamentally and essentially apart from one another. "Reality" is not a singular and objective given that will always elude comprehension—something always just beyond our grasp. It is an always negotiable and changing expression of co-implication—a horizonless process of mutual enfolding out of which we may or may not abstract "agents" who make use of "natural resources" in accordance with their "individual self interests." We are not thrown into a preexisting world that will always elude our full comprehension—something always beyond our grasp. We live in/through multiple realities, each characterized by a specific kind or quality of attentiveness.

Berger and Luckmann were careful to insist that this should not be seen as a capitulation to metaphysical relativism—a position that assumes our independence from one another as experiential monads and hence the impossibility of anything other than arbitrary consensus. Not only are our realities always *socially* defined, these processes of defining what is real are always embodied (Berger and Luckmann 1966, 116). The body is not a dividing line between the realms of the subjective and objective, but rather an expression of their irreducible given-togetherness—an expression of what the Vietnamese Buddhist Thich Nhat Hahn has referred to as our "interbeing." We necessarily live not just in and among, but also through one another. Realities are constituted relationally.[18]

From such a perspective, there are no economic givens. This means that there cannot be any ultimately valid grounds for asserting the unavoidability or necessity of, for example, income and wealth inequities. But it also means that whatever significantly affects relational quality— our modalities of personal, social, political, and cultural embodiment— is also likely to significantly affect economic realities. The increasing scope and scale of the attention economy signals, then, much more than Polanyi's envisioned reembedding of economic processes within society; it signals the crossing of key complexity thresholds through amplifying the interdependence and interpenetration of the personal, social, economic, political, cultural, and technological domains—the advent of what Lars Qvortrup (2003) has termed the "hypercomplex society." Or, to put this in terms that draw out a key ramification of the constructivist thesis forwarded by Berger and Luckmann: changing qualities and patterns of attentiveness and changing economic realities are intrinsically coemerging and co-implicating.

Seen in this light, mass media thus present us with something of a paradox. As argued persuasively by Niklas Luhmann, the societal function of mass media is to create a sense of common reality, doing so through communication technologies that allow interaction among those copresent to be circumvented and effectively rendered impossible (Luhmann 2000, 15–16). According to Luhmann, like all functional subsystems in a given society, mass media are distinguished from other operational systems and are sustained by consistently behaving in accordance with their own unique code. In politics, for example, the operational code is power. In mass media, the code is information—or, more properly stated, the differentiation of information and noninformation.

Importantly, the functional logic of information entails that repetition equals devaluation. In other words, *presenting information triggers the process of its own obsolescence.* Indeed, the act of becoming apprised of and absorbing information is inseparable from that of converting it into noninformation. Thus, having learned a friend's phone number, being presented with it again is no longer informative. And, as contemporary neuroscience has made evident, the fleeting nature of information holds true even at the most basic level of perceptual processes. Perception is an ongoing process of scanning for differences that may appear anywhere within the emergent, relational complex of brain/body/environment.[19] Information that is re-presented quickly passes from foreground to background and then into the perceptual limbo of the unnoticed—something that is neither fully present nor absent.[20]

It is in light of this equivalence of absorbing information and its conversion to noninformation that we must understand the imperatives for novelty and exclusivity, not only in news reporting and entertainment, but even in scientific or scholarly communication. Only the previously un-presented conveys or (more accurately stated) embodies information. Thus, for mass media to perform their function of constituting a common reality by informing the consuming public, they must construct new information continuously. From the early modern broadsides printed only irregularly when something newsworthy occurred, we "progressed" eventually to dailies making public "all the news that's fit to print" and then to Internet media—especially the noncorporate blogosphere—in which content is continuously updated in pursuit of sustained noteworthiness.

The imperative to produce information continuously has reached such a scale and scope that it has begun generating what is now widely known as information pollution and overload (Shenk 1997). As mass mediated publics are directed to pay increasing attention to ever-changing evidence of the depth and novelty of change or differentiation, the concomitantly rising incidence of information pollution produces needs to seek out effective information filters—metainformational services—that determine what should be considered worth paying attention to, opening opportunities for commercializing the process of discerning what is worthwhile. It is in connection with media or information overload that Luhmann's observation that the obverse of information production is attracting and retaining attention assumes crucial significance.

Contemporary mass media saturation of the sort earlier noted can be described as a maximum loading of information into society—a maximizing of differential novelty. But with equal validity it can be described as a maximizing of attention turnover, as a hypersensitivity to difference, and as a proliferation of realities open to being experienced as at once common and uncommon. Ours is an era in which Franck is in many ways correct in characterizing mass media as "reality factories." Under conditions of overload, these factories must also deliver increasingly differentiated guidance regarding what realities are desirable.

At current scales and scopes, the imperatives for mass media pursuits of novelty and exclusivity cannot be separated from processes of at once *magnifying* and *multiplying* commonalities and realities. In short, while the logic of mass mediation dictates the proliferation of categories of notice and associated kinds and qualities of attentiveness, it also compels accelerating production of new patterns of affiliation and identification, new classes of belonging. There is a sense in which, beyond a certain threshold, mass mediation becomes profoundly and yet seductively unsettling.[21]

In this regard, Luhmann very usefully notes that the process of continuous information production is, simultaneously, one of generating uncertainties that must be addressed with still further information. That is, mass media "increase the complexity of contexts of meaning in which society exposes itself to irritation through self-produced differences," ever-expanding horizons of expectation that mass mediation then continuously shatters (Luhmann 2002, 82). If we accept Gregory Bateson's minimal conception of information as "any difference which makes a difference in some later event" (Bateson 1972, 381), mass media's function of producing and publishing ever-varying information must also be seen as one of generating ever more variously constructed and shared meanings. In addition to producing realities that are at once common and uncommon, mass media also produce publics that forward ever more differentiated interpretations of interleaving, but ultimately discontinuous, realities.

Beyond an always indefinite threshold, this leads not to mass identity consolidation, but rather to a manifest proliferation of perspectives and considerations—the predominance of fleeting commonalities and fashionable affiliations, and an apparently patternless differentiation of meanings. The explosive expansion of the kinds of content being transmitted via mass media would seem to affirm that appearance is, in this case, reality. To a degree never before witnessed (or technically possible), the media sphere is one in which virtually "anything goes." And this appearance of unpatterned or rhizomatic differentiation has been reinforced for many by the impression that cyberspace is a topologically peculiar space in which all points are equidistant from all others—a pure space of information lacking any intrinsic structure. However true this might have been in the early days of the Internet, the topology of cyberspace now is both highly structured and expressly complex. Indeed, I would argue that because mass mediation takes place only as a technological phenomenon, the appearance of unpatterned differentiation can be only that—an apparition.

Although technologies do not determine how we use the tools produced through them or for what purposes, technologies are nevertheless systematizations of how we have conceived and promoted our ends or interests and are thus never value neutral. And because technologies have thresholds of utility beyond which they begin producing the conditions of their own necessity, generating problems of the sort that apparently can only be solved by more technology, heavily deployed technologies not only become ever more deeply embedded in daily life, they exert ever-greater influence on the relational dynamics taking place therein. Especially after crossing their utility thresholds, communications technologies and mass mediation begin altering both the means and meaning of being present.

Because of their distinctive technological character, and their function of continuously marrying and divorcing information and attention, mass media can be seen as "responsible for the production of modern society's 'Eigenvalues'—those relatively stable orientations in the cognitive, the normative and the evaluative domains which cannot be given *ab extra* but rather arise out of operations being applied recursively to their own results" (Luhmann 2002, 99). And, somewhat ironically, it is in their unsettling combination of providing access to realities and meanings that are simultaneously and dynamically both common (jointly experienced) and uncommon (experienced as new or distinctive) that we most clearly discern the core orientations produced by the recursive operation of mass media: a powerful convergence on *autonomously embodying* the technological and market values of *choice* and *control*.

Importantly, the relational scope or bandwidth of mass mediated choice and control are quite restricted. The realities to which mass media provide access are realities that can only be engaged through a process of abstraction from our immediate surroundings. That is, the benefits that accrue from mass mediation occur within specifically mediated environments. This is most apparent in online gaming and the realization of virtual online economies, but holds in some degree for all mediated activity. The choice and control afforded by access to media-produced realities do *not*, in other words, manifest as (or translate readily into) relating more freely in unmediated contexts. To borrow a term from the psychology of consciousness, the core benefits of mass mediation are "state specific." And to the degree that mass mediation crosses the threshold of its own utility in terms of providing program content (information) to which consuming publics pay attention in order to find out what they like, increasing choice and control have the ironic effect of driving an ever-accelerating proliferation of self-oriented and self-orienting desires.

There are many reasons to be concerned about the effects of a steady expansion and intensification of desire. It is difficult, if not impossible, to name a major religious or ethical tradition that has not invited critical reflection on the ills of (at least) unchecked or inappropriate desire. And, worries about a progressive "dumbing down" of sensibilities and sensitivities—a freefall toward the lowest possible common denominators of taste and appetite—have been a staple of moral (and often moralizing) discourse for much of modernity. Indeed, such concerns can be found in an early Buddhist text, the *Cakkavatti-Sīhanāda Sutta* (dating from roughly the fourth or fifth century BCE). Such concerns and worries can and have been contested, of course, and no doubt should be in the interest of guarding strenuously against any tendencies to slip from affirming universal "rights to think" into universal formulations and enforcements of "right thinking."

But for reasons that I have articulated at length elsewhere (Hershock 2002), I do not want to focus here on the recursively evolving impacts of media program content. As significant as these impacts are, more salient for our present purposes are effects correlated with the fact that mass media generate shared meanings by attracting and retaining attention in ways that not only *displace*, but also *replace*, relational immediacy.

Exporting Attention as Economic Stimulus

If the global economy is seen as a complex set of flows—of goods, services, information, and attention—then it is crucial to ask about what shapes the dynamics of those flows, their rates, directions, and contours. If we have begun making a transition from industrial to mental capitalism, and from a material to an attention economy, we must ask how the attraction and retention of attention are—or are not—linked to the rising inequities that the global economy is apparently generating with respect to income, wealth and opportunity. The geographies of such differences, including the resurgence of issues of class, ethnicity, and nationality, can no longer be plausibly assumed to be a function simply of disparities in respect of natural and human resources, or of discrepancies in the realization of maximally free markets.

Keeping in mind the complex nature of the interdependencies shaping contemporary geographies of difference, I want to draw out some relevant implications of what I have called "the colonization of consciousness," a process coeval with the emergence of complex markets that depend for their growth on the global extraction and redistribution of attention energy. How has mass mediation contributed to exporting from our midst this most basic of resources needed to make differences of the sort that make a meaningful difference?

The technologically enabled expansion of the reach and density of media markets over the nineteenth and twentieth centuries underwent phenomenal acceleration with the invention of transistorized consumer electronics. Over the past half century, continual advances in the miniaturization and digitalization of media tools combined with rapidly falling consumer prices as a function of economies of scale to make affordable both highly individualized and spatially ubiquitous media consumption.

As demonstrated by the statistics already provided on media use, the reach and density of mass mediation have no historical precedent. On average, homes are bought once or a small handful of times over the course of a life. Clothes are purchased much more regularly, but typically only a few dozen items in a year. Food is of course consumed more regularly still, with a stereotypical ideal being "three meals a day." For the global majority, mass media are consumed almost continuously. And, as we have seen, the operational logic of mass mediation ensures that the publics attending to mass media are not only growing in absolute volume, but are becoming ever more finely differentiated. The varieties of media options—the realities to which media provide access—are not literally infinite, but they far exceed the consumption capacities of any individual or community.

Importantly, because mass media provide diets of virtually unbroken streams of information in the form of *maximally distracting* entertainment, news, and social networking options, the attention turnover associated with the consumption of mass media content affords only the most ephemeral rewards. Mass media provide a diet that is more successful the *less* it provides lasting satisfaction. As economically viable purveyors of information, mass media must not only provide novel and exclusive goods/services, they must do so in such a way as to increase the public's appetites for the novel and exclusive.

Simply stated, mass mediation effects an industrial *extraction* and *export* of attention energy. As Nicholas Georgescu-Roegen has argued (1971), in thermodynamic terms, industrial production is in general not a generative process, but a dissipative one. That is, industrial growth is a necessarily asymmetric process of dismembering ecological and social relations to *extract high order energy* from industrial peripheries—for example, natural resources and labor—and exchanging for them *high entropy* "goods" and "services" destined for accelerating consumption and de facto conversion to waste. The cumulative result is accelerating capital accumulation at industrial centers and the *relative exhaustion* and *relational impoverishment* of developmental peripheries. Seen from this perspective, the most deleterious effects of media saturation do not lie in the program content being consumed as continuously as possible by the global majority. The most profound and wide-reaching effects of mass mediation are the export of attention from consumers' immediate environments, where it is crucial for maintaining local relational ecologies, and the resulting breakdown of these ecologies, which serves in turn as a recursively amplifying stimulus for the continued growth of the nonattention economy.

We are all well aware of how daydreaming and distraction can negatively affect both our productivity and the quality of our personal and professional relationships. One could argue, of course, that—like modest amounts of daydreaming—mass media use can be extremely useful both personally and professionally. The quality of news and entertainment available today may be uneven in quality, but is almost miraculously detailed and broad in scope. Access to research libraries and high-quality websites for everything from construction trades to medicine is readily available via the Internet. But most people, most of the time, are not engaged in active learning via mass media and the Internet, much less in formal research. The compelling nature of mass media and Internet offerings and their increasing capabilities for inducing the highest possible rates of attention turnover practically guarantee that the costs of attention paid to the media far exceed the benefits gained. Mass mediation—including the so-called peer-to-peer mediation conducted by the Internet—has crossed its utility threshold to begin creating the conditions of its own necessity: the multiplication and magnification of needs for ever more differentiated and autonomously experiential options.

The ill effects of mass media program content on family life, personal development, and public culture are quite real.[22] But the most prevalent and relationally powerful effects of mass mediation derive from how effectively it extracts and exports attention from our homes, schools, workplaces, neighborhoods, and communities. Time spent consuming mass market media is time *not* spent attending to the needs of one's family, home, neighborhood, or local community. Like gardens deprived of sufficient sunlight and water, when left too long unattended, relational ecologies suffer.

As we have already noted, the global daily average per capita export of attention via television alone is nearly 4 hours, totaling about 26 billion hours per day. This is time *not* spent developing new relational capabilities, *not* acquiring new skills or refining existing ones, *not* passing on personal or cultural traditions, and *not* making use of locally available resources to meet other basic human needs by, for example, cooking, designing and making clothes, building or repairing one's home, caring for the ill or aged, inspiring and refining learning activities, creating new works of art, music, dance, and drama, or participating in public debate, policy formation, or democratic governance. If we take the U.S. average of roughly 9 hours of total media consumption as a figure and discount that by 33% to reflect the fact that the distraction of attention is not total, Americans alone are paying out nearly 2 billion hours per day of attention energy. The global average daily media consumption per person can currently be assumed to be substantially lower, but the total still might be conservatively placed at 30 billion hours per day.

Of course, figures like these can be contested from any number of angles.[23] My aim here is not statistical precision, but rather to make the point that the costs of mass media consumption are not limited to money spent on media tools and on direct programming or access costs. These are not insignificant, of course. They now constitute, in fact, a major portion of the global economy calculated along familiar lines. But factoring in the costs in attention energy assures mass media top billing among global industries. There are two major components of cost involved.

First, there are costs associated with what is *not being done* with, let's say, the 20 billion hours that globally are devoted solely to media consumption each day. What goods and services are not being produced? What care is not being given? What acts of charity, skill transmission, and creativity are being foregone for the sake of media engagement? But there are also costs associated with relationships that are not sustained or invigorated with regular and sufficient attention—compromises of relational health, including lowered resilience and responsivity, an overall atrophy of relational strength and depth. And these costs will more readily affect the more fragile relationships—those that are most difficult to achieve and sustain, and that often represent the highest flourishing of human sociality. The very substantial body of literature that links performance quality and self-esteem might be criticized for its at times naïve understanding of social causalities and its expression in an idiom of self-valuation that works well only in a handful of societies worldwide. But the basic insight of work on the social psychology of excellence is incontestable: receiving attention is relationally nurturing. Attention energy spent in media consumption is *not* available for contributing directly to the welfare of others or realizing more appreciative relational dynamics.

As such, media consumption works *against* realizing and enhancing diversity. This is true even given the remarkable variety of content to which media and ICT grant access. Indeed, because the realms into which mass media and ICT attract our attention exist with high degrees of autonomy—that is, very limited interdependence—media consumption establishes a habit of taking experience to be ideally structured in terms of continuously available choices. The seemingly limitless realms of distraction and desire afforded to consumers by mass media—each with an experiential depth proportionate to the prominence it comes to enjoy in globally mediated circuits of information exchange—are not related ecologically. Each such realm has a distinct structure of significance or meaning. But these structures are discontinuous with one another, and the common/uncommon realities associated with each are not conducive to the embodiment of anything other than state-specific meaning-making practices. That is, mass mediation conditions consuming publics to make choices as if they neither have lasting ramifications outside of the specific experiential domains to which individual media provide access, nor real impacts on others. Especially once it has crossed its utility threshold, media consumption *is* a powerful inducement to experiential and relational variation, but *not* diversification.

It must be stressed, again, that the ill effects of mass media on public culture and the appreciation of (or sympathetic resonance with and adding of value to) local environments are not a direct function of media content. Attention is exported just as powerfully by so-called public broadcasting, documentaries, and locally produced news or entertainment as it is by commercial, global media. Media use functions very much like the *asrava* identified by early Buddhist practitioners as the primary impediment to liberation: as effluences of attention energy that, whatever personal enjoyment or sense of freedom they afford, ultimately prove to be relationally compromising, wasteful, or polluting.

Attention implies a certain quality of engagement and readiness for response. Attending to our surroundings right now will entail not just being present in our current circumstances, but present to and for them. Attending to the needs of a small child or an elder involves both caring-for and caring-about them. The quantity and quality of our available attention energy is an index, then, of strengths for being carefully and caringly present. Stated more operationally, attention energy is that without which appreciation is impossible. That is, *attention is required for both attributing and adding value.* The global extraction of attention via media and ICT means a mass compromise of capacities for valuing and adding value to our own immediate situations, and thus a mass deflection of commitments to enhancing the relational dynamics constituting them.

Granted this, a hugely significant, cumulative effect of media saturation will be an increasing reliance (and eventual dependence) on market-designed and market-delivered *nonmedia* goods and services that might otherwise have been produced personally or communally. The twenty to thirty billion hours daily spent paying attention to mass media are a tremendous windfall to nonmedia industries. The extraction and export of attention from homes, schools, offices, and communities is a powerful stimulus to global economic processes, establishing and sustaining relational conditions that are highly conducive to professionalizing the means of production for meeting the full range of human needs; a progressive rationalization of physical, mental, and emotional labor; and the erosion of local production ecologies.

Bluntly stated: attention energy "spent" in media consumption functions as a key input for both media and nonmedia industries. The distribution and intensity of media-attracted attention flows provide globally continuous feedback on what is being perceived as both different and interesting—a highly detailed index of changes in the topography of prominence that enables, in turn, the most profitable possible production and marketing of material goods and services. The more accelerated attention turnover is in the global economy, the greater the facility with which markets are able to respond to the needs of ever more variegated consuming publics. Or otherwise stated, the more abbreviated attention spans tend to be globally, the more readily, accurately, and profitably markets are able to produce desirable new information, goods, and services, as well as populations happily opting to construct their ever more individuated and various realities and identities through and around them.

Because of the individualization of the means of media consumption, the export of attention occurs in a maximally distributed manner and we can rightly praise its embodiment of the modern values of autonomy and equality. At present, the cost of ICT devices is low enough to allow the majority of the planet's people to have access to basic mass media—a much better record of equal access than holds for education, health care, or meaningful employment. Indeed, it can be argued that mass mediation and ICT are playing crucial roles in providing a "space" for reconciling the modern values of autonomy and equality—values that, when expressed together in unmediated environments, will tend to be in tense and at times openly conflicted relationship with each other and with social solidarity.

If acting autonomously means acting expressly in my own interest, in substantial disregard of any impacts my choices might have on others, then according everyone in society an equal right to exercise autonomy is workable only if everyone's choices and actions mesh miraculously, or if the primary space within which autonomy is individually expressed allows freedoms-of-choice to occur in relative isolation. This is precisely the kind of space opened by mass-produced, extremely low-cost, and maximally portable ICT devices—a space within which even diametrically opposed experiential preferences can be expressed without conflict.

But this should not be confused with declaring that mass mediation and ICT use operate equitably. Attention flows are not symmetrical. And while the growth of the attention economy does open opportunities for new kinds of economic advantage for new kinds of economic agents, the shift of emphasis from productive power to the power of prominence by no means ensures a just and fair distribution of the benefits of economic activity. On the contrary, in the absence of strong countervailing dynamics, the likely impact of increasing access to ICT by the global majority will be an increasing exacerbation of uneven outcomes and opportunities. Over the period from 1980 to 2007, when ICT development and use exploded, of the total increase of income in the United States, 80% went to the top 1% of the population (Reich 2010), and there is much to suggest that the next generation of ICT development and use will simply extend this upward transfer of income globally.

There is, of course, a trend recently to see much promise in the "interactive" turn in both mass and personalized mediation. But in fact, the geographies of prominence and wealth remain both tightly related and precipitously uneven, and the disparities emerging along with the explosive growth of the attention economy have the potential to far outstrip even those generated by monopolistic industrialism.[24] Mapping the effects of uneven attention exchanges is not, of course, as easily accomplished as with the effects of disparately distributed material wealth. As Michael Goldhaber has pointed out, attention is not quantifiable in traditional economic terms and is thus difficult to factor into standard calculations of inequity as an independent variable.[25] Still, if we do not see the attraction and retention of attention as an end in itself, but rather as a stimulus for the global economy as a whole, then the increasing unevenness of the benefits of economic globalization can be regarded as an approximate index of mounting inequities linked to the systematic, mass mediated extraction and export of attention.

EMPOWERED INDIVIDUALS, ELECTIVE COMMUNITIES

Inequity is never just an accident of power. Their relationship is far from simple, however, and this is especially true of the inequities and patterns of empowerment emerging and being sustained through the new economics of attention. Contemporary mass mediation expresses a profound functional merger of modern and market values—a unique interfusion of modalities of appreciation directed toward autonomy, equality, control, competition, convenience, and choice. It is these core values that define and direct the complex relations between inequity and power obtaining within the attention economy, and that bias it toward the subordination of diversity to variety. The ramifications of this are particularly acute with respect to the relational dynamics constitutive of persons-in-community.

As already noted, the experiential diet produced by mass media develops in recursive relationship with the growth of global markets and expresses powerful, intrinsic biases toward the novel and exclusive. This diet has the signal effect of producing a distinctive kind of hunger: a yearning, not for something in particular, but rather for *something different*, including different kinds and degrees of belonging. The quantitative success of this diet and the market-media recursion through which it has become normalized is startlingly evidenced by the 6.6% annual growth rate of the global entertainment and media industry—an industry with revenues of $1.6 trillion in 2007,[26] or roughly 3% of the global GDP of $59 trillion. To put this in perspective, entertainment and media revenues in 2007 rivaled the record-breaking $1.9 trillion earned by the oil industry.[27]

I would argue that a large part of the media industry's success can be attributed to the distinctive way in which it simultaneously creates and meets the hunger for something different. By radically tightening the consumption-to-waste cycle and accelerating attention turnover, mass mediation squeezes out opportunities for directly appreciating—both valuing and adding value to—either the goods and services we purchase or our immediate relational environments. The mutually reinforcing valorizations of choice undertaken by markets and media affect both our relations with the goods and services we consume and our relations with one another, functionally reinforcing (and eventually enforcing) preference for novel and purposely selected experiences. At least beyond certain use thresholds, mass media and ICT use tend to instrumentalize communication practices, fostering the construction of personal and community identities—our most intimate and public senses of belonging—as essentially elective in nature. Changing the means-to community deeply affects the meaning-of community.

One effect of information overload is stress—a health-compromising distortion of body-mind functions. This often occurs below the threshold of consciousness. But information overload also has the effect of inducing conscious experiences of both immediate and mediated environments as dense with obsolescence. In Buddhist terms, information overload can be seen as correlated with an economy of dissatisfaction rooted in the production of *papañca* or the proliferation of situational blockages—the steadily expanding experience of disappointment, trouble, and suffering (*dukkha*). This is because in a fully realized attention economy, only what is current has experienced value. That which is relatively lasting may be necessary—for example, transportation and communications infrastructure, or the buildings in which we live and shop—but increasingly only as means to the satisfaction of ever more fleeting desires. As attention turnover accelerates, so does the rate at which information—whether presented immaterially in the form of media content or materially in the form of a currently fashionable good or service—is converted to noninformation and thus rendered economically inert, incapable of further attracting, holding, and directing attention.

This effect of accelerating attention turnover is not restricted to objectively acquired goods and services, however. Accelerating attention turnover is subjectively equivalent to a shortening of attention spans—the curtailing or fragmentation of commitments to attending or both caring-about and caring-for others. The technological advances that globally empower us to exercise almost instantaneous access to practically unlimited arrays of media content present us as well with historically unprecedented capabilities for affiliation and disaffiliation. The means-to this freedom of association and the increasing preference for and prevalence of wholly and explicitly elective forms of community dramatically affect the meaning-of belonging. The widening interpersonal divide to which Bugeja alerts us has its roots in a drastic transformation in the meaning of sociality. In our age of technologically mediated communication, we have reduced down to a single and explicitly reversible digital event the requirements for entering a community of like interests, for participating in the joint consumption of entertainment and information, or for engaging in the construction of shared realities, interpretations, and meanings. One need only electronically assert, by the click of a computer mouse or a voice command, that "I want to experience this" or "I do not want to experience that" for it to be so. As means and end, choice and community together are being effectively disengaged from commitment.

In what I take to be a dystopian view of a "pure" attention economy, all of our needs for goods and service could be instantaneously "satisfied" in media environments. In such a "virtual world," the seamless exercise of freedoms-of-choice would render infinitesimal the gap between consumption and waste or obsolescence. With sufficient technological support, the unhindered growth of the attention economy would result both in a nearly total *dematerialization* of the economy and a nearly total *ephemeralization* of experience. Physically consumed food, for example, could be utterly generic, so long as one could—at appropriate cost—virtually enjoy a stunningly wide variety of flavorful and exquisitely presented "foods." Like avatars in massively multiple-player domains, we could dress in "clothes" and "body types" suited to our mood or anticipated social occasions, while being physically garbed in simple tunics or (perhaps more likely) full-body virtual-reality suits.

In such a "world," we would not need to wash our "clothes" or exercise our "bodies" to maintain peak appearances. Our patterns of association could be entirely elective. Substance would be almost entirely subordinated to style; the material economy both hidden and dwarfed by the immaterial. And, because the pace of consumption would not be tied as fully as it now is to the use of natural resources (other than those needed to technologically sustain realistic, or hyperrealistic, mediated experience), such an economy could even be advertised as a "green" alternative to material production. Eating real mangos in the company of actually present friends and family under a naturally occurring canopy of shower tree branches might become the exclusive privilege of the stratospherically wealthy.

Thankfully, such a "perfection" of the attention economy is likely to remain the stuff of science fiction. But such fictions do make a point: exercising ever more unlimited freedoms to determine what we experience, as well as when, where, and with whom, is conducive to so valorizing choice, convenience, and control that concerns for the actual might ultimately be almost wholly displaced by the optional. Put in terms of the mutual conditioning among values, intentions, and practices on one hand, and outcomes and opportunities on the other: the better we get at getting what we want, the better we will get at wanting; but to get better at wanting requires being continually in want, so we won't be able to want what we get.[28] Under such karmic conditions, the optimal and the optional become nearly indistinguishable.

As relational optimality comes to be seen as a function of securing or holding open relational options, the *possibility* of choosing begins assuming greater prominence than actually making choices. That is, choice begins taking on the character of a basic *right*—something to be protected, respected, and exercised as an expression of one's own empowerment. But somehow the exercise of choice will seem always to leave us still wanting.

To the degree that the *right to choice* is being technologically secured, it manifests practically as a *capacity-for and entitlement-to withholding or deferring commitment*: keeping one's options unquestionably open. This is now mundanely exemplified in the new ethos of appointment setting. Whereas it was once common practice to set meeting times in advance, and regularly to keep those appointments, mobile phones have made it feasible to abort such plans at almost any point, enabling us to change our course of action more or less as desired, with what many now regard as minimal social condemnation. Empowered individually to hold open for ourselves spaces of maximum variability, we entertain almost continuously shifting arrays of possibilities for changing our direction—to be or do something different.

This power for moment-to-moment determinations of what we will (or will not) do and be necessarily impacts relational quality. As the relationships through which we are constituted as persons-in-community are shaped by historically unprecedented valorizations of choice, control, and contingency, there occurs a significant "thinning" of both subjectivity and intersubjectivity. Even though contemporary communications technologies make it possible for us to interact with more people more often than ever in the past, we are becoming ever more isolated through the very forms of interaction these technologies afford. That is, making use of these means to greater interconnectivity simultaneously enhances the individuation and compartmentalization of personal and social relations, rendering them more abstract and less multiplex. Indeed, the attention economy's present growth trajectory can be described as predicated on a "continuing progression of the segregation and separation of life practices into various realms" (Willson 2006, 63). As a result, attention is effectively distracted from how choices made in one realm ramify importantly in others, retarding or forestalling their critical integration.

At contemporary scales and scopes, then, technological mediation can be seen as fostering a breakdown of interdependence as a characteristic structure of feeling. And especially when a particular pattern of interdependence has been constraining or troubling in character, this breakdown can be experienced as a kind of breaking free—a very real expression of new capacities for acting autonomously in our own interests. But because this technologically mediated freedom comes at the cost of increasing distraction—a lack of awareness of the full complexion of outcomes and opportunities generated by our actions—this newfound autonomy has the ironic effect over time of rendering us ever more deeply and dramatically liable to predicament.

The more variously we express our freedoms-of-choice, the more independent and indirect our modes of social interaction and belonging will be; the more abstract our contributions to others become, the thinner and more fragile our realization of diversity-enriching interdependence and shared flourishing will be. Systematically exporting attention from our families and communities renders them increasingly vulnerable to disruption and degradation, and, increasingly, this lost resilience will escape our notice. That is, the more completely and complexly we are informed by media that inculcate expectations of autonomously achieved experiential preferences, the more fully and continuously we will be distracted from our immediate situation and the possibility of attending effectively to the health of its constitutive relations. The patterns of differentiation emerging therein will be keyed ever more closely to the play of our desires, but in ways that celebrate variety and forestall critical engagement. The colonization of consciousness—the power-shifting restructuring of attentive and relational dynamics—emerges with and as a conscience-dissolving self-colonization.

Implications for Equity: Some Preliminary Considerations

If equity is an index of the degree to which members of a given population act in their own self-interests in ways that are deemed valuable by others, the compromises of relational depth and resilience induced by the mass mediated export of attention will be correlated with both decreasing diversity and increasing inequity. This runs counter to contemporary intuitions formed on the basis of associating equity with equality of opportunity and "diversity" with tolerance for those who are different. As we have noted repeatedly, ours is an era in which differences are not only increasingly recognized and respected, but actively engineered in pursuit of appeasing our increasing hunger for the new and exclusive. It is also an era in which tensions between equality and autonomy have been technically eased to the point that the most optimistic proponents of technological mediation claim we are on the verge of a new epoch of radically democratized opportunities for individually pursuing our own ends and interests—an epoch of unprecedented freedom to do, be, and have what we wish.

Contemporary mass media and ICT have opened new and incontestably exciting domains of agency, bringing fabulously multiplying options for controlling the content of experience to ever-expanding and more var-ied populations. The expansion of real freedoms-of-choice afforded by mass mediation and the fluid dynamics of the emerging attention econ-omy are without doubt individually empowering. Yet, along with these freedoms and the merging of the optional and the optimal have come a progressive ephemeralization and commodification of experience; the increasing contingency of community and belonging; and an apparent weakening of both capacities-for and commitments-to not just differing-from others, but skillfully differing-for them. These are structural effects of media and ICT, and should not be confused with the kinds of individual uses to which they are put. The regime-challenging "Arab Spring" of 2011 demonstrated, among other things, just how powerful ICT tools can be in organizing mass movements. But the dramatic skewing of income, wealth, and resource use in favor of a narrow global elite over the last half century is no less a demonstration of the power-reconfiguring effects of globally deployed media and ICT.

Ironically, the very means-to more powerfully and autonomously determining what we will experience, when, and with whom, work as well to compromise the kinds of responsive strength needed for relating-freely. More specifically, they compromise the kinds of strength expressed in actively valuing and adding-value to our situation in ways that eventuate in our being ever more valuably situated, with ever-greater opportunities and resources for contributing creatively to ever more broadly shared wel-fare and flourishing. Although we may become increasingly adept at solv-ing ever more narrowly conceived and experienced problems, we will also become increasingly disposed to ignore the predicaments being generated by differentiation processes systematically oriented toward the erosion of social, economic, political, and cultural diversity. And predicaments are never resolved by being ignored.

The fluidity of experiential engagement afforded by an attention econ-omy configured in alignment with modern and market values is clearly conducive to reconfiguring power dynamics. But there are very good rea-sons to be skeptical about whether this reconfiguration will serve to bring about more equitable social, economic, political, and cultural relations.

One of the ramifications of a shift from a material economy to an attention economy is that the exercise of power need not entail mate-rial force. This has been a crucial factor in the rise of the discourse and practice of "soft power" in the arena of international relations. Another ramification is that the exercise of power need not be centralized. The ICT-enabled advent of what Manuel Castells has termed the global "net-work society" has brought about a significant alteration of the organiza-tional dynamics of power. While the value of membership in a hierarchy is a function of one's distance from the center or top of the hierarchy, the value of membership in a network is a function of both the number of nodes or members in the net and the informational quality of exchanges among them.

The combination of ICT-informed shifts toward "soft" power and network organization can be seen as promising insofar as it suggests real possibilities for the emergence of new, more highly differentiated and responsively influential sets of political, economic, social, and cultural actors. But, once again, it is important to distinguish between the uses of tools and the impacts of technology. The regime changes of 2011 that were orchestrated from "below" in the Arab world were not all peaceful in nature or clearly oriented toward promoting diversity-enhancing patterns of interdependence. The hyperdifferentiated dynamics of the blogosphere, the instant fames and notorieties generated via YouTube and Facebook, the rise of open-source knowledge clearinghouses like Wikipedia, and the cyber-vigilante actions of the group known as Anonymous all offer undeniable evidence of an ongoing redefinition of the conditions for achieved authority. But it is far from clear that this restructuring of the means-to acquiring authority will prove conducive to inflecting differentiation processes toward diversity rather than variety—redefining authority as a function of demonstrating relational *strength* rather than one of individually exercised *power*.

The emergence of an industrially fueled attention economy that fosters highly individualized and continuous exercises of choice and control over the contents of experience can be seen as the most massive empowerment of humanity in history. Yet, it would seem to be entirely compatible with ever-widening gaps in income, wealth, and resource use, and—especially for the roughly one-third of all city dwellers in the world who live in slums—increasingly degraded relational dynamics (Davis 2006). And in this light, it is telling how readily and successfully China has been able to marry a highly conservative and authoritarian political regime to the attention-driven dynamics of global free markets. According to the dominant strands of post–Cold War political economics, in the absence of parallel political reform, the phenomenal and unrelenting growth of the Chinese economy since liberalization in 1979 should not have been possible. The growth of free market processes should have either spurred democratic reform or stuttered into stagnation. But in fact, China has demonstrated the viability of vibrantly marrying ultraconservative politics to neoliberal economic policy, demonstrating as well that increasing individual freedoms of experiential choice and consumption options is quite compatible with breathtaking rates of increased inequality and relative (if not also relational) impoverishment.[49]

If we have an interest in equity, we should beware. The Buddhist teaching that, for the purposes of resolving trouble and suffering, we should see all things as impermanent compels recognition that the attention economy and our roles within it are continuously changing. These changes need not work against human dignity and global flourishing. But if we are to orient the attention economy toward greater equity, we will need to reconfigure the values shaping who we are and what we mean for one another, dissolving our tendencies to equate the optimal with the optional and to define freedom solely in terms of experiential choice and control. We are in need of a diversity-enhancing global ethics.

CHAPTER SIX

Ethics and Differentiation

Turning Away from the Same

The aporia of difference signals our arrival at a global climax of both modernity and marketization—our arrival at an historical vantage from which it appears necessary for the pursuit of equity to begin with imagining a world no longer organized around modern universalisms and the market's endless proliferation of experiential options and elective identities. In such a *post*modern and *post*market world, personal and public efforts might dovetail in shared commitments to reorient the dynamics of global interdependence, moving obliquely to the modern and market tensions between control and choice, and to the diversity-denying opposition of individualism and collectivism.

That, of course, is not our only possible future. One alternative would be a "business as usual" world in which globalization-driven fragmentation and fractiousness continue unabated. In such a world, it is possible that a point would be reached at which the valorization of individualistic self-interest and consumer sovereignty might so severely contract our scopes of concern that collective action rooted in robustly shared commitments will be rendered practically impossible and no longer even popularly desirable. In all likelihood, already great disparities of global opportunity and wealth would become even more precipitously amplified, though this might occur ever more "invisibly" as global attention is increasingly distracted into the realm of virtual experience—the realization of a market dystopia.

Another world might be one in which market realities fall so far short of market ideals that a cancerous sense of betrayal begins spreading through the more than 50% of humanity denied access to even 1%

of global wealth—a global majority that might then erupt in repeated and ever more concerted and aggressive forms of antimarket backlash. These might assume the character of fervently collective class movements dedicated to delivering some version of elite-prosecuting justice, or that of religious or cultural fundamentalisms intent upon "restoring" unity through rigorously enforced sacred or secular collectivism. The market idealization of choice then might be swamped by all-encompassing desires for control and increasingly conservative visions of right living—a world "flattened" in compartmentalizing celebrations of conformity.

Whether any one of these—or other more favorably imagined or feared—futures come to be actualized will depend on our global karma: the constellations of values, intentions, and actions by means of which we engage our increasingly complex interdependence. Actually realized *means-to* change are finally inseparable from our constructions of the *meanings-of* change. Because of this, they are also inseparable from how (and how well) we evaluate and align our ever more deeply interpenetrating histories. The scale of interdependencies and the depths of interpenetration involved ensure that the challenges of responding effectively to the aporia of difference will be profound. But no less profound will be the required self-transformations involved.

Troublingly, the ways in which inequalities and inequities are being exacerbated by the confluence of forces currently orienting globalization processes ensure that this confluence is also conducive to weakening capacities-for and commitments-to critical self-transformation of the sort needed to mount effective responses to those forces. As complex systems, the interdependencies characteristic of contemporary globalization exert "downward" causation on their constitutive subsystems.[1] As we have seen, the growth of industrial systems not only entails the development of new production technologies, but also the production of new kinds of labor and laborers. Global markets produce not only goods and services, but also individuals and populations in need of them. The attention economy not only grows through global circulations of increasing amounts of attention energy, it also alters the character or qualities of attention in economically useful ways. This same complexity, of course, also allows for "upwardly" propagating causalities. Values systematically expressed anywhere within the total complexion of global dynamics have the recursive potential to affect those dynamics as a whole. Thus, the ongoing shift from an era of problem solution to predicament resolution signals the need for a proactive, difference-sensitive ethicization of the public sphere—a shift from the dominance of the technical to that of the ethical.

This will not be a simple, linear transition. From our present vantage, two broad currents of downward causal dynamics stand out as particularly important for shaping any viable response to globally mounting inequalities. First, from the mid- to late nineteenth century onward, global economic growth has been sustained only through increasing market density by infusing market-designed and -delivered goods and services into every possible aspect of daily life: an *economy of dissatisfaction* growing in proportion to how many new needs and domains of commodification it produces. Correlated with this has been the emergence of a distinctive structure of feeling—a hungering to have something new, to do and be something different. Second, with the advent of truly global mass media and great advances in communications technology over the last thirty years, there has emerged an increasingly dematerialized *economy of distraction* in which further growth is not fueled most crucially by coal, oil, or nuclear energy, but rather by the practically seamless export of attention from local relational ecologies into ever-accelerating global circulation.

Among the effects of pairing dissatisfaction and distraction as key economic drivers has been a disabling of the mass social and political resistance that Polanyi envisioned as natural responses to inequalities produced by freely operating markets. Global free markets have secured unprecedented degrees of consumer sovereignty, steadily expanding the range of experiential choice and control, and ever more prolifically and precisely defining our options for being human. At the same time, they have been steadily expanding the scope and scale of inequalities emerging with respect to who and what gets noticed, and hence which and whose needs are addressed, with what priority, and how.[2] The optimization of the optional has had the somewhat ironic effect of constraining the scope of what we, personally and communally, feel we *ought* to do in response to global inequalities—a circumscription of the *social ought* by *individual choice*.

AVOIDING THE OUGHT: NEUTRALIZING THE PUBLIC SPHERE

Until relatively recently, this has led to a significant lessening of public engagement with issues of values conflict—an evacuation from the public sphere of explicitly moral and ethical forms of evaluation. The broad historical precedents for this neutralization of the axiological dimensions of the public sphere are, of course, the early modern separation of religion (church) and politics (state), the consequent compartmentalization of private and public selves and identities, the promotion of equality and tolerance as key public values, and the canonization of objectivity as a hallmark of rationality. And, although there has been a rise of values discourse in the public sphere over the past half century (M. Taylor 2004), it has (for reasons we will discuss later) served more as a statement of public need than it has to galvanize sustained public efforts of the sort needed to concertedly engage issues of difference and respond to emerging predicaments with forcefully shared clarity and commitment.

One the face of it, this is not surprising. As modern/market dynamics have progressively linked the optimal to the optional, they have tended to transpose qualitative concerns about values (the worthwhile) into quantitative questions of the value (worth) of choice, displacing public deliberations about what *ought* to be done by public definitions regarding what *may* or *may not*. Hence, the protection of choices and the rule of law have come to be linked with (and championed as crucial insurance for) the maximal achievement of freedom and fairness. This circumscription of the social ought by individual options is now essentially canonical in the United States, as was amply illustrated in the 2009 congressional and media debates about universal health care.

It can, of course, be argued that a preference for rule of law over moral and ethical discourse is effective in responding to the need for institutions capable of constraining socially disruptive conduct in a world where, for example, socioeconomic interactions cross ethnic, cultural, and national boundaries. But the public dominance of legal institutions also amounts to a systematic deferral of truly public engagement with issues on the basis of predicament resolution. The modern notion of law as blind to difference and silent with respect to matters of individual conscience centers on defining and delimiting permissible interactions among generically autonomous individuals. Laws determine, first and foremost, what *must not* be done, and only secondarily and quite weakly specify what *should* be done to avoid penalty for negligence. As such, legal systems are essentially aloof from relational appreciation and aspiration.

In a world of global-scale predicaments, the progressive circumscription of the ethical by the individually optional and the legal is itself an ethical concern of the highest order. And, indeed, several high-profile incidents in recent years have led to widespread questioning of the wisdom of evacuating the public sphere of explicitly moral and ethical considerations. The exposure in 2001 of corrupt accounting and fiscal reporting practices at the global energy corporation Enron led not only to its bankruptcy liquidation and the demise of its no less globally prominent accounting firm, Arthur Andersen, but also to calls for greater corporate accountability and for honoring other than merely fiscal bottom lines. The stunning implosion of global markets in the fall of 2008, triggered by unsound mortgage practices and risk leveraging by global investment giants, similarly has led to questioning the "profit by whatever means possible" mentality that has long dominated on both "Wall Street" and "Main Street." Most recently, the fall 2011 Occupy Wall Street movement and comparable, loosely organized movements in Europe and Asia are an expression of profound public skepticism that the pursuit of what is legally just will ever result in what is socially fair.

But in these cases and the many others that might be cited, such questions have tended to devolve into quintessentially modern debates about how to balance choice and control (Wagner 1994)—debates often framed in terms of a "turf war" between liberal values and governmental regulation. Importantly, this "war" is typically not fought on moral or ethical grounds, but rather on technical ones. It is a framing conducive to treating global inequalities as evidence of underlying problems, not predicaments. And the ease with which this is done—the ease with which felt needs for strengthening moral and ethical considerations are translated into needs for technical fixes—is itself telling evidence of the degree to which addressing widening inequalities of wealth, income, resource use, and relational potentials will require a revision of our shared global karma, raising questions about the interplay of values, intentions, actions, and relational dynamics of a sort and scale to which modern ethics are, by nature, ill equipped to respond. We are in need not just of an ethicization of the public sphere, but an approach to ethical engagement that is freed from the axiomatic, modern conviction that we are essentially independent individuals who enter rationally into social contracts with one another for the primary purpose of maximally securing our own self-interest.

DISTINGUISHING AMONG MORALITY, ETHICS, AND LAW

Paradigm shifts occur for complex reasons, but often pivot on surprisingly simple revisions of basic assumptions. With a view to anticipating an ethics of interdependence and interpenetration—a nondualistic ethics of differentiation—it is useful here to sketch out some conceptual precedents for challenging two key assumptions underwriting modern approaches to ethics that have become globally dominant over especially the last two hundred years.

The first assumption is that the basic unit of moral and ethical concern is the choice-making individual. A close corollary of this assumption is that it is by scaling up protocols for evaluating individuals' choices that we are best able to address the individuating/integrating, singularity/commonality dilemmas of sociality. The second assumption is that the value of equality must be foundational for any contemporary response to issues of difference. As I understand them, these assumptions cannot be challenged by merely reaffirming modern ethical imaginaries or by "going back" to their premodern antecedents, however helpful some of the concepts and values embedded in and embodied through these imaginaries may be. To enact the paradigm shift needed to ethically engage contemporary realities, the logically "basic" duality of sameness and difference must be called into question.

To set the stage for challenging these modern assumptions and characterizing the anticipated turn toward a relationally focused, nondualistic ethics of differentiation, let me first distinguish between morality and ethics as distinct approaches to values discourses that would merge the personal and the public, and to contrast them with law as strategies for social cohesion. These distinctions will help in critically relating modernization and marketization to the late twentieth-century unfolding of profound tensions between ethical universalism and relativism as complementary expressions of the axiomatic affirmation of individuality and equality, and in envisioning a nondualistic route beyond them.

From Persuasion to Punishment and Proof

One lesson of the social constructivism proposed by Berger and Luckmann (1966) is that care must be taken *not* to presume that the categories of our engagement with the world and one another are fundamentally natural or given. Concepts like "person," "community," "society," "humanity," "reason," "emotion," "purpose," "meaning," "identity," "order," and "common good" develop through complex, temporally and spatially extended processes, and are best seen as highly recursive distillations of practices that embody continuously revised constellations of values and intentions.

Analyzing and evaluating such concepts as ideas and ideals is, of course, the bread-and-butter occupation of philosophers, whereas anthropologists have tended to document and describe how these concepts factor into actual life practices and social institutions. The great range and disparities among their various efforts amply support the constructivist thesis: the concepts crucial to moral and ethical discourses are not foundational in the way we can comfortably assume the ninety-four naturally occurring chemical elements are. In spite of their apparent commonness, these concepts turn out to have situationally/historically distinct internal structures, and how they are deployed is often highly contested, not only across but also within cultures and societies. This is perhaps especially true with respect to the discursively more general and normatively charged concepts of "morality," "ethics," and "law," the overarching character of which insures that controversies regarding their content and meaning are almost never coolly matter-of-fact. Debates about morality and ethics in particular are not for the fainthearted. Granted this, let me nevertheless distinguish between morality and ethics in a way that I find helpful in critically engaging the looming obsolescence of modern approaches to resolving the individuating/integrating dilemmas of sociality in an era of complex global interdependence and interpenetration.

Morals and morality consist in a matrix of customary perspectives and practices by means of which a particular group of people has come to assure its own survival and welfare, and that *define* and *instantiate* the meaning of both personal and communal flourishing. The values and dynamics of the moral sphere, in other words, are not abstract; they are practically *embodied*. Morality explicitly emerges as a function of first tacit and then formally explicated injunctions and proscriptions regarding individual behaviors, character traits, experiences, and goals, how these manifest in daily life, and how they are to be inculcated and applied. Eventually, morality comes to encompass modes of justification, ranges of appropriate and inappropriate feelings, systems of rules and standards, and a general perspective on "our" place in the cosmos (Edel and Edel 1968).

Historically, moralities have lacked universal pretentions. Self-consciously identified with setting the behavioral and attitudinal standards of a specific tradition or community, an operative assumption of each moral system is apparently that other communities "naturally" have their own standards and thus different—and not necessarily commensurable—moralities. If there is a "universal" moral stance regarding "others," for much of human history it seems to have been one encapsulated in the oft-repeated idiom: "to each their own." Moral membership involves acknowledging both a sense of unaffiliated *otherness* and a sense of natural *commonality* or mutual belonging—a simultaneously exclusive and inclusive sense of how *we* do things and why.

Contrastingly, ethics can be seen as emerging when conditions favor (or compel) expressing and justifying prescriptions and proscriptions—senses of the good and ill—that are relevant to all, regardless of the specific tradition or community to which one belongs. Otherwise stated, ethics signal the attempt to articulate a moral system binding "everyone," and not just "all of *us*." Most often, this shift has involved movement away from stressing the palpably felt, emotionally charged sense of communal relatedness that bonds the members of a moral community as an integral and identifiable whole. Instead, emphasis is placed on rationally determining the nature of the good life, and of right and wrong conduct in pursuit thereof. Ethics *advance* universally applicable ways of living together.

The shift from conservative *moral sensibilities* to critical *moral reasoning* subordinates the bodily and emotional to the mental and cognitive—a turn away from the practices or patterns of conduct that bind us together and define us as *a people* toward what we each are rationally bound to acknowledge as exemplifying *humanity*. Thus undertaken, the ethical turn is from a relatively narrow to a vastly broadened conception of how we are the same. Instead of appealing to ontologically thick definitions of who *we* are in determining what should be done, appeal is made to anonymously thin criteria for what *anyone* should do under the circumstances in question. With this turn, moral community is, in effect, subordinated to moral agency; collective prescriptions give way to individual decisions; justifiable practices yield to just principles.[3]

Living in one moral community, moral "others" can be simply left alone. Barring some event that forces explicit normative engagement, those living in other moral communities are *not morally relevant*. Other peoples clearly differ from "us" in terms of practices and principles. But that makes little if any difference for the most part, most of the time. At least so long as our respective communities are sustained in essentially independent ecologies of material subsistence and social cohesion, our differences can be safely ignored.[4] The advent of an explicitly *ethical* society appears historically to have been tied to intensifying interaction among such ecologies and their associated moral spheres, and ultimately their progressive interpenetration. Moral reasoning is forwarded in response to moral frictions and the need to negotiate relatively intimate forms of purposeful and mutually gratifying cooperation. That is, ethics emerges as we extend moral consideration to *others* in contexts that compel relinquishing moral boundaries in pursuit of common human interests, ends, and admirations.[5] Ethics presupposes, in short, that in critically significant ways, we are all the *same*.

One reading at least of historical evidence is that the transition from moral communities to ethical societies was typically mediated (and perhaps spurred) by the advent of formalized systems of laws in the context of large-scale state formation. For example, the oldest extant record of a code of law is associated with the unification of Upper and Lower Egypt under King Menes circa 2925 BCE. And, other ancient codes like the twenty-second-century BCE Babylonian code of Hammurabi, the sixth-century BCE Athenian laws instituted by Solon, and the legal conceptual frameworks outlined in such Indian texts as the first-century BCE work the *Manusmriti* all seem traceable to efforts aimed at ordering and securing newly consolidating, culturally and religiously heterogeneous societies, effectively transforming loose and often conflict-ridden aggregations of peoples into self-sustaining polities.

In this light, legal systems might be seen as externalized, artificially collective (rather than naturally communal) moralities stripped of the affective dimensions of mutual belonging. That is, laws become socially operative by objectively criminalizing socially disruptive acts rather than by passionately condemning them and valorizing specific attitudinal correlates of proper conduct. Unlike the after-the-fact, often violent retributions of the sort characterizing small-scale community responses to felt transgression, legal codes aim to deter transgression by forwarding proactive threats of appropriately severe physical and financial consequences. And, even in premodern times, legally defined justice was often explicitly framed as founded on being blind to differences of family, wealth, class, and political status. In short, legal systems establish universally binding standards for what is *not* acceptable in morally heterogeneous societies, establishing explicit boundaries for what may and may not be done.[6]

Significantly, arguments on behalf of impartially administered legal justice as a tool of statecraft were often paired with assertions about the practical shortcomings of morality. While moral systems might work well as means to social cohesion in homogeneous societies, they are much less effective when great differences obtain within society regarding the meaning of moral conduct and conscience. Laws are necessary precisely because everyone is not similarly inclined to moral conduct and self-cultivation, and because it is natural for people to act in ways that are self-centered. Although this line of argument and its underlying presuppositions about "human nature" assume bedrock status with the development of modern social contract theory, it can be found in appeals for the marriage of law and statecraft throughout the ancient world.[7]

A classic example of the premodern formulation of this argument can be found in the work of the third-century BCE Chinese thinker Han Fei. According to Han Fei, it is essentially human to have likes and dislikes, and to make use of power and authority to insure that one gets what one wants, as often and as surely as possible. Attempts to order society through moral development assume that it is both possible for all and preferable for most to cultivate capacities for harmonizing with others, achieving social order through personal self-transformation. But in fact, all are not equal in their inclination or abilities for moral self-cultivation. And, because power and authority equally benefit both the morally worthy who would order the world and the unworthy who would disorder it; because the unworthy far outnumber the worthy; and because the acquisition of power itself invariably nurtures human beings' selfish and tyrannical tendencies, social cohesion and harmony cannot reasonably be entrusted to hopes of a majority acting honestly and with good will. Thus, trust ultimately must be placed in a legal system that leaves nothing to chance, instilling order through impartial and exceptionless determinations of punishment and reward.[8]

To generalize Han Fei's claims: laws have the advantage that they do not assume either the presence of good intentions in all, or the presence of sufficiently powerful capacities-for and commitments-to acting upon them. The advent of law marks an emphatic shift from intentions to institutions as the key to a securely ordered society—a shift from idealizing exemplary persons to realizing behavioral conformity.[9] Crucially for Han Fei and many others, not only in classical China but also throughout the ancient world and later in the modern West, the legal route to social ordering is inseparable from a dual affirmation of a common (typically self-interested) *human nature* and of the unavoidable individuality with which this nature expresses itself. This dual affirmation underwrites the necessity of turning to legal institutions (rather than personal intentions and conscience) as means to disciplining public behavior and to framing these institutions in ways that are immune to claims of exception. [10] Laws are able to bind all because they are blind to the uniqueness of each, equally regarding all members of society as such—not as fathers or mothers, as heirs to great fortune or none, as the favorites or foes of those in positions of military and political power, or as either morally or immorally exceptional. As argued in the ancient world as well as the modern: laws are effective to the precise extent that they ignore relational differences, submitting each and all to the same standards of judgment.

A powerful counterargument, of course, is that these standards do not simply fall from the sky, and differences of the sort that are ignored by the law are often constitutive for who we are as persons and as peoples. Legal systems are not all created equally, and impartiality in the execution of legal justice may well simply enforce a particular brand of prejudice, systematically undermining certain expressions of human nature in favor of others. In short, the rule of law is itself no guarantee of fairness. The justness of legal determinations of justice is always open to question. Indeed, the Confucian critique of Legalism rests precisely on the threat to humane considerations of difference—and embodied patterns of deference—that are posed by governing through "rule of law" alone. To the degree that justice is blind, it is liable to stumbling.

In the Western tradition, the potential for a tragic disparity of the legal and the ethical is dramatically driven home by the sentencing to death of Socrates by Athenian courts on moral charges (his "misleading" of Athenian youth). Socrates' sentencing is symbolically a sentencing of the right to question authority, whether in the form of social custom, cultural norms, political power, economic might, or religious revelation. And his refusal to avert his own execution demonstrates the thoroughness with which those aiming to act ethically must be freed of prejudice, but also of relational ties that might seduce them into violating their own rationally derived principles of right conduct.

The shift from moral persuasion to moral reasoning and the emergence of a distinctively ethical approach to framing the meaning of personal well-being and social cohesion might well be seen, then, as countering that from morality to law. Ethics not only rationally engages issues of human aspiration, it opens possibilities for critically evaluating whether legal systems qualify as truly just and whether particular moral systems are conducive to realizing personal and communal well-being in morally plural societies. And in this sense, ethical claims might be seen as transcending those of morality and the law.

In actuality, of course, morality, law, and ethics are not always so readily separated or sequenced. The complexity and recursivity that characterize human societies practically guarantees that the moral, legal, and ethical spheres will be interdependent, if not fully interpenetrating. And, given this, it is not surprising that, at any given time, their dynamics are mutually entrained by the presence and persistence of some crucially shared values. Until very recently, a factor in the mutual entrainment of modern moral, legal, and ethical discourses has been their valorization of equality and autonomy, and the tendency to construct "difference" as normatively sterile. In each of these discourses, while difference has been acknowledged and even allowed, it has *not* been valorized. Differences have tended to be seen as morally, legally, or ethically unproductive, and focus has been trained on affirming that—whether as members of a moral community, as citizens within a polity, or as rational exemplars of human-ity—we *are* essentially the *same*.

Simple affirmation, of course, is not always enough. In response to dif-ferences that cannot simply be ignored or discounted, the moral response has traditionally been that of *persuasion*, often in face-to-face encounter where the (physically and emotionally) felt social and cultural pressures to belong together can be brought fully to bear. Persisting to be different is to become isolated or outcast. The ethical response has more often been that of *proof* or providing arguments that rationally close off alternative criteria for judging whether specific aims and actions are good or ill. Per-sisting to be different is to be dogmatic or irrational. To those unable to be persuaded or argued onto significantly common ground, the societal response typically has been drawing behavioral "lines in the sand"—the appeal to law and the *punishing* of difference. Where differences cannot be dismissed, they must be disciplined.

SCALING UP THE SCOPE OF THE SAME

Now, there is no doubt whatever that the nature of and relationships among morality, law, and ethics—and the interplay of persuasion, punish-ment, and proof—have varied greatly, globally as well as historically. And I would argue that these differences in how morality, law, and ethics have been constructed—and conceived as relating—constitute deep reservoirs of potential insight. There is much to learn, not just about these differ-ences, but from them.

Nevertheless, it seems safe to say that, until the latter part of the twentieth century, morality, law, and ethics have answered questions about how best to order both personal conduct and social interactions, and that these answers have generally valorized convergence and assumed that divergence induces disorder. Even in societies like that of Vedic India, where social order was envisioned as rooted in strong caste differences, active differentiation has most often been associated with deviation. In short: the tendency has been to treat order as scaled to the possibility of realizing common social norms, behavioral standards, and personal aspirations: a tendency to actualize and idealize agreement as a means-to instantiating the meaning-of our essential sameness.

The interconnections among morality, law, and ethics and their use of persuasion, punishment, and proof as means of subordinating difference to sameness became significantly more complex, however, with the twin births of modernity and global markets. We have already discussed some of the conditions involved in this: the growing prevalence of truly global constellations of commitment to the values of universality, equality, autonomy, objectivity, competition, choice, and control; a rapid industrialization of production that enables and requires new forms of material and human infrastructure, new organizational structures and new skills; an intensification of both homogeneity and heterogeneity across the social, economic, political, and technological spheres; and the simultaneous amplification of capacities, incentives, and rationales for both massification and individualization.

As they matured, modernity and markets brought about an astonishing scaling up of interdependencies and an increasing depth of interpenetration. This resulted in a no less astonishing rise of dynamics (including those of vastly increased physical and social mobility) favoring the emergence of multicontinent empires, but also extraordinarily uneven and multilayered geographies of commonality and sameness.[11] Although the degree to which identity formation and patterns of affiliation now demonstrate the prevalence of "distant proximities" or senses of commonality and sameness that are largely independent of physical location is certainly unprecedented, accelerating processes of identity dislocation and lifeworld delamination have been characteristic of the modern/market patterns of change virtually from the outset. And in the context of increasingly interdependent and interpenetrating social, economic, political, cultural, and technological dynamics, the complex interaction of integrating and fragmenting forces has reverberated with mounting intensity in the relationship among morality, law, and ethics.

As Michel Foucault (1997) has masterfully shown in his book *Discipline and Punish*, modernity and markets together brought both historically distinctive possibilities and needs for new kinds of people and social organization, and an amplification of the scope and scale of authority and power. The technological control revolution that enabled modern industrialization and globalization also enabled visions of automating and internalizing the mechanisms of discipline, rendering power (economic, social, and political) both increasingly invisible and incisive: visions of a perfectly ordered society in which individualization (fragmentation) and massification (integration) would go happily hand in hand. Modern institutions like the family, the school, the military base, the hospital, the factory, and the prison effectively differentiated individuals within interlocking, normalizing, and hence essentially juridical regimes. And through them, disciplinary societies assumed global dominance from the eighteenth through the middle of the twentieth century, efficiently reconciling the individual (symbolized by his or her signature) and the mass (symbolized by a number locating each person in society as a whole) within a societal body of power relations.[12]

Parallel to the conceptual and concrete efforts of modernity to institutionally reconcile the individual and the mass, there developed significant moral, legal, and ethical visions organized around the joint valorization of individualism and universalism. Jeremy Bentham, who along with John Stuart Mill was one of the founders of utilitarianism, went furthest perhaps in concretely envisioning both the productive marriage of individualism and universalism and the disciplinary fusion of ethics and economics. Bentham's vision fused morality, law, and ethics in a "final solution" to the problem of achieving and maintaining socially, economically, and politically productive order: a society structured according to the principles of the panopticon, a prison in which inmates are spatially disciplined into self-surveillance (Bentham 1995).

Bentham saw the Panopticon principle as affording "a new mode of obtaining power of mind over mind, in a quantity hitherto without example"—a means of perfectly merging external control (law) and internal constraint (morality) with the greatest possible utility for each individual and for society as a whole (ethics).[13] He claimed that if employed rigorously, this principle would yield both maximal individuation and maximal integration by inducing each member of society to automatically discipline himself or herself in accord with the needs of all. The result: a politically secure, economically vibrant society in which both the poor houses and prisons would be emptied and then closed.

Bentham's quintessentially modern vision, though it did inform the reconstruction of the British penal system in the latter part of the eighteenth century, was technologically premature. It was not, in fact, until the media technology revolution of the twentieth century and the emergence of the attention economy that the individual and utterly ubiquitous experience of power could be truly globalized. What Bentham did not envision was that the technology of the global panopticon could also effectively merge the automation of discipline with the exercise of autonomy—a marriage of control and choice that would be instrumental in carrying modernity to the verge of its own obsolescence, and that would force confrontation with the limits of morally, legally, and ethically valorizing the Same.

THE MODERN IRONY:
THE ETHICAL RESURGENCE OF DIFFERENCE

The multiplication and magnification of differences associated with contemporary patterns of globalization and complex interdependence are rendering all forms of identification porous, not just those associated with geography or politics. Along with the dramatic proliferation of goods and services upon which the growth of the material economy depends, and the no less dramatic proliferation of lifestyle and experiential options fueling growth in the attention economy, has come an intensification of disparities of aims, interests, and values. The complexly dynamic results have been: the continued breakdown of traditional social and cultural structures and identities; a splintering of nation-states; widening gaps of income, wealth, and health; intensifying "culture wars" pitting cosmo-politanism against multiculturalism; the rise of global fundamentalisms; and, ultimately, what I have termed the transition from an era of problem solution to one of predicament resolution. As evidenced in increasingly sharp contentions regarding the meanings of art, music, and literature; of gender, parenthood, friendship, hospitality, and neighborliness; and of education, entertainment, sport, and health, ours is an era of profoundly *recursive struggles* over the means-to and meanings-of difference. And this recursivity of engagement with difference clearly is not limited to the domain of so-called objective or external relations—those regulated by law. It extends well into the "internal" provinces of the moral and ethical where attention economies also operate, and where issues of position and perspective are no less crucial.

The internal differentiations within ethics itself are particularly tell-ing. Today, it is customary to distinguish among metaethics (concern-ing how we derive ethical guidelines or principles and the meanings of basic concepts), normative ethics (concerning the selection of criteria for evaluating principles, practices, interests, and aspirations), and applied ethics (concerning specific issues like abortion or stem-cell research and the stances we should have toward them). Normative ethics itself is highly plural, organized primarily around theories of virtues (what we should affirm as character ideals), duties (what we must affirm as universal and rationally binding obligations), rights (what we are granted by nature and must respect in others), and consequences (defined egoistically as good for me, altruistically as good for everyone else, or through utilitarian calcula-tions of what is good for all). To this taxonomy—already well developed by the nineteenth century—have been added such twentieth-century eth-ics as those centered on the structure of care (as in some feminist ethics) and the quality of roles (as in Confucian ethics). Within each of these categories and theories of ethical engagement, differentiation is ongo-ing. Positions and perspectives are proliferating and accorded fluctuating degrees of prominence in reflection of wider societal dynamics as well as those within the professional field of ethics itself. But just as is the case for the more "external" manifestations of global multiplications and mag-nifications of difference, while the present moment can be characterized as infused with unparalleled potential for diversity, it is the expression of variety that is so strikingly evident.

Translated into an ethical idiom, the aporia of difference with which we are being ever more forcefully confronted has taken the form of a tension between endorsing relativist particularism and all-inclusive universalism, the individual merits of which would seem to be mutually exclusive. In fact, it might well be said that the opposition of relativist and universalist positions and perspectives epitomizes the tensions between emerging postmodern realities and modern ethical discourses and ideals. That is, relativism and universalism represent polar extremes of a spectrum of ethical stances and views, the entirety of which is biased against realizing and enhancing relational diversity.

The Ethical Options of Certainty and Skepticism

The contrariety of universalist and relativist responses to issues of difference has become an iconic marker of the transition from modern faith in progressive integration to postmodern skepticism about all metanarratives. And, while there are many who would argue against the intelligibility of a strictly relativist approach to either ethics or epistemology,[14] the trope of opposition between universalism and relativism does shed critically useful light on the limits of dichotomizing sameness and difference and of conceptually grounding equity on equality.

The conceptual roots of the opposition of universalism and relativism can plausibly be traced back to the earliest strata of philosophical disputation. In early Greek thought, one might align these stances, respectively, with Platonism and Skepticism; in early India, with Vedanta and Jainism; and in early China (albeit more tenuously), with Mohism and the Daoism of Zhuangzi. But in actuality, most of these early oppositions amounted only to countering moral certainty with moral skepticism—a lack of conviction that we are in a position to arrive at objective and universally binding moral or ethical convictions, or that we would be able to know it if we did. Moral skepticism of this sort was quite compatible with the empirical evidence—documented, for example, in early Greek and Chinese histories—of moral variety or the presence of distinctly differing moral traditions in different societies.[15]

The stronger claim that all moral and ethical views are historically embedded and irreducibly relative to culture—a denial of the possibility of moral or ethical objectivity and universality—was not explicitly forwarded until the late nineteenth and early twentieth centuries in the context of both intensifying economic and political globalization and scientific paradigm change. Global trade had from earliest times made moral differences undeniable, and evidence suggests that encounters with moral others were not infrequently accompanied by feelings of moral and cultural superiority. The Chinese imperial tribute system, for example, was from the Han dynasty onward (206 BCE to 220 CE) predicated on the cultural superiority of China and the "natural" tendency of all others to gravitate toward China as the world's center of cultural florescence (*zhonghua* 中華). But in the context of European colonialism and imperialism, feelings of moral superiority began to be buttressed "scientifically" as the concept of evolution was married with that of teleology to produce theories according to which all societies and cultures could be categorized as being at one stage or another along a single, universal trajectory of development, and in which European societies unsurprisingly were understood to be the most advanced.

It was against such theories that anthropologists like Franz Boas first forwarded the explicit counterclaim that there are no objective grounds for ranking cultural norms and moral systems. Claiming in effect that universalism is nothing more than European ethnocentrism, proponents of antiobjectivism and moral relativism insisted on the irreducibility of cultural differences. The scientific revolution that had occurred in the premier discipline of physics at the turn of the century added credibility to such claims. Einstein's theories of relativity, Heisenberg's uncertainty principle, and quantum mechanics combined to effectively dissolve the foundation of modern science, "proving" both the observer-laden nature of even such basic phenomena as space, time, and matter, and the presence of uncertainty as a necessary concomitant and condition of observation. In short, absolute objectivity is a fiction.

Values Pluralism: The Basis of an Alternative Ethics?

For reasons and with implications that we will explore in some detail later, in the decades following the Second World War relativism and universalism began assuming their contemporary status as conceptual poles of a purportedly exhaustive spectrum of views on difference and how to respond to it. In a seminal paper on the concept of liberty, Isaiah Berlin (1958) tacitly directed attention to these ethical poles, appealing for movement in the direction of "value pluralism" rather than lapsing into either the Cold War battle of absolutist "true believers" or into amorphous abdication to relativism-blinded nihilism.

Veering in the direction of the relativist pole involves expressing (with varying degrees of emphasis) the conviction that there are no culturally (and perhaps personally) transcendent principles, rules, duties, or virtues. Like it or not, there are many ways—not one way—of being human. Veering toward the universalist pole expresses the opposite conviction that norms need not be culturally determined or bound. Granted our common "human nature," it is possible to derive norms under which the many ways of being human can all be subsumed.

Relativists will hold that differences—especially with respect to culture, values, social norms, and patterns of personal, sexual, social, and political identity—are to be acknowledged as real and as irreducible to some common point of reference.[16] Hybridity can be celebrated, but the possibility of incommensurability among perspectives, perceptions, and practices must be admitted. Differences announce occasions for tolerance. Multiplicity is embraced as at once a fact and as an order-constraining value. In contrast, universalists will hold that differences are to be understood as historical contingencies that can, and (at least under some circumstances) should, be dissolved or subsumed within more rationally encompassing commonalities. Incommensurability is an appearance generated by either inadequate commitments to the pursuit of common ground or an unwillingness to admit its ego-challenging possibility. Unity is embraced as a practical ideal and as an order-establishing value. Relativists deny intelligibility to the univocity of reasoning; universalists deny validity to claims of irreducible multivocity.

For Berlin, the choice between the poles is a false one. Historical evidence indicates that values can conflict and that they often do so in situationally specific ways that do not permit establishing a permanent and universally applicable hierarchy among them. At the same time, however, moral communication is always possible. We are not locked into independent moral spheres, and choosing among values is part of what it means to be human. Under the right conditions, value pluralism holds out the promise of articulating a hybrid moral space encompassing the best insights of the particularist/relativist and the absolutist/universalist.

This is a promising approach that has been remarkably influential in shaping contemporary discussions of liberty and the social role of values. Yet, Berlin's construction of pluralism as a context-specific blending of many people and perspectives falls short of offering an approach to realizing ethical diversity. Berlin's pluralism was worked out from the standpoint of his own commitments to liberal political theory and advocated the centrality of rational choice among values and value systems in ways that some have seen as inconsistent with the very concept of pluralism as a process of reconciling values tension while at the same time conserving rights to differ (Gray 1996). Moreover, while his liberal pluralism is a plausible corrective response to the relativist-universalist tension, it is grounded in a conviction that it is the very nature of being human to have conflicts over values that are "an intrinsic, irremovable part of human life" and that "collisions of values are of the essence of what they are and what we are" (Berlin 2002, 213). Given this, and given Berlin's conviction that values may be both incompatible and incommensurable, values pluralism falls short of providing a means of working toward a global ethics of interdependence of the sort needed to respond to predicament-rich contemporary realities.

THE IRONIC FAILURE OF DISARMING DIFFERENCE

The complex, interdependence-rich, and predicament-laden character of contemporary realities is variously conducive to increased public engagement with morality, law, and ethics. The fragmenting effects of global social, economic, political, cultural, and technological dynamics can be seen as conducive to both new and retrenching forms of morality—the resurgence of explicitly conservative and at times aggressively justified contractions of values discourses, perspectives, practices, and principles relative to specific communities or traditions. Their integrative effects can be seen as aligned with appeals to greater scopes of application for law—the amplification of efforts to develop consequentially enforced behavioral standards of the sort needed to realize and sustain the conditions for safe and just global interactions. And, the limits of morality and law—the limits, respectively, of communally narrowed constructions of what "we" mean by the good and public blindness with respect to societal aspirations—can be seen as factors in surging appeals for incisive, ethical engagement with the evolutionary dynamics of the global public sphere.

Thus far, however, the turns toward morality, law, and ethics have not proven effective in responding to evident needs to articulate both the meanings-of and means-to pursuing global equity and public good. Granted the ways in which I have defined morality and law, their ineffectiveness can perhaps be seen as a function of the specific scopes of concern. It is oxymoronic to talk about a global morality or aspiration-defining laws. But this cannot be said of ethics. And yet, although ethics and values discourses more broadly have evolved over the past century in ways that have been recursively entrained with global dynamics of integration and fragmentation, the resulting spectrum of universalist, pluralist, and relativist perspectives has not proven capable of significantly affecting the ever more inequitable patterns of outcome and opportunity accompanying complex global interdependence and interpenetration. This is true even when they nominally have held equity to be among their central values. In the Buddhist terms introduced earlier, while the ethical differentiation that has taken place over the last century can be seen as having resulted in considerable good, it has not been *kusala*.[17] Conflicts and disparities of wealth, income, resource use, and relational opportunities and outcomes have intensified; global predicaments of manifestly increasing urgency remain unresolved.

One explanation for the shortcomings of contemporary ethics would be that the global dynamics to which they are responding are simply beyond influence. According to such a view, modernization, industrialization, and globalization are perhaps akin to natural processes like the change of seasons and tectonic plate movement—things we can adjust to, but not halt or direct. Or perhaps they are like a runaway train or a "Frankenstein" that we might have set in motion but that for all intents and purposes has assumed practical autonomy. Whatever the metaphorical scalar, such a "thesis of intractability" would insert contemporary social, economic, political, cultural, and techno-scientific dynamics into a comprehensively deterministic causal matrix that cannot be squared with ample evidence of emergent phenomena within and linking each of these dynamic domains—phenomena that in principle could not have been anticipated even if they can, after the fact, be placed within some network of linear causal relations. The intractability thesis involves assuming what empirical evidence disallows concluding.[18] At its worst, this amounts to simply rationalizing irresponsibility.

Another explanation is that the poor record of efforts to address globally mounting social, economic, political, cultural, and technological inequities is evidence of faulty implementation—a failure of will, of translating theory into practice, of sufficient "buy in" by all the relevant stakeholders and centers of power. On its side, this explanation has considerable factual weight and compatibility with globally mounting public cynicism. People often wish for more than they manage to will, poorly execute their own best-laid plans, and pay lip service as needed to preserve personally and communally favorable forms of status quo. Unfortunately, the "human error thesis" amounts either to an ad hominem attack on those who have tried to address inequity or to a fallacious inference of faulty efforts on the basis of faulty results. Either way, critical leverage for improvement is effectively undermined. It's not our ethics that have failed us; we have failed ourselves.

A third explanation is that the spectrum of ethical perspectives arrayed between absolute universalism and particularist or culturalist relativism—a spectrum that might be presumed exhaustive—does not afford us the kinds of conceptual resources needed to articulate effective means-to and meanings-of equitable interdependence. For reasons not dissimilar to those that led the historical Buddha to refuse locating his own teachings in relation to the philosophical poles of hedonism and asceticism or materialist atomism and spiritualist monism, reorienting global dynamics in ways that are truly *kusala* requires opening an ethical "middle way" angled "obliquely" to the spectrum of existing views.

In the present case, I would argue that this means challenging two commitments common to the current ethical spectrum: 1) the commitment to taking the individual to be the basic unit of ethical analysis, whether understood as a person, a community, a class, a corporation, or a nation; 2) the commitment to the critical centrality of equality. The first commitment runs counter to the distinctive ontological character of the contemporary public sphere. Although the traditional Buddhist perspective has always been that the possibility of *kusala* personal conduct depends on appreciating the irreducibly relational dynamics of interdependence and interpenetration, this is now unavoidable for realizing *kusala* patterns of outcome and opportunity in the public sphere. The second commitment has, of course, been a cornerstone of public discourse since the birth of the modern era. But it is rendered critically counterproductive by the accelerating rates, expanding scale and scope, and complexity of contemporary processes of multiplying and magnifying social, economic, political, cultural, and technological differences. As we will discuss in more detail later, as powerful a fiction as equality has been, it is nevertheless a fiction, and one that no longer carries the force needed to reorient our interdependence.

The Ethical Kinship of Universalism and Relativism

While universalism and relativism are often understood as diametrically opposed, this is misleading. They are more aptly understood as a hereditary pair—the result of bifurcating commitments to the ontological centrality of the individual and the axiological centrality of equality. Seeing why this is the case enables anticipating the means-to and meaning-of moving oblique to their apparent opposition.

While strict relativists will affirm the reality and incommensurability of uncommon values, relativism affords little in the way of conceptual resources or incentives for reconciling or appreciatively coordinating them. In denying all transcendence, however, relativists effectively affirm the *equivalence* of all perspectives and the impossibility of establishing anything more than their nonhierarchic coexistence. Hence, the relativist can readily acknowledge the contemporary proliferation of predicaments regarding difference, but not the presence of real prospects for fully resolving them. For relativists, global predicaments are a function of current geographies of interaction and the only feasible response is to establish regimes of relative isolation and tolerance. The liability of doing so, of course, is that relative isolation eventuates in relational deprivation—a long-term recipe for social degradation.[19]

Strict universalists will, in contrast, deny the ultimate significance of differences in favor of pursuing unassailably common values. From this perspective, the point is to dissolve the conditions under which one would identify with being essentially different from others. To adopt a universalist position is to assume the original and ultimate *equality* of each and all, and to use common values to rise above the grounds on which conflicts might take root and persist. But the ideal of taking a position transcendental to the factual ground of difference-generated conflict is not the same as responding to real-world tensions originating in the complex dynamics of differentiation-accelerating global interaction. The universalist idealizes a world stably united under a single set of values. The liability of this, of course, is that "right thinking" ends up trumping "rights to think" in a complexly structured world prone to the emergence of unpredictable and yet significant turns of events.

Thus, in spite of their overt opposition, relativism and universalism are grounded in a common strategy of effectively *disarming difference*. For the relativist, differences among cultures and value systems ultimately cannot matter because they cannot be put into productive conversation; the incommensurability thesis forces acceptance of differences only to disallow their making any global difference. For the universalist, differences among cultures and value systems ultimately do not matter because they are historical accidents that fail to express any important truths about the essence of being human. Differences may be entertaining, but they are a critical distraction. For both, tolerance is an important subsidiary value because it is (as in engineering) a definition of precisely what kinds and degrees of difference can be comfortably ignored. Where relativism and universalism are at odds—the basis of their bifurcation—is in how to properly define the *scope and content* of equality or sameness.

In simple terms, relativists grant equality to peoples.[20] Adjudication among different systems of principles, practices, and perspectives is impossible because each is the equivalent of all others as a way of life. Universalists grant equality to persons. Adjudication among different systems of principles, practices, and perspectives is not only possible, but productive because these systems are historically and geographically contingent overlays on an essentially common, human core.[21] Relativist equality directs attention to a descriptive topography of appropriate coexistence. Universalist equality directs attention to a normative topography of appropriate communion. Pluralism is a hybrid of these approaches—an attempt to reconcile the descriptive/normative equality of peoples and persons without questioning the roots of their bifurcation. None of these theories signal movement in the direction of a global ethics of diversity-enhancing interdependence.

By rejecting the possibility of transcendental perspectives or absolute objectivity, the relativist also rejects the possibility of contesting the basic equivalence of all sets of principles, practices, and perspectives. This means that the relativist is committed to grant equality infinite scope (excluding none and encompassing all that distinguishes a people as such), but also infinitesimal content. Although we are equal as peoples, that equality affords no resources for developing a common definition for a good society. As a universalist would have it, relativists take up fictional residence in a kind of "moral flatland" where it is impossible to measure and comparatively rank even diametrically opposed views and practices—a world in denial of moral depth perception. Although everyone in this world is "equal," relativists insist that there is no one who can ultimately say if there is anything *significantly* common to them all.

By averring the ultimate contingency of differences among persons and peoples, and the existence of a fundamental and common human nature, the strict universalist is inclined to define equality or sameness as having infinitesimal scope (including only what is most essential to us as human beings), but potentially infinite content. Since we are essentially equal as persons, we have common ground on which to develop a definition of a good society. As a relativist would have it, universalists take up no less fictional residence on "ethical highlands" that afford ever-wider horizons to those most assiduously ascending the slopes of their world's single, cloud-hidden peak—a peak from which the details of their prior lives below can only appear blurred and inconsequential. Everyone in this world is also "equal," but this becomes apparent only as they leave their homes and native places, ascending together in view of the peak from which the significance of all grounds ultimately derives.[22]

But however the scope and content of equality/sameness is defined, seeing things or situations as equal/the same implies the telling of a disarming fiction in which the relational dynamics of *differentiation* are editorially "leveled down" or "evened out" into an internally vacuous characteristic—a status or garb that is either worn or shed depending on what kind of fiction is being told.

Because of their restricted (and restrictive) imagination of difference, neither relativism nor universalism affords effective resources for addressing issues of inequity and sustainably reconfiguring the complexly intertwining arcs of change comprised in contemporary globalization processes. In fact, as if pivoting on the fulcrum of an excluded middle between sameness and difference, universalism and relativism have worked in seesawing concert with the very dynamics that have been globally intensifying rather than alleviating inequity.

Although universalism, relativism, and pluralism have conceptual origins, breaking free of them—and breaking through the aporia of difference posed by the dynamics of modernization, industrialization, and marketization with which their development has been entrained—cannot be a matter of purely intellectual fiat. Concepts are distillations of lived relational dynamics. Developing a diversity-enhancing ethics of interdependence and changing the *akusala* patterns of outcome and opportunity being experienced by an increasingly large global majority will entail working out from within the conditions of climax modernity and climax markets "as they have come to be"—that is, as karmically inflected historical phenomena continuously and recursively shaped by prevailing constellations of values, intentions, and practices.

CHAPTER SEVEN

Convergence on Variety

Modern Irony, Postmodern Ideal

The current, predicament-rich complexion of contemporary global dynamics is a karmic function of an historically extended interplay among locally, nationally, regionally, and globally dominant patterns of values, intentions, and actions, including those involved in the practices of envisioning, building, and maintaining social, economic, political, cultural, and technological institutions. Reorienting these dynamics to realize new and more equitable complexions of outcomes and opportunities is necessarily a process of altering those patterns—a process that requires keen attention to the interdependence and interpenetration of the conceptual and the concrete, the intellectual and the material.

Thus far, we have examined these dynamics from two distinct historical perspectives, mapping them in the domains of what David Harvey (2006) has termed absolute and relative space-time. The first brought into view (over the course of Chapter 4) what might be considered a global geography of "tectonic" and "climatic" shifts playing out culturally, socially, economically, politically, and technologically over a period of roughly half a millennium. The second (in Chapter 5) brought into higher-resolution focus one particular feature of that dynamic geography: the crucial role played by mass mediation relative to the transition from industrial capitalism to mental capitalism and from a material economy to an attention economy.

If, however, histories of the climax of modernity and global markets are to provide guidance for establishing more equitable arcs of change than those within which we are now embroiled, we must take on an additional burden. As Timothy Brook (2005) has framed the task, our considerations of recent history should not rest content with attempting what are purportedly objective or value-neutral readings of the past, but should be keyed instead to discerning within the past resources needed for realigning historical dynamics. That is, we need to critically engage the value-infused dynamics of relational space-time.

To this end, I want to suggest seeing the contemporary aporia of difference and the relational challenges it poses as a result of the merger of two sets of dramatic currents flowing out of the stock market crash of October 1929, the subsequent global economic recession, and the rise of fascist antimodernism and moral nativism. The more concrete current flows through a set of era-defining techno-scientific advances set in motion during the Second World War, the emergence of the military-industrial-communications complex, the technologically driven displacement of the hierarchy by the network, and the eventual triumph of consumption-maximizing market capitalism. The second, more conceptual current flows through the hegemony-seeking competition of capitalist and communist universalisms, the canonization of rational choice theory as a policy tool under conditions of nuclear brinksmanship, the ethical declaration of irreducible intersubjectivity and relativity, and the idealization of fully elective identities.

The confluence of these currents marks a turning of global social, economic, political, cultural, and technological dynamics from sameness toward difference. But thus far, and more specifically, it has meant a shift from modern valorizations of global unity to postmodern valorizations of free variation. That is, although global dynamics have favored the increasing importance of issues of difference over the last century, they have been inflected in ways that have *not* been conducive to enhancing diversity as a global relational commons and public good. Seeing this, however, is also to see possibilities for reinflecting these dynamics, working out through them to generate movement in the direction of more resolutely *kusala* global futures.

MARKET FAILURES AND TOTALITARIAN THREATS: THE GREAT DEPRESSION

The Great Depression that followed the New York stock market crash of October 1929 is still regarded as the most traumatic event in economic history.[1] In addition to skyrocketing inflation and overnight losses of corporate fortunes and homeowner equity, the Depression brought, for example, a 50% drop in overall global industrial production and official unemployment rates reaching upwards of 25% even in major economies like those of the United States, Germany, and Great Britain. Although the precise causes of the Depression are still actively debated, it is generally

agreed that the seemingly intractable recession that afflicted most economies worldwide over much of the 1930s was a function of multiple national
and international factors. Whether emphasis is placed on financial market instability and/or irresponsibility, ill-conceived regulatory policies
and political misguidance, credit and consumption crises, a dysfunctional
international monetary standard, or global overproduction combined
with failures to adequately distribute the economic gains of the "roaring
twenties," the results were a widespread and crippling lack of confidence
in the "system of the world" that had been established in pursuit of modern and market ideals, and equally widespread resort to finger-pointing.[2]

As the Depression dragged on in spite of the general economic and
political embrace of the salvific "gospels" of consumerism and government spending, criticisms of industrial capitalism and free markets from
the perspectives of labor unions, socialist intellectuals, and communist
activism grew steadily in terms of apparent relevance and credibility. But
so did an opposing critique offered by fascism.[3]

The labor, socialist, and communist movements all had roots in
nineteenth-century discontents regarding ever more egregiously skewed
distributions of the benefits of market capitalism and apparent failures to
make real the progressive modern ideals of universality, equality, autonomy, and sovereignty. What the labor, socialist, and communist movements offered were alternative visions of and means to universalistic
modernity. In sharp contrast, German fascism developed over the 1920s
and 1930s as an emotionally charged response to what were seen as the
disastrous consequences of modernization, including the rise of individualism and materialism, social atomization, personal alienation, and the
decay of traditional cultures and identities. And as demonstrated by the
intellectual fervor and street demonstrations associated with the rise of
fascism throughout much of the 1930s and across much of Europe, these
sentiments of disenchantment with modernity were far from isolated.
Expressing contempt for both rationalism and the pretensions of egalitarian universalism, fascism forwarded a distinctive cult of nation that was
racially constituted and that politicized difference—cultural, intellectual,
and political as well as racial—as the root of all betrayal.

Hitler's rise to power in 1933 occurred as Germany was suffering
deeply from the effects of the Great Depression and as conservative elites
looked with fear at the growing popularity of communism. The Nazi party
promised a "third way" opposed to both capitalist liberalism and communist collectivism. Steeped in overtly moral appeals to the "pure" and
"indigenous" values and blood ties of the German folk, Nazi ideologues
constructed a crypto-religious mythology of national rebirth that would
inaugurate a "Third Reich" or successor state to the German empire of
the nineteenth and early twentieth century (the Second Reich) and the

medieval and early modern Holy Roman Empire (the First Reich). But crucial to the claims for fascist Nazi "legitimacy" was the decisive turn-around of the German economy, which grew phenomenally and against global trends from 1934 as Germany undertook aggressive remilitariza-tion and brazenly "outsourced" the costs of rapid growth to its expanding (non-German) territorial domain.

TECHNO-SCIENTIFIC SALVATION: THE RISE OF THE MILITARY-INDUSTRIAL-COMMUNICATIONS COMPLEX

The internal and international consequences of fascist Germany's preda-tory stance toward difference—the staggering losses in lives and dignity that resulted from the Holocaust and the Second World War (estimated at some fifty million deaths worldwide)—are too well known and too tragic to rehearse here. What I would like to draw attention to instead are how global responses to German fascism (and the affiliated phenomenon of imperial Japanese hyper-nationalism) helped to set in motion develop-ments that would come to play crucial roles in the advent of both the con-temporary dynamics of the attention economy and postmodern thought.

The Allied defeats of the German-Italian-Japanese Axis can be traced to any number of military and technological advances, the most popularly renowned of which was the invention of the ultimate weapon: the atomic bomb.[4] But as much as nuclear weapons would come to shape international relations during the Cold War (and remain relevant into the twenty-first century), the effects of digital computing advances have proven to be much more generally significant. While the obliteration of Hiroshima and Nagasaki set the overt doomsday context of Cold War competition for global hegemony, it was the advent of computational science and its rapid technological deployment that would prove crucial in so thoroughly transfiguring the means of global competition that the bipolar world of Cold War international relations would dissolve into a much more com-plexly differentiated world of continuously shifting multilateral alliances and individual consumer sovereigns.[5]

There were two main lines of war-effort research and development (R&D): the first centered on developing digital computers capable of out-performing assembly lines of humans in calculating artillery firing tables and in precisely aiming weaponry; the second focused on advancing capa-bilities for electronic surveillance and for breaking German and Japanese communications codes or encryptions.

The first line of R&D effectively laid the foundation for industrial applications of servomechanisms and real-time computing, spurring a mechanization-to-automation transition that over the next five decades would lead to revolutionary changes in manufacturing and the explosive growth of the electronics industry, but also to no less revolutionary changes in the work of science as computer data crunching and mathematical modeling became both extremely fast and cost-effective.[6] The second line of R&D laid complementary material and theoretical foundations for building relational databases, natural language recognition systems, and artificially intelligent systems that would completely and complexly transform the nature of commercial transactions and communications by the final decades of the century, driving the world irreversibly forward into an increasingly dematerialized "information age."[7]

As the Cold War intensified, the United States and the U.S.S.R. invested heavily in both lines of R&D. Pursuing competitive advantages in the nuclear arms and space races, and in broad-spectrum and highly detailed surveillance, conditions were created for the emergence of a self-propelling trinity of political, military, and commercial interests that by 1961 constituted what outgoing U.S. President Dwight D. Eisenhower termed a "military-industrial complex." The iconic nuclear showdown (and eventual stand-down) precipitated by the Cuban Missile Crisis of 1962 had the dual effect in the United States of intensifying already deep-cutting debates about how best to defend America's democratic capitalist and individualist interests and values against Soviet communism and collectivism, and of stimulating equally profound concerns about the liabilities of centralized military and government communications and decision making in the event of a nuclear strike.

In government, military, and academic circles, these debates and concerns occupied many of the best minds of the generation, often in the context of virtually apocalyptic narratives of conflict between American political and economic liberalism and opposing Soviet (and later, Maoist) totalitarianism. But they resonated with particular forcefulness and to eventually great effect at the RAND Corporation. A unique interdisciplinary, nonprofit, government-supported "think tank" established in 1945 to connect military planning with decision-making processes in research and development, RAND was home to an elite corps of aeronautics engineers, computer scientists, economists, physicists, psychologists, and social scientists. Its early reputation was based on its development of a distinctive "systems analysis" approach to decision making in relation to military procurements and tactical organization. A purely quantitative method for solving strategic and logistical problems of any degree of complexity, systems analysis was later applied to studying and proposing strategies for addressing a wide range of key social and economic issues.

The very first (1946) RAND publication detailed the design, production, and uses of Earth-orbiting satellites, and can well be seen as the point of origin for the orbital surveillance and communications networks that began being assembled after the Soviet Union won the race to launch the

first orbital spacecraft in 1957. Five years later, the Cuban Missile Crisis led
to another seminal RAND study that would fundamentally transform the
structure of communications networks: a proposal to develop a decentralized national network capable of surviving nuclear attack. Designed around
principles of transmission and organization that now underlie the World
Wide Web, the first iteration of this network was actually built in 1969 by
the Advanced Research Projects Agency (ARPA) with U.S. Defense Depart-
ment funds.[8] Fourteen years later, the network was split into military (MIL-
NET) and nonmilitary (ARPANET) nets, and in 1989 the nonmilitary net
was renamed the "Internet." Due in large part to the combination of these
two communications advances, the Cold War marriage of political, military,
and commercial interests has morphed over the past quarter century into
a much more nimble and decentralized *military-industrial-communications
complex*, a primary result of which has been the explosive growth of state,
military, and commercial surveillance and data analysis capacities.

Together, then, these two lines of wartime and postwar R&D initiated and nourished geometrically expanding networks of innovation that,
in addition to their direct applications in the transformation of military
technologies, also enabled a global shift from a Fordist model of centralized mass production to one of decentralized just-in-time production, vastly
compressing the demand→design→production→marketing→consumption
cycle, and greatly accelerating global flows of goods, services, and people. As
we have seen already from a different angle, this in turn made both possible
and necessary a shift of dominance from material to mental capitalism
and the eventual emergence of a global attention economy, generating as
well an entirely new set of challenges and metaphors for understanding
self and society.

In addition to propelling the phenomenal scaling up of industrial
and commercial activities, these lineages of techno-scientific innovation were contributing to heightening the complexity of the relational
dynamics linking military, industrial, and communications systems and
interests, and to destabilizing traditional social, economic, political, and
cultural institutions. Over the last half century in particular, advances
in communications and computing have contributed to a paradigmatic
restructuring of global power dynamics—a shift from the predominance
of highly centralized hierarchies to increasingly decentralized networks
(Castells 1996, 1997, 1998). The significance of this shift cannot be over-
emphasized. Networks are dynamic structures that grow as a nonlinear
function of both negative (i.e., stabilizing) feedback and positive feedback
that *accelerates interactions* and *amplifies differentiation*. Thus, even though
the growth of military-industrial-communications complexes was fueled
initially by efforts to maximize security, as the impacts of these efforts
matured and were generalized, the ironic result has been an ever-greater

entrainment of growth with both increasing variability and volatility—a signal characteristic of what Castells has referred to as the "network society" and "global informational capitalism."

Thus, although widely celebrated, the scaling up of industrial and commercial activities combined with the shift toward network organization has been shadowed by the coalescence of conditions for the advent of a new, reflexive phase of industrial modernization in which continued industrial and economic growth entails the production of unpredictable threats, risks, and hazards in the face of which responsible decisions nevertheless must be made (Beck, Giddens, and Lash 1994). Simply stated, beyond certain thresholds of scale, scope, and complexity, conditions are created for the emergence of "world risk society" (Beck 1992, 1999) in which it is no longer possible to externalize the environmental, social, economic, and cultural costs of sustained growth. Yet, because of the predominance of network organizations that grow through accelerating interaction and amplifying differentiation, it is impossible as well to inhibit the percolation of risks and hazards into virtually every aspect of life, or to forestall the intensification of compulsions to choose under conditions of continuously heightening ambiguity and uncertainty.[9]

RISK, RATIONAL CHOICE, AND STRATEGIC BETRAYAL: A COLD WAR PUBLIC POLICY LEGACY

Nothing perhaps so well illustrates the historical complexity of the rising prominence of deliberately assumed risks and the self-defeating triumph of modern emphases on universality and individuality than the Cold War nuclear arms race and the broader ideological and material struggles for global power between American "democratic" individualism and Soviet "totalitarian" collectivism. And, as it happens, a key role was again played by the RAND Corporation in framing the drama of nuclear brinksmanship: the formulation of rational choice theory and its rise to the status of the premier approach to engaging social, economic, and political issues and to shaping public policy in strategic relation to them.

In her masterful account of the origins and aims of rational choice theory, Sonja Amadae (2003) details how rational choice theory crystallized around work—much of it done at RAND or by researchers associated with RAND—in applied game theory, the mathematical modeling and simulation of risk-laden and uncertain environments, expected utility theory, and cybernetics, and then came to serve as the linchpin of the capitalist democratic West's ideological triumph over the socialist authoritarian Eastern Bloc in the Cold War.[10]

Initially developed during the most intense period of nuclear brinkmanship in the early to mid-1960s, rational choice theory offered a means of optimizing decision results in highly volatile and fundamentally competitive environments, logically and mathematically "proving" that autonomously pursuing individual interests affords better results than collective decision making and action. Inspired by Kenneth Arrow's (1951) seminal argument that collectively rational and optimal group decisions are logically impossible, rational choice theory poised its adherents to strike a preemptive blow against Marxist, idealist democratic, and totalitarian approaches to realizing social welfare. Once one accepted the premises of Arrow's "impossibility" theorem, there was no avoiding the conclusions that collective determinations of social welfare are either unintelligible or irrational, and that "rationality, objective and universal law, and individual freedom over subjective choices represent the bases of capitalist democracy" (Amadae 2003, 122). According to Arrow, individual preferences—and individual preferences alone—are the information out of which legitimate collective decisions are to be realized.

Choice as a Prisoner's Dilemma

Rational choice theory took over Arrow's axioms of instrumental rationality, transitively arrayed desires, the interpersonal incomparability of preferences, and the sovereignty of the individual, along with his conclusion that deliberatively maximizing collective benefit is irrational, and converted them into defining characteristics of human nature. As exemplified in its canonical illustration—the Prisoner's Dilemma—rational choice theory forwards an axiomatic approach to decision making that assumes the essential autonomy of actors naturally and rationally inclined to instrumentally pursue their individual, transitively organized interests.

In the Prisoner's Dilemma, you and another prisoner are independently offered a deal: if both you and the other prisoner remain silent, you'll both get light sentences; if you confess (defect) and the other remains silent, you go free and he/she gets a heavy sentence; if you remain silent and the other defects, you get the heavy sentence; if you both defect, you each get a medium sentence. According to rational choice theory, defection is the best strategy since each prisoner gets a better outcome than if one decides to cooperate (remain silent) and the other does not.[11] In short, rational choice theory concludes that, all other things being equal, and human nature being what it is, betrayal is the best bet.

In a manner uncomfortably akin to the fascist treatment of otherness as an index of the possibility of betrayal, rational choice theory treats others as excludable from moral consideration and purportedly establishes betrayal as quintessentially rational. From a rational choice perspective, one can dispense with trying to take others' preferences or ultimate good into account in making decisions. One should simply act on the basis of one's own nature, remaining unwaveringly committed to pursuing one's own self-interest.

For those inclined to valorize altruism and cooperation, this is a hard pill to swallow. Two generations of scholars have attempted to circumvent the logical necessity of doing so on what might be called humanist grounds; and, within the game-theoretic community, the wider application of rational choice theory and its reading of the Prisoner's Dilemma have been greeted with sustained logical and mathematical critique. Nevertheless, rational choice theory has assumed nearly canonical status in the social sciences, in the business community, in legal circles, and in the world of public-policy making, and it is not trivial to ask why.

The key, I think, lies in a fact stated with great clarity by the game theorist and economist Ken Binmore. In the rational-choice framing of the Prisoner's Dilemma, "the dice are as loaded against the emergence of cooperation as they could possibly be," and the bottom line is that "rational players don't cooperate in the Prisoner's Dilemma, because the conditions necessary for cooperation are absent in this game."[12] Intent on establishing the utter rationality of noncooperation in the context of competitions between would-be global hegemons, the original proponents of rational choice theory simply rigged the game. By fusing a unique set of assumptions carried over from Arrow's "impossibility" theorem to a one-stop (rather than an indefinitely repeated) Prisoner's Dilemma, the framers of rational choice theory were able to draft their conclusions into service as parts of the purportedly most rudimentary game rules for decision making in competitive environments.[13]

The influential results of their efforts can be read as an index of the degree to which rational choice theory "proved" what many wanted to hear: that it is rational to ignore the preferences of others and the possibility that cooperation might prove most beneficial to all. In the midst of the arms race, the ever-present specter of nuclear Armageddon, and a direct standoff between the global powers arrayed under the banners of competing universalisms—capitalist liberalism and communist collectivism—a theory which proved that the best possible results would flow from narrowly self-interested action undertaken in denial of external constraints was precisely what many felt the doctor should order.[14]

Depicting rational choice liberalism as originating in the dramatic currents of the Cold War has the effect of historicizing its successes and demonstrating their contingency. Set against the broader complexion of events leading up to the Second World War, including the global economic collapse and recession of the 1930s, and the intensification of antimodern sentiments around which German fascism crystallized, rational choice theory emerged as a metaethical response to the crisis of modernity—a response triggered by the aggressive postwar expansion of powerfully opposed visions of modernity. Rational choice theory forwards a powerful set of metaethical axioms: that all human beings are ultimately the same, sharing the same basic nature as rationally self-interested individuals; that the only relevant differences among individual humans and the societies they create are differences of desire or preference; that desires are not interpersonally comparable; and that rationality is both transcultural and singular in nature. Together, these axioms serve as the cornerstones of an ultramodern ethics of autonomous independence in which reflections on overall good are subordinated to strategies for securing the interests of each individual—an ethics, ironically, in which "others" are morally irrelevant because their preferences and decision-making processes lie behind a veil of mutual ignorance that is itself normatively justified because the advantages of last-minute defection or betrayal are so rationally (and hence "naturally") compelling.

For the champions of global capitalism and democratic liberalism, jointly committed to the sovereignty of the citizen-as-consumer and individual liberty, such an ethics of autonomous independence tells the most compelling (and comforting) of stories about how best to deal with the emergence of difference within the bosom of modernity: a story in which we are ethically compelled to protect and promote the "sanctity of individuals' preferences as the bulwark against coercive totalitarianism" (Amadae 2003, 108). The moral relativity assumed and then asserted by rational choice theory—the utter atomization of personal patterns of desire and preference—acts as a rationally incontestable solvent on the interpersonal mortar without which the foundations of totalitarian, collectivist structures simply and necessarily crumble. The singularity of self-interest as an ethical means and end is *given* in the primacy and essential privacy of the decision-making agent. Bluntly stated, rational choice theory "proves" that selfishness is actually the natural and best foundation for decision making. Although not going so far as to make the deontological claim that individually self-interested action should be affirmed as a duty by and for all, rational choice theory issues purportedly incontestable warrant for claiming the universal merit of selfishly calculated courses of action.[15]

THE POSTMODERN TURN: FROM SAMENESS TO OTHERNESS

Historicizing the rise of rational choice theory, and the metaethical considerations informing it, is also useful in drawing attention to their distinctively American origins and character, however broadly they have come to be disseminated. At roughly the same time that the foundations were being laid in the United States for the construction of rational choice liberalism as *the* response to Soviet totalitarianism, there began coalescing in France strong currents of antifoundationalism expressing a comparable, but distinctly alternative, set of counters to totalitarianism. Like those inclined by Arrow's "impossibility" theorem and rational choice theory to turn "logically" toward moral relativism and a de facto horizontal ordering of individual differences/preferences, the poststructural, postmodern approaches developed in France in the 1950s and 1960s—by, for example, Michel Foucault, Emmanuel Levinas, Jacques Derrida, and Gilles Deleuze—deeply opposed appeals to any form of transcendent order and externally enforced norms. And as with their counterparts across the Atlantic, the trope of imprisonment would factor importantly into how the case against social, political, and philosophical authoritarianism was critically framed.[16] Where the American and French responses varied most crucially was in the ethically constitutive role the latter granted to otherness and difference.[17]

Mounting disenchantment with the realities of global market capitalism had insured attention to difference on global socioeconomic and political agendas from at least the middle of the nineteenth century, most notably at first from Marx and his heirs and then from more broadly democratic anticolonial perspectives. But parallel to the search for competing, but no less universal, modern ideals and institutions, skepticism about the project of modernity as such began growing. This was not only in fascist or romantic circles. Spurred in part by the paradigm changes occurring in the sciences—most notably the bracketing of religious creationism by Darwinian evolution and the eclipse of Newton's mechanistic worldview and physics by Einstein's relativity—paradigm-challenging movements in philosophy began developing in the late nineteenth and early twentieth centuries. These included the logical positivism of the Vienna Circle, American pragmatism, German phenomenology and hermeneutics, and French existentialism. Yet, it was not until after the Second World War that there began developing, in France, a movement to invert the value statuses of sameness and difference.

Although highly variegated, this broad movement—often identified as poststructuralism, deconstructionism, or simply postmodernism—can be seen as originating in the widely felt need to theoretically secure possibilities for differing from prevailing normative and institutional structures. With the memory of the German occupation still fresh, the ravages of the war and incomplete reconstruction still very much evident all across Europe, and ever more chilling developments in the Stalinist Soviet Union and McCarthyist United States, it was perhaps natural for the postwar generation of French intellectuals to see securing the freedom to differ as crucial, and to see this as requiring a complete dismantling of transcendental claims and imperatives—a resolute dispersal of the determinative force of all political, economic, social, cultural, and conceptual systems. In practice, this meant adopting a critical stance toward all givens, all hierarchies, and all metanarratives, including narratives of "natural" community—an arc of change that culminates ontologically in Deleuze's subordination of identity to difference and ethically in Levinas' subordination of subjectivity to relationality.

At one level, then, the work of poststructural and postmodern French thought has been focused on undermining modern claims (most clearly articulated, perhaps, in Descartes) for the intelligibility and possibility of complete and certain knowledge—the final disciplining of our knowledge of the world according to ultimate categories. This philosophical skepticism or humility with respect to ultimate metaphysical and epistemological foundations is combined, however, with a normative assault on all forms of totalitarianism. This explicitly meant a rejection of all forms of political authoritarianism, fascism perhaps first and foremost. But as Todd May has noted, this assault eventually took aim as well at any projects—including those embodied in social, economic, political, and techno-scientific institutions—that would "constrain people's lives and identities within narrowly defined parameters" (May 1997, 4). As the twentieth-century history of Europe had made entirely too evident to those living in postwar France, such structural constraints on the freedom to be different are all too easily translated into forces for marginalization and elimination, and against these forces existentialist individualism had proven impotent. The task at hand, finally, was to challenge the ontological and ethical subordination of difference to sameness and identity. And taken to its logical limit, this entailed nothing short of the deconstruction of fixation: ultimately, a complete deconstruction of (and freedom from) the past or all that remains and would force a reiteration of the same.

The Origins of Ethics in Encountering Difference: Levinas

Without doubt, Emmanuel Levinas was at the forefront of efforts to undertake a paradigmatic, ethical inversion of the statuses of identity and difference in response to both modern propensities to marginalize differences and totalitarian threats to eliminate them. Levinas knew firsthand the atrocities that could be committed—and "morally" justified—by identitarian true believers.[18] Born into a Jewish family in what is now Lithuania (then Russia), Levinas went to Germany in the 1920s, where he studied under Edmund Husserl and met Husserl's most influential student, Martin Heidegger, before emigrating to France. Drafted into military service at the outset of the Second World War, Levinas was captured during the invasion of France and spent five years in a German prisoner-of-war camp. Although his wife and daughter were kept safely in hiding throughout the war, other family members were deported and never heard from again or, like his father and brothers, killed outright by the Nazi Secret Service.

Levinas' breakthrough work, *Totality and Infinity* (1961), is a remarkable phenomenology of the face-to-face encounter of self and other that aims to demonstrate that the origins of human subjectivity must be traced to intersubjectivity, and that ethics is inseparable from encountering and embracing difference. In the year of its publication, as the Cold War escalated toward the Cuban Missile Crisis, France was awash in riots. Peaceful demonstrations for Algerian independence resulted in the arrests of tens of thousands of French-Algerian Muslims, a stream of state-orchestrated "disappearances" and killings, and finally (on October 17) the massacre of several hundred demonstrators by French military and police. In this social environment, *Totality and Infinity* made the timely and powerful normative claim that to encounter another is at once to be called to respond and to be called into responsibility. For Levinas, to encounter the other is to be made aware of precisely who one *is*—a comprehension of one's own particular identity and totality—by being addressed by what one *is not*. Indeed, the totality of one's own self, as all that can be assimilated as "the same," only appears as such through confrontation with the infinity of another who cannot be comprehended or fully grasped, exceeding or exhausting all representations, categorizations, and claims of identity. Difference, ultimately, is constitutive of who we are.

But as Levinas is at pains to insist, the primordial encounter with difference in the face of the other reveals a structure not of need, but rather of fathomless desire. The awakening of subjectivity is an affective event, not one that is coolly rational, instrumental, or physically compelling. If, as the proponents of rational choice theory maintain, our "individuality" is founded most fundamentally on the interpersonal incommensurability of our desires and preferences, it is a "foundation" thoroughly marbled with difference. Our most primordial desires are desires *for* another. And as made clear in Levinas' insistence that the basic encounter with another always includes a "third party," our own totality and constitutive desires occur always in the context of a considerate weighing of desires and necessarily infinite responsibilities—a concern regarding the meaning of justice. Yet precisely because the third party signals the need to compare the incomparable and limit our responsibility to *the* other in view of *all* others, justice is a kind of violence—a primary "economy" based on the assumption of an original equality among all others. As such, it is the origin of the State, a necessity, but not itself ethical.[19]

For Levinas this is crucial, because ethicality is not something added onto our human nature, but is rather the very dynamic of our subjectivity. Our ethicality is not optional, though it can be limited, even repressed. Ethics arises as the originary, precognitive calling into question of our own spontaneity and totality under the gaze of one who is infinitely (and so, indefinitely) other. Ethics thus precedes logic and metaphysics as a "first philosophy" rooted in the irreducibility of the different to the same. In this sense, it cannot rest on any sort of calculation or control. It cannot consist of a disciplining of self and desire—whether as a pursuit of objectively given principles or virtues, or as an expression of rationally mandated duties or senses of ought. Ethics cannot be imposed; not even self-imposed.

Importantly, however, Levinas' emphases on the ineradicable ethicality of encountering otherness and his location of goodness in interpersonal relations is not undertaken under any veil of ignorance regarding the prevalence of violence and competition in human history. His question is rather *how* responsibility, generosity, and hospitality occur within such a history. Or as he later insists with more precision (Levinas 1981, 176–77), how do we struggle against violence so as not to instantiate and institute violence in the course of that struggle? Levinas' phenomenology of totality (self) encountering infinity (other) can be seen, then, as a response to (and as taking responsibility for) the historical trauma of Nazism's "genocidal" pogrom against racial, ethnic, religious, and political difference, and the ever-present threat of its repetition. But it can also be seen as a historically sensitive response to the ethical trauma inflicted by the logic of the Prisoner's Dilemma.

As it is framed in the context of rational choice liberalism, the Prisoner's Dilemma axiomatically affirms what Levinas reveals in the encounter of self and other: the impossibility of forcing others into sameness with ourselves. But Levinas rejects the classic liberal assumption of the originality of the autonomous and rationally calculating individual, even if he affirms that the other must be presumed equipped to resist all our attempts at persuasion, to refuse following along with our proofs, and, in the end, to reject cooperating in ways we can neither predict nor control. Whereas the rational choice liberal interprets this as establishing a disjunctive symmetry that justifies excluding the desires and preferences of others as in principle beyond our grasp, Levinas sees the encounter with the other as an irreducibly asymmetrical event through which the foiling of our impulses and efforts to grasp, possess, or comprehend the particularity of the other *is* precisely the unfurling of those desires through which our own particularity is revealed. In short, contrary to the axiomatic assumption in rational choice theory that we are all given first and foremost as atomic, wholly independent individuals, Levinas and his kin affirm the irreducibly *interactive* nature of individuality.

Since encountering the other is inseparable from our own individuality and humanity, we cannot deny, betray, or destroy the other except through ultimately self-destructive acts. As Levinas puts it, "violence is to be found in any action in which one acts as if one were alone to act; as if the rest of the universe were there only to receive the action"; yet violence is also concomitant with "any action which we endure without at every point col-laborating in it" (Levinas 1990, 6). Consideration, solicitude, cooperation, sharing, and mutual participation: these are the ultimate bulwarks against violence and totalitarianism. To play the Prisoner's Dilemma according to the rules of rational choice theory is to guarantee loss.

Levinas' phenomenology of the origination of subjectivity in the rela-tionship with another carries us to the brink of a paradigmatically new engagement with difference. The discovery of a constitutive difference between the self as a totality of the same and another who is immediately present as an infinity irreducible to the same, its concepts and categories, affords a conceptual vantage from which it is possible to see the experi-ence of difference as an opening for mutual contribution, and thus as inti-mating possibilities for critically assessing how differentiation processes are oriented. But the phenomenological character of Levinas' method—its rootedness in the immediacy of experience—gives away as much as it provides. By beginning necessarily in individual experience, the infin-ity of the other is viewed from within the phenomenal horizons of total-ity. There is, in short, a chasm between the total and the infinite which, once invoked, cannot be simply revoked. Levinas is, in his own words, a defender of subjectivity (Levinas 1961, 26). And, while his idea of subjec-tivity may be founded in the idea of infinity, it is by definition only the subject that could assume centrality in his vision of originative relational-ity. His is not yet a fully nondualistic ethics.

These difficulties are raised by Derrida in his denial that Levinas suc-ceeds in displaying the transcendent nature of the Other vis-à-vis the self as the Same.[20] The infinity and exteriority to which Levinas refers us in laying out the relational origins of subjectivity and its intrinsic ethicality cannot be presented except as expressions of the finite and interior. Stress-ing the paradox in any phenomenological articulation of the infinity of the Other, Derrida points to the impossibility of speaking about the infinite except as the "in-finite": we are not carried beyond our own finitude and totality by simply announcing their indebtedness to another. To say of the infinity of another that it cannot be categorized or comprehended is still to characterize it in terms of our own categories and comprehension—a linguistic knot that Levinas takes great pains to undo in *Otherwise than Being* by turning language against itself, avoiding the verb "to be" and all references to the "exteriority" of the other. And, it is in light of this cri-tique, incorporated into the body of Derrida's own very influential work, that we must understand Levinas' (1987) later avowal that the difference of the other is present ultimately only as a transcendent *absence*, as a *trace* of that which in fact has never been there.

Whether Levinas' attempt to force "the said" (the finite, ontological, historical) into revealing "the saying" (the infinite, ethical, transcendent) succeeds in its own terms can be left for his readers to decide. But as means for resolving the contemporary aporia of difference and responding to the irreducibly historical expansion and deepening of the *occurrence* of inequity, his approach to delivering difference from subordination to sameness results in what could be called an ethical miscarriage. As trace or absence, the difference to which we owe our own subjectivity, the transcendence that calls us into acting responsibly and not just instrumentally, calls us from and to what is beyond history, beyond the workings of society. Thus conceived, difference is in no position either to impose or to offer.

On the positive side, granted that difference plays a constitutive role in the co-origination of subjectivity and ethicality, conceiving of difference as trace or absence warrants the ultimately unconditional nature of agency, its freedom from historical or material determinism. This is crucial to Levinas' defense of subjectivity. Whereas the dominant traditions of Western liberalism assert the inherently sacrosanct nature of the individual axiomatically, Levinas defends subjectivity—called forth through encounter with the infinity of another, under the gaze of the third party or humanity—because it is the only possible locus of responsibility for the Other, especially against the violent reasonableness of historically realized social, economic, political, and cultural institutions and hierarchies. Again, individual subjectivity, as intersubjectively constituted, is the final bulwark against totalitarianism.

But precisely because there is access only to *traces* of infinity—to a sense of its *absence*—while Levinas might successfully lead us to the point of rejecting the premises of the modern dualism of subjects and objects, selves and others, stating explicitly that "[to] be or not to be is not the question where transcendence is concerned" (Levinas 1981, 3), he cannot take us beyond having only a *vantage* on nonduality. The constitutive role of difference does not imply or necessitate a contributory role; and given that we ultimately encounter only traces—evidence of absence—it is hard to see how the difference of the other even *could* be capable of making any particular and significant difference.

And so, while the fecundity or creativity of difference is widely championed by those working from what we can broadly term "deconstructivist" or "postmodernist" vantages, it is a kind of creativity that is ill suited to redressing inequity. More ironically than might be generally appreciated, because postmodern stances against hierarchies of power and advantage are grounded in a radical distrust of all metanarratives and forms of objectifying transcendence, the vantages they yield afford access to a bewildering array of "vistas" that nevertheless have in common a distinctly flattened aspect. As expressed most graphically by Gilles Deleuze and Felix Guattari in their several jointly authored books, engaging difference from such perspectives involves a refusal to reach out toward difference through the vertical, arboreal metaphor of roots, trunks, and branches, and instead to regard differences as occurring on open-ended "planes of immanence"—entirely surface phenomena that play out only horizontally or rhizomatically.

This rejection of verticality and hierarchy is, of course, explicitly connected with the desire to forestall even the possibility of drafting difference into the service of totalitarian thinking and practices. But safeguarding difference against its use in justifying exclusionary practices or worse is not to assure its activation as the basis of mutual contribution. In fact, since any concrete act of contribution expresses the asymmetry of strengths in a given situation and at a certain time, establishing however temporarily a hierarchic tilt in relational dynamics, contribution requires recognition of "verticality." The mutual contributions involved in the emergence of diversity are not surface phenomena. Conceived as an "even exchange," mutual contribution is merely symbolic—a trading of like for like, same for same. In effect, the postmodern insistence on the absence of a vertical dimension prohibits commitment to any realizable *arcs* of change. The arrow of postmodern insight into the *importance* of difference falls short of its aim of *making* a difference, released without the requisite relational strength on a trajectory hugging too close to the plane of the horizontal.

Of course, too much can be made of the postmodern metaphor of rhizomatically proliferating differences. But in spite of the very critical assessment of global capitalism offered by Deleuze and Guattari (1983, 1987), it is significant how naturally this metaphor has come to inform cyberculture discourses that celebrate distanceless interaction, the practically limitless experiential options offered by the attention economy, and the relational subordination of commitment to choice. And it is no less significant how well and readily the metaphor resonates with rational choice–affirming, neoliberal convictions (Friedman 2005) that contemporary global market competition is proving, after all, that "the world is flat." Common to all is a mythically scaled imagination of the level playing field: a profoundly modern utopia on/in which each can claim equality with all.

The Limits of Flat-World Rationality and Ethics

This apparent convergence of postmodern patterns of criticism, consumption, and competition on equality, whatever its complex causes, should make us wary. If the ethics of responsibility to the other forwarded by Levinas and then taken up distinctively by Derrida, Deleuze, Luce Irigaray, Jean-Luc Nancy, and others provides us with a first draft of an ethics of difference, the daringness and necessity of their efforts should not blind us to the possibility that the vantages they offer on difference may well yield only an ethics of variation. Rational choice liberalism, as profoundly opposed as it is to postmodern sensibilities in other ways, particularly in its explicit rejection of cooperation as a strategy for maximizing either individual or collective good, can be seen as a competing ethics of variation. Neither is of much help in addressing the contemporary aporia of difference.

One shared weakness of such horizontal or flat-world ethics is that their means to recognizing and valorizing difference work against realizing the meaning of difference *as a value*—that is, as a modality of appreciation, a qualitatively inflected and accelerating pattern of change. Appreciation can only occur as the expression of relational dynamics oriented "perpendicularly" or "obliquely" to the plane of the ordinary—a recognition and realization of the extraordinary or exemplary. More specifically stated, appreciation involves *enhancing*—literally heightening (Latin: *in* [an intensifier] + *altus* [high])—relational sensibilities and sensitivities, but also expanding capabilities and strengthening commitments.

A second weakness of flat-world ethics is that their projection of conflicts of interest onto an idealized level playing field significantly distorts the "map" of power dynamics. In a world characterized by highly recursive, scale-crossing interdependencies, seeing differences as two-dimensional conceals complexity and has the liability of directing attention to superficial proximities or co-incidences in ways that compress or conceal both underlying and overarching causal networks. Attempting to realize specific goals on the basis of such a view of power dynamics can be as fruitless as it would be to set a course for a specific star in the absence of depth perspective, armed only with the (quite faulty) assumption that "adjacent" lights in the night sky are equivalently nearby destinations.

These are serious liabilities in responding ethically to predicament-generating arcs of change. Problems can be solved "horizontally," within already given orderings of values and priorities. Successful solutions reproduce the conditions of *ordinal continuity*, conserving existing patterns of ends and interests through compatible, even if significantly new, practices. Predicament resolutions involve *ordinal discontinuity*—the realization or emergence of new hierarchies of values and priorities, new patterns of ends and interests. Ethical approaches that foundationally insist on equality, however universal their aspirations may be, are not likely to be effective in shaping responses to predicaments arising in multicultural, multisectoral contexts. By supporting fictions of equivalent agency and independence, adhering to the principle of leveling the playing field is conducive to aggravating, not alleviating, inequity.

"PROGRESS" UNDERMINED AND REDEFINED

What is brought into critical perspective by charting the dramatic currents flowing from the stock market crash of 1929 to the roughly contemporaneous formulations of rational choice theory and postmodern ethics of difference? What do these currents reveal about the "global karma" shaping the dynamics of global interdependence and interpenetration? And, more specifically, how does viewing them in tandem help us to discern resources for responding to the intensification of moral, legal, and ethical tensions regarding identity, individuality, community, equality, freedoms-of-choice, justice, and difference, and for activating potentials therein for equity-enhancing change?

The market collapse of 1929 and the subsequent worldwide recession made painfully evident to all that the processes of globalization-as-modernization that had prevailed worldwide since at least the late seventeenth or early eighteenth century were neither infallible nor inevitable. "Progress" could be halted and even reversed. Cosmopolis, ever only half built, could be dismantled and its pieces scavenged for other ends. The rise of fascist totalitarianism and Nazi moral nativism drove an ideological stake into the universalist heart of modernity through refusing to ignore or tolerate differences and mounting a totalistic, communal assault on difference. Against the purportedly level playing field invoked by Western liberalism and its modern biases toward equality, autonomous individuality, and a contractual understanding of social relations, German fascism insisted on a hierarchic ordering of cultural differences; the sanctity of common traditions, language, and blood; the power of belonging and communally felt superiority; and the right of unifying the world not according reason but by force of will.

The eventual defeat of the Axis powers, however, was not a function of the superiority of universalism and the power of modern moral, legal, and ethical ideals. It was accomplished through an ad hoc, multicentered coalition armed with the results of collaborative, cutting-edge scientific and technological research and development. Germany was not defeated by a single competitor for global dominance, but by a culturally and ideologically disparate *alliance*. And, although important roles were played by the development of new kinds of weapons and delivery systems, the crucial factor in turning the war's tide was Allied *communications* advances. It was access to superior *information* resources yielded by breaking Axis codes that halted and reversed German and Japanese military advances.

The defeat of Nazi Germany militarily meant also the defeat morally of its core values of cultural commonality and ethnic purity. But as symbolized by the coordinated invasion of Germany by American and Soviet troops from along the Western and Eastern Fronts, it was a defeat that also brought American and Soviet visions of modernity—their contrary individualist and collectivist universalisms—into face-to-face confrontation. The scientific, technological, and industrial means to Allied victory had the unexpected consequence of sparking the cybernetics revolution of the second half of the twentieth century, but also of setting the terms of

Cold War competition between the powers that assumed global leadership for the material reconstruction and axiological revision of cosmopolis.

The Iron Curtain that soon dropped between the Soviet-aligned East and the American-aligned West not only polarized global political dynamics, it also polarized the dynamics of military-industrial development and communications. The military engagements of the Cold War were primarily prosecuted through proxies against a backdrop of increasingly sophisticated surveillance and espionage. The Cold War's ideological engagements were, of course, prosecuted most visibly and synoptically in the media as a standoff between Soviet and American universalisms. But the most decisive measure of their competitive advantages was neither military nor ideological in nature; it was the quantitatively "objective" metric of economic growth. And it was in economic terms—not conceptual ones—that the advantages of Western market liberalism came to be correspondingly evident.

Although great advances were realized through both Soviet and American Cold War R&D, it was in the context of the market-driven, choice-multiplying, and autonomy-engendering dynamics of the democratic West that the results of Cold War R&D were most rapidly, effectively, and widely translated into nonmilitary applications and civilian benefits. In comparison with the American model, the Soviet combination of a command economy and centrally coordinated, government-censored communications stifled rather than stimulated innovation. As Western industry and commerce were infused with the results of Cold War R&D, geometrically expanding gains were made in promoting communication, choice, and consumption. The result was a dramatic biasing of global circuits of economic exchange in favor of Western-style entrepreneurial industrialism, the rise of the network, the increasing valorization of individuality, and the growing power of immaterial economic "engines" that did not run on material fuels, but rather on sustainably captured attention.

The disparate outcomes of Soviet and American efforts to demonstrate ideological, military, and economic superiority might be seen as a warrant for announcing the triumph of the latter's vision of progress. But insofar as the agendas of Soviet and American universalism were framed in strategic response to a world torn asunder by fascist totalism and both German and Japanese ethnocentric communalism, this conclusion requires greater nuance. The Soviet Union and the United States were able to *compete* precisely because they both forwarded a vision of modernization in which the identities and traditions of the past were to be progressively discarded, not unlike stages of the rockets by means of which they began launching satellites into orbit around the Earth in the late 1950s. Seen from a certain angle, the Cold War was fought in defense of distinct approaches to achieving the modern ideal of national (and eventually, global) unity in the face of historically acute differences. The Soviet Union geographically incorporated and institutionally bound a remarkable range of European, Central Asian, and East Asian ethnic groups and nationalities, and differences among them were disarmed through promises of achieving a prosperous and egalitarian collective destiny. The United States, through immigration and the effects of the transatlantic slave trade, incorporated people from across Europe, West Africa, and Pacific Asia, and undertook disarming differences among them by promising equal opportunity to each individual and guarantees of liberty for all.

For those sensitive to the plight of people(s) who are denigrated and persecuted on the basis of being different, however, it was by no means clear that either of these strategies for progressively responding to the modern "fact of plurality" was ultimately better than the other. Neither was it clear that the goal of building cosmopolis was in fact one that would be universally beneficial. Over the 1950s and 1960s, especially for those still with fresh memories of fascist occupation and the Holocaust, or those caught up in the battle between American and Soviet interests, it was especially hard not to worry about the coercive potential resident in all universalisms. And even within the United States and the Soviet Union, universalistic promises of progress were by no means ringing true for all. French postmodernism was formulated in the context of American counterculture, civil rights, and antiwar movements, surging dissidence in the Soviet Union following Brezhnev's decisive repeal of Khrushchev's "thaw," and predatory designs on global hegemony emanating from both Washington and Moscow. And in that historical context, postmodernism can be seen as giving incisive expression to globally felt needs to renounce any and all attempts at erasing difference, whether under the aegis of totalitarian nativism or that of either individualist or collectivist universalism.

If the Second World War is seen as a defense of modernity against the threat of a communalist, fascist reconstruction of premodernity, the escalation of the Cold War can be seen as having forced a defense of difference against the threat of a potentially apocalyptic Third World War between competing universalistic visions of hegemonic Sameness. Against all single-order visions of cosmopolis, Levinas, Derrida, Deleuze, and their heirs argued that the most sound and sustainable route beyond intolerance and the violence of all centrally imposed hierarchies was not to circumvent or supersede differences by whatever modern means necessary, but rather through valuing—and changing the meaning of—difference itself.

As influenced by Levinas, postmodern thought called into question whether the individual could or should be seen as the basic unit of ethical analysis. With memories still fresh of the tragic and totalitarian ramifications of Nazi German invocations of commonality, Levinas and his heirs sought to locate ethicality neither in the individual subject nor in communally defined practices and values, but rather in the relational dynamics of the intersubjective. Crucial to this was an epistemic rejection of univocity and an ontological affirmation of hierarchy-denying mutuality. As it happened, however, while conceiving of epistemology, ethics, and ontology as investigations of difference—understood as articulations of absence—did prove effective in countering modern metanarratives and biases toward presence or the myth of the given, it also dovetailed quite well with market imperatives for maximizing the spatial and temporal density of consumption through hyperindividuated valorizations of choice. That is, the at least tacit relativism of postmodern approaches to issues of difference coincided with global market needs to expand the scopes of personal autonomy and consumer sovereignty, and with liberal political emphases on voluntary association and elective participation—a combination conducive to the percolation of self-interested decision making into virtually every aspect of daily life and identity construction.

Strangely, then, the confluence of conditions through which postmodern thought came to be formulated and then lifted into academic and popular prominence by the late 1970s was also conducive to the ascent of rational choice theory from its think-tank origins to its ranking as the premier perspective on strategic governmental and corporate decision- and policy making. On the surface, postmodern thought and rational choice theory would seem to be in critically sharp tension if not diametric opposition. Rational choice theory insists, after all, that the individual is and should be the natural unit of analysis in efforts to optimize decision making outcomes. But with roots in Arrow's assumption that individual ends and interests cannot be intersubjectively ranked, rational choice theory naturalizes horizontally arrayed differences, interpreting individuality quite literally as indivisibility. In this, it has much in common with postmodern tendencies toward relativity rather than universality, and toward seeing differentiation processes in rhizomatic rather than arboreal terms. And, in essential agreement with postmodern thought, rational choice theory does *not* invoke a world ordered from above on universal principles, promoting instead a self-organizing world with intimate connections to the automatically optimizing behaviors of free markets. In short: postmodernism, rational choice theory, and free market liberalism converge on the ideal of *free variation*.[21]

From Cosmopolis to Netropolis

The confluence of dramatic currents to which we have been directing our attention thus suggests seeing the contemporary aporia of difference as marking the site of a basic and karmically charged shift of *agendas*: a transit from the utopian, universalistic, and fundamentally hierarchic project of seamlessly merging natural, social, economic, political, cultural, and techno-scientific orders to a no less utopian project of realizing a relativistic "anarchy" of free variation. Given the current dominance of the tropes of networking and the World Wide Web, we might characterize this as shifting from the social construction of the *grid* to that of the *net* (Taylor 2001)—a shift from the idealization of *cosmopolis* to that of *netropolis*.

To date, much of the thinking about the interdependent (and, indeed, interpenetrating) arcs of change in which we find ourselves has focused on the multiple and pivotal roles being played by information and communications technology; hence, the tendency in both popular and policy circles has been to proclaim our entry into the "information age." But as Lars Qvortrup (2003) has rightly insisted, the emphasis on information is too narrow to capture the dramatic nature of the shift in which we find ourselves. Ours is a "hypercomplex" era, the dynamic character of which is most clearly brought into view by emphasizing the structural transformation being wrought by the technologically mediated processes and domain-crossing valorizations of the network (Castells 1996, 1997, 1998).

As noted by Castells, network structures bias change dynamics toward collaboratively significant, yet spatially discontinuous and temporally variable, patterns of interest-focused interaction. For many, networks have an intrinsic potential for fostering utopian mergers of the real and the ideal. Some have gone so far as to see the advent of the Net and the birth of essentially elective and egalitarian "virtual communities" as signaling the dawn of an era in which new means-to community are opening new meanings-of community: an historically unprecedented expansion and alliance of the meanings of immediacy and democracy (Rheingold 1993, 2000). If the metropolis was the symbol of modernity—the city or *polis* as uterine mother, *mater*—then modernity's obsolescence is signaled by the cinematic dissolve of hard, grid-work metropolitan spaces into holographic nets wherein distance cannot matter because *each* space is capable of granting access to *any* space.

Cosmopolis expressed a utopian vision of a world ordered "from above"—a world explicitly organized around rationally derived universal principles in which differences are ultimately rendered contingent and subordinate to our shared "human nature." Cosmopolis conjures a society of equals set on a trajectory of controlled and irreversible progress toward ever more fully engineered and unifying means-to and meanings-of the good life. Netropolis expresses a no less utopian vision. But it is instead a vision of a world that is dynamically self-originating and self-regulating—a world in and through which nothing is imposed, in which everything is implicitly subject to autonomously exercised choice, in which differentiation is associated with play and yet understood as necessary, and in which the means-to and meanings-of a good life are irreducibly plural and ever varying.[22]

The narrative I have sketched about the past half century suggests an arc of dissolving modern values, intentions, and practices/institutions leading to the end of cosmopolis as an epochal ideal, not as a function of external factors, but rather as an ironic and complex function of its own successes. This is a point stressed by Beck, Giddens, and Lash (1994) in their joint elaboration of the dynamics of "reflexive modernization." The internally related vectors of convergence on the idealization and realization of netropolis—that is, the postmodern valorization of difference, the validation of rational choice theory's strategic celebration of individualism, and the global-market reconciliation of tensions between autonomy and equality through the medium of an infinitely burgeoning attention economy—suggest global movement away from hierarchy to anarchy, from the bias for *being-as-presence* to that for *presence-in-absence*. With this, the modern conception and idealization of progress have been undermined.

There cannot be a "master plan" for netropolis. It is not that kind of utopia. The increasing force of the vectors of convergence on free variation has the effect, finally, of a möbius-strip twisting of the modern ideal of progress so that public utopianism is rendered apparently distinct, but in actuality inseparable, from the realization of personal autonomy. The hidden *agenda* of modernity is not so much abandoned in netropolis as it is subjected to a critical recursion that reveals it as a continuous expression of the means-to and meanings-of exercising ever less limited individual *agency*—an "inalienable" right to differ-from all others.

THE FUTURE AS FREE VARIATION

My charting of the historical currents from the market crash of 1929 through the rise of German fascism and moral nativism, the Cold War competition between individualist and collectivist universalisms, the hyperindividualizing consumer and communications revolutions, and the parallel rise of rational choice liberalism and difference-valuing postmodernity has *not* been presented to suggest a pattern of teleological change. Much as the "rise of the West" in the early period of global industrialization is best understood as a contingent function of an array of factors that could easily have been otherwise (Goldstone 2001), the contemporary pattern of multidomain and multiscale convergence on paradoxical celebrations of and conflicts over difference is *not* an expression of global destiny. At the same time, however, it is not just a phase in an essentially random sequence of events. The global confrontation with the limits to universality, the problem-to-predicament transition, the dramatic advent of world-risk society, and the intensifying aporia of difference describe a distinctive *arc of emergence* that, while it was not and perhaps could not have been anticipated, is nevertheless profoundly meaningful.

Moreover, in drawing attention to difference-biased internal relationships among ethical, sociopolitical, and economic vectors of change, it has not been my intention to discount the real and ideal ramifications of globalization's simultaneous production of integrative dynamics. These have been and continue to be tremendously significant. Instead, the narrative I have presented has aimed at making visible how these integrative tendencies, epitomized by the modern agenda of cosmopolis, have come to be transmuted into (and not simply replaced by) the differential biases of netropolis. The climax of the narrative, then, is not the sudden demise of universalistic ideals or their blunt subordination to relativistic realities, but rather their dual sublimation into what might be called agent-focused virtuality.

Finally, charting these currents through the domains of economics, politics, and ethics as I have should not be taken as in any way exhaustive. Many other mappings of the relational dynamics of the twentieth century could have been undertaken. But calling attention to resonances among the economic, political, and ethical dimensions of these dynamics is particularly effective, I think, in revealing the critical liabilities of treating issues of difference as problems rather than as predicaments. Just as the meaning of globalization varies greatly depending on how and where one is positioned with respect to its constitutive flows, engagements with and valuations of difference differ dramatically. But perhaps more importantly, attending to resonances among ethical, sociopolitical, and economic patterns of change helps bring into focus the complexity of globalization-driven multiplications and magnifications of difference, forcing us to abandon the comfortingly modern tendency to construct issues of difference in linear and dichotomous terms. If we are to understand and critically engage the "hidden agenda" of netropolis, we must at the very least factor into our considerations the recognition that difference is not only a cause for *celebration* or *conflict*, but also a locus of intensifying *commodification*. Indeed, as has been made powerfully evident by the cascade of events following the financial sector collapse in the fall of 2008, issues of difference occurring in any one domain can only be effectively addressed by seeing them as interdependent with those occurring in others.

This last point bears some further adumbration as it links us to the next turn in our conversation. Although the emerging attention economy has over the past quarter century made the value of difference a matter of explicit and central concern, as David Harvey (1996) has eloquently and extensively argued, the vibrancy of global capitalism—even in its most resolutely industrial and materially oriented phases—has always been intimately tied to the production and, indeed, proliferation of geographies of difference. The modern bias toward individuation plays out across scales as localities, cities, nations, and regions compete with one another for global capital, attracting the greatest possible proportion of economically relevant attention possible through strategic differentiation. In language that has global ethical implications: the growth of free markets depends— as Adam Smith insisted—on the production of inequalities or hierarchies of advantage and disadvantage. Indeed, it could be argued that all value can be traced back to difference, be it biological, cultural, social, political, or techno-scientific. Generically stated: adaptive responses both depend on and enhance capacities for differentiation. At least for sentient beings, *discerning and making differences is perhaps the most basic subsistence need.*

Stating matters this way allows us to bring our relational narrative into more pointed focus. If Ivan Illich (1973) rightly observed that any commodification of a basic need institutionalizes a new class of the poor, what are we to make of the apparently deepening interdependence among celebratory, conflicted, and commodifying patterns of ethical, sociopolitical, and economic convergence on difference? If we admit that the production of differences, including differences that take the form of inequalities of both outcomes and opportunities, is not an accident of contemporary industrialization and globalization processes but rather inherent to them; if these patterns of differentiation are not simply linear matters of fact, but rather recursively amplifying expressions of systematically deployed constellations of values; and if these patterns of differentiation are evidence of disparities in wealth, income, resources and relational outcomes/opportunities, then are we not compelled to admit as well that the ideals of netropolis and its agenda of free variation are relationally impoverishing?

The relational arcs of change in which we find ourselves embroiled are neither necessary nor accidental. They are processes for which *we* are responsible—not individually or collectively, but rather complexly and interdependently. In Buddhist terms, these arcs of change are our karma, a function of consistently configured arrays of values, intentions, and actions. To break away from the currents of change carrying us from cosmopolis to netropolis, from universalism to relativism, from singular vertical orders to multiple horizontal ones, and from progress to free variation, we must change our karma in relation to difference. The means-to and meaning-of realizing greater equity is not free variation, but enhanced diversification.

CHAPTER EIGHT

Delinking Equity and Equality

Over the course of the last several chapters, I have tried oscillating between historical and philosophical optics to generate depth perspective on the emergence of difference as a crucial contemporary issue and concern. Historically, my aim has been to compose a convincing set of precedents for seeing that the predicament-rich character of contemporary realities is not an anomaly, but rather a significant (and ironic) result of the complex interplay among modernization, individualization, marketization, and globalization processes. Philosophically, I have tried to establish the plausibility of seeing the unevenness and inequalities of contemporary global dynamics as critically entrained with aporetic confrontations with difference that call into question the longstanding bias—dominant in the modern global West and North— toward regarding the individual human being as the basic unit of moral, legal, and ethical concern. At the same time, I have tried to raise questions about the adequacy of modern/universalist and postmodern/relativist perspectives on ethics and justice for effective engagement with this unevenness and inequality.

When set against our opening discussions of differences as irreducibly oriented processes of differentiation—that is, as qualitatively distinct *occurrences* of relational modulation—this oscillation has the intended effect of bringing into view the progressive coalescence of conditions for the coemergence of contemporary concerns about difference and revived and substantially revised concerns about equity. That is, it brings into focus both increasingly explicit needs to address the values-infused conjunction of economics and ethics, and critical precedents for two claims made thus far only in passing: 1) that, in the context of complex global interdependence, diversity and equity should be seen as global relational commons and public goods; and 2) that realizing greater equity entails enhancing, not equality, but diversity.

THE DIVORCE OF ETHICS AND ECONOMICS

The imperative to critically address the interplay of ethics and economics is nothing new. We can see in fourth- and fifth-century BCE classical Greek and Buddhist analyses linking poverty and wealth inequalities with civil unrest, crime, social disintegration, contracting horizons of care and concern, and moral decline, that the relationship between economics and ethics was understood as intimate and as deserving critical engagement at least from early antiquity. Attention given to issues of economic justice in eighth- and ninth-century Islamic jurisprudence, in the eleventh-century reforms of Wang Anshi in Song dynasty China, in the thirteenth-century writings of Thomas Aquinas, and in the social contract theories of social justice proposed by Thomas Hobbes, John Locke, and Jean-Jacques Rousseau in the seventeenth and eighteenth centuries demonstrates an ongoing and critical marriage of ethics and economics that remained vibrant through the early part of the modern era.

Convictions that morality and ethics are naturally and properly in critical interplay with economics first began breaking down perhaps with the mercantilism of the fifteenth to seventeenth centuries. But their "great divergence" accelerated decisively following Adam Smith's groundbreaking, 1776 treatise on modern markets, *The Wealth of Nations*. From this point forward, their divorce was imminent, and by the end of the nineteenth century it was for all intents and purposes an accomplished (if not entirely unprotested) fact. Throughout the modern era to the final third of the twentieth century, the clearly dominant trend has been for the ethical to be forcibly extruded from economic theory and method—an intellectual parallel of what Polanyi described as the progressive disembedding of the economy from society as a functionally autonomous system.

There is much to be learned from this extrusion of the ethical regarding our current prospects of responding in equity-enhancing ways to the kinds of domain- and scale-crossing predicaments that increasingly characterize local, national, regional and global dynamics. Consciousness of tensions between economic realities and ethical ideals was widespread in the eighteenth century. The unevenness of modern/market development was by midcentury, for example, at the heart of heated debates across Europe regarding whether the supply of subsistence needs should be left to free market mechanisms or undertaken under governmental supervision. As widening gaps became apparent in the distribution of benefits accruing from market-directed economic growth—and along with this, increasingly aggravated class stratifications—the jeopardy into which overall social well-being was placed by unconstrained and eventually industrially powered markets was quite palpable, and it was deemed by many to be both morally repugnant and politically reprehensible.

From the Moral Work of Markets to the Mathematics of Economic Justice

Smith attempted to meet these concerns head-on, arguing on historical grounds that, far from being morally worrisome, market-generated inequality is best seen as a morally justified concomitant to securing basic needs for all.[1] In terms that two centuries later would be vigorously applauded by his neoliberal redactors, Smith averred that market-produced inequalities would naturally redound to the benefit of all, as if guided by an "invisible hand." Smith's aim was to demonstrate that market dynamics were shaped by natural economic laws and that market processes were the best means by which human beings, in keeping with their God-given nature, could make use of and allocate the resources over which they had rightful, divinely bestowed dominion. For his own part, Smith did acknowledge the limitations of markets in supplying the full range of goods beneficial to society as a whole. With at least tacit allegiance to sensibilities expressed in his earlier *Theory of Moral Sentiments*, he was a seminal advocate of state-provided "public goods" like education and transportation infrastructure as crucial elements in avoiding market failures and assuring uninterrupted economic and political growth. His legacy, however, was less complex: since markets regulate themselves naturally in ways that result in the best possible uses of resources and allocations of wealth, human agency—at least in terms of its moral valence—could be left out of direct economic account.

From the beginning of the nineteenth century, inclinations to accord ethics even a tangential role in shaping economics were being pressed out of the mainstream with ever deepening resolve. Most notably through the theoretical and methodological contributions of David Ricardo, the extrusion of ethics from economics began to assume canonical status as economics came to be viewed as a universal, objective, and value-neutral scientific enterprise. Indeed, as economic theory and method assumed an ever more thoroughly mathematical character in open emulation of science and especially physics, many intellectuals came to see economic laws—like other empirically revealed laws of nature—as intermediate between the eternal law of God and temporally realized human law.

This trend, in its main outlines, was no less evident among those who were *not* persuaded by Smith's defense of market-produced inequalities and who were inclined instead toward envisioning critical alternatives to market economics. Like the classical market theory forwarded by Ricardo, socialist economics was predominantly framed as a scientific extension of the natural history of economic and social relations. As evidenced in the work of J. C. L. Simonde de Sismondi and then that of Johann Karl Rodbertus and Karl Marx, nineteenth-century socialism sought to reveal the operation of natural laws destined to carry humanity beyond life within and in service (or servitude) to capitalist markets. In Marx's vision of postcapitalist modernity, issues of fair distribution would not be solved, but rather *dissolved* through the historically inevitable realization of universal and scientific socialism, rendering obsolete the culture-bound, bourgeois moralities previously needed to manage conflict. Thus, in spite of drawing attention to the dynamics of exploitation that fueled capitalist markets, and implicitly granting socialist modernity a kind of ethical superiority, Marx and his heirs can be seen as substantially in league with classical market economists in their efforts, first, to naturalize the subordination of ethics to economics, and then to instigate their full and final divorce. The social function of ethics could be taken over by economic science.

There were, of course, those like John Stuart Mill who insisted on the integration of political economy and social philosophy, and for whom economics was deemed sterile in the absence of social conscience. But, as Douglas Vickers has succinctly observed, the dominant intellectual climate of the nineteenth and early twentieth century "abetted the rush to establish a value-free enquiry and to separate from economics the impact of ethics and its normativities" (Vickers 1997, 6). From John Neville Keynes' formulation of positivist economics, to Lionel Robbins' location of economics in the objective behaviors and structures linking ends and scarce means, to the aggressive mathematicization of economics initiated in earnest by Leon Walrus, on to the nascent neoliberalism of Friedrich Hayek and Milton Friedman, the overwhelming orientation in economic theory and methodology through the final third of the twentieth century was toward the strict (and some would argue, ultimately just) exclusion of ethics.

This trend began showing substantial signs of weakening only over the final quarter of the twentieth century, in apparent sympathy with, on one hand, postmodern philosophical contestations of universalism, rationalism, and value-free objectivity, and, on the other, with social constructivist qualifications of such core, market liberal concepts as freedom, equality, utility, and the autonomously rational, self-interested individual. With ever-widening acknowledgement that the means-ends distinction is at best relative rather than absolute, and that the relationships between persons and communities—and by extension between economic actors and systems—is complex, recursively structured, and prone to nonlinear, emergence-rich change, the supposition that economics could and should be purified of ethics as a value-neutral science came to strike many as an unsustainable and self-contradictory fiction in the process of being shattered.[2]

A TURNING POINT: PLACING EQUITY IN JOINT ETHICAL/ECONOMIC CUSTODY

If Smith marks a turning point beyond which economics would vigorously dissociate itself from explicit normative considerations for the better part of two centuries, John Rawls' (1971) *Theory of Justice* marks an equivalently significant turn back toward joint economic and ethical critical engagement with normative issues. Much as Smith remained essentially true to the commitments expressed in his *Theory of Moral Sentiments* in his theoretical justification of market economics, Rawls remained very much true to his inheritances from the eighteenth- and nineteenth-century liberal social contract theories of Hobbes, Locke, and Rousseau, and from Kant's deontological approach to ethics. In framing the political and economic foundations of justice as fairness, Rawls unabashedly modern aim was to provide a generic/universal solution for all problems of fair distribution by thinking through the implications of making choices regarding socioeconomic and political structures and processes from an "original position" located behind a "veil of ignorance." Rawls' conviction was that if rational individuals had no knowledge of facts about themselves or their circumstances of the kind that would affect their choices, then their deliberations about how best to organize society would assure that each individual would have equal rights to obtaining the most extensive possible array of primary goods (including liberties) that is consistent with all others enjoying the same rights; that any inequalities would be such as to afford both benefit to all and the greatest benefit to society's least advantaged (the "maximin" or "difference principle"); and that every position in society would be open with equal opportunity for all.

Upon publication, Rawls' a priori construction of justice began drawing criticism that would eventually encompass libertarian, communitarian, feminist, and postcolonial perspectives. A key point of contention for many critics was the explicitly ahistorical and purely hypothetical nature of the Rawlsian "original position"—a position that expressed allegiance to an unapologetically modern conception of persons as essentially autonomous, rational individuals rather than concretely situated and relationally constituted. These immediate and pointed criticisms make all the more striking the tremendous impact of *The Theory of Justice*, over precisely the period of time (from the early 1970s through the 1980s) when liberalism-challenging postmodern sensibilities were coming into the critical foreground. This impact seems explainable in part by Rawls' efforts to delink justice and law, reclaiming for justice explicitly moral and ethical dimensions, and arguing on behalf of their relevance for responding to issues of inequality falling within the domains of politics and economics.

But, in addition (albeit in ways consonant with prevailing canons of market liberalism), Rawls also insisted on the inclusion of robust considerations of difference in any socially just construction of political, economic, and social relations. However hypothetically, his "maximin" or "difference principle" explicitly linked justice with difference in ways that gave at least tacit warrant to reviving aspects of a rich historical tradition in which invoking considerations of equity functioned as a counter to unfair and morally troubling consequences of adhering strictly to the letter of the law and the (fictitious) equality of all before it.

Equity as Taking Differences into Account:
An Alternative to Universally Mandated Justice

In the nominally "Western" lineage from which Rawls drew direct inspiration, the earliest iterations of the concept of equity can be traced back to the foundational philosophical works of Plato and Aristotle. In the *Statesman*, for example, Plato allowed that because of the complexity of human circumstances and the nonuniformities characteristic of them, universal and standardized law codes are not always able to determine what *should* be done in a given case. There is a fineness of grain in our lives as persons-in-community that no generically formulated systems of rules and precedents is going to be capable of taking into account. Often, however, doing precisely that is crucial to insuring fairness of outcomes. Following this reasoning, Aristotle positively characterized equity as involving corrective attention to particularity and difference in the pursuit of justice. Situations arise in which strictly applied statutory laws prove to be defective in delivering justice, precisely because of their universality.

This conception of equity as a route to justice that takes primary account of difference and particularity carries forward through Roman times into medieval Europe. This was perhaps most explicit in the institutionalized English conception of equity as a moral complement to statutory law—a separate "court of appeal" originally associated with the office of the king and later with the Chancery as the locus of royal, moral conscience. Active Courts of Chancery could be found in England well into the early modern period, and were operative in several of the American colonies, even after gaining independence. In sum, through the birth of modernity, the function of appeals to equity was to assess the effects of equality before the law in pursuit of greater fairness.

Not surprisingly, perhaps, this began changing as modern institutions matured, as the breakdown of sociocultural traditions and industrialization processes intensified, and as the values of objectivity, autonomy, and choice assumed greater and more general prominence. Legal disputes began to range across social classes and societies. The explosive growth of commerce and the crafting of new structures of political power had the combined effect of progressively undercutting the determinative effects of heredity, complementing (if not spurring) philosophical and religious claims that one's life circumstances mirror one's strengths and qualities of volition, choice, and agency. Under these conditions, appeals to equity came under conceptual criticism as irreducibly subjective and as liable to resulting in unpredictably variable rulings.[3] As John Selden famously remarked in the seventeenth century, using equity as a measure of justice was like taking the length of a foot (twelve inches) to be equal to that of the changing feet (or consciences) of successive occupants of the Office of Chancery. Eventually, the institutions for contesting the delivery of justice through equality before the law were dismantled.

Equity as a Function of Financial Accounting

As the conception of equity as a difference-sensitive corrective to legally defined justice was losing it institutional basis, an economic notion of equity was consolidating that would in many ways come to overshadow its ethically inflected kin: equity understood as the capital-generating and thus productively exploitable difference between the market value of a good or property and claims against it—a ratio of circumstantially varying assets and fixed liabilities. Equity in this financially inflected sense is a fundamentally quantitative concept that relates ownership, the distribution of startup and operational costs, the contingency of changing circumstances, and distributions of benefits in joint business and investment ventures.

From the late nineteenth into the early twentieth century, in the context of deliberations regarding a broad class of issues surrounding problems of fairly distributing or allocating goods and burdens in society as a whole, qualitative and difference-sensitive concerns about fairness came to be paired with quantitative assessments of rights, claims, and values. As mentioned earlier, the increasingly uneven distribution of the costs and benefits of industrialization and marketization was of great concern to those committed to realizing truly progressive political economies. And especially from the turn of the twentieth century onward, wide-ranging critical responses to the realities of unequal development were being mounted on the basis of emerging welfare, social choice, and social justice theories that aimed at rationally managing the dynamics of economic growth. In contrast with the premodern considerations of how universally applied laws might fail to bring justice to particular persons/families under certain circumstances, a decidedly modern and fundamentally economic conception of equity coalesced around public considerations of the general impacts of development on different population aggregates—the working classes, women, children, immigrants, and so on. Here, while inequalities were taken as given, the question of equity was an essentially quantitative one of determining the point at which inequality was not only unfair, but developmentally counterproductive.

Where Ethics and Economics Came to Meet: Equity as Opportunity Justice

As we have already seen, the first phase of modernization (from roughly 1750 to 1950) was characterized by the dissolution of traditional *communities* that were organically sustained through ongoing rehearsals of shared meaning, and their replacement by malleable and readily manageable *collectives* of individuals organized around shared interests. This blending of emancipatory and disciplinary dynamics fostered a practical bifurcation of the subjective and objective poles of experience, as well as the normalization of explicitly instrumental constructions of social relations.

The dominant trend in ethics over this period was to focus concern on rationally defining the foundations of appropriate individual behavior. Although virtue ethics emphasizing personal character development still held considerable sway, the defining ethics of the modern era—Kantian deontology and Bentham's utilitarianism—understood the path to appropriate behavior and social relations to be a process of aligning subjectively formed intentions and consequent actions with either universal rules and duties or universally desired results. Equity thus came to be associated with establishing conditions for maximizing and integrating *expressions of individual agency* as the basic motive force in society.

As just noted, over the same time, economics was first largely purified of ethical oversight and thereafter formulated an essentially quantitative conception of equity around considerations of the degree to which developmental goods and burdens were being distributed in ways that maximized collective welfare and continued growth. Equity in this sense consists in an *objective structural achievement*—a condition that predominant, late modern currents of economic theory framed as being realized as a result of inexorable historical processes (Marxist dialectics), no less inexorable market processes (Smith's "invisible hand"), or mathematically warranted logistical interventions (Walrasian general equilibrium).

Thus, in spite of their practical divorce, modern economic and ethical constructions of equity converged on a common inclination to regard equity as resulting from consistent *compliance with universal laws*. These laws might be derived mathematically (resulting, for example, in Pareto-optimal distributions of income and wealth via competitive market-clearing exchanges) or ideologically (resulting, for instance, in granting full rights of social participation to women and minorities). What mattered was that the relevant laws were not arbitrary expressions of personal whim, but rather the yield of rational deliberations undertaken on the basis of universally applicable principles. Thus, in the context of both empirically framed scientific economics and conceptually framed universalistic ethics, the overarching tendency was to legitimate disregard for the exceptional as methodologically just. Achieving equity was understood, ultimately, as a design issue—a function of material and/or moral engineering.

Through roughly the middle of the twentieth century, then, the concept of equity can be seen as being reshaped by apparently opposing but ultimately complementary intellectual and practical currents: one moving in the direction of increasing objectivity and quantification, the other in the direction of increasing subjectivity and abstraction. The combined result was a decisive orientation away from the traditional identification of equity with ensuring discursively attained and qualitatively just *concrete outcomes* for specific persons as members of a relationally dense community. Instead, equity came to be seen as a public state of affairs in which structurally attained and quantifiably just *generic opportunities* were guaranteed for all as members of irreducibly plural societies. This definitively modern conception of equity, while it ambitiously shifted focus from what is fair for a particular person to what would be fair for the greatest number of people, also had the effect of progressively masking the line between manifest facts of difference and increasingly convoluted fictions of equality.

EQUITY AS A UNIVERSALLY DEFINED
CONDITION OF FAIRNESS

To summarize the discussion thus far: along the main lines of conceptual and institutional development from Plato and Aristotle through the English courts to public responses to twentieth-century socioeconomic and political confrontations with problems of fair distribution, equity issues can be seen as primarily revolving "around the question of how *differences* in claims—due to disparities in merit, desert, contribution, need and so forth—should be taken into account" (Young 1994, 12). Especially in the period from the late nineteenth through the mid-twentieth century, this came to be understood as a matter of paying attention to how decisions made in the context of specific circumstances might comparatively affect particular legal individuals (whether persons, corporations, towns, voting districts, or nations). That is, the prevailing conceptions of equity through most of the twentieth century evidenced a significant premodern heritage that emphasized addressing differences as contingent factors that might be irrelevant in most cases but that will occasionally warrant direct and careful attention. Even in its minimally ethical economic formulations, equity issues continued to be seen as arising when impartiality in the form of strict adherence to the fiction of equality would result in given individuals—of whatever scale—being unfairly treated.

The shift of equity considerations from concrete outcomes to generic opportunities marks a decisive departure from this premodern heritage— a shift that was taken to its logical limit in the kind of equity that Rawls envisioned as being essential to any just society. Yet, while Rawls' conception can be seen as quintessentially modern, it is a concept that (like Smith's conception of morally justified markets) would prove to be both highly influential and ironically transitional. In the context of his overarching theory of justice, equity is functionally aligned with correcting or compensating for potential *structural* inequalities through a preemptive derivation of universally applicable principles and rules. Rather than directing attention to specific individuals or to society as a collective whole, attention is focused on imagined public (not private) identities and classes. In effect, equity concerns in his hypothetically just society do not bear on *who* I am, but rather on *the kind* of person I *might* be. While the consideration of difference remains crucial to equity, the locus of consideration turns from specific persons/groups in concrete situations to generic individuals/groups in a maximally abstract situation. Equity does not depend on empirical determinations of what is fair. Actual persons and populations are, in fact, entirely irrelevant. Equity is ensured through a completely and purposely a priori method.

As it happened, this universally framed, ideologically liberal and a priori approach to conceiving and socially attaining equity resonated powerfully with key dramatic currents of late twentieth-century modernity and markets. The idea that society could be proactively and equitably structured in accordance with modern values that would ensure maximal autonomy, freedoms-of-choice, resource access, and social opportunity to all was (and remains) profoundly seductive. Developed in the context of ongoing civil rights struggles, the rise of feminism, and increasing sensitivity to issues of ethnicity, Rawls' theory of justice asked that every individual in society consider the implications of being born into any position in society and to structure society accordingly. And the requested liberation from how things are gave credence to a wide range of progressive beliefs in possibilities for change.

But in a complex and network-organized world in which growth entails accelerating interaction, amplified differentiation, and emergent— that is, in principle unpredictable and yet significant—change, Rawls' approach to imagining a more just future easily devolved into ethical and institutional distraction. While it can be seen as having contributed to the development of a conception of equity sensitive to the contemporary aporia of difference, it did not provide the resources needed for breaking through that aporia. In part, this was because of his theory's primary focus on taking purely potential differences into account. In part, however, it was because of continued allegiance to a construction of personal identity and agency that was being rapidly undermined by emerging socioeconomic realities.

REFLEXIVE MODERNIZATION AND THE MYTH OF EQUAL VANTAGES

Roughly from the end of the Second World War, as trajectories of scientific and technological change steepened in the context of Cold War competitions, the ambit of instrumental rationality and technological control grew with extraordinary rapidity. This dramatically expanded the scope, scale, and complexity of modernization, industrialization, and globalization processes, as well as their impacts in the personal, cultural, social, economic, and political spheres. As these processes crossed crucial quantitative and qualitative thresholds, a new era of "reflexive modernization" (Beck, Giddens, and Lash 1994) and "world risk society" (Beck 1992) was ushered in—an era in which sustaining economic growth depends on continuously amplifying risks and generating unforeseeable threats in the face of which responsible decisions nevertheless have to be made (Beck 1999; Wynne 1996). Importantly, this production of threats, risks, and hazards is not evidence of the *failure* of modern industrial, market, and expert systems; it is evidence of their *successes*. Reflexive modernization begins when the successes of these systems bring about such dense, extensive, and efficient patterns of global interaction that it is no longer possible either to externalize or fully insure against the (environmental, health, social, cultural, and political) costs of further growth.[4]

Much as the emancipatory dynamics of the first phase of modernity had their disciplinary shadow, the dynamics of reflexive modernity are shadowed with substantial irony. This is particularly evident in connection with the individuation processes central to modernization. At the point of becoming reflexive, individuation processes no longer consist solely in disruptions of traditional relationship structures that progressively free people to define the terms of their own lives; they begin to disrupt the unity of the self, shattering the ontological cornerstone of liberal ideology—the autonomous, purportedly "atomic" individual.

Whereas traditional societies are organized around communal identity structures and hereditary values, and modern societies around collective identity structures and elective values, reflexively modern societies are dynamically biased toward the "progressive freeing of agency from structure" (Lash, 1994: 119) In effect, agents are required to respond to ever-greater scopes of (and demands for) choice or decision making, and to assume responsibility for "reflecting" critically on the rules and resources constitutive of prevailing societal structures. This critical turn is not taken in a value-neutral environment, however, or on anything like a level playing field. Under conditions of reflexive modernity, the market logic of continuously expanding ranges and densities of experiential choice and consumption exerts pressures on each individual (agent/consumer) to question existing social forms (especially those related to work, family, and gender), to continuously construct (and reconstruct) his or her own identities and life narratives, *and* to do so under conditions of heightened ambiguity, uncertainty, and risk (Giddens 1992)—all even as one's attention is being systematically captured and sent into circulation as a basic "fuel" of the global economy. Being given continuously expanding choices with respect to an expanding array of real-life issues is, under these circumstances, to be given ever-greater opportunities for making the *wrong* choices, with more and more at stake.[5]

Two points must be emphasized in this connection. First, the freeing of agency from structure is ultimately also a forfeiting of essential self-definition. Under conditions of reflexive modernity, *the unity of the self is not a given.* Second, the resources for skillfully undertaking the kind of reflection needed to engage skillfully in identity construction and responding to risk are by no means evenly distributed. In the context of free market exchanges and a global attention economy, the proliferation of opportunities and imperatives for identity construction is inseparable from the magnification and multiplication of real quantitative and qualitative differences of access to material, conceptual, and relational resources. Fairness can hardly be expected to be a *result* of granting equivalent opportunities for choice to all when the resources and conditions for *making choices* are themselves not fairly distributed or structured.

On one level, then, as the construction of self and personal growth are ever more powerfully tied to assuming amplified individual risk, freedom from meaning-conferring structures and the prescriptive unity of the self easily translates into mounting stress and heightened insecurity.[6] Given this, it is not surprising that stress-related illnesses have become major public health concerns over especially the last half century. On another level, however, granted the contemporary reality that in matters of identity we have no choice but to choose, and given the increasingly uneven distribution of resources for making timely and apt decisions under conditions of complex change, it is also not surprising that as industrial modernization processes have become reflexive, there has been a dramatic widening of wealth, income, and resource use gaps that translates ultimately into exacerbations of relational disadvantage.[7]

The percolation of ever-greater scopes of decision making throughout all sectors and scales of social relations cannot be dissociated from sharpening and deepening divisions between "reflexivity winners" and "reflexivity losers" (Lash 1994, 127–35). Or stated in terms that more directly beg questions of equity, the global nature of the risks, threats, and hazards associated, for example, with climate change do not necessarily result in globally equal impacts (Beck 1999, 5–6). Just as the truism that "pollution follows the poor" makes the point that the greatest impacts of environmental degradation are felt by those least able to afford, avert, or adapt to them, the distributions of risks, threats, and hazards concomitant with reflexive modernization further disadvantage those already most vulnerable to the global effects of predicament-generating growth and development. The era of reflexive modernization has thus also seen the emergence of ever more finely fractured geographies of development, the unevenness of which is historically unprecedented and stretches beyond the geopolitical, socioeconomic, and environmental domains to the cultural, somatic, cognitive, and emotional (Beck 1999, 5).

If the characteristic conflicts of the first phase of modernity centered on how best to balance the private and public provision of goods needed to advance the good of society as a whole, those of reflexive modernization are ever more apparently centered on distributing the burden of risks, threats, and hazards that accompany continued growth and development, and on mitigating the impacts of unavoidable public bads like urban blight, toxic waste, particulate and thermal pollution, ecosystem degradation, and human-induced climate change. With reflexive modernization, underdevelopment can no longer be seen as a precursor stage en route to full development; it is a by-product of a certain kind or direction of development. Reflexivity winners and losers are *not* arrayed on a single arc of change with current losers occupying positions closer to some hypothetically neutral point of developmental departure; they are on entirely different trajectories, heading in ever more widely differing directions.

Whose Equity?

The ways in which reflexive modernization transforms individuation processes can be seen as validating Rawls' redirection of deliberations about how to achieve justice from *who we actually are* to the *kinds of people we might be*. This focus on possible positions in society takes on even greater critical gravity in the context of complex change dynamics that are in principle unpredictable. Nevertheless, Rawls' vision of justice remains fundamentally liberal. The questions posed behind the veil of ignorance are formulated as questions about how to ensure the maximal scopes of freedom and opportunity possible for each and every one of us as self-interested individuals. However, under conditions of complex, network-organized reflexive modernization, we cannot be assured of stable identities and interests. Instead, what is assured is the manifest presence of ever-varying arrays of options for self-construction.

As noted by Richard Stivers, we seem to have reached a technologically occasioned point where "one looks to the group to secure one's rights and acquire political power," not primarily because of the safety or power of numbers, but precisely because "the individual has become the sum total of her group identities" (Stivers 2008, 53). Under conditions in which all identities are multiple, equity concerns naturally shift from "atomic" individuals to situationally defined *identity arrays* organized around joint interests. Hence the expanded importance and discursive space granted to civil society organizations since the 1960s, the (for many, quite unexpected) resurgence of religious affiliation worldwide since the late 1970s, and the explosion of "occasional" groups organized around specific interests or support needs, in contingent response to a specific event (as in mass protests), or in spontaneous and fundamentally ad hoc celebrations of grouping as such (the flash crowd).

Significantly, this movement toward constructing self-identity by means of ever-radiating arrays of group affiliation is not classically liberal. But neither does it involve a communitarian retreat to the holism and hierarchy of traditional societies. Instead, the last half century has witnessed the rise of a politics centered on group member appeals for the recognition (and respect) of differences "that in their view are not incidental and trivial but spring from and constitute their identities . . . those chosen or inherited characteristics that define them as certain kinds of persons or groups and form an integral part of their self understanding" (Parekh 2000, 1). Coincident with the freeing of agency from structure and essence, and with the postmodern networking agenda of free variation, the rise of the politics of chosen as well as inherited differences begs, at the very least, a basic redefinition of community.

But perhaps more importantly, identity formation through circumstantially changing group affiliation not only links us to others through jointly chosen practices of belonging; it also opens us to specific flows or circuits of exchange that, while informing us about the kind of people we are and affording us with specific kinds of power and access to goods, also conduct us into globally accelerating currents of hazard, risk, and threat distribution. Insofar as this occurs as a function of the successes—not failures—of modern, market-driven industrialization and globalization, and their embedded systems of expertise and strategies for problem solution, identity formation itself becomes a primary engine for amplifying the scale and scope of predicament generation. Reflexive modernization not only dissolves the myth of equal vantages, it exposes as fiction the modern hope of effectively and justly responding to mounting inequality by engaging in a priori derivations and applications of universal principles.

At a conceptual level, then, the freedom from structure and forfeiture of essence that occur with reflexive modernization can be seen as conducive to asking pointedly liberal questions about justice like those posed by Rawls. But they also can be seen as aligned with the development and spread of postmodern ethics of difference and the skepticism expressed therein about the common essences and values that are often invoked from communitarian perspectives. If equity does not pertain to individuals, to groups of individuals or to society as a whole, then to whom—or what—does it pertain? And what, ultimately, is the critical benefit of linking equity to the pursuit of equality of opportunity in a world in which experiential and identity options are constantly being expanded, alongside exposures to unpredictable risks, threats, and hazards? To suggest an oblique angle for answering these questions by posing a further question: are we not being pressed toward an ontological revision of the meanings-of and means-to greater equity?

FROM BLIND JUSTICE TO RECOGNITION: MOVING TOWARD RELATIONAL EQUITY

Considered in the context of the dynamics of reflexive modernization, the combined, late twentieth-century rise to global dominance of free market neoliberalism and the politics of recognition and respect take on an extremely keen edge. As is well known, neoliberalism favors maximizing deregulation, market integration, competition, and privatization while simultaneously minimizing taxes, state welfare, and governance superstructures, thus fostering a progressive shift from deliberation-guided pursuits of greater equity to so-called market solutions produced by open competition among essentially self-interested agents.[8] Over especially the last thirty years, this has resulted in a widespread transfer of responsibility for providing such "public goods" as health care, education, transportation infrastructure, and drinking water from the state to the private sector—a transfer that unsurprisingly has tended to exacerbate (rather than alleviate) disparities in accessing/using such goods and in taking advantage of the relational opportunities that they open. Moreover, as regulatory regimes have been dismantled, there has been an accelerating production and increasingly skewed distribution of public bads. In sum, the spread of neoliberal ideology has been conducive both to increasingly uneven and fractured spatial and social patterns of risks, threats, and hazards, and to heightening probabilities of ever-greater populations being subjected to regimes of both state and market *indifference* and *inattention*.

Rawls' theory of justice invokes blindness as to our future position in society as a deliberative tool to facilitate the design of a just society based on what might be called opportunity egalitarianism—a strategy that takes differences into account only to subsume them within procedural guarantees of impartial access to bundles of broadly desirable goods. For those systematically disadvantaged by (racial, ethnic, gender, or religious) differences, this may be an interesting thought experiment, but it can hardly be seen as a route to real social, economic, or political justice, especially in the context of modern assumptions about individual autonomy and rationally self-interested agency. For the systemically disadvantaged, differences are not abstract possibilities; they are concrete expressions of historically extended relational dynamics.

The politics of recognition that began coalescing in the 1960s and 1970s calls attention to the significant critical bias embodied by taking difference to be an *external* relation—a contingent matter of fact that can be stripped away to reveal an essential human core. It demands instead an eyes-wide-open, not eyes-closed-shut, approach to difference that refuses to rest content with any representative politics in which those who differ may be seen and counted, but (like children in the idealized and authoritarian American family of the 1950s) not really heard. The politics of recognition insists on the recovery of lost, perhaps never fully utilized voices. If one is not both seen and heard, rights to public participation and equality of opportunity finally have only imaginary value.

Consider in this connection the sober remarks offered by World Bank President Robert Zoellick in the spring of 2008 as basic food prices skyrocketed globally as a result of complex factors both within and outside of the food industry: those most severely affected are those who can least afford it; and the crisis is not a matter of lost meals or increasing social unrest, but of lost learning potentials and stunted intellectual and physical growth that in the future will likely manifest as shrunken options for employment and for social, political, and cultural participation.[9] The impacts of world hunger are not a set of problems to be solved. They are dynamically emerging articulations of unresolved predicaments. And for this reason, simple recognition of those bearing the brunt of food insecurity is not enough. That too easily consists simply in acknowledging coexistence without coresponsibility. Strongly interpreted, the politics of recognition is a plea for responding fairly to the terms of our interdependence and interpenetration—a plea for confrontation with the inadequacy of modern presuppositions about the ontological primacy of autonomous individuals, the essentially external relationship between individuals and institutions, and the absence of alternatives to assimilation and accommodation as means to addressing issues of significant difference.

Merging Recognition with Respect

In this sense, the politics of recognition cannot be seen as an extension of liberal principles. To the extent that recognition is seen as entailing shared responsibility, it directs us toward critical engagement with the *internal* or constitutive nature of relationships and differences. This is a direction taken by Christine Koggel in her effort to develop a relational theory of equality in which considerations of equality of opportunity, wealth, resources, well-being, life prospects, capabilities, and outcomes are complemented by an "equality of respect" approach in which different perspectives are explicitly enabled to make a difference in existing structures and norms rather than being either assimilated or tolerantly accommodated. Her focus is to create what might be called a *differential space* for breaking free of oppressive relationships in pursuit of greater autonomy, an approach that provides nuance to Amartya Sen's capability-focused work on development. "Relational theory begins," she argues, "with the ontological significance of relationships, and shows how relationships structure identities, create dynamics of power and control, and become interactive sites of struggle, confrontation, and change" (Koggel 1998, 241–42). Defining differences relationally, as constitutive, and as socially and politically significant, Koggel asks us to shift attention from questions about what moral equals need to flourish and develop as individuals, to questions about what moral equals "situated, embedded and interacting in relationships of interdependency need to flourish and develop" (p. 242).

There is, however, a relational tension in Koggel's continued allegiance to equality as part of the conceptual core of both justice and equity. Equality is *not* an internal relation, but rather an external one that implies neither interdependence nor interpenetration. Grounding equity in equality—as has been the norm in global discourses on equity at least since the UN's 1948 Universal Declaration of Human Rights—is to ground equity in what we ideally have in common, but do not actually share in the real and mutually constituting way that we share meals, dances, or parenting responsibilities. Being equal through rights that we generically have in common does not situate us in the shared space of mutual contribution, but rather defines or circumscribes our minimal possessions as human beings who are only contingently male or female, old or young, rich or poor, a resident of the global North or one of the global South.

Equal rights do *grant* a measure of *power* to those who might otherwise be powerless—a set of legal *options* that they are abstractly capable of exercising. But that is not the same as *generating* the relational *strengths* needed to insure that *capacities-for* and *commitments-to mutual contribution* are truly and actively shared by all. Equality of opportunity to act in one's own interests—the core of liberal consensus on equity and a presupposition of rational choice theory—does not necessarily result in actions of the skillfully sustained, *kusala* sort needed to actually make a relationally significant difference.[10]

Indeed, the gap between options and actualities is endemic to any construction of equity that is conceptually grounded on equality. As already noted, claims about equality are functionally inseparable from disregarding purportedly contingent differences en route to establishing claims that various individuals or groups are essentially the same in particular, relevant respects. That is, as a value or particular modality of appreciation, equality directs attention toward the progressive articulation of what we have in common, effectively minimizing the salience of situational/relational specificities. As such, equality can serve as a powerful tool in establishing, for instance, precedents for a positively "blind" legal justice system or for realizing international consensus on thresholds of indignity that enable distinguishing between minimally humane living conditions and those that will be deemed inhumane. Yet, since seeing persons and peoples as equal always entails an extensive editing of their historical and relational uniqueness, it is always unavoidably counterfactual.

The point here is not the trivial one that each person or people can be seen as "numerically" unique—that is, unique in the way that every quartz crystal or grain of sand is a unique instantiation of a particular molecular array. Persons, peoples, and cultures are complex systems that continuously incorporate the histories of their constitutive relational dynamics into the always ongoing process of their own environmentally responsive self-articulation and evolution. Complex systems are learning systems. As such, they are not only unique in numeric terms; they are unique in narrative or dramatic terms. Persons, peoples, and cultures are continuously revising what they mean. Seeing them as equal is to ignore their distinctive and significant dynamism. The equality of persons, peoples, and cultures is, ultimately, a fiction.

Fictions, of course, can be very compelling. Where inhumane conditions are an ongoing reality or continual threat, the pursuit of equality (whether on universalist or relativist grounds) can be a powerful corrective. But the pursuit of equality should be understood as tactical triage, not as a strategic ideal.[11] In a complexly changing world wherein differences are being multiplied and magnified in unpredictable ways, bringing about increasingly widespread and deep predicaments in virtually every dimension of the public sphere, appeals to equality are counterproductive. First, they deflect attention from actual relational dynamics in ways that leave real persons, peoples, and cultures out of account—legitimating ignorance of how things have come to be. This, in turn, makes it impossible to inflect ongoing patterns of change in the way needed to work out from within current conditions to realize superlative and sustainable arcs of change. To reconfigure our conduct in the ways needed to address—and redress—the kinds of relational disadvantage, distortion, disruption, and degradation that characterize our era of predicament-laden complex interdependence, we have to go beyond a "relational theory of equality."

FROM COMPARATIVE TO RELATIONAL EQUITY: TAKING DIFFERENCE INTO POSITIVE ACCOUNT

On the basis of assuming that persons are fundamentally individual and autonomous agents, much of contemporary thinking about equity—whether by economists or ethicists—is focused on calibrating how much power, wealth, access, and opportunity are being distributed to various independent (externally related) individuals or collectives thereof.[12] Equity in this sense is an objectively measurable state of affairs—a potentially deliverable good. The degree of equity or inequity present can be determined by comparing the statuses of various individuals or groups with respect to a standard set of measures (e.g., access to education and health care, income, and political participation). For convenience, we might call this "comparative equity."

Working out, instead, from the perspective of an ontology in which relationality is understood as more "basic" than things-related, equity considerations necessarily shift from *comparisons* of the "estates" of various individuals or groups to *evaluations* of the patterns of interdependence and interpenetration that are constitutive of their shared presence. This might be called "dynamic" or "relational equity."

Achieving greater equity in its now dominant, comparative sense would mean achieving a specific measure of equality, in relation to some relevant good or opportunity, for some set (for example) of gender-, ethnicity-, or nationally-defined individuals or groups. If we are trying to determine the equity of access to education, from a comparative equity perspective any differences in access among, for example, individual ethnic groups—the *absence* of sameness or equality in this respect—will be seen as a measure or index of inequity. Equity is achieved when any differences among ethnic groups in this respect are insignificant. We will not be concerned about whether educational institutions are undergoing substantial differentiation in response to market pressures or elite demands for effectively separate and superior private alternatives to open-enrollment public schools. We will not be concerned about whether the differences among various ethnic groups in society are conserved and incorporated into the educational process in a productive way, if they are celebrated and yet marginalized through "culture days," or if they are paved over with behavioral and achievement standards that are ostensibly universal but that may reflect the biases of the dominant ethnicity. Since differences are precisely what is to be eliminated in pursuit of equality of access or educational opportunity, a comparative conception of equity implies strategic agnosticism regarding how such processes of differentiation are oriented. Whether comparative equity exists or does not exist is *not* a function of the quality and direction of differentiation processes.

Relational equity is not a deliverable *state of affairs*; it is an index of the prevalence of a distinctive, qualitative *direction* of dynamic interdependence and interpenetration. Returning to an earlier Buddhist detour, we can say that equity in this relational sense is nondualistic. It does not depend on establishing a basis for equality, but rather on the evaluative— and, indeed, normative—inflection of differentiation processes. Accordingly, inequity does not denote a conceptually vacuous absence. Relational inequity consists in the critically substantial *presence* of differentiation processes that are inflected in such a way as to eventuate in the occurrence (or further proliferation) of debilitating or degrading relational patterns: the situational compromise of strengths or capacities for relating-freely, often in the context of deepening power asymmetries. Contrastingly, relational equity is enhanced insofar as differentiation processes eventuate in the occurrence or further adumbration of appreciative relational dynamics: the situational enhancement of strengths or capacities for relating-freely—even in the absence of any new freedoms-of-choice—most commonly in the context of attenuating power differentials.

A significant implication of conceiving of equity as relational and nondualistic, and thus with seeing the pursuit of equity as concurrent with building *strengths* for relating-freely and with attenuating *power* differentials, is that equity cannot be a deliverable. More equitably orienting difference-generating global dynamics is *not* a "finite game" in which the meaning of winning is predetermined and the means-to doing so are already defined. Realizing relational equity can only be undertaken as an "infinite game" played in such a way as to keep the process going in ways that recursively enhance the value of continuing to play—a de facto refusal to take the rational choice option of self-serving betrayal of the interests of others. Stated otherwise, enhancing equity is at once a *means-to* and *meaning-of* realizing the conditions for articulating and sustaining appreciative and contributory virtuosity.

Equity as the Appreciation of Diversity

This *functional* characterization of equity as an evaluative process aimed at normatively inflecting and strengthening relational dynamics begs questions, of course, about precisely what *form* situationally apt and self-sustaining virtuosity takes.[13] If relational equity is not reducible to purely quantitative comparisons, what impact does (or could) pursuing it have on such quantifiable differences as those associated with increasing inequalities of wealth, income, resource use, and risk distribution? Given that differentiation processes are now structurally crucial to continued economic growth, in what ways must differentiation be *qualified* to be equitably inflected? Or more pointedly stated, if equity is not to be aligned with achieved equality and autonomy (core values of liberal, comparative equity), in accord with—or expression of—what values is it to be pursued?

Over the course of our discussion, I have several times framed equity as the distinctive quality and direction of relationality that occurs when all present in a given situation manifest both *capacities-for and commitments-to furthering their own interests in ways that are deemed valuable by others*. That is, I have characterized equity as emerging insofar as differentiation eventuates in greater diversity—the relationally concrete enhancement of mutual contribution to sustainably shared welfare. Although orienting the difference engines of complex globalization and reflexive modernity toward greater equity will require substantially altering the distribution of benefits and burdens associated with them, this alone is not enough. Indeed, insofar as relational equity is conceptually correlated with diversity, moving in the direction of a more equitable global future is expressly *not* to move in the direction of a developmentally "flat" world in which each of us enjoys the same complexion of benefits and suffers the same costs as every other.

Much as realizing Buddhist nonduality is *not* what Japanese Zen master Hakuin (1686–1768) derided as the experience of some "all-frozen sameness," but rather the demonstration of fluidly responsive and wisely and compassionately inflected interaction, realizing relational equity does *not* entail eliminating differences. A world without differences would be one of maximum entropy—a world without differences of the sort that would allow the making of any significant differences. Realizing relational equity involves sustaining conditions that are "far from equilibrium"— conditions that demonstrate the presence and activation of enriching potentials for meaningful interaction. The aim is not the modern one of erasing differences, or the postmodern one of respecting and enabling the rhizome-like proliferation of differences, but rather reorienting differentiation processes in ways conducive to diversification. Realizing a more relationally equitable future involves moving obliquely to the global dynamics arcing from modern valorizations of global unity to postmodern valorizations of free variation—the demonstration of meaningful alternatives to both cosmopolis and netropolis.

Affirming that there ultimately is *no equity without diversity* is to affirm that the primary locus of our personal and public concerns about equity should not focus on *how much* we do or do not *differ-from* each other, but rather on *how well* we *differ-for* one another. The pursuit of equity thus implies commitment to developing and exemplifying, not an ethics of universal duties, maximizing generic well-being or cultivating individual virtue, but an ethics of relational virtuosity oriented toward *appreciation* as a "structure of feeling" alternative both to assimilation (modern politics of representation) and accommodation (postmodern politics of recognition).

Importantly, since diversity occurs as a value—a distinctive modality of appreciating difference—both within and across scales and domains, it has the potential of functioning as a *global relational commons*, serving as both means-to and meaning-of realizing equity as a distinctive *global public good*. Crucially, affirming this internal relation between diversity and equity opens concrete possibilities for extending equity considerations beyond the scope of solely human concerns in the articulation of a coherently global ethics of interdependence—an ethics functionally and formally devoted to globally coordinating predicament resolution.[14]

CHAPTER NINE

Diversity and Equity

Global Relational Commons and Global Public Good

P ublic goods are now generally understood to be goods, services, or institutional arrangements which are clearly beneficial both to individuals and to society as a whole, which are nonexcludable in terms of the distribution of their benefits, and which are nonrival in terms of their use or consumption. Commons are domains from which generally useful resources or goods can be readily and beneficially extracted, but that are subject to exhaustion or degradation over the long term.[1]

Public goods are typically associated with *problems of provision* and the concept of market failure: the inability of markets to supply such goods in the necessary quantities due to the scale of initial and ongoing costs and the low returns or profitability of doing so. Commons are associated with particular liabilities to market-serving overexploitation and *problems of protection*. Generally accepted as shared by both are the so-called free-rider problem of users or consumers who allow others to bear the total costs of provision and/or protection, and a related set of issues summed up by the Prisoner's Dilemma which calls attention to the presence of rational limits to cooperation among self-interested actors—problems that become particularly acute with respect to supranational (international, regional, or global) public goods and commons.[2]

These basic definitions have been considerably qualified, especially over the last quarter century. It is now customary to distinguish between pure and impure as well as intermediate and final public goods; to note the importance of both positive and negative externalities and the production and circulation of "public bads"; to recognize the techno-scientific production of new resource commons (e.g., geo-stable orbits and the human genome); and to call attention to the disparate connotations (and contested legitimacy) of the concept of the public in relation to various goods, services, and scales of interest.[3] Moreover, it is now recognized that, far from being impermeable, the categories of public goods and commons are historical in nature; are open to considerable distortion or porosity as a result of technologically or institutionally enabled changes in the costs of their production and/or extraction; and are importantly subject to the vagaries of shifting power relations within and among societies. Not unexpectedly, as the concepts of commons and public goods have been applied to concerns of global scope—resource domains and goods that reach and afford benefits across borders, populations, and generations— their inherent complexity has been greatly accentuated.

The emergence of concepts of global commons (GCs) and global public goods (GPGs) over the past twenty years can be seen as evidence of a watershed of critical engagement away from nationally biased approaches to maximizing economic growth and human security, and toward approaches sensitive to issues of scale and complexity in advancing specifically human well-being as part of overall human-with-planetary welfare. At least implicitly, this also marks the advent of shared commitments to engage sustainability as a distinct value or modality of appreciation and to critically appraise and potentially reorient the historical trajectory of development and globalization processes.

As has been made apparent in efforts to understand and address such key issues as global climate instability, world fisheries depletion, and access to drinking water, activating these commitments requires not only an extraordinary depth of normative consensus, but also recognition and respect for the very real differences that obtain both in how these issues are understood and in how forcefully their impacts are felt. In short, the imperatives and challenges of negotiating how best to conceive, provide, and protect GPGs and GCs are precisely those of answering the aporia with which we began: the apparently contrary needs of taking differences ever more deeply into account while engendering ever greater clarity about and resolve in relation to joint and globally coordinated action. In the context of emerging twenty-first-century realities, the critical force of GCs and GPGs rests on their respective roles in the *recursive appreciation of diversity and equity*.

One justification of this claim is that valorizing diversity opens a detour to consensus that bypasses the competing approaches arrayed along the universalist-relativist spectrum that would disarm differences and reductively index equity to the achievement of comparative equality. The appreciation of diversity as a global relational commons entails resolutely conserving and coordinating differences across ever greater scales and complexity, and recursively indexing equity to the heightening realization of dynamically shared well-being. In short, the internally related pairing of diversity and equity as relational commons and public good constitutes both the means-to and the meaning-of enabling the interdependence of the ethical, economic, and ecological domains to be meaningfully and sustainably appreciated.

RESOURCE COMMONS AND PUBLIC GOODS: IMPERATIVES FOR AN ONTOLOGICAL SHIFT

Interpreting diversity and equity in this way is, in fact, invited by the advent of complex systems of global interdependence that encourage critically marrying the previously separate conceptual genealogies of resource commons and public goods. A brief sketch of precedents for this marriage will help bring into focus some wider implications of this interpretation of diversity and equity for resolving the contemporary aporia of difference.

In his seminal paper "The Tragedy of the Commons," Garrett Hardin (1968) revived the concept of the commons to critically engage the possibility of limits to industrial and economic growth. Citing evidence that meeting the needs of a rapidly expanding global population was possible only at the cost of a degradation and eventual collapse of global resource commons, Hardin presciently argued that averting this collapse could not rest solely on discovering new technical solutions, but required instead a "fundamental extension in morality." The contemporary tragedy of the commons, in other words, is not a function of local problems, but rather one of intensifying and ultimately globally felt predicaments.

In recommending a merger of expressly quantitative (scale) and qualitative (ethical or moral) concerns, Hardin stood firmly in a lineage of utilitarian thinkers like Bentham and Mill who have called attention to the ethical significance of scale and sought to develop what might be called a global calculus of care. This utilitarian thread remains quite influential in both GCs and GPGs discourses, as well as in broader theories of distributive justice.[4] But most significantly, Hardin's appropriation of the concept of the commons to frame human impacts on the integrity and long-term viability of global ecological systems effectively shifted attention from the conservation of what hitherto had been treated as independent material resources to conserving patterns of interdependence or relational dynamics as such. This not only set the stage for a merger of economic, ecological, and ethical concerns, it opened possibilities for seeing commons as productive *processes* rather than simply as finite *pools* of already existing resources, thus blurring the conceptual dividing line between public goods and commons.

These possibilities resonated well with developments in public goods discourse. As already noted, Adam Smith can be credited with acknowledging that it is necessary to temper the workings of private enterprise and free markets with the public provision of certain goods if the conditions of continual growth were to be effectively realized and the inequalities of the market morally justified.[5] As evidenced in the World Bank's *2006 World Development Report* and its vision of long-term complementarity (rather than endemic trade-offs) between increasingly equitable distributions of global wealth and growth-accelerating, market-realized efficiency, this moral linking of economic vitality and the delivery of key public goods has retained at least its rhetorical power, even in the context of globally ascendant neoliberalism (Ferreira and Walton 2005).

The modern concept of public goods alloyed compelling insights that markets are not sufficient to insure either public welfare or the conditions for accelerating wealth generation; that there is potential for enhanced efficiency as a result of reconciling ethical and economic values; and that publicly provided goods play a key role effecting this reconciliation. In the context, however, of the recursively structured, self-organizing, and novelty-generating systems of interdependencies that are now emerging across multiple scales and sectors, translating these insights into effective action requires their significant amplification and refinement.

A first and indispensable step in this direction is to confront the fact that the deepening stresses correlated with contemporary patterns of social, economic, political, cultural, and technological interdependence are *not* evidence of market failures, but rather of reflexively modern market successes. One of Smith's most important admissions was that market solutions are always partial in both senses of the word: both incomplete and biased. Taking this seriously, it follows that the function of public goods is not only to compensate for market failures or address market incompleteness, but also and more importantly, to correct for the market's partiality in distributing the benefits and burdens resulting from its successes. Given this dual function, public goods discourse can be seen as carrying on work traditionally associated with the pursuit of equity. And, indeed, equity and social justice have themselves begun to be regarded as global public goods (Kaul et al. 1999).

In the context of globally complex systems of interdependence and interpenetration, however, this work cannot focus solely on bringing about comparatively just distributions of benefits and burdens among individual and essentially autonomous stakeholders. Instead, the locus of public goods concerns must extend to include the quality and direction of relational dynamics as such and their impacts on fluidly constituted groups. Once we begin taking seriously the epochal nature of the shifts from industrial to mental capitalism and from material to attention economies, it is difficult to avoid recognizing that *the modern ontology of independently existing agents and things acted upon affords insufficient critical traction to address the justice issues that are crucial to reconciling ecological, economic, and ethical considerations.* Yet in the context of these shifts, especially engaged from the perspective of a relational ontology, global public goods begin looking much less like deliverables than like patterns of values-articulating relational interventions. That is, over especially the last quarter century, GPGs have been undergoing a dematerialization comparable to that characterizing the economic shifts just noted.

Thus, contemporary realities invite, for example, a transition from focusing on the provision of education as a key public good—for instance, through state-financed school construction, teacher training, and curriculum development—to realizing relational conditions that are conducive to sustained educational innovation and improvisation.[6] Since educational innovation and improvisation cannot be separated from quality issues—including how well educational practices respond to and in turn affect current social, economic, political, cultural, and technological dynamics—it becomes clear that as *a* public good, education cannot avoid addressing issues of *the* public good. In effect, public goods discourses are being pressed beyond a *compensatory* role vis-à-vis market processes to an increasingly normative or *evaluative* one. Relational GPGs thus straddle the distinction between being "*a* public good" and serving "*the* public good," effectively undoing the ontological divide between means and ends or issues of provision and purpose.

This merger of compensatory and normative or evaluative roles can be seen, indeed, as mandated by what I have termed the global problem-to-predicament transition. The severe global recession that began in the fall of 2008 with the global collapse of financial markets was not evidence of *problems* "resulting" from a sudden piercing of the U.S. mortgage industry bubble—problems for which appropriate technical or institutional solutions were lacking. Rather, the sudden onset of global recession was a complex consequence of pervasive, persistent, and profound *predicaments*, generated and sustained by conflicts within and among patterns of values and priorities, and in which each and every one of us is implicated. Phenomena like this drive home the point that, in the context of complex interdependence, a key function of explicitly *global* public goods must be to facilitate and foster scale- and domain-crossing predicament resolution. Doing so may require providing new kinds of goods or establishing new institutions. But more importantly, it will also entail generating new depths of global resolve—the realization of ever more globally coordinated and yet differentially activated commitments to revising our shared and evidently troubling patterns of values and priorities.[7]

Deliverable Goods and Exploitable Resources or Relational Domains?

The shift from regarding GPGs as deliverables to regarding them as relational interventions carries us in the direction of conceptually marrying

GPGs and GCs. And in fact, since Hardin's early articulation of precedents for expanding the notion of commons to include more than essentially material resources, there has been steadily increasing readiness to
acknowledge that explicitly relational domains like geo-stable orbits and
the Internet should be seen as new and crucially important commons.
In contrast with pools of naturally occurring and potentially exhaustible
material resources—e.g., forests used for collecting firewood, fisheries, or
environmental features like rivers or the atmosphere that are capable both
of being used directly and of serving as sinks for public bads like industrial heat or particulate pollution—such commons are humanly produced
media through which specific and evolving types of relational networks
are being realized. That is, rather than being valued as sites for extraction
(of desirable materials) or deposit (of undesirable wastes), these are commons valued because of the relational benefits they afford.

Global commons in this broader sense can be seen as consisting of
distinctive spaces of appreciation or value-enhancing intercourse. Crucially, unlike traditional commons that are susceptible to overuse, the
more widely relational commons are accessed and used, the more fully
and effectively they facilitate interaction, thus taking on characteristics
traditionally definitive of public goods. As such, relational commons raise
important questions about the limits to regulatory governance and the
technological valorization of control. If these spaces or relational domains
function to promote increasingly wide and deep coordination among different users, restrictions applied therein would seem destined to constrain
coordination and could easily result in their becoming vehicles for the
production of inequity-generating inequalities. At the same time, there
is no disputing that the relational opportunities afforded by such global
commons are more readily empowering for some users rather than for
others. Networking is not power neutral, especially not in the context
of reflexive modernization and the complex interdependencies through
which the globalization-driven multiplication and magnification of differences are recursively shaped according to interwoven sets of values.

The Complexity of Relational Intervention

Here, Amartya Sen's cautions about the liabilities of both "grand universalism" and "national particularism" in the pursuit of global justice
assume critical salience. As we think through the meaning of equity as
a global public good, we must be aware that ours is a world of not only
multiple actors and interests, but also of fluidly interpenetrating "plural
affiliations" (Sen 1999a). Far from being discrete atomic units, the persons and communities to be benefited by the normative protection and
provision of GCs and GPGs are intrinsically differential and complexly
interrelated across a wide and often shifting range of social, economic,

political, cultural, and technological boundaries and scales. The task of equitably coordinating the values and interests that inflect the dynamics of fluidly constituted affinity groups and publics far exceeds the parameters of any Prisoner's Dilemma of independent actors instrumentally choosing between cooperation and competition, regardless of whether these actors are persons, civil society organizations, states, corporations, or intergovernmental associations.

One of the merits of adopting a relational ontology is that it becomes evident that the indeterminacies surrounding the beneficiaries of GCs and GPGs must also permeate the benefit-conferring practices associated with GCs and GPGs. Indeed, as Robert Keohane and Elinor Ostrom have pointed out, the globalization of concerns regarding public goods and the commons forces confrontation with the fact that these concepts do not mimic divisions in the real world, but are instead constructed in nonuniform and historically variable ways in keeping with both explicitly recognized and tacit patterns of stakeholder values and norms (Keohane and Ostrom 1995, 13–15). What we mean by GCs and GPGs is fluidly determined on the basis of the abundance of particular resources given the functions they perform in specific socially, economically, politically, culturally, and technologically conditioned circumstances. Because of this, we must take evaluative account of the fact that not only are GCs and GPGs irreducibly relational in nature, the authority regimes and structures of (social, economic, political, and cultural) power informing their construction are not stable entities. The complex interdependencies that are emerging as nonlinear outcomes of contemporary globalization processes do so against a background of simultaneously fragmenting and integrating dynamics characterized by transiently marbled patterns of affiliation and concern, and hence spatially disjointed and highly ephemeral solidarities and publics.

Because predicaments evidence conflicts among ends and values, the shifting complexion of nominally individual stakeholders, affinity groupings, and publics results in a continually morphing play of conflicts and power contests that cannot be addressed effectively through any calculus aimed at balancing fixed and abiding interests. The global predicaments with which we find ourselves increasingly confronted are themselves changing—often unpredictably—and this is instrumentally unsettling. In the absence of any fixed frames of reference, predicament resolution cannot be methodized or standardized. Ours is a world of flows within flows in which the logic of accumulation is dissolving into that of circulation, and in which power no longer implies or imputes permanence.

Market Processes: Intervening and Evaluating

This observation is crucial in outlining the full scope of the challenges associated with the development of any viable alternative(s) to traditional market-based constructions of GCs and GPGs. To begin with, in the context of such dynamics, public goods and the commons have themselves become fluidly constituted and predicament-rich sites for struggles over the meaning and legitimacy of differences with respect to publics crystallizing and recrystallizing, for example, around identities focused on consumption practices, gender, ethnicity, rights, political ideologies, cultural ideals, and wealth. Moreover, because of the role played by mass media in the coalescence of identity groupings, significant feedback and feedforward circuits obtain among global markets and the transient arrays of publics involved in struggles over how to define GCs and GPGs. These publics and the modes of affiliation they express are not innocent of market influence. Indeed, markets benefit considerably from inducing a persistent *variety* of interests and desires that insure shifting perspectives on the significance of GCs and GPGs, bringing about conditions that *work against the scales and scopes of resolution needed to begin equitably addressing the predicament-generating dynamics of global interdependence.*

As we have seen, this skewing of dynamics toward variation expresses values crucial to the ways that complex market economies have been shaping their component systems of production and consumption to sustain inequality-generated and inequity-generating growth. The partiality of markets toward variation favors the preemptive dominance of essentially *external* relations within and among the flows constitutive of the ecological, economic, and ethical domains. In the present context, this recursive relationship—between, on one hand, the global dynamics that GCs and GPGs are intended to affect and orient more equitably, and on the other, the fluidly constituted publics struggling over the meaning of GCs and GPGs as means-to greater equity—assumes acute critical significance. There is, in reality, no outside or transcendental position from which to articulate even the traditional conservative and compensatory functions of global commons and public goods discourses, much less the explicitly evaluative relational functions we have claimed to be crucial to enhancing equity through expanding and deepening diversity. The resolution—both clarity and commitment—needed to more equitably orient global interdependence and interpenetration can only emerge from within and through differentiation.

It would seem, then, that we are led to seeing GCs and GPGs as furthering critical, evaluative engagement with market processes. The dominant modern conceptions of common pool resources and public goods were formulated in critical sympathy with market biases, with commons protection and public goods provision conceptually linked to market needs and capacities. Hence the mainstream dominance of the idea that publicly financing the production of key goods, for example, is justified only when default to market processes would result in underprovision—an essentially quantitative assessment. By contrast, a self-consistent conception of GPGs involves seeing "public goods in a way that does not leave the task of identifying 'public' and 'private' solely to the market" (Kaul and Mendoza 2003, 87), and that focuses instead on positive interventions aimed at activating the contributory potentials generated by already ongoing processes of differentiation so that they serve as catalysts for the emergence of equitably shared well-being and flourishing.

In practical terms, this entails realizing that there are, for example, forceful social and cultural reasons to resist allowing the provision of traditional public goods like basic education or drinking water to be turned over to private, for-profit industry, simply because it has become possible to do so. The market feasibility (i.e., potential profitability) of providing a particular good may be a necessary condition for transferring responsibility for its provision to the market, but it should no longer be seen as a sufficient condition for doing so.[8] More importantly, if GCs and GPGs are to perform predicament-resolving—rather than merely problem-solving—functions, they must ultimately work to realize and sustain conditions for the *strengthening* and *normative coordination* of relational dynamics as such, both within and among the economic, ecological, and ethical domains.

FROM AGENT-DRIVEN PROGRESS TO VALUES-ORIENTED EMERGENCE

This conclusion raises new questions. Problems are solved from the outside. Confronted with the failure of existing practices and techniques, we develop new resources and methods better suited to current situational dynamics. Problem solution confirms that we exist, literally "standing apart from" the situations in which we exercise our power to transform the world in accordance with abiding interests and values. Such an external relationship to the world, however, is a block to predicament resolution, which requires revising the complexion of our values, intentions, and practices—transforming relations that are irreducibly internal or constitutive. Predicament resolution alters what we mean for one another and thus ultimately also who we are. Given the recursion-rich relationships just sketched among market processes, relevant affinity groupings, and publics, and the predicaments to which GCs and GPGs are responses, this raises questions about exactly how and by whom the strengthening and coordination of relational dynamics is to be accomplished.

To the extent that GCs and GPGs are to facilitate equitably resolving global predicaments from within, in ways that enhance social, economic, political, cultural, technological, and ecological diversity, we cannot ground their evaluative functions in presuppositions of a universal human nature. The presence of profound global predicaments already indicates a plurality of constitutive dispositions rather than the unanimity presumed by a purportedly universal human nature. But neither can we ground these functions in the autonomy of individual agents whose preferences are not directly comparable, and whose basic values may well be critically incommensurable, since the essentially external ontological and axiological relations between such agents effectively inhibits (if not prohibits) their engagement in sustained diversification. Universalist *assimilation* and relativist *accommodation* are at bottom problem-solving methods that deny creative relevance to our differences, disarming or dissolving the very resources needed to engage in global predicament resolution. It is not by asserting either our essential unity or our manifest variety that predicaments are resolved, but only through the harmonizing *coordination* and *appreciation* of our differences.

The difficulties of doing so would be hard to overestimate. The modern values of autonomy, independence, equality, sovereignty, and freedom-of-choice are very deeply incorporated within our institutions and our practices of self-articulation. But in addition to conceptual and institutional inertia, the task of taking into account the disparate interests and needs of all relevant groups and publics—the basic units of the politics of recognition and respect—is increasingly complex since as we have already noted, it is not just that we all now have multiple identities, but that globally prevailing social and economic conditions in particular promote the multiplication of identities we acknowledge as our own. Our modernity-enabled freedom from fixed social, economic, political, and cultural structures has meant also the loss of any fixed essences. And with reflexive modernization has come not only deepening imperatives to compose our own life narratives, but to do so in an ongoing and recursive fashion.

This could be a liberating admission. Realizing our lack of defining structures and essences explodes any presumptions we might have about our lots in life being a function of fate or necessity. We are not human beings, we are human becomings. And the freedom that we have in shaping who we become is not an abstract function of having some essential human nature; it is a concrete function of the dynamic interdependencies that are constitutive of precisely who we are becoming, moment-by-moment. If individuality entails indivisibility, we can no longer claim to be individuals.[9]

But the admission that we are no longer in any significant sense individuals also raises troubling concerns about the meaning of agency. What is agency in the absence of ontologically discrete and abiding agents? Is there a limit to how much we are influenced by "outside" forces? If we do not have an essential and unchanging core, then to what does our freedom attach? Who possesses the freedom to become this way or that? The mutual dissolution of structure and essence marks the dissolution of both independently existing agents and the purportedly "external" things on which they act. And with this, can we really speak of *action*? Or can we only speak of *conduct*, where conduct connotes being "led together"—a directed complexion of dynamics without any director? [10] Realizing that we ultimately are not individuals is to realize that appeals to unidirectional causation, instrumentality, and the modern segregation of means and ends are merely conventions.

This is something that we know at a certain level. But much as we persist in talking about the sun "rising" and "setting" in spite of knowing that at dawn and dusk we are in fact witnessing the spinning of the Earth on its axis, we persist in thinking about change in terms of "agents" who engage (or fail/refuse to engage) in "actions." Because of this, we assume that equity and diversity are necessarily going to result (or not result) from actions we undertake (or fail to undertake). This is to revert to thinking of equity and diversity as states that we can cause to come about. But in the relationally robust senses forwarded here, equity and diversity are neither the products nor properties of individuals—whether real or imagined, either summed together as a generic "everyone" or considered separately as instantiations of "anyone."

The ecological metaphors for change that we explored in Chapter 3 provide us with a bridge out of the conceptual habit of agent-directed change, drawing our attention to dynamic networks of mutual influence and transformation. Given the absence of a transcendental or outside-stander position from which to reorient the dynamics of global interdependence and interpenetration, and the unprecedented degree to which these relational dynamics are now characterized by the multiplication and magnification of differences, contrary to modern expectations, realizing greater equity cannot be assumed to entail a convergence on *the same* (ideals, interests, practices, institutions, etc.). Realizing greater equity entails "ecologically" strengthening and coordinating processes of differentiation—a revision of relational dynamics from within and throughout that, because of the complexity of these dynamics, cannot be expected to result in achieving anticipated outcomes in a clear and linear demonstration of progress. With the advent of recursively structured, complex systems of global interdependence and interpenetration, engineered change yields to emergence.

This does not mean that predictable patterns of change and precisely engineered outcomes have become a thing of the past. Just as classical mechanics was not so much discredited as delimited by the physics of general relativity and quantum mechanics, controlled change—whether as a function of natural laws or human artifice—is not dispelled as illusory by the increasing relevance of emergence, but rather displaced from a position of critical prominence. That is, what has changed is the global significance of engineered changes in comparison with changes occurring in ways that we might in the language of complex systems theory call autopoetic (self-making) or in the more conceptually consistent language of early Chinese Daoism, *ziran* or self-soing.[11] Increasingly, it is not planned events, but rather uncontrolled, impossible to anticipate, and yet value-conditioned emergence that most significantly shapes the *creative* dynamics of global interdependence.

Strengthening and coordinating processes of skillfully differing-for one another—the "work" done by equity as an overarching global public good—is thus not best conceived primarily as a matter of consistently enacting outcome-oriented strategies and tactics. These may, of course, do some of the work needed, but not all of it. This is already clear from the nearly half century of efforts expended on behalf of realizing equity through programs and policies aimed at equalizing opportunities to acquire primary goods and act on basic rights. Counterintuitively with respect to habits of reducing all causation to a function of linear and ultimately mechanical influences, the most effective way of orienting the dynamics of emergence-prone complex systems is by *affecting* the complexion of their informing values.[12] Granted this, realizing greater equity is best understood and undertaken as a qualitative function of *reconfiguring axiological resonances* within and among ecological, economic, and ethical domains.

Issues of Freedom

The Buddhist concept of karma affords distinctive access to the nature of this process of value reconfiguration in response to jointly experienced predicaments. Recall that in Buddhism, karma refers to the patterning of experienced outcomes and opportunities in consonance with sustained values, intentions, and practices, in the context of a relational ontology of horizonless interdependence and interpenetration. Or put somewhat differently, the topography of change is not *determined* as a linear function of efficient (realist) and final (idealist) causes, but is rather an emergent function of continuously and recursively interfusing patterns of personally- and lifeworld-embodied commitments. The Buddhist teaching of karma, then, enjoins recognizing both the inseparability of the ontological and the axiological, and their dynamic openness. Hence the Buddha's striking claim that it is precisely karma (a term that in earlier Indian traditions implied a lawlike system of cosmic retribution) that warrants the possibility of liberation from troubled and suffering-inducing patterns of interdependence.

From the perspective of Buddhist practice, sustainably redirecting troubling relational dynamics involves dissolving present karma. Doing so involves altering the complexion of values, intentions, and actions in consonance with which our experience is being shaped. Given that our thoughts, feelings, and behavior are themselves expressions of our karma, dissolving our karma might be dismissed as being just as unlikely as pulling ourselves up off the ground by tugging on our own shoelaces. But, in practice, "bootstrapping" is not necessary. The practical key to dissolving our present karma is to realize no-self (*anatman*): the absence of any binding structures (*saṃskāra*) and fixed essence. Realizing no-self does not mean the absence of experience as such, but rather the absence of any independently existing and self-identical subject who possesses or undergoes various experiences, and who acts in instrumental pursuit of various objects of desire.[13] Realizing this absence is not, however, a matter of "removing" the self—an action that would be possible only by assuming a position independent of the self and applying some force to placing it elsewhere. This approach ultimately produces an infinite regression of selves, not a realization of no-self. Realizing the absence of self occurs as the "ontological gap" between experiencing "subjects" and experienced "objects" is dissolved. No-self *means* the absence of any distance to be closed, any blockages to be removed, and anything to be overcome—a realization of the nondualistic emptiness (*śūnyatā*) of all things as the fullness or repletion of relational possibilities.

This meaning of emptiness is most clearly brought out in Mahayana traditions, where sustaining the realization of emptiness is associated with the bodhisattva's responsive poise and the limitless capacity for demonstrating the virtuosity (*upāya*) needed to inflect situational dynamics toward the expression of liberating patterns of relationality. Emptiness—the absence of fixed structures and essences—is not an erasure of our differences, but rather the vibrantly improvisational activation of our differences as the basis for relationally appreciating mutual contribution.

This, of course, is what I have been describing as the emergence of diversity. What recommends diversity as a value for reconfiguring the patterns of normative resonance shaping contemporary global dynamics is, in part, that it is conducive to actualizing coordinative arcs of change without forcing or establishing precedents for convergence on sameness or singularity. Diversification resolves the one-many, self-other dichotomies that undergird both utilitarian and deontological constructions of global public good, providing evidence that enriching who we *are* is inseparable from enhancing what we *mean* for one another. But the valorization of diversity is also recommended by the fact that diversification, unlike variation, is not a process that can be engineered or imposed; it can neither result from nor result in the exercise or accentuation of power. Diversity implies an emancipatory coordination of differences without the disciplinary shadow that attends all exercises of control. It is the ongoing articulation, in our conduct, of means-to and meanings-of nonduality.

The Buddhist teaching of karma alerts us to the relationally constituted nature of experienced realities, and to our intimate implication in the inflection or direction of their dynamics. But it also alerts us to the interpenetration of the real and the ideal, and to the inseparability of experienced realities and responsibility. The imposition of an ontological gap between self and other—what in Buddhism is often referred to as the "wound of existence"—enables the experience of being independent or cut free from felt responsibility to and for others. This experience of autonomy or feeling free to be who or what one wants without needing to take others' wants into critical account is a very seductive feeling—the result of taking the wound of existence and turning it into a source of pleasure. It is this sense of empowerment that animates the almost religious championing of rational-choice liberalism and free markets by both the very wealthy and powerful who benefit most greatly from their prevalence, and by the majority of those who are most thoroughly disenfranchised by reflexively modern industrial and market regimes.

But while some measure of control over our circumstances and our own responses to them is better than none at all, valorizing control and structuring society so as to maximize individual exercises of control is ultimately self-defeating. The karma of control is that: the better we get at getting what we want, the better we get at wanting; but the better we get at wanting, the better we must get at getting what we want, only to find that we don't want what we get. Improving our capacity for control requires that we experience our situation as both continuously *open to* and *in need of* control. If control karma is sustained long enough and with sufficient energy, it eventuates in the *akusala* proliferation of risks, threats, and hazards in the face of which we cannot but feel compelled to exercise still more control. Valorizing diversity disrupts this karmic cycle, not by directly opposing control, but by fostering the situationally specific, relational appreciation of contributory virtuosity.

The agendas of modern universalism and postmodern relativism are seemingly opposed, with the former promoting cosmopolis (the world as rational "grid") in pursuit of global unification, and the latter promoting netropolis (the world as differential "web") in pursuit of free variation. But the ideals of modernity and postmodernity have in common commitments to valorizing autonomy, equality, and choice: commitments to realizing conditions for the experience of control that, however distinct in the scales of their practical expression, work decisively against enhancing diversity and realizing truly relational equity.

As we are now finding out at a global scale, while all circularities are not vicious, those produced by control eventually are. What our Buddhist detour brings into view is that, as things have come to be, realizing greater equity requires working out through, but not against, the control-confounding dynamics of complex emergence. As is often said in

Mahayana Buddhist texts, the ultimate reality (*paramārthasatya*) of liberating relationality can only be expressed or articulated through conventional reality (*samvrtisatya*). The point is not to engage in oppositional forms of *resistance* that in practice will only reproduce precisely the karma of control and power that we are hoping to dissolve; it is to *redirect* relational dynamics.

In conceptual terms, this means moving obliquely to the tensions between such dichotomous stances as those of realism and idealism, universalism and relativism, or individualism and collectivism, embarking on a trajectory of improvisation that ultimately calls into question both modern and postmodern presuppositions about the means-to and meaning-of freedom. If there is a core "structure of feeling"—an affective root—of modernity and postmodernity, it is the experience of exercising and expanding freedoms-of-choice. Resolving the contemporary aporia of difference and orienting global dynamics toward enhanced equity will require articulating and embodying an alternative construal of freedom.

Thus, while Sen (1985) is entirely correct in calling attention to a detrimental bias in much of GCs and GPGs discourses toward focusing on resources rather than freedoms, it is crucial to resist understanding freedom either as an achieved state of affairs or (as Sen does) as an achieved set of capabilities for exercising real choices in pursuit of one's own, individual interests. If, as argued earlier, dynamic equity is a function of attenuating self-other and individual-collective polarizations of interest, the extent to which freedom can be affirmed as a focus of GCs and GPGs discourses is the extent to which it connotes demonstrating contributory and appreciative virtuosity, not the dualistic, self- and other-reifying exercise of choice.

The difference-multiplying and difference-magnifying dynamics of contemporary realities can be seen as generating conditions that favor foregrounding the merits of conceiving equity itself as a key public good or public policy outcome.[14] But understood karmically, these conditions also invite seeing that, in order for this accentuation of differences to prove conducive to enhancing equity, the market values of control, competition, and conveniently exercised freedoms-of-choice should be subordinated to (though not necessarily supplanted by) those of contribution, coordination, and the cultivation of commitments-to and capacities-for relating-freely. Indeed, this values-reconfiguring approach is ultimately the surest path to insuring that the processes of differentiation intrinsic to contemporary systems of complex global interdependence veer away from the production of increasing variety toward ever more robustly realized diversity and relational equity.

In developing the concepts of diversity and equity as a global *relational* commons and global public good, I have been responding to the complex historical dynamics to which we have turned from different angles and at different scales over the course of our conversation thus far. Attending to the differentiated nature of difference and breaking the conceptual dependence of equity on equality are indispensible to reorienting global interdependence in ways that have real prospects for enabling all mothers, fathers, sons, and daughters to live dignified lives.

But I have also been responding to the evident need for values that have predicament-resolving, coordinative, and evaluative potential within and among societies and across multiple scales and domains. This means a dramatic shift away from conceiving GCs and GPGs as resource pools and deliverable goods that are useful in meeting autonomous needs, and toward conceiving them as distinctive relational values that foster the emergence of self-coordinating and sustainably strengthening patterns of human-with-planetary flourishing. That is, diversity and equity can be seen as modalities of appreciation that are conducive to realizing new structures of feeling—new affective modalities—within which relationally enhancing capacities-for and commitments-to global predicament resolution can readily be improvised. Transitioning from the modern/postmodern era of problem solution to an era of predicament resolution impels social, economic, political, cultural, and technological modulations from the affective priority of freedoms-of-choice to relating-freely.

CHAPTER TEN

Making a Difference

Toward a New Structure of Feeling

Contrary to postmodern orthodoxies, something like a metanarrative is required for us to critically engage and effectively transform the kinds of global processes that are currently serving as engines of inequality and inequity. The complex realities of contemporary globalization require us "to go beyond the particularities and to emphasize the *pattern* and the systemic qualities of the damage being wrought across geographical scales and differences" (Harvey 2000, 81). To use an old Zen saying, anything short of this would be no more effective than "a mosquito biting an iron ox."

This is not to deny that there are very good reasons for postmodern skepticisms about metanarratives and for postcolonial politics of identity which would construct cultural plurality as a shifting array of resolutely particular "localisms." But these responses to the coercive potentials of universalism as a cultural project have also been troublingly coincident with the widening global dominance of neoliberal ideology and free market institutions. This coincidence suggests that, absent something like a critical metanarrative, efforts to redress inequality and inequity will be ineffective precisely because they will be "partial, focused on short- and medium-term goals, fragmented, and temporally and spatially discontinuous" (Luke 2005, 20). To effectively address the large-scale structures that are fostering ever-widening gaps of income, wealth, opportunity, and relational quality, we are in need of a holistic and restructuring vision.

The historical and philosophical narratives woven together over the preceding chapters hopefully will have served, among other things, to establish strong convictions that this restructuring vision must not

amount to a cosmetically altered universalism—a repackaging or reimag-
ing of unity as a socioeconomic, political, and cultural ideal. Our attempts
to critically restructure and reorient the dynamics of global interdependence and interpenetration cannot take the form of overwriting cultural
boundaries and the differences they imply with essentialist affirmations of
commonality and homogeneity. At the same time, we have reason to resist
aligning this restructuring vision with postmodern valorizations of variety and hybridity. Globalization- and market-driven processes of variation and hybridization have proved to be no less conducive to deepening
and expanding power asymmetries than their unifying and homogenizing
polar opposites. In spite of the disparity of their overall visions, the metanarratives of global unification (*cosmopolis*) and free variation (*netropolis*)
have in common the effect of disarming differences, subverting the conditions needed for "making distinctiveness itself possible" (Kompridis 2005,
332), inflecting global interdependence in ways that work against realizing
contemporary potentials for new scopes and scales of mutual contribution.

    In contrast with the metanarratives of unification and variation, valo-
rizing diversification entails a nondualistic refusal either to render differences impotent or to endorse zero-sum competition in de facto acceptance
of the inevitability of irresolvable conflicts of interest—a refusal that positively entails realizing the appreciative and contributory potential of difference. As previously noted, however, diversity *emerges* relationally and
cannot be the result of prescriptive exercises of control, no matter how
well intended. Stated otherwise, neither the process of diversification nor
the metanarrative of diversity are structured around a *predictive/prescrip-
tive logic* of "if this, then that." Rather, they express a *performative logic* of
"first this, then that"—a narrative logic in which surprising aptness, not
rule-expressing rigor, is the root index of excellence. In practice, then,
diversification—and by extension, the realization of enhanced equity—
cannot be engineered; diversity can only be evoked or elicited.

    This phrasing makes it sound as if enhancing diversity and equity may
be less a political process than a poetic one, and perhaps this is not entirely
misleading. Politics is commonly defined as the art of government—a
revealing statement in light of the fact that to govern literally means to
direct, control, guide, decide, and determine. As commonly defined, then,
politics is a process of distributing and exercising power. And as such, if it
is not inherently in tension with diversity, it would at least seem to be in
tension with the emergent dynamics of diversification as a nonlinear process of qualitative, relational transformation. Whether it is autocratically,
democratically, or by some means in-between, politics aims at *getting things
done.* But in the context of the multiplication and magnification of differences that characterize contemporary global realities, the risk proliferation
associated with reflexive modernization, and the tightening network-fos-
tered correlation of economic vitality (and hence political legitimacy) with

volatility, getting things done has itself become an increasingly complex and nonlinear process. Given this, the politics of the twenty-first century seem destined to be less an exemplification of the art of governing than that of negotiating coherent policy pathways through continuously shifting and profoundly contested terrains—an art, finally, of building confident (belief-inspiring) bridges between existing economic, social, and cultural realities and jointly imagined ideals. Seen in this way, politics appears to be a not very distant relative of poetry. Like poetry, politics has become a deeply metaphorical process of cantilevering bridges out from the actual and familiar in the direction of the unknown and yet-to-be.

Seeing the political as poetic encourages asking whether political systems are best evaluated in terms of their effectiveness and efficiency, or if other less instrumental and more qualitative dimensions of performance should be seen as equally (and perhaps more) important. What would characterize political practices conducive to the emergence of movement oblique to the contrariety of modern narratives of unification and postmodern narratives of variation? What kinds of political bridges are most likely *not* to fold back on themselves and render politics a resolutely conservative process of *legitimizing what has been* rather than *realizing the yet-to-be*?[1] That is, what sort of political processes are most conductive to allowing our differences to make real political differences, contributing to the articulation of arcs of change characterized by enhanced diversity and equity?

These are questions that will occupy us over the first part of this chapter. But it will be important to consider further whether these questions, with their "realist" biases toward political practices and institutions, already give too much away to the association of politics with government. Indeed, as already intimated, the greatest likelihood would seem to be that the politics of diversification will prove no more readily definable in terms of governmental institutions or policies, than poetic excellence is in terms of the presence of specific rhyme schemes and meters or the use of a particular vocabulary. The politics of diversity may well be best characterized by the surprising and yet apt advent of a distinctive ethos and structure of feeling—one that I have referred to as "relating-freely." It is to this possibility that we will turn in the second half of the chapter, asking: what relational values and qualities foster the emergence of creative and yet resolutely coordinative relational dynamics?

POLITICS AND THE CONSERVATION OF DIFFERENCE

The history of modern politics has been a history, first, of the global rise of the nation-state and, second, of the global ascendance of the democratic polity as a governance ideal. This means that modern politics has also been, more or less openly, a politics of responding to and managing differences. The institution of the geographically bounded, multiethnic and multireligious nation-state originated as a "battlefield emergency" amid cataclysmic social, economic, and political circumstances, and among the many legacies of its rise to global dominance has been that all modern societies must address the "fact of plurality" (Rawls 1971). But this plurality has never been a simple given. As we have already noted, a key feature of modernization has been the "emancipatory" dissolution of traditional *communities* and their replacement by *collectives of individuals* organized around shifting arrays of shared interests—a transformation with a long history of being regarded as crucial to the rise of both civil society and modern democracies.[2]

Positively evaluated, modernity has been politically inseparable from questioning the legitimacy of historically given ideals and institutions—a questioning of the familial, the local, and the traditional that has inculcated sustained awareness of possibilities for crafting new ways of being human, including new rights, new roles, and new patterns of affiliation and aspiration. This positive reading notwithstanding, modern individuation processes have been continuously shadowed by the evolution of what Foucault (1997) has termed "disciplinary" societies committed both to reconfiguring power relations and to producing populations suited to advancing the interlinked aims of nationalization, marketization, and industrialization. In short, throughout their intertwined histories, modernization and its central political institution, the nation-state, have been characterized by the joint and often tense valorization of both freedom and control (Wagner 1994).

Given their combination of "emancipatory" and "disciplinary" forces, it is not surprising that, in spite of being fueled by shared convictions about human capacities for autonomously realizing progressively better lives for each and for all, the various utopian projects of modernity have from the outset begged questions about how "better lives" are to be defined and about precisely where the benefits and burdens of progress are to fall. Thus, in addition to the tension between freedom and control, modernization and nation-building processes have been continuously characterized by almost "marital" tensions between valorizations of the individual (as freed from traditional forms of community) and the collective (as the locus of voluntary membership), and between contrary *universalist* and *particularist* conceptions of the good life and human flourishing. Pertinent to our present concerns, and especially those belonging to the second half of the twentieth century, these tensions have come primarily to be expressed politically in contrasting liberal and illiberal conceptions of democracy.

Contrasting Liberal and Illiberal Poles of Democratic Practice

In principle, democracies would seem to be well suited to enacting a politics of difference capable of undertaking the norm-evaluating process of responding to the contemporary aporia of difference and our increasingly predicament-rich global realities. Democracies, after all, are governments constituted "by and for the people," and for any modern nation-state, "the people" is actually shorthand for a plurality of peoples with distinctive perspectives and patterns of preferences. The modern eminence of the democratic state is in large part a function of its substantive and procedural commitments to insuring that each and all within its borders are free to participate meaningfully in political processes, in accord with their own values, needs, and interests.

In practice, however, there are many variations on the theme of democratic government ranging from such liberal states as the United States, Great Britain, and India to such illiberal states as Singapore, Korea, and Iran, and they are by no means equivalent in how they address issues of difference. Indeed, given the fact that some of the widest gaps in income, wealth, resource use, and relational opportunity are found in democratic states, it is by no means evident that even the global ubiquity of democratic governance would ensure the more equitable inflection of ongoing global magnifications and multiplications of difference. Since democracy has proven in so many other respects to be well suited to dissolving the conditions for social, economic, and political exclusion, this raises disquieting questions about whether the spectrum of liberal to illiberal constructions of democratic politics affords the resources needed to realize resolutely diversity- and equity-enhancing patterns of global interdependence.

Liberal democracies assume that the individual is the basic unit of political analysis, that the autonomy of the individual is sacrosanct, and that the political complexion of society is best determined through a free exchange of ideas and through insuring the right of all to participate significantly in political processes. The primary responsibility of the liberal state is to realize conditions in which all individuals can craft life plans in accord with values, aims, and interests that they have freely chosen, generating at least the possibility of a real plurality of voices at all times. In liberal democracies, balancing the various—and perhaps contrary— interests found in a pluralistic society is undertaken procedurally through regular, free, and fair elections open to all citizens. The very real threat of a "tyranny of the majority" is addressed through comprehensive and well-enforced systems of constitutionally protected political, civil, and legal rights. Importantly, these rights serve the dual purpose of both safeguarding the expression of individual and minority interests, and protecting citizens against potentially coercive state practices. In keeping with its core values of freedom of choice, equality, and a tolerance for difference, the liberal democratic state maintains an explicitly neutral stance with respect to the nature of the good life. Policies are determined (at least ideally) by constitutionally mandated processes of fair competition among contending views—an essentially *"market"* approach to governance.

The merits of liberal democracy and the protections afforded by the rights regimes that are crucial to its fair engagement with plural interests are well known. But even within the West, where the liberal tenet of individual autonomy has often assumed the status of a factual given rather than a challengeable presupposition, the liberal articulation and practice of democracy has come under considerable scrutiny by those who see it as overvaluing individualism and rationalism; as unduly focused on procedures rather than principles; and as morally anemic. Communitarian worries, expressed by both the political right (MacIntyre 1984) and left (Taylor 1989; Sandel 1982), critique liberalism's overemphasis on individual autonomy and equality, arguing that it threatens to reduce the democratic process to a purely quantitative balancing act, producing policies bereft of any coherent and qualitatively rich vision of the common (e.g., national) good.

The liberal rejoinder is that outside of the arena of intellectual debate, passions often trump moral virtues. As made evident in the populist rise of the religious right in the United States and of Hindu communalism in India, the disturbing fact we have to confront is that political passions can often assume *exclusionary* religious or communal forms. Indeed, as is now all too familiar, the political mobilization of passion—whether on the side of democracy or autocracy—can easily take on an intolerant and totalizing (if not totalitarian) edge that is readily directed to excising those who happen or dare to differ (Nancy 1991).

In illiberal democracies, society itself is taken to be the unit of political analysis, not the private individual. In keeping with this focal shift from persons to the public as a collective whole, ensuring the good of society is not taken to be a function of competitively ranking sums of individual interests through representative voting mechanisms. Rather, it is understood to be a function of state-organized deliberations. Here, the state has no pretension of being neutral with respect to the nature of the good life and actively undertakes its articulation and implementation. Not surprisingly, illiberal democracies reserve the right to establish the proper range of life choices consistent with achieving the maximally productive and harmonious development of society as a whole—a process that is corporately managed by a rationally motivated, techno-bureaucratic elite. In practice, if not in principle, this entails being keenly attuned both to communitarian concerns about the excesses of liberalism, and to the dangers of passionately constituted communalism. And so, whereas liberal democracies work to insure the possibility of a plurality of politically salient values and interests *within the state*, illiberal democracies are inclined to insist on the right to the plurality of interests and evaluations of the good *among states*. Rather than appealing to a market-like mechanism of competition among views and values, illiberal democracies hold that government properly plays an essentially *"managerial"* role with respect to difference.

Illiberal democracy has proven—very much against the expectations of some—to be highly compatible with stimulating and sustaining rapid economic growth and modernization. Visitors to Singapore, for example, are invariably impressed with the quality of its public infrastructure, the safety of its streets, and the vibrancy of its economic life. But illiberal democracies are also targets of pointed social, cultural, and political critique. The denial of political intelligibility—and in some cases, legal status—to a "loyal opposition" has inclined illiberal states toward actively limiting freedoms of expression, especially expressions of political dissent. By thus subordinating the "right to think" to state-defined "right thinking," illiberal states open themselves to questions about their capacities for fully understanding and then acting in the best, and necessarily plural, interests of the modern societies they govern.

Perhaps even more damagingly, illiberal democracy's technocratic approach to addressing the kinds of challenges facing contemporary societies is itself open to critical challenge. While the complexity of contemporary realities practically compels governments to make use of "expert systems" in shaping public policy, we now also know that these same systems of expertise are profoundly implicated—however ironically—in the increasing volatility and expanded scales and scopes of hazards, risks, and threats associated with reflexive modernization. Expert systems are well suited to solving problems, working within preexisting parameters and values; they are not suited to the significantly ethical—and not merely technical—task of predicament resolution. Illiberal prohibitions of publicly expressing and exploring significantly different understandings of the common good and its core values is likely to compound the considerable liability of any state's reliance on techno-bureaucratic systems of expertise.

Differing: How Much versus How Well

Granted that there is no equity without diversity, one explanation of democratic failures to induce globally robust arcs of equitable change is that, in spite of assuring spaces for a politically salient multiplicity of perspectives, democratic states are not necessarily capable of or committed to insuring that differentiation processes result in more than mere variation. In spite of their otherwise sharply contrasting characters, liberal and illiberal practices of democracy are alike in their commitments to protect the right to *differ-from* one another as equals. In *liberal* states, this is construed as the *right of individual citizens to exercise choice* in their personal pursuit of well-being. In *illiberal* states, it is construed as the *right of individual polities to exercise control* of the sorts needed to insure the well-being of society as a whole. That is, the spectrum of liberal to illiberal possibilities in the practice of democratic politics reproduces an animating tension at the heart of the modern conception of freedom: the tension between choice and control. Where liberal and illiberal democracies differ is in how they locate autonomy—as an inalienable property of the individual or of society as a whole—and the proper scope of its exercise. That is, what ultimately distinguishes liberal and illiberal democracies is the vector of their commitment to conserving *political variety*, not how committed they are to valorizing and realizing *political diversity*.[3]

When *how much* we *differ-from* one another—the root index of variety—is of primary concern, it is natural to see conflict resolution as a function of balancing interests by *weighing* and then differentially *weighting* disparate *claims to power*. The liberal democratic ideal (yet to be realized) is that the claims of all individuals and freely associating groups within society are originally and institutionally equal.[4] The illiberal democratic ideal (also yet to be realized) is that the claims of all sovereign states and free associations thereof are originally and institutionally equal. Stated otherwise, liberal and illiberal democracies—like universalist and relativist ethics—are in agreement about the primacy of the value of equality: "we" should all be treated the same. In neither liberal nor illiberal states is difference itself understood as something to be appreciated—something to be both valued and resolutely enhanced.

When *how well* we *differ-for* one another is of primary concern—the root index of diversity—concerns about how to balance interests (an essentially quantitative endeavor) yield to those about how to best *coordinate* them (a resolutely qualitative one). Realizing political diversity is not easily reconciled with the kinds of agency and institutions that inspire and regulate the finite games crucial to the *politics of power*—games that are played for the purpose of winning and that must end in dichotomously opposed experiences of victory and loss. Political diversity consists in our deepening implication in a *politics of strength*. That is, political diversity does not result from wielding capacities for determining or controlling how things are and will be, or from autonomously exercised freedoms-of-choice. Rather it emerges as a complex function of the capacities and commitments needed to play well the infinite game of according with our situation, responding as needed to sustain and further the interests of all involved.[5] In short, if political variety is a *relative* function of the power to autonomously exercise *freedoms of choice*, political diversity is a *relational* function of strengths for *relating-freely*.

Granted that the modern, secular state originated as a mechanism for balancing the interests of contending, often profoundly opposed religious and ethnic factions, it is not surprising that it has been characterized by the valorization of political variety. The conservation of variety can be centrally managed. And since the conservation of political variety involves securing relatively equal rights to choose, it is also not surprising that the modern era has been dominated by national and international politics of power structured centripetally on answering questions of who is in control and to what degree. Whether the answers have been framed in accord with the liberal bias toward guaranteeing rights to vary within a given state or in accord with the illiberal bias toward maintaining conditions for variety among states, the result has been a relationally thin pluralism grounded in the valorization and practice of tolerance.[6]

This relationally thin engagement with difference works against the emergence of diversity and brings about conditions in which equity becomes an ideal for which no one is responsible. When refracted through liberal and illiberal interpretations of autonomy and equality, this relational thinness has proved to be instrumental in realizing the basic plausibility condition for both moral monadism and moral monism: the conviction that how "we" do things—as individual human beings or as members of a particular community/country—is at once natural and right.[7] While the former angle of conviction takes the form of assuming that there should be only contingent differences of values among societies, and the latter assumes that this should be so within society, the effect either way is a disinclination to engage difference as relationally significant and as both ethically and politically crucial.

The "inconvenient truth" is that neither the universalist and individualist biases of liberal democracies nor the particularist and culturalist biases of illiberal democracies are conducive to the kind of open deliberation among value systems that is necessitated by such global threats and risks as climate change. In taking account of the fact of plurality, liberal and illiberal democracies alike are inclined toward treating difference as something to be disarmed or overcome—whether through assimilation or special accommodation. In keeping with their disparate emphases on the individual/person and the collective/nation as the central unit of moral and political consideration, this drive toward *inclusion* can result, ultimately and ironically, in failures to engage differences in the resolutely appreciative way needed to address global predicaments. At least insofar as it implies uniformity or the fiction of equality, inclusion is no more conducive to realizing political diversity or predicament resolution than are exclusionary appeals to variety-legitimating claims of essential or irreconcilable differences. Given the scales and scopes of predicament resolution compelled by contemporary realities, and given the depths of the differences that obtain among basic values and perspectives within and among contemporary societies, the opposition of difference and sameness is both ethically and politically crippling.

POLITICAL DIVERSITY AS AN
EMERGING STRUCTURE OF FEELING

Whatever their other merits, there are very real shortcomings common to both liberal and illiberal forms of democracy with respect to realizing political diversity of the extent, depth, and intensity needed to equitably resolve the predicaments with which we are being globally confronted. Given this, we must take seriously the possibility that the *politics of diversity*—a politics that is still yet-to-be—may *not* be a fundamentally *governmental politics*. Rather, it may be a politics centered on the shared realization of a distinctive "structure of feeling"—the realization of a shared lifeworld infused with a distinctive complexion of affectively charged sensitivities and sensibilities.

Exploring this possibility must be undertaken with "eyes wide open." As has been made all too painfully obvious over recent decades, there are dangerous liabilities in turning toward passion-fueled politics as a means to addressing manifest differences of identity, interests, and values. We need only recall the history of racial terror perpetrated by the Ku Klux Klan in the United States, the thousands of deaths resulting from the Hindu-Muslim riots in North India after the destruction of the Babri Masjid, or the communities and people being literally torn apart by suicide bombings in Palestine, Iraq, and Afghanistan to understand just how powerfully communal sentiment can run contrary to the activation of our differences as the basis of mutual contribution and sustainably shared welfare. If the politics of diversity cannot be built on a set of foundational governmental structures and institutions, but instead can only be induced to emerge from within a shared structure of feeling, it is clear that not just any feeling will do and that it is our burden to discern precisely what feeling opens relational dynamics in the direction of diversification.

Moreover, as Jean-Luc Nancy (2000) has pointed out with particular keenness, we must be careful not to confuse *shared* structures of feeling with those that are experienced in/as *common*—a structure within/through which we each have "the same" feeling(s). A truly *shared* structure of feeling in Nancy's terms would be one in which we each have a distinctive, contributory stake—a structure that incorporates and enables the activation and further articulation of our differences. This is an important distinction. In contrast with the difference-revealing experience of a shared structure of feeling, the experience of a common structure of feeling is one of being swept up indistinguishably into a compelling whole—the experience of being essentially *the same*. This may take the transient form of the single-mindedness of a mob; but it can also take on the more permanent and pernicious forms of social, economic, political, cultural, and technological totalitarianism. Nancy himself forwards a conception of "inoperative community" to call attention to the need to delink community from any sense of literal communion or common essence—whether "naturally occurring" as claimed by German fascists, or consciously crafted for ultimately disciplinary purposes—and, instead, to align community with sustained and creative differentiation (Nancy 2000, 59).

This alignment with creativity or the living dynamism of human sociality is, in fact, crucial to Raymond Williams' insistence on the herme-
neutical and critical importance of structures of feeling. For Williams, the
apparently oxymoronic combination of "structure," with its connotations
of fixity and objectivity, and "feeling," with its connotations of fluidity and
subjectivity, is a way of directing attention to *emerging* relational dynamics—a counter at once to modern, especially capitalist and nationalist,
metanarratives of teleological progress and development, and to Marx-
ist/socialist metanarratives of materialist determination. As a particular
quality of historically distinct social experiences and relationships, a given
structure of feeling is in actuality a structuring process through which
elements of impulse, restraint, tone, and tension come into abiding and
yet continually changing constellation with both felt and thought aspects
of consciousness and relationality: "practical consciousness of a present
kind, in a living and interrelating community" (Williams 1977, 132). In
discerning a given structure of feeling, then, we are not encountering
an already established set of fixed institutions or societal formations, but
rather "social experiences *in solution*, as distinct from other social semantic
formations which have been *precipitated*" (pp. 132–33) as specific features
of "society" or "the economy" or "politics." Structures of feeling are evident only "at the very edge of semantic availability" (p. 133) as distinctive
"changes of presence" that holistically affect experience and action, even if
we are not yet able to define, classify, or rationally explain them.

Unlike the "spirit of an age" which infuses a given lifeworld as its
essential and defining character, or a socioeconomic, cultural, or political agenda in accordance with which all of our pursuits are organized, a
structure of feeling is more akin to a qualitative crescendo of relational
dynamics—a crescendo emerging from within what is soon to be no-lon-
ger, in coalescent intimation of what is still not-yet. That is, structures
of feeling are not completed works, or even works in progress, but rather
expressive embodiments of what is *newly working*. It is in light of this that
Williams notes that we become *aware* of the structure of feeling emerging
at any given place and time through the experienced ways in which we
differ in constituting a qualitatively shared lifeworld. In other words, we
find ourselves co-implicated in the expression of a new structure of feeling
precisely through realizing how we differ meaningfully from one another.

My suggestion that the politics of diversity will emerge as/through
shared capacities-for and commitments-to differing-for and not merely
differing-from one another builds on Williams' insight into the nondualistic, relational nature of structures of feeling. That is, *the politics of diversity can be seen as a still-emerging structure of feeling at once resulting-from
and resulting-in ongoing amplifications of our differences as the basis of mutual
contribution—a structure of feeling dynamically aligned with the appreciation*

of strengths for relating-freely. Far from implying or implicating us in some fixed governmental framework or institutional architecture, the politics of diversity consists distinctively in the coalescence of differentially realized patterns of ever-strengthening readiness for shared, value-generating relational improvisation.[8]

As the "oxymoronic" nature of the term suggests, structures of feeling are ontologically ambiguous and cannot be accurately categorized as either "objective" or "subjective," as both, or as neither. Necessarily, this would be especially true for any structuring process of emerging strengths for relating-freely in improvised expansion of the scopes and scales of diversity across the full range of interdependencies constituting the contemporary world. As a cogently affective and practical expression of what is newly working, the structure of feeling through/as which the politics of diversity is emerging is not any sort of stable *foundation.* It is a distinctive *modality* of change processes—a modality of appreciating difference that cannot be reduced, as more generally noted by Williams, to some "epiphenomena of changed institutions, formations, and beliefs, or merely secondary evidence of changed social and economic relations" (2000, 131). On the contrary, the crafting of new institutions and formal relations will only in retrospect give evidence of the working-out-from-within-the-present of diversification as a newly coalescing value or modality of relational appreciation.

One of the purposes of crossing back and forth, as we have done, over several centuries of global history, at different levels and along different arcs of association, has been to elicit an appreciation of prospects for qualitative changes—emerging from within the ascent of difference itself as a crucial contemporary issue and concern—that would express the advent of relational dispositions oblique to both modern discourses of progressive unification and postmodern discourses of free variation. As I have described it, the "obliqueness" of these dynamics is a complex function of their conduciveness to differential expressions of readiness for value-generating relational improvisation—a readiness for qualitatively transforming how we differ. Speaking of this new structure of feeling as one of *relating-freely* is in part a way of stressing its relational nature—the fact that the politics of diversity exceeds the possibilities of being either subjective (a transformation of the agent) or objective (a transformation of the acted-upon), being both, or being neither. But it is also in part to direct attention to the phenomenological distinctiveness of "freedom" in this emerging politics.

Among the most troubling disclosures of the wayfaring undertaken thus far is the coincidence among the emerging attention economy; network- and market-generated proliferations of choice; and the progressive concentration of wealth and power in an ever-smaller portion of the global population. To the degree that we would work out from present global dynamics in the direction of enhancing diversity and equity as a global relational commons and public good, this coincidence suggests the need for exercising particular care *not* to confuse relating-freely with the experience of *being-free*, especially as "equal" and "autonomous" agents. To be sure, the feeling of being-free is preferable to that of not being free, just as having choices is preferable to having none. Indeed, whether interpreted liberally as a key factor in realizing "justice" (as Rawls does) or illiberally as crucial to securing national "sovereignty" (as the Communist Party of the People's Republic of China does), there is much to recommend both the immediate subjective sense of being-free and its more objective political expression. But insofar as being-free is understood as inseparable from the conditions for jointly assured equality and autonomy, it implies the production of situational dynamics inflected toward increasing variation—a modality of differentiation that does not entail attention or commitments to the qualitative transformation of relational dynamics as such.

Identity, Difference, Recognition, and Respect: From the Formal to the Felt

In fact, insight into the insufficiency of even quite substantial autonomy and freedoms-of-choice to bring about significant, equity-enhancing relational transformation has factored crucially into the development— especially over the last half century—of increasingly incisive forms of other-than-governmental global politics. One of the most important concurrences of the second half of the twentieth century was that of intensifying Cold War competition between would-be Western and Soviet-bloc hegemonies, and intensifying critical engagement with the legacies of colonialist, capitalist, and classist exclusion. As exemplified, for example, in the 1960s by global intersections among the civil rights, women's, student, antiwar, environmental, and postcolonial movements, and over the 1970s by a surge of indigenous rights, nationalist, and subnationalist movements, engagement with issues of identity and exclusion against the background of competing "individualist" and "collectivist" models of social well-being had the politically explosive result of fusing considerations of difference with those of justice and good governance.

Although far from uniform in expression, the politics of identity can be seen as rooted in two key insights: first, that each of us is differentially embedded—socially, economically, politically, culturally, and technologically—in local, national, regional, and global dynamics; and, second, that the resulting differences in opportunities and outcomes cannot (by those most adversely affected) and should not (by those more fortunate) be imagined away. Especially when such differences are a result, not of personal shortcomings, but of structural exclusion—due, for example, to religious affiliation, ethnicity, or gender—they command explicitly political attention and response.

The practical result of identity politics was in most cases legally guaranteed political recognition and representation, augmented in some cases by formal compensatory mechanisms. But its most important ethical ramification was forced confrontation with difference as a historically dynamic *relationship* the breadth, depth, and quality of which are neither fixed nor a matter of chance. What quickly became apparent, however, is that redressing past and ongoing injustices requires much more than being legally guaranteed rights as political "equals" and perhaps being granted some measure of institutionally delivered compensation. From roughly the middle of the 1980s, the politics of identity and difference began giving way to a politics of recognition which insisted that, in addition to the legally guaranteed freedoms from social, economic, and political exclusion, individuals and groups whose differences set them "apart" are also due genuine respect—that is, respect accorded, not *in spite* of how they are different, but rather in affirmation of them *as* different (Kruks 2001, 85).

The demand for respect moves us in the direction of explicitly acknowledging the political salience of a felt dimension of difference-expressing relationships. Respect is not a product of cursory and inconsequential encounters. It is evidence of positively evaluated and obligation-structured interpersonal dynamics that meaningfully constrains personal autonomy. The politics of recognition and respect thus brings into focus some important liabilities of according political primacy to exercising freedoms-of-choice in the pursuit of diversity and equity. As Charles Taylor observes, "in the flattened world, where the horizons of meaning become fainter, the ideal of self-determining freedom comes to exercise a more powerful attraction . . . [and it] seems that significance can be conferred by *choice*, by making my life an exercise in freedom, even when all other sources fail" (Taylor 1992, 69). But, in fact, what allows us to have truly *shared* focuses and projects and not merely parallel ones is not just being able to exercise freedoms-of-choice. What we need above and beyond choice is an organically constituted and affectively rich set of "the ways people imagine their social existence, how they fit together with others, how things go on between them and their fellows, the expectations that are normally met, and the deeper normative notions and images that underlie these expectations" (Taylor 2004, 25). It is only in the context of such dense and value-rich relational dynamics that we are likely to enjoy the trust necessary to open ourselves to being *enhanced* by the differences of others.

The politics of identity rightly insists that the cosmopolitan stance toward difference as contingent, and hence politically irrelevant, is not acceptable. The politics of recognition and respect adds to this the conviction that not only is tolerating difference is not enough, guaranteeing rights to political representation and participation is not enough. The experiences and effects of exclusion are not eliminated by the factual achievement of coexistence or even the idealization of exceptionless inclusion. Differences must be understood *and* appreciated.[9] And yet, respect and appreciation cannot be forced any more than affection can. Respect for those who differ—whether because of their ethnicity, race, gender, or religion, their sexual orientation, age, or disability, or even because of such seemingly elective categories of difference as lifestyle and affective citizenship (Mookherjee 2005)—cannot be effectively legislated. Respect can be earned and it can be offered, but it cannot be compelled.

The politics of recognition and respect thus not only insists that we acknowledge the political salience of the felt dimensions of relational dynamics, it also points us toward considering the limitations of governmental politics in bringing about the conditions for political diversity. This said, however, it is not clear that recognizing and respecting those who differ—even insofar *as* they are different and not *in spite* of it—will suffice to orient differentiation processes toward greater diversity. After all, recognition and respect can be earned and offered without us ever coming to see others as differing from us in ways that contribute significantly to realizing mutually enhancing arcs of change. That is, we can recognize and respect others *as* different without activating our differences as the basis of mutual contribution. The politics of recognition and respect emerged in response to the realization that formally ending exclusion is not the same thing as fully functional inclusion, and it has first and foremost been a politics aimed at bringing about the conditions needed for full and authentic self-realization. But being-free and even being encouraged to articulate our own individual and collective identities—as important as that is—is also not the same thing as realizing the kind of qualitative, relational transformation that is both the means-to and meaning-of equity-enhancing diversification.[10]

It is entirely possible, for example, for me to *respect* Islamic injunctions against charging interest on loans without feeling compelled to evaluate seriously its relevance to my own society and the equity issues involved in the corporate facilitation and financing of consumer debt. I can respect the Chinese valorization of resolutely hierarchic familial relations without feeling critically bound to question my own, American culture's recent idealization of "democratic" family dynamics in which children and adults have equal voices in family decision-making processes. In other words, recognizing and respecting others can be done without opening ourselves to the depths of evaluative engagement with different value systems that are needed to develop coordinated and resolutely equitable responses to the global predicaments with which we find ourselves increasingly and ever more powerfully confronted.

One approach to moving beyond this shortcoming of the politics of recognition is to examine the perhaps ironic consequences of its conceptual linking of respect and authentic self-realization. As Nancy Fraser points out, the concept of self-realization disposes the politics of recognition toward subjectively or psychologically framed indicators of political success, thus reproducing the common modern and postmodern bias to treat the individual as the basic unit of ethical and political analysis.[11] And while many of the most prominent exponents of the politics of recognition explicitly declare that self-realization is an irreducibly dialogical process, unless interpreted in a purely metaphorical sense, it is the individual communicative agent that remains ontologically basic, however significantly informed by linguistically mediated encounters with others. Moreover, since conceptions of self and of the good life vary dramatically across societies, linking the politics of recognition with self-realization runs the risk of placing politics at odds with the realities of ethical pluralism, especially if one tacitly and erroneously assumes that the elements of self-realization and the character of the good life are already agreed upon by all (Fraser and Honneth 2003).

Put into practice in culturally plural environments, the "politics of recognition" has an unwelcome potential to result in what Cillian McBride (2005) has termed an "excessive deference" that works against the depth of inclusion required for robust and effective democratic contestation and deliberation. Recognition, respect, and multiculturalism then become part of a legitimating code for skirting the deep and expanding predicaments in which we find ourselves embroiled—a rationale for contenting ourselves with variety-conserving policies that McBride sees as conducive to a "re-feudalization" of the public sphere rather than pressing forward with the difficult interactions needed for the emergence of either cultural or political diversity.

Finally, with this risk in mind, it bears recalling that the politics of recognizing and respecting difference emerged in the context of an historical confluence of the end of the Cold War and the apparent triumph of market liberalism; the intensification of risks and volatilities associated with reflexive modernization; the exponential growth of network structures and their propensities for accelerating differentiation; and the advent of a global and media- and information-driven attention economy. This combination not only fostered the philosophical and political ascent of difference, but also a *growing instability within and among the categories of politically relevant difference*. It is not just that familiar kinds of differences and patterns of exclusion are finally being taken into critical, political account, and that awareness is mounting of the need for transitioning from a relationally thin politics of identity to a relationally thick politics of recognition and respect. The range of politically relevant differences is itself undergoing significant differentiation. In this context, the politics of recognition and respect—however necessary, useful and promising in other ways—can easily and ironically slide into an endorsement for ongoing and critically immune, finite games of political variation.

IMPROVISATIONAL READINESS: THE POLITICS OF OPENING

The politics of recognition and respect importantly foregrounds concerns about the felt dimension of difference, particularly where difference is understood as an affectively charged relationship. And, as interpreted by those who, like Fraser and McBride, are unwilling to delink politics from issues of distributive justice and value pluralism, it is a politics with potential to significantly *qualify*—that is, to qualitatively transform—the meaning of freedom.

At the same time, however, as a function of its roots in the politics of identity and its emphasis on expanding the ambit of social, economic, and political inclusion through commanding a voice for each and all, it is also a politics curiously well aligned with the maintenance of existing geographies of power. In the context of network-enabled global capitalism and an attention economy in which social networking portals enable everyone with a computer to have a published voice and face, and in which the expansion of experiential choices is a key mechanism or circuit for preserving and accentuating power hierarchies, the multiplication and magnification of politically salient differences has ironically great potential to work as insurance *against* the coalescence and amplification of holistic global movements actively committed to greater political, economic, social, and cultural diversity and equity.

Admitting this is not to conclude that respect is politically irrelevant with regard to realizing a robust and global politics of diversity. Mutual respect is undeniably crucial to the kind of international and intercultural deliberation required to resolve global predicaments like climate change. But while necessary, recognition and respect alone are not enough. Something more *original* is needed, where original means both creative and primordial, where *creativity* consists in significant innovation, and where the *primordial* consists in relational initiation (Latin: *primus* + *ordiri*, or "the first to begin a web").

Thus far, I have tried to point in the direction of this originality by characterizing political diversity as emerging with readiness for relating-freely in newly working expressions of mutual contribution to sustainably shared flourishing—that is, with the origination of a structure of feeling in which relational improvisation is not just a fact, but a recursively amplifying value or modality of appreciation. Here I want to try fleshing out this characterization by discerning what must occur or flow together for such a structure of feeling to emerge. Given that diversity is not able to be engineered or imposed, this is not a matter of trying to discover what external conditions need to be established for this structure of feeling to occur. Instead, the task we are confronted with is a phenomenological one of discerning what distinctive dispositional dynamics occur in social experience with the expression of strengths for relating-freely. What distinguishes the activation of readiness for relational improvisation?

The descriptions offered thus far of the politics of diversity suggest that we approach this task from two directions. The first approach would be from the perspective of attention to the experiential meaning of shifting from the predominance of individual concerns about how much we differ-from one another to that of concerns about how well we differ-for one another. This is what I have termed a nondualistic engagement with our differences. The second approach would be from the perspective of attention to the shift from seeing politics as a finite game played to acquire, distribute, and retain power, to seeing politics as an infinite game played in expression of strengths for practically articulating means-to and meanings-of shared flourishing. This is what I have termed the expression of relational—and more specifically, appreciative and contributory—virtuosity.

Seeing improvisational readiness as a function of nondualistic engagement with difference and relational virtuosity, as appealing as it may be philosophically, will for most of us suggest counterproductively that the politics of diversity must lie at the far margins of the realm of possibility. For most of us, experiences of nonduality and virtuosity are assumed to lie in the provinces of mystics, geniuses, and other exceptional beings. As I hope to make clear, however, this is in large part a matter of misconstruing nonduality and virtuosity. The distinctive structure of feeling that I have referred to as "relating-freely" is in fact quite familiar.

Parenting: An Exemplification of Readiness to/for Change

Take, for example, the arc of change that occurs with becoming a parent. Although the process of becoming a parent can be plausibly seen as beginning with the birth or adoption of a child, or perhaps at the moment of conception or the decision to adopt, becoming a parent is not a momentary event. We do not *become* mothers or fathers, as if arriving at a preestablished goal or having had something final befall or happen to us. Instead, if we can speak of motherhood and fatherhood as states, they are states of continual *becoming*—a ceaseless, differential process of discovery or disclosure through which we come to differ-from who we were and might have become by differing-for the welfare and flourishing of our child. Parenting changes the ways we are changing. It is not a finite game played in order to finish, something to chalk off our list of adult aims. It is an infinite game that requires not just strength, but ever-changing kinds of strength.

The verb "to parent" literally means "to bring forth" or "breed" and directs attention to the act of "giving birth." But "giving" has the objective connotation of an act of bestowal—an act complete in and of itself—and this is misleading. Parenting is immersion in a continuously transforming process of mutual offering, the fruit of which is a life shared with our sons and daughters—a new kind of life in which distinctively differing contributions merge in ways that are often surprising and challenging. It is, in fact, only through ongoing processes of *relational differentiation* that there emerges what we *mean* by mother, father, son, and daughter.

Put another way, parenting entails continuous, relationally expanding, and interdependence-enhancing improvisation. We can glean insights and draw inspiration from others—especially our own grandparents, parents, siblings, and friends—who have been en route, becoming parents, for longer than we have. But becoming a parent is not just a matter of replicating what has been done by others with whom we abstractly have parenting *in common*. Becoming parents is a process of continuously learning with our children how to most fully and intimately *share* in creating and recreating the relational meaning of family, changing who we *are* by revising what we *mean* for one another. Other adults, societal norms, and cultural institutions can help us see and weigh different options for solving the many common problems of family life, providing us with a store of "tried and true" conventional wisdom. But it ultimately is only through moment-by-moment and unpredictable collaboration with our children that we engage in the processes of predicament resolution through which the meaning of family is expressed as a unique and truly shared arc of qualitative, relational transformation.[12]

In sum, becoming a parent is not just an *alteration* of who we have been. It is not a matter of "tailoring" ourselves—our habits, impulses, thoughts, feelings, daily practices, and desires—to fit the completely novel situational dynamics into which we find ourselves placed by accepting the roles of mothers and fathers. Parenting means full-scale *revision*, a holistic undoing and redoing of what we mean by being human. And the profusion of parenting manuals notwithstanding, this is never finally revision "by the book" or according to a predetermined plan. Parenting always and only takes place live—an improvisation in response to ever-changing dynamics, in real time, with no time off and no time outs.

Now, to be sure, this improvisation can be done well or poorly, with virtuosity or with fixed stances and troubling resistance. Like all other patterns of interdependence, the interdependence among mothers, fathers, sons, and daughters can—and all too often, does—go awry. Improvisations are not all of a single quality. And there are times when even the attempt to improvise fails in hot or cold assertions of power, with all-too-tragic and sadly familiar consequences of both threatened and real abuse and abandonment. But what we are most concerned with here is not the "result" of parenting—the specific outcomes and opportunities that in retrospect define a family's dynamics over time. Instead, we are concerned with the distinctive *quality of presence* that occurs with both embarkation on and full commitment to the parental path of improvising what we experience as entirely new directions and qualities of relational dynamics. This is not the experience of *being ready* to become a parent: the experience of defining ourselves as "parents-to-be." Being ready happens the very moment that we not only recognize and accept the *fact* that we are involved in a pregnancy or adoption, but also choose to carry through biologically or legally to take on the responsibility and status of a mother or father. The quality of presence that I am invoking is something very different—an openness to/for change that is at once values-infusing and values-challenging: a resolutely sustained, creative and primordial *readiness*.

This distinctive way of being present is never something general and abstract, but quite specific and concrete. In my own case, this improvisational readiness did not occur until six months after the birth of my first son. For half a year, although I was already a "father," I had not yet committed myself fully to becoming a parent. Living with my wife and son in a small garage apartment with a kitchen and a bedroom joined by a bathroom at one end and a stairwell landing at the other, I was running and lifting weights in the morning; buying, selling, and trading musical instruments and sound systems during the day; playing guitar an hour or two daily; jamming past midnight once or twice a week with a shifting collective of like-minded musicians; meditating every evening at sundown; reading the world's great religious texts; writing a novel; cooking, cleaning, and in general trying to break through the confines of conventional consciousness and experience into something other and more. In short, I was a new, twenty-five-year-old father living pretty much the same, largely self-centered life I had led before the birth of my son, only with less sleep and with regular and increasingly unwelcome interruptions of my efforts to pursue my own interests.

The turning point came not long after my wife began working again part time and I found myself home alone with our son for an entire day. It was a steaming hot summer day of the sort common along the Gulf Coast of Florida—days when the barometer goes haywire as clouds mass overhead for evening thunderstorms, causing migraine-like headaches and potentials for both real and emotional riot. I had planned to write

throughout the day as my son played happily in his crib, mobiles spinning in the morning breeze coming through the open windows, and as
he napped throughout the afternoon. The breeze never came. By midaft-
ernoon, after hours of trying to entertain, feed, carry, rock, cradle, and
console him—all to no avail—I placed him in his crib and decided to let
him cry himself to sleep. He didn't. And after a half hour of his choking
wails of want and indignation, I cracked. Throwing my typewriter onto
the bed, I stomped across the room, screamed down at him with all of my
considerable might, jerked him up out of his sweat-soaked crib, and felt
an almost blindingly muscular compulsion to hurl him out the window.
This surge of violent intent was so sudden and severe that I momentarily
came free of myself, as if moving half a yard to the side to see myself bel-
lowing in frustration.

Luckily, what I saw shocked me into immobility. I gazed down at my
now silent, wide-eyed baby boy and realized how close I had come. I realized that if I continued thinking first and foremost of myself and my own
interests, the day would come when I would not stop. I realized that it was
my cravings and unchecked desires that had led to his conception; my
choices that had led to living in this cramped garage apartment with an air
conditioner we could only afford to run a few hours at night; my dreams
and delusions of talents untapped that kept me from being present enough
to stop his crying and make him gurgle with unthinking glee. I realized
that if I didn't merge his interests with mine, everything else would sooner
or later come undone anyway. So I "gave in" and began offering him my
attention wholly whenever I was with him. If this meant stacking wooden
blocks for an hour, arranging them in new patterns only to knock them
down and start over, then so be it. If it meant playing in the sandbox for
an hour, so be it. What I discovered—much to my surprise—was that it
was possible to do this: attuning myself to his experience and yet responding as needed to keep things interesting for both of us, at once widening
and strengthening the quality of our interactions. Committed finally and
fully to becoming a parent, for a long time thereafter, he was my greatest
teacher and my most rewarding partner in relational improvisation.

In my own experience of becoming a parent, the readiness for improvisation came only at the point that I relinquished my essentially dualistic
discrimination between what my son wanted or needed and what I wanted
or needed. Prior to that moment, I had taken for granted that I had to
carefully weigh his interests against my own and make choices that fairly
distributed my time and attention (my most basic resources). I realized,
of course, that this would mean compromising the energy with which I
could pursue my own interests. But in making choices between the vastly
different interests of a twenty-five-week-old infant and a twenty-five-year-
old man, it had also seemed evident that my interests were intrinsically

"superior" in terms of their conceptual, emotional, and physical scopes and considerations. Realizing the ultimate interdependence of our very different interests dissolved the basis for making such judgments.

Quite to my surprise, I then realized that not imposing my judgments on my son was at the same time freeing myself from the impositions of my own past—the self-sustaining complexion of my values, intentions, and actions to that point in my life. This did not mean that my son and I became "the same," as if I suddenly had lost any sense of the vast differences between us. Neither did it mean that I strictly subordinated my interests to his, inverting my previous judgment about whose interests had priority. Rather, I simply stopped seeing our differences as impediments and instead began *experiencing them with him* as sources of mutual insight and delight. This was a shift away from both attempting to balance our disparate needs and denying any need to balance them because one set would have absolute priority—a shift, finally, in the direction of heightening responsiveness to the quality of what we ultimately shared: our relational dynamics.

Especially when told in the first person, a story like this might easily be dismissed as the recounting of a melodramatic instant that is philosophically and politically impotent with respect to our tasks of discerning an original sense of readiness for relational improvisation and somehow realizing the emergence of a politics of diversity. And for many, especially those with memories of dysfunctional family life or the depredations of authoritarian elites, the very idea of using parenting or the family as a source of political insight will itself seem highly problematic. Using parenting to gain insight into the meaning of the readiness to improvise through and with differences could easily devolve concretely into crafting a paternal (or maternal) politics in which an older and purportedly wiser elite takes responsibility for the growth and development of the rest—a generationally defined illiberal politics that, for reasons already discussed, could hardly be conducive to political, social or cultural diversity.

At the same time, however charitably we interpret it, the parenting metaphor does not point us toward a liberal politics grounded in presuppositions of a common human nature or common rights as individuals—assumptions that would view all interests as "equal" and that would eventually lead us back in the direction of balancing different needs and interests, whether indirectly through voting mechanisms or directly through formal deliberation. While there are those who would liberally regard family members as essentially equal and autonomous individuals, the practical reality is that all families are hierarchically ordered, at least in terms of responsibilities, and the roles assigned to mothers, fathers, sons, and daughters varies dramatically from society to society and from culture to culture.

Taken together, of course, these "disadvantages" illustrate precisely why parenting might be usefully recommended as a primordial expression of readiness for relational improvisation. After all, it is in the effects on the family of change dynamics within and among the social, economic, political, technological, and cultural domains that we most personally and profoundly experience the predicaments characteristic of our particular historical and environmental circumstances. And it is in the family that we first and perhaps most immediately confront issues of power and prejudice, experiencing together with others conflicts that we cannot simply turn our backs on or treat as problems that we can "solve," remaining essentially unchanged in the process. The family is a relational ecology. And if we are fortunate enough, it is one in which we originally witness and participate in the activation of differences as the basis of mutual contribution to sustainably shared flourishing—the emergence and enhancing of diversity.

This said, the fact remains that familial dynamics have also served as theaters of relational degradation and as incubators of threats to diversity—source lessons in ecological failure and collapse. If parenting can be used as a bridge to understanding and realizing the readiness-to-improvise in joint realization of the social experience of relating-freely, it will require refraining from either amassing the detailed particulars of "real" family life in this or that culture and time, or attempting to transcend such particulars through abstract articulations of universally valid familial "ideals."[13]

Improvisation: Toward an Aesthetic of Original Change

There is now a growing body of work that aims at understanding and enacting improvisation as crucial to opening movement from within current economic, social, political, technological, and cultural circumstances in the direction of greater social justice and equitable change.[14] As Fischlin and Heble (2004, 11) argue, at the heart of this critical conception of improvisation is the recognition that improvisation involves the "lived, enacted performance of being differently in the world"—a process of evaluative differentiation expressing, from within our present situation, "possibilities excluded from conventional systems of thought and thus a locus of resistance to orthodoxies of the imagination (knowing), of relations with others (community), and of relations to the materials of the world around us (instruments)." Yet this envisioning of possibilities for critical differentiation is not only a matter of distinguishing ourselves from others and subverting their truths, revealing them as ideological constructs. Improvisation "challenges indifference: the smug knowledge that one's own view of the world is self-validating and can be imposed unproblematically on others" (p. 16). To improvise is to challenge our own tendencies to lapse into habit, inattention, and the presumption of rights to exercise of power over the experiences and aims of others.

When, for example, two jazz saxophonists trade solos in an ever-intensifying crescendo of harmonic, melodic, and rhythmic permutation, it is not a contest to see who "wins." It is a sharing of strengths in which each solo builds on the previous one, with each player responding to the notes offered by the other to hold open new dimensions of playing in which all references to "leading" and "following" lose relevance. This is dual soloing, not a duel. And when it works, both of the lead players and their supporting musicians find themselves together propelled out beyond the prior horizons of their musical and interactive imaginations. As the improvisational guitarist Derek Bailey has said, what improvisation affords are new possibilities, and at its most unexpected (and yet desired) "something happens that so disorientates you that, for a time, which might only last for a second or two, your reactions and responses are not what they would normally be." The original—creative and primordial—nature of improvisation is just this: the discovery that "you can do something you didn't realize you were capable of" (Bailey 1992, 11).

At one level, then, a primary intention of improvisation is "to produce *beginnings*" (Peters 2009, 37). But this is not just doing something different. All moments are different from those that have come before. A beginning is something other and more than this. Beginnings signal changes in the direction or quality of change processes. Improvising involves not only keen attention to ongoing relational dynamics, but also an attunement to possibilities for breaking away from familiar trajectories of change. In ways that we will explore more fully later, this improvisational attunement to possibilities for changing the way things are changing significantly parallels the practical intent of Buddhist teachings of impermanence, and with similar implications for societal transformation. In the context of Buddhist practice, seeing all things as impermanent is in part directed to enabling awareness that our attempts to hold onto things and seek permanent forms of security is counterproductive and lies at the roots of a great deal of our human sufferings. But seeing all things as impermanent is also seeing that there are ultimately no intractable situations. No matter how impacted or blocked a situation may seem, at some scale, in some dimension, it is already changing. All that is in question is the way change is being inflected—its direction and quality. With sufficient relational virtuosity, any situation can be opened in liberating expression of new beginnings, new directions of relational unfolding.

As a means to realizing new beginnings, then, improvisation is a moment-by-moment revising of the meanings, quality, and direction of change. Improvisation *interrupts* the familiar, not simply to avoid repetition, but to creatively *advance* through what is currently taking place. Improvisational beginnings are not instantaneous events that are simply different-from what has gone before. They are exploratory and expressive relational occurrences that demonstrate the dynamic distinction between merely differing-from what has been to differing-for what has yet to be—a process of extending and enhancing the quality and scope of relational dynamics, be they musical, dramatic, commercial, or political.

Importantly, as a qualitative advancing of presently occurring relational dynamics, improvisations do not occur in historical vacuums. Improvised beginnings are not like the "beginnings" invoked in myths of transcendent creation—events that happen along the edge of time where temporality and eternity blend indistinguishably. Improvised beginnings emerge *from within* history and in response to it. Improvisation is not *creatio ex nihilo* or "creation from nothing"—the "paradigm of all power relations . . . that require the tensions among component elements to be resolved in favor of one of the components" (Hall 1982, 249). Improvising is *creatio ab intra* or a strength-expressing "creating from within"—an irreducibly reflexive and transactional creativity that interrupts the flow of time, in real time, not to determine what will happen, but to work out from whatever is now occurring as means-to expressing the meaning-of relating-freely.

As many improvisers claim, this making of new beginnings entails being fully "in the moment," not as a blank slate, waiting for something to happen or be transcribed in, on, or through us. It is presence of the concentrated kind that brings all of our past (personal and cultural) resources to the verge of expression and then refrains from allowing them to determine where we go from within *this* moment, and the next, and the next. Improvisational interruption, then, has the character of continuous *departure*—a continual movement that is not *from* this place *to* that one (movement focused on a predetermined destination), but rather *from* this place *toward* no place at all (movement in a new direction). And in this sense, all improvising is transutopian activity—a departing for what the jazz innovator Sun Ra points toward as "the other side of nowhere." Improvisation ultimately consists in taking all previously played or imagined music—or all previously realized or imagined dramas, families, economies, or politics—and working with and through them as *metaphors* or bridges cantilevered *out* toward something still unknown and not-yet. Improvising is opening new *headings* within situational dynamics: *new arcs and modalities of appreciation.* It is the ongoing explication or unfolding of new values and meanings from within things as they have come to be.

In this sense, it can be said that culture originates and flourishes in and through improvisation. The infinitesimal difference between the human and the animal invoked by Mencius—the capacity-for and apparent

commitment-to opening new domains of value within such familiar animal activities as eating and procreating—is an improvisationally realized
difference. For Mencius, what distinguishes humans and animals is not
learning. All animals change behavior in response to changing circumstances, solving problems commensurate with the scope and scale of their
awareness. What is distinctively human is improvising—the opening of
qualitatively new kinds of relational dynamics, new and recursively amplifying arcs of appreciative resolution (both clarity and commitment). It is
in this light that we should understand the Confucian claim that it is not
the *dao* or natural patterning of things that extends the human, but rather
the human that extends the *dao* (*Analects* 15/29). Changing circumstances
alone do not cause a broadening of what it means to be human; rather,
it is the distinctively human capacity for qualitative differentiation that
broadens the meaning of the *dao*, opening up new headings within (and,
indeed, for) the world.

Given the characterization of improvisation as metaphorical conduct
without destination and yet directed toward the "other side of nowhere,"
and given the origination of cultures in shared and qualitatively distinct
arcs of change, it is perhaps to be expected that it is also distinctively
human to open possibilities for the experience of predicament or conflicts
among values. Interrupting the already given and familiar to advance into
the unknown and not-yet affords no guarantees of remaining together.
It is always possible—and, indeed, likely—that we will not all cantilever
relational bridges along the same arcs of appreciation. Beginning together
does not assure staying together. This is true whether we are improvising musically, dramatically, romantically, or politically. If a collective
improvisation works, there is an interweaving of the arcs of appreciation
undertaken by all of those involved, and what each offers functions as a
contribution that sustains and further enhances the relational dynamics
underway. And, as we know from the histories of our own families, if it
does not work, then things either revert to what is habitual or fall apart.
In musical improvisation, the result is either safe repetition or cacophony.
More generally, we might simply call these "reversions to the status quo"
or "noise"—the demonstrated failure of our joint efforts at advancing relational dynamics to cohere or hold meaningfully together.[15]

The crucial question, however, is what is occurring when conflicts are
perceived by all involved as productively resolving in ways that not only
allow them to share in relating-freely, but also to surprisingly enhance the
quality with which they are doing so. How is it that we avoid falling into
and becoming mired in conflicts over what to appreciate, or over what new
modalities of appreciation to open and how to constellate them? What
enables us to share in cantilevering interactions out into the unknown,
and to *not* have them collapse beneath us?

Improvisation and Conflict Resolution: A Buddhist Perspective

I would like to begin responding to these questions by means of a final Buddhist detour, this time through a specific text—the *Atthakavagga* (or Octets Chapter) in the *Sutta Nipāta*, one of the earliest collections of teachings attributed to the historical Buddha. In this text, as elsewhere in especially the earlier strata of the Buddhist canon, the primary focus is on offering both conceptual and practical strategies for authoring our own liberation from trouble and suffering, understood as the experiential results of conflicts among our own values, intentions, and actions: our karma. That is, the teachings in the *Atthakavagga* are directed first and foremost toward generating clarity about how troubling and predicament-expressing patterns of interdependence occur and, second, toward realizing commitments of the kind needed to change the way things are currently changing. As such, they are teachings aimed at stimulating insight into both the meaning-of and means-to doing what we have not yet done: eschewing repetition to begin improvising truly liberating relational dynamics.

Three of the *suttas* (recorded teachings of the Buddha) included in the *Atthakavagga* directly address conflict and contention, their root causes, and the means-to and meaning-of dissolving them.[16] In keeping with our earlier discussions of nonduality, these *suttas* locate the ultimate source of conflicted relational dynamics in the self-articulating tendency to set up things as "pairs of opposites." This can take the familiar and apparently innocuous form of perceiving one thing as pleasant and another as unpleasant, or one as desirable and another as not. But it can also take epistemic form in the expression, for example, of the conviction that "this is true, all else is false" or the rank ordering of things, ideas, people, and processes as "superior," "equal," or "inferior." Thus, in sharp contrast with the experience of improvisationally manifest arcs of contributory appreciation, the experience of conflict reveals identification with a self standing apart from things in judgment of them—the assumption of a position of power, a position from which to calculate the merits of various behavioral options and to determine what is or is not optimal. That is, the advent of conflict is inseparable from reducing freedom to freedoms-of-choice.

As these and other Buddhist texts make evident, however, the route to ending conflict is *not* the eradication of choice. In fact, the elimination or refusal of choice is itself an example of setting things up in "pairs of opposites"—in this case, choice and no-choice, exercising "free will" or submitting to "fate" or "chance." Buddhist liberation is not a function of choosing or refraining from choosing. It is a function of *realizing* the meaning of nonduality as hindrance-less relational dynamics: the situationally apt expression of attentively poised responsive virtuosity. The end of conflict is thus also not the elimination of differences, but rather the readiness to accord with ever-differing situational dynamics, responding without appeal to any fixed views and principles, without any reliance on past knowledge, traditional rites, or set rules and methods.[17] In other words, the process of dissolving the roots of conflict and contestation—even when these occur in the course of improvisation—can be realized only improvisationally.

This should not be confused with acting at random or indiscriminately. The realization of Buddhist nondualism is not equivalent to achieving a strictly value-neutral presence in the world. The Buddha's teaching career, after all, was devoted to providing effective strategies for liberation from trouble and suffering, not for simply accepting things however they have come to be. In terms introduced earlier, Buddhist nondualism means practically differentiating between *akusala* patterns of outcome and opportunity—that is, patterns judged as good, bad, or neutral—and those that are *kusala* or virtuosic. Buddhist nonduality is not entering into a state of adamantine detachment from things, but rather discerning the meaning of *kusala* engagement with them.

The improvisational nature of *kusala* conduct is signaled, in fact, by the metaphorical depiction of Buddhist teachings as a raft, and Buddhist practice as a passage by means of them toward an unseen "other shore." In sharp contrast with sacred texts understood as containing the absolute truth about the world, Buddhist teachings are explicitly understood as conveniences, assembled out of what is near to hand, that are to be abandoned once they have performed their intended function. At the same time, this function is clearly open-ended since the "other shore" is itself not a well-defined goal, a fixed destination. The very term used to qualitatively anticipate the "other shore"—in Pali, *nibbana*, and in Sanskrit, *nirvana*—makes this quite clear; it literally means "blown out" or "cooled down." Asking about the location or nature of the "other shore" is like asking about the location or status of a candle flame once it has been blown out. There is no intelligible way of answering such a question because it results from a kind of category mistake. The Middle Path is traveled by improvised means, not to arrive at some predetermined state of liberation, but in active expression of the meaning of liberating, relational virtuosity.

One implication of this understanding of conflict, its sources, and its resolution is that we cannot expect too much of the embrace of tolerance and respect as the foundation for a global politics of difference. Tolerance and respect are both conceptually wedded to the notion of independently existing selves and cultures. Experientially, they connote the possession of real options for ignoring and/or deferentially acknowledging those who differ significantly from us—options for enjoying purely external and contingent relationships in which we remain completely "free" to abstain from the critically self-transforming process of differing-for others. Resolving improvisational conflicts requires going well beyond simply refraining from dogmatism or the prescriptive universalization of our own convictions.

Improvisation occurs with the advent of new beginnings, but without the imposition of expected or desired endings. As was stressed earlier, improvisation is not an endeavor undertaken in order to finish, a "finite game" from which we expect to walk away having won, lost, or played to a draw. Improvisation is playing without fixed destinations or predetermined rewards: an "infinite game" that can only be played well by playing with or outside the rules—a playing that refrains from prescribing where things can, should, or must go. Yet, playing with or outside the rules— resulting at its best in playing with utter abandon, exceeding all known capabilities—is not equivalent to acting randomly or in self-centered and self-seeking disregard for others. Initiating and sustaining improvisation requires of us a resolute readiness to go beyond merely hearing to truly *listening*—and not just with our ears, but with all of our senses. That is, improvising requires us to be both *fully attentive* and *actively open* to what is occurring.

In his phenomenology of music listening, the sociologist Alfred Schutz (1976) describes listening to music as a process of "mutual tuning-in," an opening to experiencing a continual unfolding and flowing forward of the music *along with* the musicians. Truly listening to music is to experience the flowing together of consciousnesses in "vivid simultaneity"—a sense of "growing older together." For Schutz, this mutual tuning-in is the originary social experience. And, for him, this means that—unlike the Pythagorean theorem, for example, which can be grasped monothetically or all at once (even if we can no longer remember how to prove it)—social meaning cannot be seen at a glance; it can only be realized polythetically, in a moment-by-moment unfolding. That is, like musical meaning, social meaning cannot be explained—literally, laid out completely on a single plane. It can only emerge over time as we "keep time" with others in shared experience. In short, improvising requires both *listening* and *remembering*—a continuous weaving together of what has been, what is, and what is yet-to-be. Indeed, it is only through both listening and remembering that we have the opportunity to avoid repetition and cliché, to play something that is not only different, but that also makes a *meaningful* difference (Peters 2009, 81–86). Improvisation is not the abandonment of history, but rather its interruption and, if successful, its meaningful revision and reorientation.

Sustaining the mutual attunement required to improvise meaningful social experience requires a qualitative shift in attention. And among the several reasons for turning to musical improvisation for insight into the meaning of this shift, one is that we are quite comfortable noting the qualitative distinction between merely hearing and actively listening. In fact, however, we can only hope to engage in meaningful social, economic, political, and cultural improvisation if we also go similarly beyond not only "merely" seeing, tasting, smelling, and touching, but also beyond perceiving things through "merely" thinking and emotionally feeling.[18] And, with important political implications, this shift of attention also entails going qualitatively beyond merely recollecting. Recalling things does no more than to bring them into experiential coexistence, without any implication of significant relationship among or with them. Remembering things is a process of actively accentuating and revising the dynamics of significance at play among and with things in ways that affect us in the most intimate way possible: from within. In sum, improvisation involves demonstrating what might be called horizonless attention: a being present that is utterly and *originally* attentive to reconstituting the meaning of presence.

In Mahayana Buddhist traditions, this attentive readiness and capacity for history-revising remembrance is epitomized by Guanyin, a bodhisattva or enlightening being who is often represented as having a thousand arms with eyes in the center of each hand, and whose full name (*guan-shi-yin*) literally means "perceiving world sound" or more figuratively, "perceiving the cries of the world." As symbolized by Guanyin's thousand eyes, bodhisattvas are not restricted or attached to a single perspective on things. But neither are they restricted or attached to one method or another of engagement with others. To be a bodhisattva is to embody or manifest limitless *upaya* or situationally apt, responsive virtuosity. Importantly, this is not understood to be an intrinsic capacity or evidence of superior talent or natural abilities. Rather, bodhisattvas' responsive virtuosity is understood as an emergent function of the specific vows they have taken: the modally distinct and proactive complexion of commitments they have promised to activate resolutely for the purpose of helping all sentient beings realize freedom from trouble and suffering. This is explicitly understood as an unending task—an infinite endeavor. And given the continually changing nature of all things, keeping such vows requires unflagging readiness both for and to change—a readiness to improvise with and through the present situation, as it has come to be (*yathabhutam*), expressing ever-evolving means-to and meanings-of liberation or relating-freely.

This is a very grand vision of improvisational genius, of course. Encountered from the right angle, it might serve quite inspirational purposes. But for most of us, the very grandeur of such a vision is likely to serve as license instead to absolve ourselves of any responsibility for taking it seriously. It is hard to imagine either emulating or drawing politically relevant insight from a being capable of simultaneously sustaining a thousand points of view on every situation and yet responding to each with singular and liberating virtuosity. And, while we might be able to angle our engagement with the image of the thousand-eyed Guanyin to see it as a metaphor for a truly functional democracy that resists classification as either liberal or illiberal, from slightly different angles it would not be hard to see it as a metaphor for either Bentham's utopian panopticon or Foucault's dystopian vision of the same.

Yet the point of introducing this image of improvisational virtuosity is not to distract us into esoterically "inspiring," but politically irrelevant, musings. Neither Buddhist teachings about the responsive commitments and capacities of bodhisattvas nor those about the causes of conflict and the means to resolving it were developed in search of or support for an esoterically experienced ideal world. On the contrary, they were developed and delivered in the daily life context of eliciting a readiness for improvisation among unapologetically practical villagers and townspeople whose lives revolved around farming, modestly scaled local manufacturing, and growing urban and regional trade. The Buddha's audiences were by all accounts well-versed in transcendental visions of eternal and soul-freeing merger with a reality above and beyond mundane experience, but also in materialist visions of the total extinction of the experiencing self upon death, and in complex traditions of rituals and sacrifices ostensibly effective in bringing about experientially better lives here and now. What the Buddha offered was not an esoteric alternative to these approaches for understanding and responding to the trouble and suffering that were so very much a part of the lives of people then, as now. Rather, what Buddhist teachings offered was an invitation to immediacy—an invitation to begin changing the way things are changing through strengthening commitments-to and capacities-for relating differently.

As is made evident both by the inclusion of men and women from every sector and strata of society in the early Buddhist community, and by the numbers of laypeople who realized full liberation in the course of the Buddha's own teaching career, accepting this invitation was understood as something that could be undertaken in the midst of daily life.[19] In the *Atthakavagga* chapter of the *Sutta Nipāta*, practical emphasis is placed on realizing nonoppositional engagement—the practice of nonreliance and the relinquishing of all fixed perspectives—as key to changing the quality and direction of relational dynamics. Elsewhere, the realization of nondualistic immediacy is more positively characterized as the practice of mindfulness or nonjudgmental awareness—a practice that, when sustained, is understood as concomitant with the deepening and expanding suffusion of one's situation with the appreciative relational headings of compassion, loving-kindness, equanimity, and joy in the good fortune of others. Or more generally stated, conflict resolution ultimately is a function of attuning to potentials—already present in our situation, as it has come to be—for amplifying and accelerating relationally manifest mutual appreciation.

Embodying the readiness for improvisation through mindfulness and the qualitative transformation of relational dynamics was understood as being well within the capabilities of all whom the Buddha engaged, including not a few political leaders. I believe that this remains true today, and that the cultivation of mindfulness and responsive virtuosity are crucial to realizing a global politics of diversity that would not merely secure rights to differ *from* one another, but that would also demonstrate the meaning of working out from within contemporary realities, as they have come to be, in the direction of enhancing strengths for and commitments to differing *for* one another, improvising resolutely exceptional (*kusala*) arcs of change. In short, the readiness to relate differently is the condition of possibility for the emergence of truly shared expressions of global flourishing—a readiness that is elicited through ongoing critiques of both self and culture as primordial (or relation-initiating) nexuses of the values, intentions, and practices shaping our personally and socially experienced patterns of outcome and opportunity.

FROM READINESS TO REALIZATION: POLITICAL DIVERSITY NOW

The good thing about this Buddhist perspective is that it optimistically warrants our ability to do something concrete toward the emergence of a global politics of diversity. In Buddhist terms, we can cultivate greater wisdom (*prajñā*), attentive mastery (*samādhi*), and moral clarity (*śīla*) through the interleaving practices of heightening our appreciation of the interdependent origination of all things, expanding our capacities for flexibly concentrated awareness, and increasing the resolution (both clarity and commitment) with which we perceive and respond to the experience-shaping interplay among values, intentions, and action in an increasingly complex and predicament-laden world. And in an ideal world, these practices would be well within our personal reach, and it would be entirely feasible to translate them—for example, through paradigmatically new forms of public education open to all—into socially relevant forms of relational cultivation. Ours, however, is not an ideal world.

This is a fact about which there is no debate whatsoever among the nearly half of the world's population that subsists each day on less than what $2 can buy in the United States, where the official poverty line is established at just over $20 per day or $29,000 per year for a family of four. Poverty makes a real difference. Indeed, this is a point acknowledged again and again in Buddhist discourses, especially those in which the Buddha engages political leaders. The elimination of poverty is a *prerequisite* for realizing a flourishing society, not a result thereof. The Buddha openly acknowledged that the strategies he offered for authoring our own liberation from trouble and suffering could *not* be consistently and effectively applied by those without adequate food, clothing, and shelter, or those without access to basic education and health care. Entering the neighborhoods of Port au Prince, Haiti, in the aftermath of the 2010 earthquake with only invitations to the practice of mindfulness and relational cultivation as a response, would *not* be skillful means and would *not* bring about *kusala* eventualities, evoking superlative arcs of change from within those communities.

This is not to deny, of course, that having already embarked on the path of such practices would positively affect how persons and communities respond to such tragic crises. Nothing would be more valuable in such circumstances than a well-developed readiness for improvisation and widespread embodiments of compassionately responsive virtuosity. But, as always, the affirmation of a counterfactual offers the scantest possible solace to those who are already in the midst of suffering the collapse of everything on which they had previously relied. And we are left with resurging questions about how to bring about a readiness for improvisation—a structure of feeling evoked by heightening capacities-for and commitments-to relating-freely—when the conditions of possibility for living with even just the hope of a dignified life do not obtain for all. Are we not caught in a vicious circularity, with realizing greater diversity and equity depending on a global readiness for improvisation that cannot be realized in the absence of more equitably oriented and diversity-enhancing patterns of local, national, regional, and global interdependence? What would it mean to break out of this cycle?

Given the historical and philosophical case made thus far for the coemergence of diversity, equity, and responsive virtuosity, it should not be expected that answering these questions could take the form of drawing a "road map" specifying both routes and destinations. The way forward will be improvised, not planned. But having said this, much can be learned about the kind of conduct that will support the emergence of a politics of diversity by thinking through the way in which exponents of democratic deliberation have responded to similar charges of circularity leveled against the politics of recognition as a means to achieving difference-respecting social justice.

Parity of Participation, Deliberation, and Cooperation in the Politics of Difference

Recognizing and respecting those who differ, precisely insofar as they are different, places a special burden on those responsible for crafting and maintaining the institutions needed to frame and implement social, economic, and political policy. Realizing a coherent political community in a culturally, ethically, and morally homogenous society is one thing; doing so in a profoundly heterogeneous society is another. Even granted that democratic institutions are the best yet developed for balancing perhaps quite disparate individual and group interests, practical questions arise as to how to insure that these institutions operate in ways that are just in fact, and not merely just in principle.

At one level, these questions center on the means to and meaning of participatory parity. Occupying one end of a spectrum of possible responses are theorists like Iris Young (1990, 2000) and Will Kymlicka (1995) who would argue on behalf of special representation of groups that for a host of reasons might otherwise be effectively excluded from political participation; at the other end are those like Charles Taylor (1994) and Alex Honneth (1996) who would argue that guarantees of individual rights and representation are sufficient to insure parity of participation. But whether group or individual differences are seen as analytically basic, or whether the importance and impossibility of categorically ranking both is accepted, the fact remains that in a society where significant differences obtain among constituents' basic values, it is important not to exaggerate "the possibility of harmonious co-operation" in anticipation of what Simon Thompson (2006, 144) characterizes as a "symphonic" political community—a community in which no difference or contribution will conflict with others, and which thus naturally forms an integrated or organic whole. Indeed, the evidence that we are now in an era of reflexive modernization characterized by ever-increasing scales and scopes of predicaments suggests that overoptimism in this regard is potentially disastrous.

At a deeper level, however, these questions open out beyond concerns about balancing individual and various scales of group rights and representation to considerations of the relative priority of democratic deliberation and justice. While it is widely and perhaps quite reasonably assumed that democratic deliberation will play a crucial role in governing and policy-making processes in any society committed to respecting the plurality of values and interests, without having first realized a functional degree of distributive parity, it is hard to imagine how deliberation could be anything other than a formal mechanism for majority and/or elite self-legitimization. That is, while democratic deliberation may be the best extant difference-respecting approach to determining the *meaning* of justice, the disconcerting fact is that justice is itself a precondition for democracy since—in its absence—it is inevitable that some members of society (those who differ most from majority/elite views) will be effectively excluded from real participation. In other words, democracy and justice would seem to be in an irreducibly recursive (chicken-and-egg) relationship. As Thompson pointedly asks, "is democracy necessary in order to determine what recognition is due, or is recognition necessary before democracy can exist?" (Thompson 2006, 157).

This practical circularity may not be as damaging as it might at first appear. What it alerts us to is the impossibility of establishing a fixed means-ends relationship between democracy and justice—an impossibility that is in broad accord with the complex understanding of causality that is required by the shift from an ontology of individual existents to one of irreducibly relational dynamics. Like all things, democracy and justice arise and develop interdependently, and by interpreting deliberation and recognition as dynamic processes, possibilities open for seeing the interplay of democracy and justice as a spiral rather than a circular phenomenon (Thompson 2006, 158). Once initiated, every reiteration of this cycle will result in deliberatively expanded conceptions of and commitments to justice that will then recursively increase the depth and scope of subsequent democratic deliberations.[20]

A reasonable question would be whether this reiterative and ostensibly open-ended interplay of deliberation and recognition and its progressive deepening of both means-to and meanings-of democracy and justice can be identified as a practical basis for improvising political diversity. Or, does it (perhaps ironically) implicate us in an ever-amplifying and increasingly complicated oscillation between political unification and variation? One of the criticisms directed at appeals to deliberative processes as a means to taking differences into political account *within* a given society is that the likelihood of these processes proving successful is proportionate to the degree to which its citizens are committed to working toward an already acknowledged common good. That is, appealing to deliberation as a universal means to addressing political differences is only plausible if we assume counterfactually that everyone in a given society is already in substantial agreement on what is meant by the "common good"—a difficulty that is greatly compounded if we extend the scope of deliberation to include taking account of differences *among* societies. But if deliberation and recognition are in a feedback-feedforward relationship, once initiated, their recursive interactions over time will in fact *produce* increasing consensus on an ever more comprehensively articulated set of common interests and commitments. In other words, a consistently maintained spiral of deliberation and recognition has great potential for effectively converting political predicaments into political problems.

In fact, this would seem to be part of the conception of deliberative democracy as a response to the shortcomings of liberal and illiberal models of democratic government. As articulated by Amy Gutmann and Dennis Thompson (1996), deliberative democracy is built around four interlocking commitments: to the respectful exchange of ideas (*reciproc-ity*); to transparency (*publicity*); to a concern for enabling the interests of all to be represented, including future generations (*accountability*); and to understanding moral and political principles as open to revision (*provision-ality*). Together, these commitments are understood as creating conditions within which individuals (and groups) are enabled to debate fundamental moral and political differences in ways that are conducive to arriving at mutually binding decisions grounded in mutually justifiable reasons. That is, to the extent that democratic deliberation works, it does so by provid-ing a forum for first bringing into decisive focus how much we differ-from one another in basic and significant ways, and then going on to determine the proper scope of, and identify concrete prospects for, cooperation.

Quite clearly, the deliberative process is intended to interrupt polit-ical "business as usual" by providing a safe forum for articulating and comparatively weighing politically salient differences in values and con-ceptions of our common, social good. Deliberation offers an alternative both to the market approach of liberal electoral politics and to the mana-gerial approach of illiberal elite politics, one that focuses on engaging dif-ferences not as grounds for conflict but as potentially useful resources. And under ideal circumstances, it could be seen as bringing about condi-tions within which it would be possible to politically confirm mounting empirical evidence that heterogeneous groups capitalizing on divergent cognitive approaches, heuristics, interpretations, and mental models can outperform homogenous groups of individually exceptional experts in both problem solving and prediction (Page 2007). At the very least, demo-cratic deliberation can be seen as serving the function—absolutely crucial in an era of the accelerating multiplication and magnification of differ-ences—of initiating and sustaining significant *political innovation*.

At the same time, however, the features that make democratic delib-eration a means to empowering those who differ also ensure that it is *not* a process that is ultimately conducive to realizing a self-sustaining and diversity-enriching politics of strength of the sort needed in a world of deepening and truly global predicaments. That is, while it offers an important alternative to liberal and illiberal constructions of democratic government, the practice of democratic deliberation does not gener-ate movement oblique to the current spectrum of political possibilities. Precisely because of its decisive alignment with cooperation as a seminal political value, it is at best a metaphor for—not an embodied realization of—*political improvisation*.

Although innovation and improvisation are clearly related, it is useful to draw a distinction between them, much as it is useful to distinguish between variation and diversification. Innovation is a task-specific activity that takes place within well-defined parameters of success, the results of which are new techniques or strategies that effectively advance an existing set of aims and interests, typically in response to changing circumstances. Political innovation is, in other words, essentially instrumental—a process undertaken for the purpose of problem solving, where the terms for what would count as a solution are already well defined. In contrast, political improvisation is an explicitly destination-less practice that works out from the familiar, not toward already anticipated ends, but in expression of a situationally responsive arc into the unknown—a process of articulating new, shared aims and interests which can be advanced only through ongoing predicament resolution.

As a process of political innovation, democratic deliberation is both practically and conceptually a finite endeavor. While it can be reiterated indefinitely, it is initiated with the explicit intention either of arriving at concrete decisions about specific issues or of laying stable (if not permanent) foundations for broad classes of decision making. Broadly implemented, deliberation yields a comprehensive and issue-focused "topography" of differing perspectives on a specific issue—a "map" of public opinion that can be used to chart viable routes for reaching existing political goals. Rather than new and meaningfully *shared* values or modalities of appreciation of the sort hoped for in political improvisation, the immediate result of successful deliberation is a set of *common* parameters for compromise, and a more comprehensive calculation of benefits, costs, and liabilities than could be arrived at either by independently operating stakeholders simply exercising voting rights or by a centralized managerial elite. The assumption in entering deliberation is not that those involved will be profoundly changed by the process, but rather that grounds will be established for bringing competing evaluative metrics into sufficient agreement to productively *define cooperation* in regard to specific issues or classes of issues.

Of course, there is no denying that defining the terms of social and political cooperation is a valuable, if not indispensible, process. And, indeed, the finite nature of democratic deliberation is crucial insofar as endlessly expressing our differences without ever arriving at any relevant decisions is equivalent to enabling the status quo to persist unchanged. Yet, we must be clear that deliberation is not entered into only to express our individual (personal or group) interests and gain the recognition (and hopefully respect) of others, precisely as we are. The deliberative process is also entered to maximize how many of our distinctly different interests—crucial, perhaps, to our identities and our sense of social and cultural well-being—are in fact politically acknowledged and factored into the lives of the communities in which we live. While cooperation is the desired end result, the process is unavoidably a competitive one. And as rational choice theorists have asserted with widespread assent, while it is entirely rational to cooperate with others, especially under conditions of uncertainty, it is also entirely rational to curtail cooperation whenever it becomes evident that our own individual interests are likely to be better served by doing so. We can dispute whether such behavior truly qualifies as rational in a world of deepening and expanding global predicaments. But it is behavior that remains globally evident and entirely in accord with the biases toward political realism that inform contemporary political confrontations with difference, both within and among societies.

Many of the world's religions, of course, encourage us to aspire to less self-centered and more caring modes of engagement with others and, indeed, with the planet as a whole. Charitably understood, this tendency to subordinate competition to care can be seen as one factor in the global resurgence of the political salience of religion over especially the past quarter century. The trouble is that the presence of a competitive bias within deliberation is not simply a fact about human selfishness or our collective failure to understand that interdependence is an internal relation, not an external one—a function of human fallibility that might be corrected given a sufficiently powerful will to do so. The trouble is not with our intentions as we enter deliberation, but rather with the deliberative value of cooperation.

On one hand, as is illustrated, for example, in market operations and sporting events, competition requires cooperation. Undisciplined by commonly accepted rules and regulations, "competition" will not result in the separation of winners and losers and a "fair" distribution of benefits, whether in terms of a capital-accumulating material economy or a prominence-heightening attention economy; it will come to an end only with the "triumph" of the last to remain standing. In the absence of such rules and regulations, I can win a footrace by outrunning you, or I can do so by tripping you, by colluding with a third party to block your way, by changing the location of the finish line to my advantage, or by doing you preemptive bodily harm. In a world of completely deregulated markets, aggressive takeovers, corporate counterintelligence, bribes to politicians, product dumping, and a host of other strategies would grant ready opportunities for monopolization and the de facto end of competition. It is only within agreed-upon parameters that competition does not devolve into a process of mutually sought elimination.

On the other hand, cooperation itself implies the continued presence of disparate aims and interests. It is not merger. We do not consider cooperating or "working together" unless it is generally the case that we have not done so, and it is now the case that we can see reasons—at least for a time, and for specific purposes—why we should. That is, we seek cooperation when our usual practices of working independently seem less advantageous than working together. Cooperation does not signal the sudden realization that we have the *same* aims and interests, but rather an experience of circumstances that suggest the contingent benefits of allowing them to overlap. Cooperation is thus a conventional approach to bringing our actions into working alignment—an external relationship that we enter fully convinced that we will be able to exit essentially unchanged. The insistence in rational choice theory that competition ultimately trumps cooperation is not a function of an aberrant understanding of cooperation, but rather a logical implication of our everyday notion of what it means to *co-operate*—a manifest ability to operate in parallel or complementary ways that enable us to reach well-defined, common goals without sacrificing our autonomy. In this sense, cooperation can be seen as the realization of productive variety as an alternative to what would evidently be unproductive conflict. In other words, cooperation is bringing our differences-from one another into useful accord—judged from our own individual, not relational, perspectives—without requiring us to differ-for one another in ways that would irreversibly change who we *are*. Hence, cooperation often requires us to compromise, but by definition never to the point that our own individual, group, or national identities and interests are at risk.

As a finite process aimed at producing mutually binding decisions grounded on mutually justifiable reasons, democratic deliberation might be seen hopefully as a forum for inverting the realist subordination of cooperation to competition—a way of going beyond self-interest. Yet in practice, deliberation entails placing different stakeholder perspectives in respectfully open competition for the purpose of defining, and hence placing specified limits on, how best to cooperatively address issues of common concern. Thus, both conceptually and practically, the relationship between competition and cooperation is irreducibly one of co-implication. Cooperation opens and then conserves opportunities for competition; competition multiplies and then differentially distributes the benefits of cooperation.

Given this account of cooperation as a practice and value, it is readily apparent why democratic deliberation is understood to be an empowering process. It is a means to addressing difference in a way that is easily assimilated within already existing politics of power, enabling the definition of allowable ranges of self-determination. And, insofar as deliberation is a way of conserving differences within or among societies and staving off possibilities of elimination, it is rightly regarded positively. But by itself, the progressive reiteration of the cycle of deliberation and recognition will not eventuate in the exceptional strengthening of relational dynamics, or in a shift from *comparative* (quantitatively assessed) to *relational* (qualitatively assessed) *equity*. Deliberative innovation may result in securing the conditions for political variety, or in defining the parameters of political unity. It will not, in and of itself, foster the emergence of political diversity. For that, we are in need of something other than the joint valorization and institutional development of cooperation and competition.

Coordination, Contribution, and Strength: Opening to a Qualitative Politics of Diversity

Enacted consistently and broadly enough under ideal conditions, the core commitments of deliberative democracy to reciprocity, publicity, transparency, and provisionality would bring about what could be called a "process politics"—a politics under continuous revision that, granted ideal conditions, would over time succeed in bringing about a functional disarmament of differences within and among societies. In keeping with its axiological alignment with cooperation and competition, this would be a politics inflected on one hand toward a proliferation of increasingly well-defined, politically salient differences, and on the other hand toward ever-widening and deepening stakes in practically realized consensus and commonality. That is, it would be a politics focused on consensually balancing rights to vary from others and imperatives for acting in unison with them—a politics capable of practically merging the postmodern agenda of netropolis and the modern agenda of cosmopolis. Such a merger would securely reconcile the globalization- and network-driven multiplication and magnification of differences with our manifestly increasing needs for globally integrated responses to the threats, hazards, and risks that are the reflexive and ironic consequences of continued and progressive growth and development.

The reconciliation brokered by such a politics would be an unequivocally good thing, leading to a global political community freed from the enormous human and material burdens of violent confrontation over the means-to and meaning-of our global common good—a cooperative community within which it would be possible to differ widely and yet safely from one another, and in which competition would function as an energizing medium for both individual and collective enrichment. Yet, as good as such a political reconciliation of liberal freedoms with illiberal order would be, it would not mark the advent of a politics of diversity. Indeed, by disarming difference, it would (in however utopian a fashion) work against the global activation of our differences as points of relational departure for improvising virtuosity-expressing arcs of shared flourishing. Such a politics would in practice be good for each and every one of us. But it would not bring about superlative (*kusala*) outcomes and opportunities for all of us, or foster the truly *original* improvisations needed to resolutely and equitably address the kinds of global predicaments with which we now find ourselves faced.

As a politics that can only emerge through political improvisation, it is not possible to specify in advance what institutional or procedural forms the politics of diversity will take. But much as it is possible to use an apt metaphor to elicit intuitions of an entirely new kind of experience, I think it is possible to cantilever out from the more familiar dynamics of deliberatively realized cooperative community toward this still yet-to-be politics. The politics of diversity, like the politics of recognition, respect, and democratic deliberation, will both result from and result in responses to difference; but whereas the latter is oriented to defining the terms of and extending the practical reach of cooperation as a central political means and end, the politics of diversity, upon emerging, will turn out to be aligned historically with the relational value of coordination.

Coordination literally means "together ordering" or perhaps "mutually ordering," and is often thought of in primarily structural terms. Thus, a jobsite coordinator is someone who makes sure that all of the various people involved in a project perform their duties in the timely way needed to fit in with what is being done by everyone, bringing their efforts into proper and smoothly functioning relationship. Yet, while contemporary uses of "order" tend to be biased toward spatially and temporally regulative structures, and thus toward understanding coordination as a sort of "top down" or externally enacted process, the root metaphor implicit in the word points us in a more interactive, dynamic, and creative direction.

The Latin roots of the English word "order"—the Latin *ordo*, a row of threads in a loom, and *ordiri*, to begin to weave—can themselves be traced back to the Indo-European root *ar-*, from which are derived the English words "art" and "arm." This suggests that ordering is a process of creative articulation—a jointing of different elements into novel and productive relationship. Order is not something complete and predetermined; it emerges, much as cloth emerges from the working of a loom. Accustomed as we are to factory- and machine-produced fabrics, the almost magical nature of weaving and its force as a metaphor for order are perhaps not readily appreciated. Weaving originated some eight to ten thousand years ago with the improvisational advent of a new kind of relationship among humans, plants, animals, and minerals—a process through which dyed plant and animal fibers are brought into unexpectedly strong, highly flexible, and resilient interplay through human imagination and capacities for attentively refined bodily movements.[21] This new relationship not only made manifest an entirely novel and practically useful material that was valued enough to spur intercontinental trade,[22] but also an entirely new medium of both personal and cultural expression and differentiation. To bring order or "begin weaving" is to initiate a creative process through which familiar things are composed in ways that at once make manifest new dimensions of what they *are* and enable the expression of new kinds of *meaning*.

As a "weaving together," political coordination can be seen as a process of initiating new and transformative relational dynamics, bringing significantly differing people and their values, aims, and practices into new and systemic relationship. At the very least, as in a cooperative community, this means realizing minimal friction in the interactions among people and their perspectives, making sure that the relational system they are realizing together does not result in their individual or collective degradation. But above and beyond this, coordination entails realizing patterns of interaction through which there emerge entirely new relational qualities. That is, coordination implies both structural and aesthetic transformation, at once resulting from and resulting in qualitatively enhanced relational attunement—a process through which different stakeholders' values, intentions, and practices are brought creatively into alignment, recursively opening up new directions of relational appreciation.

This is a point worth stressing. In a highly coordinated community, differences among its members are not simply conserved or enabled to statically persist. A dynamic relational environment is realized that conduces to opening new domains or dimensions of difference, fostering what might be called ecologically evolving patterns of differentiation. Whereas the determinate end or purpose assumed in pursuit of greater cooperation allows the meaning of cooperation to be experienced monothetically, the meaning of coordination (like that of music) can only be understood polythetically through a process of mutually sustained tuning in.

This meaning of coordination informs our evaluation of certain dancers or athletes as being extraordinarily coordinated. In this usage, coordination connotes a demonstration of powerfully articulated, precise, and qualitatively distinctive movement—a refined gracefulness or elegance that is not the result of an external disciplining of motion, but rather a qualitatively distinct freeing and illumination of movement from within. In this sense, coordination implies the opening of embodied potentials for virtuosic arcs of change. What distinguishes those with a high level of coordination is not simply the accuracy and apparent ease of their movements, but an extraordinary capacity to respond to situational turbulence and the unexpected, improvising gracefully with and through whatever occurs. In this sense, coordination is not a function of body parts in precise and efficient motion; it is the expression of exceptionally refined attentive immediacy and responsive spontaneity. More generally stated, coordination is the simultaneously structural and aesthetic expression of means-to and meanings-of relational transformation in the direction of enhanced resilience, fluency, and responsive virtuosity.[23]

As a political value, cooperation establishes viable links between political variety and political unity, making possible the translation of predicament-expressing conflicts over differences of values, aims, beliefs, and practices into practically soluble problems. Cooperation yields predictable results, helping us to move from bad relational dynamics to better ones. This is very attractive, especially since any compromises cooperation entails with respect to pursuing our own individual or group interests will have been judged in advance by us as essentially worthwhile. The predicament-dissolving (not resolving) capacity of cooperation derives, in other words, from the fact that the limits of cooperation are established by individually undertaken calculations of the comparative value of what will be lost and gained through it—a conversion of conflicts of values into determinations of value.

In sharp contrast, coordination does not aim at specifiable and measurable results; neither does it impel us toward making mutually binding decisions among value systems or placing predetermined limits on the expression of difference. Indeed, coordination commits us to refraining from any attempt to establish the "exchange value" of different perspectives and practices in a predicament-dissolving "economy of values." Coordination is *not* enhanced by a comparative ranking of the distinctive patterns of opportunity and outcome associated with particular constellations of values, intentions, and practices. Neither is it furthered or more productively articulated through opposing any such constellations. As a political value, then, coordination implicates us in the open-ended strengthening of relational dynamics: the shared improvisation of new and contribution-expanding modalities of relational appreciation and flourishing. This changes the nature of political change. Whereas cooperation-inducing *political innovation* aims at carrying us forward to a common, predefined, and freely chosen destination, coordination-conducive *political improvisation* involves us in the open-ended articulation of a meaningfully shared direction.

Political diversity will emerge as we demonstrate the nondualistic readiness to interrupt conflict from within by improvising movement oblique to the relationally degrading opposition of variety and unity. Movement of this sort can only be sustained by continuously heightening and expanding the scale and scope of the resolution (clarity and commitment) with which we engage the complex dynamics of local, national, regional, and global interdependence, working out from within our conflicts, not on the basis of some lowest common denominators, but both toward and through the qualitative appreciation of means-to and meanings-of the social experience of relating-freely—the realization of a new and resolutely shared global structure of feeling.

Epilogue

The Next Step?

A s I have described it, valorizing coordination points us in the direction of an aesthetically enriching politics of strength. Widely enough realized, this would enliven a political counterculture of concerted movement oblique to the tension between free variation and unification—movement directed toward aligning our social, economic, political, technological, and cultural interdependence with increasing diversity and relational equity.

But could valorizing coordination ever be enough? Would it be enough to break us globally out of the vicious circularity implied by the fact that realizing greater diversity and equity depends on a global readiness for improvisation that cannot be realized in the absence of more equitably oriented and diversity-enhancing patterns of local, national, regional, and global interdependence? Could it be enough to begin and sustain the kinds of global transformation needed for every mother, father, son, and daughter on the planet to have their subsistence needs met in the degree and with the relational quality needed for them to have more than just inspiring but ephemeral hopes of living dignified lives? If not, then so what? Given how things have come to be, what should we be doing now? How should we be responding to the intensifying conflicts, trouble, and suffering that continue to characterize life on our planet, in spite of—and, in reflexively increasing degree, because of—the remarkable achievements of humankind?

It is fine to talk about realizing conditions that will be conducive to a new structure of feeling which expresses the meaning of relating-freely in shared improvisation of enhanced diversity and equity. And it is fine to argue that political improvisation is, indeed, the only way forward given the complexity and volatility of global dynamics and the emergent nature of diversity and equity. But if the metanarrative of diversification through improvisation yields nothing in the way of real and effective steps that can be taken to address the kinds of global predicaments in which we already find ourselves immersed, it is hard to conclude that the "spaces of hope" it purports to open are anything more than imaginary. And imagination clearly is not enough.

We know already that what we have been doing politically to realize a more peaceful and equitably prosperous world has had limited success. Deliberation, negotiation, establishing sanctions of various sorts, resorting to military intervention (for either strategic or humanitarian purposes), and setting common targets like the UN's Millennium Development Goals are all processes with which we are familiar. In one circumstance or another, each has brought about desirable results. But all have also proven to fall far short of what is needed to begin translating hopes of dignity for all into lived realities. Best efforts notwithstanding, our present era remains one of both the greatest practical cooperation and the greatest disparities of wealth and relational opportunities the world has ever known.

If valorizing coordination and improvisation is forwarded as a kind of response distinctively different from those that have been forthcoming thus far from across the contemporary spectrum of liberal and illiberal political systems and methods, it would seem to be reasonable to ask how some of the most "intractable" and troubling of our circumstances and conflicts would be addressed if we were, indeed, to begin moving obliquely to that spectrum. Even if it is accepted that movement of this sort is irreducibly open-ended—an arc into the unknown emerging in response to irreducibly particular circumstances—it nevertheless would seem reasonable to ask how we will know if we are making the right first steps, in the right direction.

Unfortunately, however apparently reasonable it is for us to ask such questions, the desire to first know and then act is ultimately not conducive to the *kusala* or virtuosity-manifesting improvisations required to realize a sustainable politics of strength. Knowledge of the sort that would allow us to determine whether a particular constellation of efforts will be successful—for example, in ending conflicts over nuclear proliferation or responding equitably to climate change—in effect would empower us to fix the meaning and direction of differentiation processes. That is, it would enable us to instrumentally prescribe what each of us *is* and can *mean* for one another. This has historically been a very seductive possibility: realizing political change as a path defined in advance as a series of finite steps from one desirable goal to another. But with respect to realizing greater diversity and equity, it would be self-defeating. There can be no guarantees—even methodological—of the kind of relational appreciation needed to realize truly shared arcs of *kusala* change.

This is very unsettling. Realizing greater diversity and equity is a process to which we can contribute, each in distinctively different ways. But it is not a process that we can aim to complete, or even a path along which we can proceed incrementally with readily measured confidence. As an infinite game, the politics of strength requires setting aside even very distant goals. An infinite path cannot be broken down into a sequence of finite steps and comforting arrivals. Indeed, the certainty afforded by being able to see, ahead of time, exactly where we are going can only be achieved at the cost of first having abandoned such a path. Along an infinite path, destinations are only to be found in the past as an experiential residue of the unexpected—a retrospectively evident series of turning points at which, like the transitions between breathing in and breathing out, we have clearly "arrived" but could never have "remained." In this sense, destinations do not tell us anything about where we are headed, but rather only help us get our bearings regarding whence we have come.

Granted this, we might contrast the protest movements that have come to be popularly identified with the phrases "Arab Spring" and "Occupy Wall Street." The Arab Spring began in December 2010 with protests against the government of Tunisia, and over the succeeding months spread across North Africa and into the Middle East. The results thus far have been the toppling of governments in Tunisia, Egypt, and Libya, and continued civil unrest and state violence in especially Syria, Yemen, Bahrain, and the Western Sahara. Incited largely through grassroots organizations and the use of social media, the revolutionary protest movements associated with the Arab Spring nevertheless have had specific political goals in mind, with a proximate focus on the restructuring of state government.

The Occupy Wall Street movement began in New York City in September 2011 and has since spread rapidly with locally coalescing "Occupy" encampments springing up in major cities across the United States and internationally. Also originating in grassroots organizing and the use of social media, the Occupy movement is being staged around the iconic contrast of the interests of the wealthiest and most powerful 1% of the world's people and the remaining 99%. Unlike the Arab Spring protests, the Occupy movement does not have the proximate goal of toppling any particular government, but rather of challenging the ways in which multinational corporations, governments, and highly privileged, global elites have entered into de facto collusion in enabling an ever more dramatic skewing of the benefits and costs of economic growth. Criticized by some for having no unified or cogently presented political and economic agendas, the Occupy movement has been successful in directing mass media attention to issues of increasing inequality, presenting an array of essentially moral critiques of global systems.

In contrasting these movements, it is useful to first note that while both began "locally," neither was initiated in a centralized manner around a single comprehensive vision or even a set of clearly stated objectives. In this sense, they are both postmodern—and not modern—protest movements. Both have been fueled by popular outrage at the ever more egregiously manifest reality of being economically disadvantaged and discounted as politically irrelevant. And both have centered essentially on rejecting existing power structures—a mass willingness to simply say "no more." The Arab Spring, however, has evolved in the direction of embracing explicitly finite goals of governmental change, while the Occupy movement has remained a more open-ended approach that might be seen as closer in spirit to what I have anticipated as a nongovernmental politics of strength. Yet, the Occupy movement has come, however loosely, to be framed in explicitly instrumental terms as trying to compel structural change. And as many municipal governments have decided, the long-term occupations of public space that are a hallmark of the movement are not demonstrations of truly alternative and scalable structures for equity-enhancing economic and political vitality, but rather highly visible and (some would argue, parasitic) "sores" on the state-, corporate-, and elite-biased body politic.

Among other things, what these movements evidence is the incompleteness of the colonization of consciousness that has thus far been a primary effect of the growth of the global attention economy. That is, they indicate: first, the widespread presence of sufficient clarity about the dynamics of global interdependence to recognize that they confront us with complex sets of predicaments, not problems that can be addressed from within existing frameworks for evaluating what works and what does not; and second, the presence of sufficiently deep commitment to break with routine and begin improvising together in response to these dynamics. At the same time, however, they do not evidence the presence of recursively structured systems of practices aligned with continuously relinquishing our personal and collective horizons of relevance, responsibility, and readiness—practices without which it is impossible to sustain *kusala* arcs of change, and without which how well we differ-for one another will eventually be subordinated to how much we differ-from one another.

One of the reasons for having taken as many Buddhist detours as we have is that Buddhist traditions have been keenly aware of the ultimate importance and yet great difficulty of relinquishing the view that practice is a means to the end of attaining enlightenment rather than its immediate demonstration. And in confronting the theoretically evident impossibility of pursuing political diversity through instrumental acts of political problem solving, it is perhaps useful to draw upon Buddhist resources in affirming the practically evident possibility of committing to an uncertain and explicitly infinite path of relational appreciation.

In the *Diamond Sutra*, a Mahayana Buddhist text that interestingly played a crucial role in the "indigenization" of Buddhism in China, the Buddha is asked what he attained with unsurpassed complete enlightenment. His simple and shocking response was: not a single thing. Asked then how bodhisattvas—those who would work for the liberation of all sentient beings—should conduct themselves and condition their minds, his response was equally simple and surprising: they should neither dwell nor rely upon anything. Demonstrating enlightenment eludes containment within the categories of either fixed means or determinate ends. Embodying limitless *upāya* or responsive virtuosity is incompatible with adhering to any set principles or methods. Relating-freely in actualizing a liberating interdependence among all beings is *not* reducible to making the right choices.

This is true even if, after the fact, it will always be possible to give a plausible account about options exercised and foregone, and how these affected our success and failure. If such a reduction of relating-freely to exercising freedoms of choice were possible, we could indeed play our liberation as a finite game. We could proceed from right choice to right choice, step-by-step coming closer to arrival at an enlightened end to all trouble and suffering. Having completed the journey ourselves, we could then map it out for others to use, guaranteeing their arrival in due course at the "other shore" of final liberation.[1] But as the Chan master Huairang pointed out to his student Mazu, triggering the latter's awakening: we cannot gaze *at* the bodhisattva path; we can only see *from* it. Realizing a politics of strength is not a function of deploying the "right" means for achieving a certain kind of relationship; it is the expression, moment-by-moment, of the meaning of relational appreciation.

Traditionally, demonstrating the bodhisattva ideal of unlimited improvisational readiness was correlated with the strength of one's vows. This correlation suggests that relational transformation of the quality and orientation needed to bring about greater diversity and equity will not take the form of a path that we can seek out and then travel to an already envisioned end. Rather, it is a way of relating made manifest as a creative function of our own expressed clarity and commitment: a recursively amplifying path of karmic revision.

From this perspective, the gradual broadening and deepening of values discourses over the second half of the twentieth century can be seen as a hopeful indicator of conditions conducive to a still-emerging structure of feeling open and resolute readiness for relating-freely in the shared improvisation of more equitably oriented patterns of global inter-dependence. Importantly, as the processes of reflexive modernization and the rise of world risk society have intensified over the last three decades, this turn toward values has taken on particular urgency. As Mark Tay-lor (2004) has argued, contrary to the expectations of those who would identify modernization with secularization, the resurgence of the politi-cal salience of religion since the early 1980s has not occurred in spite of, but rather because of, increasingly complex globalization processes and the economic, social, political, and cultural volatilities generated by them. In short, it is a response to a publicly and profoundly experienced values vacuum: the manifest absence in the public sphere of those qualities of concern and commitment deemed by many to be crucial to realizing an integrated vision of the good.

This turning toward—or returning to—religion can be seen as sig-naling awareness of the limits of both the rule of law and the workings of expert systems in resolving predicaments of the scale and scope that now confront us. And, charitably viewed, the central role played by faith in this turn toward religious values can be seen as an admission of personal, social, and political uncertainty about the best way forward. Construed with sufficient openness, the impulse toward faith can be seen as counter-ing tendencies to frame the realization of greater good as a finitely con-structed and predictably realized process. That is, appeals to faith can be seen as creating spaces for appreciating the dynamics of complex, emer-gent change.

Yet religious appeals to faith are often combined with instrumen-tally framed, salvific imperatives to adopt a particular set of principles and values as ultimately preeminent—a centripetal, moralistic turn away from plural to unitary interpretations of "the ways we do things." This combination has fostered powerful fundamentalist visions, for example, of a coming clash of Christianity and Islam, or of an imminent winner-takes-all endgame between cosmically opposing forces of good and evil. The familiar counter to such exclusive claims to truth has been to dis-arm religious differences by articulating an ethical common ground on which all traditions can find significant footing. And, the importance of opening spaces for noncompetitive engagement and for the articulation of interreligious commonalities should not be discounted. But, in the con-text of the problem-to-predicament transition, it should also not be over-estimated. The articulation of *common values* easily becomes an exercise through which differences are overwritten and conflicts of values, aims, and interests are subjected to discursive solvents rather than actually and sustainably resolved. Enhancing diversity and equity requires the consid-erably greater openness that is needed to activate differences as the basis of mutual contribution, developing situationally specific constellations of resolutely *shared values*.

If the adaptations of complex systems express characteristic sets of values that are conserved over the course of adaptation, and if predicaments arise when successful adaptations begin producing significant unexpected or ironic consequences, then predicament resolution implies a critical reconfiguration of values. In the case of predicaments occurring within a single community, this reconfiguration might take the form of changing priorities among systemically crucial values—for example, a subórdination of political loyalty to environmental justice. There are cases, in other words, in which all that is required is a reconfiguration of existing values: the articulation of substantial accord about how to better constellate values already held in common.

But there are other cases when, for example, a predicament occurs at scales and scopes that make necessary intercommunal, interreligious, international, and/or intercultural clarity and commitment—an expression of resolve that *may* entail realizing a distinctively new configuration of values, but that more importantly *will* entail the expression of new and distinctively shared values or modalities of appreciation. For example, simply shuffling environmental values further forward in the mix in various societies will not be enough to resolve the global predicament of climate change. We are in need of an entirely new conception of justice that critically evaluates the interdependence among human, ecological, and planetary processes in ways that exhibit neither (universalist) *blindness* to differences nor (relativist) affirmations of one or another form of natural, biological, social, cultural, political, economic, or epistemic *bias*. Passage through the contemporary aporia of difference cannot be secured by either tolerating or celebrating difference.

Common values are a prerequisite for problem solution. They are what allow us to define the meaning of what can be counted *as* a solution. To establish common values is to enable seeing and charting where we are going. Shared values are an emergent result of the predicament resolution process. They are a product of working out from within how much we differ from one another in regard to a specific issue and discerning how best to actively incorporate those differences in addressing it. That is, shared values result from appreciating differences as points of joint, improvisational departure. Shared values do not enable previewing where we are going; they develop as a function of sustained consonance in how we *feel* our way forward together.

The difference in feeling between having common and shared values or modalities of appreciation is nicely captured by the contrast between marching together and sharing a dance. Marching effectively together—for example, as a military unit—requires using carefully measured steps of identical length, moving only when and as directed in simultaneous iteration of a single ideal. Changes of direction are precise and carried out in ways that entail no breaking of ranks, no disturbance of the design within which each marcher has a clearly specified place. To march is to have a specific pattern of movement in common; its opposite is having no pattern in common, milling about at random. To share a dance—for example, the heavily improvised Argentine tango—requires being keenly present to and for one another, changing steps and timing as needed, but always in such a way as to allow differences in our movements to amplify in improvised appreciation of the quality of our mutual attunement.

What I have tried to do over the course of this book is to invite participation in a new kind of dance with difference. Passage through the contemporary aporia of difference cannot be secured by means of modern, cosmopolitan toleration of difference; neither can it be secured by means of postmodern, netropolitan celebrations of difference. Marching in affirmation of what we have in common will not work. And neither will our milling about in individual affirmations of our essential uniqueness. For both historical and philosophical reasons, I have pressed the concept of diversity beyond its customary usages to point toward both the means-to and meaning-of working out from present global circumstances in passage through our increasingly acute and aporetic confrontations with difference.

In doing so, however, I am fully aware that what is presented in this book are just words and that "diversity" is akin to the Zen "finger pointing at the moon" and not, after all, the "moon" itself. Thinking this, I am reminded of the situation faced by the ninth-century Chan Buddhist master Linji, after he had just finished encouraging an assembly of monks, nuns, government officials, and community members to conduct themselves like bodhisattvas or enlightening beings—refusing to set up enlightenment as a goal, and instead exemplifying it as the virtuosic and improvisational heading of all their activities. Amid the general murmur of approval, the provincial governor—the official local representative of the imperial court—stood and politely but skeptically asked Linji to explain, in simple and straightforward terms, the true meaning of enlightenment.

Taking a moment to survey the expectant faces of those arrayed before him, Linji smiled, leaned forward, and then thoughtfully noted that as soon as he opened his mouth to answer, he would already have made a mistake. He paused, sat back, and then added that, at the same time, if he didn't provide those before him with at least a foothold or a *gang* (the rope that enables a casting net to be pulled closed and drawn back to shore) they would have no means of moving forward. Linji then stood up and dramatically shook out the sleeves of his robes. Scanning the eyes of the audience members fiercely and yet with almost grandmotherly kindness, he posed a challenge. "Who among you," he asked, "is ready, here and now, to come forward without hesitation, deploy your forces, unfurl your banners, and enter into combat?" (T. 1985, 496c)[2]

Linji's response to the governor can be understood in many ways. But at the very least, his challenge transforms the situation from one unfolding within the cooperative conventions of the monastic lecture hall to one in which we are invited to cross over into the potentially chaotic and violent space of openly engaged strife and conflict. What happens thereafter is that Linji stops talking *about* enlightenment to engage whoever comes forward in improvised, relational *demonstration* of means-to and meanings-of enlightening conduct and conflict resolution. Just so, it is time to stop talking about diversity and equity. The global multiplication and magnification of differences, the reflexive proliferation of risks, threats, and hazards as conditions for further growth and development, and the increasingly acute unevenness with which the benefits and liabilities of growth and development are being distributed all ensure that there is no shortage of opportunities for activating our differences as the basis of mutual contribution to sustained and more equitably shared flourishing. Opportunities for demonstrating unwavering resolve in realizing the means-to and meaning-of relating-freely are all around us. In Linji's terms (T. 1985, 497c), we need only begin "facing the world and going crosswise."

Notes

INTRODUCTION

1. As noted by Amartya Sen (2002), one of the earliest extant printed books is a translation into classical Chinese of a Buddhist text, the *Diamond Sutra*, originally written in the Indian language Sanskrit, most likely sometime around the beginning of the Common Era. The translation was completed in the imperial capital of China in 499 CE by a Buddhist monk—the son of an "Indian" father and a "Turkish" mother—who had traveled into China along the famous Silk Road. The oldest surviving copy was printed in Korea in the ninth century CE. The global movement of goods, people, and ideas is nothing new.

2. Thomas L. Friedman (2000) hints at this process in his use of the "golden straightjacket" as a metaphor for the realities of market-driven global interdependence.

3. The effects of globalization on the construction of personal identity and emotion are much less well noted than those more objectively apparent in the public sphere. For an introduction to current thinking, see Lemert and Elliot (2006).

4. The consolidation of a distinctive transnational capitalist class, for example, is inseparable from the emergence of locally, nationally, regionally, and globally uneven geographies of development and advantage, which in turn shape the movements of transnational capital by means of which global economic elites further differentiate themselves from global majorities.

5. The publication, in 1962, of Rachel Carson's *Silent Spring* drew attention to a classic, early example of this process by means of which the multilayered foundations of common sense come unglued and, in the case in question, revealed an underlying and expanding ferment of predicament. By compiling evidence of emerging, significant, and potentially catastrophic environmental and public health costs associated with prevailing modes and scales of industrial production, Carson demonstrated the impossibility of continuing to assume that what was relevant to "the good" of the economy or the nation as a political entity could be assumed equivalently relevant to "the good" of the environment or public health. The existence of a common frame of reference across these domains could no

longer be affirmed, much less simply assumed. In effect, Carson pointed out how our means of development was recursively opening a deep predicament in the meaning—the nature and direction—of development itself.

6. The rise to power of the Taliban in Afghanistan can be seen as an extreme example of such a fundamentalist rejection of the modern, but milder versions can be found in the ultraconservative expressions of fundamentalist Christian politics in the United States.

7. With the term "provisional" and its characterization as "local coherence," I am making use of Ziporyn's (2004) philosophical exegesis of the Tiantai Buddhist teaching of the "three truths."

8. For a relatively concise exposition of support for these claims, see Hershock (forthcoming).

9. This is a position that has a long history in Asian contexts in which it has been averred that all things arise interdependently or as functions of relational dynamics. A brief introduction to Buddhist philosophy is Hershock (2003), especially pages 239–54. An illuminating consideration of Western precedents for arriving at a similar affirmation of the ontological primacy of processes and relations can be found in Harvey (1996), especially pages 49–57.

10. For those unfamiliar with the topological features of the möbius strip, cut a one-inch by six-inch strip of paper, drawing a series of circles or dots on one side and a continuous, wavelike line on the other. With a bit of clear tape ready, fold up the two ends of the strip of paper with a single twist so that the wavy line slightly overlaps the side of the paper inscribed with dots or small circles. Tape the joint. The piece of paper now has only one side and one edge, which can be demonstrated by simply running your finger along either side or edge, rotating the möbius strip as needed to keep going until you arrive back where you started.

11. A relatively accessible discussion of the general Mahayana Buddhist notion of the "two truths"—conventional and ultimate—and the more sophisticated Chinese Buddhist notion of the threefold truth can be found in Swanson (1989).

12. On collective action in relation to issues of governing common-pool resources, see Ostrom (1990). For a more general analysis of transiting from "individual" to "collective" action in providing public goods, see Olson (1965).

CHAPTER ONE. TOWARD A NEW PARADIGM OF DIFFERENCE

1. The concept of the lifeworld was developed initially in the phenomenological tradition, notably by Edmund Husserl and Alfred Schutz, and was later critically adapted by Habermas (1981) in his two-volume work on communicative action.

2. A representative range of views on the asymmetries of globalization can be found, for example, in Stiglitz (2002), Harvey (1996), Chossudovsky (1997), Korten (2001), and Harrison (2006).

3. Professor Sir Michael Marmot, interview by World Health Organization, Commission on Social Determinants of Health, http://www.who.int/social_determinants/advocacy/interview_marmot (accessed September 24, 2007).

4. The distinction between change and creativity is here intended to call attention to the possibility that some relational dynamics are not inherently

meaningful (change), while others are (creativity). The former dynamics result in increased variety, the latter in the basic conditions for diversity. In making this distinction, I am drawing on the work of John Hope Mason (2003), who has defined creativity as significant innovation.

5. As might be expected given the philosophical commitments (or refusals of commitment) associated with "postmodern" thought, there is no agreement on the nature of postmodern thought or of who is properly seen as affiliated with it. Terms like poststructuralist, deconstructivist, and postmodernist have no clearly demarcated horizons of reference, and many of the thinkers most widely associated with these terms deny their applicability and relevance. I beg the reader's charity in allowing the use of "postmodern" here in a loose, but hopefully not entirely empty, fashion.

6. I should perhaps clarify that my use of the locutions "global West" and "global Western" is intended to allow inclusion of traditions or theories that have origins outside of what are now taken to be the geographical boundaries of "the West." Significant currents of early Indian thought, for example, can easily be seen as commensurable with now globally dominant ways of construing knowledge and meaning that had their origins in the ancient, cultural West. And, in reverse, many late- and postmodern "Western" traditions of philosophy and cultural studies can be seen as commensurable with geographically Asian or African sensibilities. The qualification "global West" is a way of skirting questions about directions and degrees of influence that are of great historical interest, as well as questions about the extent to which commonalities across disparate geographical and cultural terrains are essential or incidental, but that do not bear directly on our primary aim of understanding how difference has come to assume the centrality and importance that it has, and how we might best conceive or reconceive it.

7. For a translation and commentary on Nagarjuna's major work, see Garfield (1995).

8. I am drawing here on Fazang's work *Huayan yicheng jiao yi fenchi zhang*. The Chinese text appears in the Japanese collection of the Buddhist Canon, *Taisho Shinshu Daizokyo*, Vol. 45, no. 1866, pp. 477–509. A definitive consideration of Fazang's thought is Cook (1977).

9. Readers interested in a concise conceptual introduction to Buddhist teachings and history may wish to consult Chapter 1 of my own *Chan Buddhism* (Hershock, 2005). For a more comprehensive and yet quite accessible introduction to Buddhist thought and practice, see Robinson and Johnson (1997).

10. For a succinct and insightful exposition of the notion of sympathetic resonance in medieval China, see Sharf (2002), especially Chapter 2.

11. It should be explicitly noted, however, that as Buddhist traditions have spread throughout Asia and into the West, they have typically accommodated— and been accommodated by—the various cultural belief systems with which they have entered into sustained contact. This has led, for example, to blending of Buddhist and Hindu concepts and practices in South Asia, Buddhist and animist traditions in Southeast Asia, Buddhist and Shinto sensibilities in Japan, and Buddhist and feminist discourses in the contemporary West. The conceptions of karma across the full range of Buddhist traditions are, as a result, far from homogenous,

in spite of having shared roots in the texts and teachings incorporated within the Buddhist canon.

12. For an extended discussion of the critical relevance of karma, see Hershock (2008).

CHAPTER TWO. VARIETY AND DIVERSITY

1. As I will argue later, the now dominant, qualitatively vacuous concept of difference is not natural; it is an artifact, the origins of which can be traced back to the early modern era, when space and time were similarly subjected to a "cleansing" of qualitative "distortions" and conceived as pure forms of measure. Available evidence suggests that, prior to this, spatial and temporal differences were understood in more strongly relational terms. Recognizing this is an important step toward revising our engagements with difference. But for all the deficiencies of the qualitatively evacuated, modern concept of difference, the point is not to attempt a restoration of premodern sensibilities about difference (or about space and time). While these sensibilities may be useful in contextualizing modern excesses in the direction of the universalization and essentialization of time, space, and difference, they are unlikely to afford us with the global purview and critical purchase needed to go beyond the particularist tribalisms that so often and so antagonistically characterize contemporary fundamentalist reconstructions, and that apparently held sway over the vast majority of premodern human history. We must go forward, not backward, in our engagement with difference.

2. See, in particular, Mead (1934).

3. See Hershock (2006), pp. 180ff, for a fuller discussion of problems and predicaments.

CHAPTER THREE. TIME DIFFERENCES

1. While this is certainly a mainstream view of time and change in Buddhism, there were early Mahayana and Theravada schools of Buddhism that propounded theories of temporal moments (Pali, *khana*; Sanskrit, *ksana*) that were understood as kin to atoms of matter. According to these theories, the experience of time as a flowing continuum (*santāna*) is a function of the extremely "brief" compass of these moments. These theories were criticized as being inconsistent with seeing all things as without self or empty and eventually lost currency in Buddhist circles.

2. Interestingly, many of these worries are now as common in science (especially physics and cosmology) as in philosophy, and many of the most current positions being articulated bear striking resemblance to those of considerable antiquity—for example, the appeal in loop quantum gravity theory to a "digital" view of time as a composite of temporal units of approximately $10-^{43}$ second duration, recalling two-millennia-old South Asian theories of similarly infinitesimal temporal "atoms."

3. This is a position worked out in considerable detail by Henri Bergson in his 1889 book *Time and Free Will* (Bergson 1960).

4. For a compendious consideration of this coalescence of political, social, economic, technological, and cultural realities around a distinctively modern constellation of values, see Johnson (1991). For a study on the value of control, with an emphasis on the centrality of technological transformation, see Beniger (1986).

5. For a critical assessment of the apparent inconsistency between the will to power and eternal recurrence, see Löwith (1997).

6. Bergson's ideas about change are infused in virtually all his work, but a synoptic perspective is given in Bergson (1944).

7. For a qualification of Deleuze's reading of Bergson, see Guerloc (2006).

8. Seen in this way, Bergson's identification of temporality with creativity is no more necessarily mystical than the accounts of contemporary cosmologists who depict the history of the scientifically known universe as a continuous evolution of order subsequent to the so-called Big Bang that occurred when a time-space/matter-energy singularity began differentiating or unfolding at a phenomenally high rate, *rather* than dissipating into increasing disorder.

9. A broad discussion of the technological change and the notion of thresholds of utility can be found in Hershock (2003).

10. It is this focus on locality, language, and tradition that would find favor with Nazi ideologues crafting their own alternative to modernity, ideologues with whom Heidegger seems to have had more than a passing sympathy during the Second World War—a revelation that shook the philosophical world in the 1980s (Farias 1991).

11. Heraclitus' actual claim, if the relevant extant fragment is any indication, was less definite about the universality of flux: "On those stepping into rivers staying the same, other and other waters flow." (DK22B12) Based on other fragments, it is perhaps truer to Heraclitus' own thought to say that all things consist of ceaseless oscillations among opposites.

12. For a detailed and extended examination of the contrasts between Chinese and early Western thought, see Hall and Ames (1995).

13. See "Space as a Key Word" in Harvey (2006).

14. A classic illustration from American politics is the way that winning control of Congress enables the party in power to redraw district voting lines to help insure continued electoral dominance—a tactic that understandably triggers increasingly aggressive and confrontational campaigning by the other party.

15. *Kalahavivāda Sutta*, verse 7, in the *Sutta Nipāta*, p. 102.

16. On the Buddhist advocacy of karma as the foundation for a conception of human temporality, see Gregory (1995).

17. In the case of Confucianism, sustaining continuity was most fundamentally a conservative function of appropriately conducted sociocultural rituals (*li*); for Daoists, sustaining continuity was understood as a process of according with natural patterns of relational dynamics (*dao*), often through a shedding or at least bracketing of the attributes of enculturation.

18. On the conditions of conflict and how to dissolve them, see the *Sakkapañha Sutta*, *Digha Nikāya* 21.

CHAPTER FOUR. WRITING HISTORIES, MAKING DIFFERENCES

1. In so-called radical or revisionist histories, the forward motion is more complicated since it combines a delegitimization of existing histories with attempts to clear the way forward for the previously voiceless to make themselves "heard." A good example of this genre is Zinn (2001).

2. A succinct summary of this shift, its merits, and its problems is found in Peter Burke's "Overture: The New History, its Past and its Future," in Burke (1992), accessible online at http://www.kowa.euv-frankfurt- o.de/iba_european_history/ iba_european_history_text_p_burke_new_history.PDF.(accessed May 14, 2008).

3. This is, of course, particularly true of the semiotic processes embedded within and informing complex interdependencies, but even the most basic material processes—to the extent that they are complexly structured—are affected by significant indeterminacy.

4. The geographic metaphor is, perhaps, not ideal since we think of geological formations like valleys and ridges as relatively permanent features of an abiding landscape. The image works better if transposed to the surface of oceans where the equivalent of "valleys" and "mountains" are created as energy pulses through the water, causing each point of the ocean's surface to rise and fall (without, as it appears, moving forward), continuously reconfiguring the surface topography. In this case, although the point-to-point relations at the surface of the ocean remain relatively constant—like those between "moments" of time past—their topographical arrangement or evidence of radiating influences can alter very dramatically. In this image, the "vertical dimension" is that of relational significance.

5. Although originally published in 1944, *The Great Transformation* remains a valuable, synoptic view of the history of self-regulating markets through the mid-twentieth century, and a source of considerable insight into their modern roots, their functional limitations, and the complexity of their dynamics. A recent and readily available republication, with a very useful new introduction, is Polanyi (2001).

6. Here, I would trace an arc of resistance to co-optation from the 1950s Beat generation and 1960s counterculture through the Punk and New Wave phenomena of the 1970s and early 1980s on through 1990s hip-hop and rap heterodoxies and to present-day proliferations of electively constituted communities of "peer-to-peer" personal networks that stress individual self-expression and self-promotion.

7. A very useful history of the technological evolution of control through the mid-1980s is Beniger (1986). My own reading of that history and its ramification in the colonization of consciousness is most fully presented in Hershock (1999).

8. In actuality, these phases are not strictly sequential. The unevenness of globalization processes has meant that locales of various scales have progressed through the four phases at different rates, and that even within a specific locale there are often positional differences such that it is possible to read various dynamics as expressing these phases in a range of combinations.

9. Charles F. Kettering, "Keep the Consumer Dissatisfied," *Nation's Business*, January 1929 (cited in Rifkin 1995).

10. For a persuasive presentation of this inseparability, see Harvey (1990), especially Chapter 2.

11. For a detailed and yet concise discussion of this aspect of the "great divergence," see Robert C. Allen, "The British Industrial Revolution in Global Perspective: How Commerce Created the Industrial Revolution and Modern Economic Growth," http://www.nuffield.ox.ac.uk/users/allen/unpublished/econ invent-3.pdf (accessed May 7, 2008).

12. One dimension of this was the mass drafting of women and children into wage-earning employment; another was a heightened demand for "educated" workers equipped with basic literacy and numeracy of the sort needed to manufacture and operate machinery.

13. In the global South, food production in cities remains a fact of daily life, though in an increasingly threatened manner, with clear consequences for the geography of poverty therein. See, for example, "Growing Better Cities," a paper of the International Development Research Centre, http://www.idrc.ca/en/ev-95353–201–1-DO_TOPIC.html. (accessed May 8, 2008).

14. The ultimate failure of Soviet and Chinese Maoist experiments with delinking modernization and markets, albeit with substantial commitments to control as a political and technological value, can be seen as offering some negative proof of the dependence of flourishing modern values on equally flourishing markets. But perhaps even more telling are the great difficulties experienced in post-1989 Russia and post-1979 China to combine market liberalization with equitable development.

CHAPTER FIVE. THE COMMODIFICATION OF DIFFERENCE

1. This is not to deny the growth of "media ethics" since the late 1950s. But "media ethics" have focused almost exclusively either on the ethical impacts of media content (e.g., how violence in media conditions or fails to condition violence in society) or on how media professionals should conduct themselves as morally responsible agents. Mass mediation itself, in terms for example of its societal function, typically has not been subjected to ethical evaluation.

2. These highlights of media history are drawn from the very useful timeline available on the University of Minnesota Media History Project website, http://www.mediahistory.umn.edu/timeline/ (accessed May 12, 2008).

3. See Business Net, http://findarticles.com/p/articles/mi_m3065/is_n3_v20/ai_10461679/pg_1 (accessed July 26, 2008).

4. For a summary, see http://www.ifpi.org/content/section_resources/dmr2008.html (accessed July 28, 2008).

5. See Brown (1995) and a useful summary of statistics at http://www.waynesthisandthat.com/moviedata.html (accessed July 28, 2008).

6. For one of the most detailed studies of film marketing, see *World Film Market Trends, Focus 2006*, http://www.obs.coe.int/online_publication/reports/focus2006.pdf (accessed July 26, 2008).

7. Ibid., p. 9

8. A wide array of documents related to the history of television can be found at http://www.tvhistory.tv/ (accessed July 26, 2008).

9. See http://www.nielsenmedia.com/nc/portal/site/Public/menuitem.55dc6 5b4a7d5adff3f65936147a062a0/?vgnextoid=4156527aacccd010VgnVCM100000ac 0a260aRCRD (accessed July 24, 2008).

10. Information on global television viewing trends and statistics can be found on the Eurodata TV website, http://www.mediametrie.com/contenu. php?rubrique=int (accessed July 26, 2008); for statistics on Olmypic television audiences, see the Beijing 2008 International Olympic Committee website, http:// en.beijing2008.cn/16/87/article211928716.shtml (accessed July 26, 2008).

11. For an insight-rich look at media consumption over time, see Jay Newell's "Media Saturation in Radiotown," http://www.allacademic.com//meta/p_mla_ apa_research_citation/0/1/4/5/0/pages14509/p14509–1.php (accessed July 24, 2008). This paper follows up longitudinally on Wilbur Schramm's pathbreaking 1959 study *Television in the Lives of Our Children* (Stanford, CA: Stanford University Press, 1961).

12. A comprehensive survey of youth media consumption patterns can be found in Donald F. Roberts, Ulla G. Foehr, Victoria J. Rideout, and Mollyann Brodie, *Kids and Media at the New Millennium*, a 1999 Kaiser Family Foundation Report, http://www.kff.org/entmedia/upload/Kids-Media-The-New-Millennium-Report.pdf (accessed July 24, 2008).

13. For a summary of several studies, including one conducted by Yahoo, Inc., and OMD Worldwide that surveyed youth in eleven countries about media and media multitasking, see http://www.cross-mediaentertainment.com/index. php/2005/10/08/simultaneous-concurrent-meshing-usage/ (accessed July 26, 2008).

14. For data on social networking use, the Comscore website is readily accessible and reliable source. See, for example, the Comscore March 18, 2008, press release, http://www.comscore.com/press/release.asp?press=2115 (accessed August 1, 2008).

15. A detailed consideration of the growth of online gaming businesses in China can be found in Julian Dibbell, "The Life of the Chinese Gold Farmer," *New York Times Magazine*, June 17, 2007, http://www.nytimes.com/2007/06/17/ magazine/17lootfarmers-t.html?pagewanted=all (accessed July 30, 2008).

16. For a historical perspective on the emancipatory potential of the telecommunications and computational revolutions, see Brate (2002); for an enthusiastic presentation of the promises of virtual community, see Rheingold (2000); and for an approach that envisions more radical and mixed patterns of change, see Bard and Söderqvist (2002).

17. Hardin (1968) offers the seminal and succinct statement of the fallacy of composition—the "truth" that whatever is good for each and every one of us is good for all of us. I have written more extensively about the fallacy and the occurrence of ironic consequences in Hershock (1999).

18. The implications of applying a social constructivist approach to understanding international relations have been drawn out, for example, by Alexander Wendt and Martha Finemore.

19. A concise summary of contemporary theories of perception is offered by Alva Noë en route to presenting his own enactive theory of perception in Noë (2001).

20. It may seem counterintuitive to pair the present and absent in perception, but in actuality being aware of something's absence is still to be aware of it. We

note this thing being absent, precisely because its absence is informative. A child notices, for example, the absence of a notorious bully on the playground. The unnoticed, by contrast, is that which is *not* informative, *not* relevant, and *not* taken to be constitutive of who we are.

21. A profoundly mass mediated society might be characterized as nomadic—as in Deleuze's work—were it not for the fact that the eccentricities of mass mediated publics are quite at odds with the finely tuned ecological sensibilities and often fierce commitment to tradition expressed by nomadic peoples.

22. It should be noted that the causality linking media program content and society is not linear, but complex and network-like. The linkages are, in other words, correlative—a function of interdependencies and not one of independent "causes" producing dependent "effects." The policy failure (or irrelevance) of research that is critical of the interplay of mass media and society is itself very much a function of the rarity with which one can find a "smoking gun" in media content.

23. For example, many teenagers "study" while watching television, office workers often listen to music transmitted by radio or via internet downloads, commuters check stock markets and read news updates on handheld wireless computers. The costs of distraction by media content in different cases and for different populations assuredly vary. But that some costs are incurred is hardly debatable.

24. Consider in this light the great fortunes made literally overnight and almost entirely on the basis of speculation-driven prominence during the dot. com boom, with some companies' stock values soaring several hundred percent on the first day of public trading. Or to focus more specifically on the asymmetry of attention exchanges, consider the more mundane example of an "interactive" television show like *American Idol* that invites audiences to participate in deciding who eventually becomes the season's star. But if for any hour-long show there are 20 million viewers and 10 contestants and judges, the ratio of attention exchange is 20 million to 10 (or perhaps 1000 if one allows 100 hours of support-staff time for each contestant and judge per show). Advertisers capable of affording a 30-second spot during such shows—a global corporate elite that purchases this sliver of individuals' attention for $300,000 to $650,000—understand full well the economic advantages offered by the terms of this trade in attention.

25. This unevenness of attention flows has factored into several of Michael Goldhaber's discussions of the attention economy in the web journal *First Monday*, http://www.uic.edu/htbin/cgiwrap/bin/ojs/index.php/fm/ (accessed August 22, 2008).

26. See the PricewaterhouseCoopers *Global Entertainment and Media Outlook, 2008–2012*, available through PWC at http://www.pwc.com/extweb/pwcpublications.nsf/docid/5AC172F2C9DED8F5852570210044EEA7 (accessed September 8, 2008).

27. See the *CRS Report for Congress: Oil Industry Profit Review 2007*, produced by Robert Pirog for the U.S. Congressional Research Service, http://fpc.state.gov/documents/organization/103679.pdf (accessed August 22, 2008).

28. I would argue that this karmic pattern is generally symptomatic of our technological society. But one concrete index of the power of desires for the new and different that are media induced and media enhanced—either directly through advertising, or indirectly through the effects of attention export—is

the degree to which a population meets their perceived needs through revolving credit. In the United States, revolving consumer debt in 2008 is likely to reach 1 trillion dollars (standing at $968 billion in May)—a figure that does not include mortgages or other secured debts. For recent statistics from the U.S. Federal Reserve, see http://www.federalreserve.gov/releases/G19/Current/.

29. David Harvey (2005) has a very cogent discussion of the neoconservative and neoliberal marriage in China. See Chapter 5.

CHAPTER SIX. ETHICS AND DIFFERENTIATION

1. For a discussion of downward causation and it implications in a broad range of social science and scientific disciplines, see Andersen et al. (2001).

2. In this connection, consider the responses to Hurricane Katrina by local, state, and national agencies, and the degree to which racial and class differences map onto those responses. In the United States, Hurricane Katrina washed away the thin veneer of equality of access to basic services, revealing the severe shortcomings and biases of human agency and official systems of response.

3. Contrasting morality and ethics in this manner obviously echoes the contrast of premodern and modern sensibilities, suggesting that the premodern world be seen as predominantly one of moral communities and the modern world as one of ethical societies. And there is, I think, some merit in such a reading of the contrast, though it is easily oversimplified and overplayed. In spite of the dramatic events surrounding the transit from the premodern world to the modern, these worlds are not divided or held apart by some sort of ontological null space; their clear distinction is a function of the constructive projects of history writing. The merit, if any, in distinguishing the premodern and the modern is ultimately inseparable from admitting their interwoven continuities. Similarly, conceiving of morality and ethics as distinctly differing approaches to posing and answering questions about how we should live is grounded (if at all) only heuristically. My specific purpose in making the contrast as sharply as I have is to make noticeable some significant features of the history of difference in moral and ethical discourses.

4. Such was the situation in the segregated American South prior to the Civil Rights movement and widespread bussing of school children to forcibly integrate primary and secondary education. Suddenly, the possibility of maintaining separate moral communities—separate spheres and, indeed, senses of mutual belonging and responsibility—began unraveling.

5. To pick up the theme of the preceding note, the American counterculture of the mid- and late 1960s might well be described as an ethical experiment—a presupposition-challenging critique of mainstream values that allowed (and sometimes openly endorsed) the segregating practices of mainstream American moralities. Seen in this way, the counterculture sought to unite the movements for civil rights, peace, black power, women's rights, economic justice, and cultural creativity in ways that would allow those who were distinctly and apparently different (and often in significant disagreement) to nevertheless stand on the same side. What undermined the counterculture and served to position it historically

as only an "experiment" was, I would argue, its acceptance of two key modern assumptions: that persons are fundamentally autonomous individuals and that freedom is ultimately a function of choice. Together, these left the counterculture highly vulnerable to commodification and to a steady dissolution of commitments to collective action—its gradual transmutation from a "we" to a "me" generation.

6. Of course, since transgressions aimed at challenging or undermining state authority were clearly high on the list of potentially destabilizing offenses, and since such challenges would most likely come from within elite strata of society, the impartiality of law might best be understood as grounded less in valorizing equality and impartiality as ethical ideals than in assuring all that the reach of law will be politically effective.

7. Debates about human nature were crucial, for example, in Chinese discussions of statecraft from at least the fourth century BCE. For example, Confucius is recorded as noting: "Lead the people with administrative injunctions and keep them orderly with penal law, and they will avoid punishments but be without a sense of shame. Lead them with excellence and keep them orderly through observing ritual propriety and they will develop a sense of shame, and moreover, will order themselves" (*Analects*, 2.3).

8. See the *Han Fei Tzu*, Chapter 40: "Objections to the Primacy of the Power-Base."

9. The debates about the merits of moral and legal routes to social cohesion and harmony were particularly keen and well documented in early Chinese society. The Legalist tradition, as exemplified in such works as the *Shangzi*, the *Kuanzi*, and the *Hanfeizi*, positioned itself as a realist response to Confucian, Mohist, and (to a different degree) Daoist affirmations of the political potency of personal self-cultivation. Crucial to these arguments, as would later be the case in early modern constructions of social contract theory, was a nonidealistic view of human nature—a conviction that having individual likes and dislikes is elementally human, and that persuasion is much less powerful than punishment. For a brief, but insightful, reading of the early Legalist tradition, see Graham (1989, 267–92).

10. Laws, in other words, are necessary because intentions—the signature expressions of human individuality—are not directly open to discipline. Even as torture of the most extreme sort is not always capable of forcing compliance, neither are even the most extravagant inducements capable of eliciting it. Intentionality, as existentialists of the twentieth century would insist, is the most basic manifestation of human freedom.

11. To take a single, simple example: eighteenth- and nineteenth-century patterns of rapid industrialization, labor specialization, colonial expansion, and shifting alliances among religious, political, and scientific factions combined to generate both elite and popular opportunities for social and geographical mobility, the intensification of class affiliations, and the rise of "transcontinental" British identities. British expatriates in the Americas, Africa, and Asia were distinctly British, yet also easily distinguished from those living and working in the United Kingdom proper. Intermarriages in the colonies created still other, more explicitly hybrid identities, but so did the spread of British organizational structures that in India, for instance, greatly exalted the status of (literate) members of the Brahmin caste, many

of whom adopted explicitly British social ideals, while at the same time fostering a niche identification of Sikhs with military and police service.

12. The signature and the number are invoked by Gilles Deleuze as the two poles of modern disciplinary societies, and contrasted with coding as the hallmark of societies of control that began emerging in the second half of the twentieth century. For a brief discussion, see Gilles Deleuze (1992), available online at http://www.n5m.org/n5m2/media/texts/deleuze.htm (accessed November 20, 2008).

13. Jeremy Bentham, preface to *Panopticon*, originally written in 1787 and available online at http://cartome.org/panopticon2.htm (accessed November 20, 2008).

14. For a general, but thorough, discussion of relativism, see Chris Swoyer's entry on relativism in the *Stanford Encyclopedia of Philosophy*, http://plato.stanford.edu/entries/relativism/. For a discussion of moral relativism, see Chris Gowans' entry, http://plato.stanford.edu/entries/moral-relativism/ (accessed October 1, 2011).

15. In the fourth-century BCE Chinese text the *Zuozhuan* (Commentary of Zuo), it is bluntly stated that, "if a person is not of our kin/bloodline (*yizu* 異族), he is certain to have a different mind." And in the later Han dynasty, Zheng Xuan (127–200 CE) offered an "environmental" explanation of moral differences, arguing that just as valleys and streams are variously formed, so are the people living there and their various characters and customs.

16. Some philosophers like Donald Davidson have argued that this way of formulating relativism—however well it captures popular usage—renders relativism self-contradictory. The basic claim of the relativist has the logical form, after all, of a universal statement. My own point is not to defend relativism, but only to capture something of its relevance to issues of difference and, eventually, equity.

17. This is not to deny that much good has come of responses to difference generated from along the relativist-universalist spectrum. To give just a few examples: relativist-leaning moral stances have played important roles in drawing attention to the possibly coercive dimensions of majoritarianism and cosmopolitanism, and in protesting on behalf of allowing varying weights to be given to the three "generations" of human rights; universalist-leaning stances have been instrumental in advocating for the provision of education and health care as primary public goods, in negotiating cross-border stances on human trafficking, and in crafting arguments for identifying and protecting global resource commons; and pluralist perspectives have been important in carving out public space for accepting and encouraging multiculturalism.

18. As we will see, this tactic is made use of in the construction of rational choice theory and the distinctive form of liberalism to which it has been wedded over the past four decades: a way of looking at the world that absolves us of having to go beyond the pursuit of narrow self-interest because such a pursuit makes the best of outcomes for all inevitable.

19. One might think here, e.g., of the case of North Korea and the radically different trajectory of its development vis-à-vis South Korea after the end of open conflict on the peninsula.

20. Holding that relativism extends to individual persons is empirically inconsistent since the incommensurability thesis would disallow arriving at the kinds of practical arrangements that are constitutive of social engagement.

21. As we will see later, this ethical contrast of emphasis on peoples and persons will take political form as contrasting illiberal and liberal approaches to democracy.

22. Not surprisingly, relativist valorizations of "difference" have recently come under considerable universalist, neoconservative attack as a polity- or community-threatening justification for exclusionary self-interest groups—an unjust and ultimately divisive marriage of equality and autonomy (Wood 2003). Similarly, universalist celebrations of globally integrative cosmopolitan values have been regarded with skepticism and at times outright hostility by relativists sensitive to the ways in which establishing a planetary equivalence of actors in pursuit of common values can be much more advantageous to some than to others—an unfair and ultimately coercive marriage of equality and hegemonic authority (Kompridis 2005).

CHAPTER SEVEN. CONVERGENCE ON VARIETY

1. This distinction was much in the news in 2008 as global markets were suffering in a degree and depth not witnessed since the crash of 1929, with many economists, like Paul Krugman, allowing that the long-term impacts of the crisis might be even greater.

2. For a concise summary of current thinking about the economic causalities involved in the Depression, see the E-History website entry by Randall Parker, "An Overview of the Great Depression," *EH.Net Encyclopedia*, ed. Robert Whaples, March 16, 2008, http://eh.net/encyclopedia/article/parker.depression (accessed August 26, 2008).

3. For a discussion of the growth and eventual co-optation or suppression of labor, socialist, and communist movements in the United States, see Lipset and Marks (2001). For two views of the rise of national socialism and fascist ideology and culture, see Paxton (2004) and Sternhell et al. (2005).

4. In fact, while the race to develop atomic weaponry in both Germany and the United States clearly set the stage for the subsequent Cold War arms race between the United States and the U.S.S.R., the bombings of Hiroshima and Nagasaki are now widely regarded as "insults" added to the mortal injuries already sustained by the Axis powers—events that, horrendous as they were, did not significantly contribute to the end of the war. As demonstrated by the iconic image of the mushroom cloud that hung over the world throughout the tensest years of the Cold War, the atomic bombings of Japan are best seen as a symbolic rather than military exercise.

5. The era of American neoimperialism that climaxed during the Bush administrations from 2000–2008 is, I think, best interpreted as an interregnum between U.S.-Soviet bipolar dynamics and a still nascent twenty-first-century dynamic of multipolar complexity. The disastrous political and international-relations consequences of the wars in Iraq and Afghanistan, combined with the recent collapse of global financial markets, will permanently cripple any remaining American aspirations to global hegemony. And the realities of a resurgent Russia, an ever more ambitious European Union, the rise of China and India, and the prospects of profound changes in Latin America and Africa all suggest a

more—not less—differentiated topography of power and authority in the foresee-able future.

6. Ironically, Japan's global dominance of the consumer electronics industry can be traced to the postwar constitution and economic plan drafted by the U.S. Occupation. First, the constitution made it impossible for Japan to redevelop its devastated military-industrial complex, forcing reconstruction development along new lines. But more importantly, perhaps, the Occupation forces made a request for the local manufacture of four million radio sets in 1945 to carry out its campaign to inform (and indoctrinate) the Japanese populace regarding the "new Japan." This kick-started a mass consumer electronics industry, and when the television began taking off in the 1950s Japan was able to respond to a rapidly rising global need for electronic components and almost overnight become a global supplier and eventually design innovator. For a history of the industry, see Nakayama et al. (1999).

7. A thorough, case-study approach to the relationship between government funding and the computing revolution can be found in *Funding a Revolution: Government Support for Computing Research*, Committee on Innovations in Computing and Communications: Lessons from History, Computer Science and Telecommunications Board, Commission on Physical Sciences, Mathematics and Applications, and the National Research Council (Washington, DC: National Academy Press, 1999).

8. The Rand Corporation has continued to speculate about the future of information technologies and their impacts on both civil and governmental sectors. An entry point revealing their turn of the century thinking can be found at http://www.rand.org/publications/randreview/issues/rr.12.00/transcendental.html (accessed August 28, 2008). For a brief account of Rand researcher Paul Baran's proposal for decentralized networks based on packet-switching, see http://www.rand.org/about/history/baran.html (accessed August 28, 2008).

9. We will consider the wider implications of reflexive modernization and the advent of network and risk societies in Chapter 8.

10. The list of those associated with both RAND and the development of rational choice theory reads like a virtual "who's who" of leading social scientists, mathematicians, and computer scientists, including: Kenneth Arrow, James Buchanan, Herbert Simon, Mancur Olson, John von Neumann, Oskar Morgenstern, Duncan Luce, and Howard Raiffa.

11. There are many versions of the Prisoner's Dilemma, including versions that involve multiple iterations of choices, infinite numbers of choices, and more than two prisoners. The literature on the Prisoner's Dilemma is extremely voluminous and much of it is directed toward the interests of specialists in game theory. For a broader introduction, one can access the entry in the *Stanford Encyclopedia of Philosophy*, http://plato.stanford.edu/entries/prisoner-dilemma/ (accessed September 24, 2008).

12. See Ken Binmore, "The Origins of Fair Play," p. 9, available online at http://else.econ.ucl.ac.uk/papers/uploaded/267.pdf (accessed September 25, 2008).

13. The importance of a one-stop, rather than indefinitely iterated, framing of the Prisoner's Dilemma is that in the latter, cooperation is in fact a long-term equilibrium solution to the dilemma. Betrayal does not prove to be the hands-down

winner. A major champion of applying this insight in thinking through the nature and origins of cooperation is Robert Axelrod (1984, 1997). A critical review of Axelrod's sweeping conclusions is offered by Ken Binmore (1998).

14. This would seem to be the logic operating in the George W. Bush administration's advocacy of American unilateralism and the doctrine of just preemption. The "you're either with us or against us" mentality of that administration well illustrates the rational choice theoretic approach to decision making and strategic planning. The results, alas, are also illustrative.

15. The claim that self-interested action is a duty would await statement by late twentieth-century neoliberal exponents of maximally free and differentiated markets who equated expanding deregulation with deepening capacities for self-correcting behavior from the individual up to global markets—an approach that now seems to have fostered conditions for the fall 2008 global financial, credit, and investment meltdowns.

16. As noted earlier, the most explicit use of the trope of imprisonment is by Michel Foucault (1997). But Levinas' own experiences as a Jew in a Nazi prisoner-of-war camp clearly affected his thinking about otherness and ethics.

17. By posing its foundational commitments as axioms, rational choice theory self-consciously arrogated an aura of mathematical rigor and geometric purity, structuring choice in accord solely with the dictates of universal rationality. But these commitments can also be seen as expressing in skeletal form an historically contingent and peculiarly American structure of feeling—a feeling of autonomy epitomized in the "declaration of independence" that announced the birth of the United States as a modern nation-state. Since then, American national identity has revolved around the idealization of individualism and frontiers, a merging of assimilationism and isolationism, and an assumption that the social, economic, political, and technological successes of the United States demonstrate a distinctively transcultural genius and passion for competition—American uniqueness pitched as a universal model for progressive change, as is assumed in the United States. American stresses on jointly and aggressively affirming autonomous individuality and assimilative equality—a just (though not yet realized) ideal of difference blindness—resonate forcefully with the axiomatic assumptions about human nature that undergird the hypermodern ethos asserted by rational choice theory.

18. A very insightful collection of essays on how atrocities can be committed with "moral" or "ethical" justification can be found in LaFleur et al. (2007).

19. Levinas' thoughts on justice and ethics are widely scattered and anything but systematic. However, a good starting point is Levinas (1981, 157–61).

20. See his "Violence and Metaphysics: An Essay on the Thought of Emmanuel Levinas," in Derrida (1978).

21. One of the more ironic results of this convergent valorization of variety in the context of technologically and industrially expanded capacities for control and choice has been that the climax of the Cold War did not bring what Francis Fukuyama (1992) famously referred to as the "end of history": the final triumph of Western cosmopolitanism. Far from heralding a second and final "rise of the West" and/or American hegemony, the end of the bipolar political dynamics of the Cold War has resulted in the emergence of multiple poles of global confluence and influence. The rise of China and India come immediately to mind, of course,

but also the ideological ascent of Islamic fundamentalism in Africa, Central Asia, and Southeast Asia; the intensification of ethnicity-based separatist movements in Eastern Europe, Africa, and parts of Asia; and the consolidation of sociocultural resistance movements in Central and South America. If the end of the Cold War signals the end of the fight between opposing, universalistic visions of modernity, the result has not been the triumph of the "last man" left standing, but rather the ironic triumph of an increasingly volatile mix of centripetal and centrifugal forces producing conditions for increasingly fluid polyarchy—the presence of multiple and shifting centers of power.

22. The term "netocracy" has been used to signal the potentially revolutionary political relevance of new media, particularly the Internet. But it is used in quite contrary ways to refer on one hand to the development of Internet-mediated democracy, and on the other hand—as, for example, in the work of Alexander Bard and Jan Söderqvist (2002)—to rule by a technologically advantaged and constituted elite.

CHAPTER EIGHT. DELINKING EQUITY AND EQUALITY

1. This is an argument that remains favored among Smith's neoliberal heirs who have made much use of its popularly phrased conclusion that "all boats rise in a rising economic tide." The empirical merits of the argument in Smith's time were questionable, based as it was on then-current historical/anthropological understandings of societies viewed through colonial and imperial lenses. Contemporary neoliberal justifications of inequality, similarly, rest on less-than-stable and -convincing empirical grounds.

2. For an early and, in retrospect, somewhat premature announcement of this shattering, see Heyne (1978).

3. In effect, the assumption was that if one would be ill served by equal treatment before the law, this was because one had—through one's own lack of initiative—failed to rise to a reasonable social baseline. The poor, for example, were poor because of laziness, addictive behavior, and bad choices, not for structural reasons for which society as a whole might be responsible. This sort of "blame-the-victim" perspective persists, of course, today.

4. The now widely accepted reality of human-induced climate change and variability is, of course, the most prominent and "global" example of the scale of risks associated with the second or reflexive stage of modernity. But mention can be made of the threat of future chemical and nuclear disasters like those that occurred at Bopal and Chernobyl, the potential impacts of the uncontrolled spread of bioengineered organisms, or the economic ramifications of global financial crises like those in 1997 and the fall of 2008.

5. Here it is perhaps appropriate to state clearly that the implication of this is *not* that choice in and of itself is bad or that choices should be made only by some kind of a well-informed and well-intentioned elite. Rather, the point is to call attention to a confluence of conditions that aligns expansions of choice and widening inequalities in who bears the benefits and costs of growth. What this shows

is the predicament-generating nature of a predominant constellation of values, not the intrinsic "fallibility" of expanding choices for all.

6. It is worth noting here that in Mahayana Buddhist traditions in which the perfection of wisdom means realizing the emptiness (*śūnyata*) of all things, the risks associated with the dissolution of structure and essence are openly acknowledged and offset by practice traditions that emphasize the indispensability of an enlightened teacher and the coemergence of wisdom and compassion. In these Buddhist contexts, that is, emphasis is placed on realizing liberating intimacy and responsive virtuosity—the bodhisattva ideal of realizing the emptiness of all things in order to be able to respond as needed to orient ongoing relational dynamics in ways conducive to the liberation of all sentient beings from subjection to trouble and suffering. The emphasis on contribution, in other words, is a key element in bringing about the dissolution of the conditions for stress and insecurity.

7. A useful illustration of the inequality of resources for decision making is the difference between those who have the wherewithal to hire full-time financial managers able to play stock market fluctuations in real time, taking profitable advantage of both rising and falling prices, and those whose trading practices are informed only by what they read in the newspaper and hear on television, and who seldom have the capital needed to risk buying when there is "blood" on the floor of the stock exchange or on the streets of real estate.

8. As this description highlights, neoliberalism has much in common with rational choice theory.

9. Reported in "Riots, Instability Spread as Food Prices Skyrocket," *CNN.com*, April 14, 2008, http://www.cnn.com/2008/WORLD/americas/04/14/world.food.crisis/.

10. For an argument on behalf of constructing equity in terms of equality of opportunity, see Roemer (1998). For a qualified critique of that construction, see Denis Cogneau, "Equality of Opportunity and other Equity Principles in the Context of Developing Countries," Document de Travail, Development Institutions and Analyses de Long Terme, January 2005, http://www.dial.prd.fr/dial_publications/PDF/Doc_travail/2005–01.pdf (accessed February 24, 2007).

11. I have argued, in this regard, that human rights conventions, while sadly necessary, are not a cause for pride or celebration, but rather an indictment of our collective inability to refrain from exercises of gross inhumanity. See Hershock (2000).

12. Rawls' *Theory of Justice* (1971) and *Justice as Fairness* (2001) are, of course, classics, as are Ronald Dworkin's seminal articles (1981a and 1981b) on "What is Equality? Part 1: Equality of Welfare" and "What is Equality? Part 2: Equality of Resources." Amartya Sen's *Inequality Reexamined* (1992) extends his earlier work on equality to present a theory of equity in terms—not of primary goods, as is true for Rawls—but, rather, capability or functionings—framing the outlines of what has come to be known as "equality of opportunity." This approach has been given a more quantitative, rather than philosophical, treatment in Roemer (1998).

13. Here, I should note that my use of form and function does not hearken back to the seminal Western dichotomy which accords form or essence and function or activity ontologically separate statuses. Rather, I am working through

the expressly nondualistic, Chinese notion of *ti-yong*, where *ti* (form, substance, essence, pattern) and *yong* (function, use, purpose) are understood as mutually constituting.

14. One of the liabilities of equality-grounded conceptions of equity is that they impose limits on the ethical reach of equity, allowing for only quite thin considerations of ecosystems and the species comprised within them since it is hard to imagine how we would determine significant equivalencies with or among them. Utilitarian approaches have difficulty seeing how the same interests or happiness could be ascribed to ecosystems or other species as to humans; deontological and virtue ethics likewise have similar difficulties in meaningfully ascribing duties or capacities for self-cultivation beyond the boundaries of humanity.

CHAPTER NINE. DIVERSITY AND EQUITY

1. Susan Buck (1998) provides an alternative categorization scheme based on exclusion and subtractability. Public goods are goods or services with low subtractability (the benefits accruing to one user do not subtract from those accruing to others), the usage of which is very difficult to restrict; common-pool goods or resources have high subtractability (are subject to depletion or degradation) and patterns of use or access which are difficult to restrict.

2. These relatively simple definitions, however useful, belie considerable differences in how the concepts of common-pool resources and public goods have been formulated and used, a discussion of which is properly the subject of a longer and independent work. For those interested in the wider discussion, the generally agreed-upon locus classicus of the modern concept of public goods is in Samuelson (1954). A range of perspectives is represented in Buchanan (1968), Olson (1971), and Sandler (1997).

3. For a succinct review of the challenges of conceiving public goods, see Kaul (2001).

4. For a neoutilitarian approach to issues of economic justice, see Singer (2002).

5. See, for instance, Smith (1994), Book 1, Chapter 8.

6. The distinction between innovation and improvisation will be addressed later in more detail. In brief, innovation is the kind of new thinking and action involved in problem solution; improvisation is the kind of new thinking and action involved in predicament resolution.

7. The authors of the *2006 World Development Report*, for example, seem well aware that the efficiency-equity tension exhibits the structure of predicament and that addressing the developmental liabilities of persistent (and, indeed, deepening) inequities necessarily involves a clarification and consistent prioritization of values. Their expressed conviction that increasing equity may *over the long term* prove conducive to economic growth and wealth production amounts to an implicit subordination of market to moral values. Their lack of commitment to subjecting market dynamics to ethical appraisal remains, however, a major stumbling block.

8. Marketizing goods that were previously publicly provided *can* open spaces for a variety of new actors to become involved in the provision process and may

contribute to its greater efficiency. But there is no guarantee that this widened range of actors will persist or that it will serve to foster deepening commitments to sustainably shared welfare. The record of the George W. Bush administration in the United States is ample evidence of the liabilities associated with placing market advocates and corporate/industry lobbyists in positions to exercise authority over defining public goods and commons and setting related public policy agendas. In this regard, see Kennedy (2004).

9. It is tempting to deny the critical importance of this observation by appealing to the metaphor of the ship of Theseus, which was rebuilt board by board, ever remaining "the same ship" even though it eventually incorporates none of the lumber out of which it had originally been built. Indeed, our bodies are much like this, with every individual cell being replaced in less than roughly seven years, and much the same could be said for our cities and societies. But the comfort of the metaphor comes from the supposition that Theseus' ship has a single and ever-abiding design that is maintained through replacing its component parts as necessary, and we are not such timeless, Platonic ideals. The truth of the matter is better captured by the Buddhist teaching of no-self that paying close and sustained enough attention to ourselves bodily, psychologically, and socially makes evident that the idea of a fixed and abiding self is an ontological artifact, a construction maintained through a certain way of understanding and engaging the world.

10. I have developed the concept of "conduct" at some length in Hershock (1996).

11. *Poesis* or "making" reintroduces the idea of a source of change since things made imply makers. The Chinese term *ziran* can be translated as "naturally" or more literally as "self-so," and is understood as applying to all *dao* or dynamically patterned presences.

12. We shall make more of the dual connotations of "affect" in English of influence and emotion in Chapter 10.

13. This can be thought of as refusing to make the Cartesian leap from "I think" to "therefore, I am," and verifying instead that "I think" only allows asserting that "therefore, thinking occurs"—realizing, in other words, the ongoing occurrence of thoughts without a thinker.

14. See, for example, Rao (1999) and Sen (1999a).

CHAPTER TEN. MAKING A DIFFERENCE

1. Perhaps the clearest contemporary example of such a past-legitimizing political system is that of North Korea—the Democratic People's Republic of Korea—but elements of this conservatively recursive orientation can be found, I think, in perhaps every polity that is self-consciously structured as a geographically stable nation-state.

2. This was a crucial part of Alexis de Tocqueville's nineteenth-century thesis regarding the rise of American democracy and has continued to be invoked to the present, most prominently perhaps in Moore (1966) and Rueschemeyer et al. (1992).

3. The argument can be made that deliberative democracy represents something like a "third stream" cutting across the dialectic between liberal and illiberal constructions of democracy. This possibility will be taken up later with an eye to seeing whether it suffices to generate the kind of movement oblique to the liberal-illiberal tension that is needed to align democratic practices with diversification.

4. Constraints on what is possible, of course, come from many different directions—political, economic, social, cultural, and technological.

5. I am drawing here on the distinctions between finite/infinite games and power/strength forwarded by James Carse (1986).

6. Tolerance is, of course, a key modern value. Yet while tolerance is clearly preferable to intolerance, tolerance translates practically into seeing differences as not making a significant difference. In engineering, tolerance defines the degree of difference that can be ignored, and more august rhetoric aside, this remains central to the moral practice of toleration.

7. Moral monadism assumes the primacy of individually existing entities that have a common moral/metaphysical structure—a "Leibnizian" view of the relationship between moralities. Every individual is likely to have distinct views and values, but having views and values is common to all and provides a procedural basis for bringing differences into accord. Moral monism assumes the primacy of independently existing cultural communities all the members of which have a common moral/metaphysical substance—a "Spinozistic" view of moral multiplicity. Morality is communally rather than individually determined, and while there may be significant differences between moral communities, there can/should not be any within them.

8. Here, the term "value" must be understood ambiguously as referring to both value as an index of worth, and values as modalities of appreciation.

9. For a seminal formulation of the politics of recognition, see Taylor (1994).

10. Thus, as exemplified in Nancy Fraser's (2005) lamentation that the politics of recognition seems to have led politics astray from issues of the relative distribution of outcomes and opportunities across society, the critique is focused centrally on relative considerations, not truly relational ones.

11. The individual can, of course, be a person, a nation, a corporation, and so on. The point is the assumption of individually existing things or beings as primary, rather than relationality as such.

12. It should be stressed that the rhetorical convenience of speaking about a single-generation "family" is just that—convenience. In actuality, all families are multigenerational, and the emphasis on the so-called nuclear family is a narrowing of relational scope justified only for the sake of expressive clarity. In fact, in becoming parents we do not cease being children, and the roles we play as mother, father, son, and daughter are not mutually exclusive.

13. In the extensive introduction to their translation of the Chinese *Classic of Family Reverence*, Roger T. Ames and Henry Rosemont, Jr. (2009) have forwarded the view that properly engaged, a distinctive "role ethics" can be developed that is not predicated on liberal assumptions about the autonomous individual as the unit of ethical and political analysis. This approach is further developed by Ames (2011). Although broadly compatible with the approach taken here, the Confucian

inspiration for this contemporary ethics grants lesser scope, perhaps, to relational improvisation and possibilities for revising the meanings of sociality.

14. For a succinct statement of this view of improvisation and its wider ramifications, see Daniel Fischlin (2009). For a more extended consideration, see Fischlin and Heble (2004). And for a cultural history of improvisation as a central feature of a *mentalite* of mid-twentieth-century critical opposition to the scope and power of corporate-liberal systems and ideology, see Belgrad (1998).

15. It is possible, of course, that some of those involved in a collective improvisation will feel as if things are holding together in interesting ways while others will not. They may forge on, effectively leaving the others behind to fall into "silence" or forcing their compliance, thus transforming the proceedings into a finite power play—an assertion that *this* is what we will do and nothing other than this. With this constriction of relational imagination, improvisation as it has been characterized here either ends or contracts dramatically in scope, becoming an improvisation carried on by some, but not all.

16. See *Sutta Nipata*, trans. H. Saddhatissa (London: Curzon Press, 1985), especially the Kalahavivāda Sutta, the Cūlaviyūha Sutta, and Mahāviyūha Sutta.

17. On the nonreliance on views, knowledge, rites, and rules, see the *Paramatthaka Sutta*, also in the *Atthakavagga* chapter of the *Sutta Nipata*, verses 796–803.

18. The Buddhist understanding of perception recognizes that humans have access to six sense realms through seeing, hearing, tasting, touching, smelling, and thinking, and regards each as associated with a qualitatively distinct consciousness that arises as a result of the relationship between a sensing organ and a sensed object. Thus, consciousness and perception are not uniform, but rather irreducibly differentiated. I have added emotion in as a "seventh" sense—the perception of flows and concentrations of significance.

19. This is not, of course, to deny the central role played in Buddhist teachings of "home leaving." In practical terms, engaging in the meditative and moral disciplines central to Buddhist practice is more "easily" undertaken in the simplified world of the monastic community. Yet, this was explicitly regarded, not as a retreat *from* the world, but *toward* possibilities for cultivating wisdom, attentive mastery, and moral clarity—a process that entails what I have termed both a "critique of self" and a "critique of culture." That is, monastic retreat made attaining the depths of "listening" and "remembering" required to improvise the resolution of human suffering and trouble somewhat less challenging than in the highly scripted world of northern India in the fifth century before the common era—a world of rigid distinctions of caste as well as class, and in which formalized learning and practices for heightening qualities and expanding scopes of awareness were forbidden to the majority of the population.

20. The suggestion here, then, is that seeing the circular relation of democracy and justice as "vicious" depends on taking deliberation to be a one-off affair—a finite endeavor rather than an infinite one. The parallel to criticisms of rational choice theory are significant.

21. Not insignificantly, whereas wearing animal skins required killing the animals, making fabrics out of wool sheared annually from domesticated sheep allowed for a new kind of human-animal relationship. Similarly, using cotton

fibers for weaving did not require uprooting the plant to make use of its fibers—again, a new kind of relationship.

22. Evidence suggests that fabrics were transported over continental and intercontinental distances even prior to the consolidation of the famous Silk Roads that, by the early centuries of the common era, connected the cultures and societies of East, South, Southeast, and Central Asia with the Middle East and Europe. And, if woven cloth played a significant role in early globalization processes, it was no less crucial in the modern era as the export of British machine-made fabrics brought about a drastic reconfiguration of global trade balances and made possible the realization of commercial and political empires on which the sun never set.

23. The difference between an average running back in American football and one who is highly coordinated is that the latter is able to respond immediately and fluently to the dynamics of the playing field, finding open seams through the continuously changing trajectories of twenty-one other bodies in motion. Responding with exceptional appreciation of even the most sudden and unexpected exigencies, an exceptional running back uses the imparted energy of would-be tacklers to accelerate and spin off through openings that shut immediately after passing through upfield. Placing this same athlete on a surfboard, however, may be cause for much hilarity. Being generally coordinated may help such an athlete learn more quickly than someone who is physically uncoordinated to paddle, stand up, and remain standing as the board is propelled toward shore by a wave. But to demonstrate the same kind of graceful virtuosity in motion on a surfboard as on a football field would, at the very least, take years of tuning in to both the distinctive environmental and bodily dimensions of surfing.

EPILOGUE

1. As might be expected, such an instrumental view of Buddhist practice did arise and in many cases became a kind of orthodoxy. Indeed one of the most virulent and recurrent debates within Buddhist circles has been centered on whether enlightenment is a function of gradual practice or sudden and apparently unprecedented awakening.

2. This passage is from the Discourse Record of Linji, the *Zhenzhou Linji Huizhao chanshi yulu*. Taishō shinshū daizōkyō, Volume 47, Number 1985. The translation is my own.

Bibliography of Works Cited

Amadae, S. M. *Rationalizing Capitalist Democracy: The Cold War Origins of Rational Choice Liberalism*. Chicago: University of Chicago Press, 2003.

Ames, Roger T., and Henry Rosemont, Jr. *The Chinese Classic of Family Reverence: A Philosophical Translation of the Xiaojing*. Honolulu: University of Hawaii Press, 2009.

Ames, Roger T. *Confucian Role Ethics*. Honolulu: University of Hawaii Press, 2011.

Andersen, Peter Bogh, Claus Emmeche, Niels Ole Finnemann, and Peder Voetmann Christiansen, eds. *Downward Causation: Minds, Bodies and Matter*. Ärhus: Aarhus University Press, 2001.

Arrow, Kenneth J. *Social Choice and Individual Values*. New York: Wiley, 1951.

Aveni, Anthony. *Empires of Time: Calendars, Clocks and Cultures*. Boulder: University of Colorado Press, 2002.

Axelrod, Robert. *The Evolution of Cooperation*. New York: Basic Books, 1984.

———. *Complexity of Cooperation: Agent-Based Models of Competition and Collaboration*. Princeton, NJ: Princeton University Press, 1997.

Bailey, Derek. *Improvisation: Its Nature and Practice in Music*. London: British Sound Library Archive, 1992.

Bard, Alexander, and Jan Söderqvist. *Netocracy: The New Power Elite and Life after Capitalism*. New York: Pearson Education, 2002.

Bateson, Gregory. *Steps toward an Ecology of Mind: Collected Essays in Anthropology, Psychiatry, Evolution and Epistemology*. New York: Ballantine Books, 1972.

Beck, Ulrich. *Risk Society: Towards a New Modernity*. Translated by Mark Ritter. London: Sage Publications, 1992.

———. *World Risk Society*. London: Polity Press, 1999.

Beck, Ulrich, Anthony Giddens, and Scott Lash. *Reflexive Modernization: Politics, Tradition, and Aesthetics in the Modern Social Order*. Stanford, CA: Stanford University Press, 1994.

Belgrad, Daniel. *The Culture of Spontaneity: Improvisation and the Arts in Postwar America*. Chicago: University of Chicago Press, 1998.

Beniger, James. *The Control Revolution: Technological and Economic Origins of the Information Age*. Cambridge, MA: Harvard University Press, 1986.

Bentham, Jeremy. *Jeremy Bentham: The Panopticon Writings*. Edited by Miran Bozovic. London: Verso, 1995.

Berger, Peter L., and Thomas Luckmann. *The Social Construction of Reality: A Treatise on the Sociology of Knowledge*. Garden City, NY: Anchor Books, 1966.

Bergson, Henri. *Time and Free Will: An Essay on the Immediate Data of Consciousness*. Translated by F. L. Pogson. New York: Harper Torchbooks, 1960.

———. *Creative Evolution*. Translated by Arthur Mitchell. New York: Random House, 1944.

Berlin, Isaiah. "Two Concepts of Liberty." 1958. In *Four Essays on Liberty*. Oxford: Oxford University Press, 2002.

Binmore, Ken. Review of *Complexity of Cooperation: Agent-Based Models of Competition and Collaboration*, by Robert Axelrod. *Journal of Artificial Societies and Social Simulation* 1, no. 1 (1998). http://jasss.soc.surrey.ac.uk/1/1/review1.html (accessed September 26, 2008).

Brate, Adam, ed. *Technomanifestos: Visions of the Information Revolutionaries*. New York: Texere, 2002.

Breisach, Ernst. *Historiography: Ancient, Medieval and Modern*. Chicago: University of Chicago Press, 1994.

Brook, Timothy. "Violence as Historical Time." *The Globalization and Autonomy Online Compendium*, June 9, 2005. http://www.globalautonomy.ca/global1/article_print.jsp?index=articles/RA_Brook_Violence.xml (accessed October 10, 2011).

Brown, Gene. *Movie Time*. New York: MacMillan, 1995.

Buchanan, James M. *The Demand and Supply of Public Goods*. Chicago: Rand McNally, 1968.

Buck, Susan J. *The Global Commons: An Introduction*. Washington, DC: Island Press, 1998.

Bugeja, Micheal. *Interpersonal Divide: The Search for Community in a Technological Age*. New York: Oxford University Press, 2005.

Burke, Peter, ed. *New Perspectives on Historical Writing*. University Park, PA: Pennsylvania State University Press, 1992.

Busch, Lawrence. *The Eclipse of Morality: Science, State, and Market*. New York: Aldine de Gruyter Press, 2000.

Carse, James. *Finite and Infinite Games*. New York: The Free Press, 1986.

Castells, Manuel. *The Rise of the Network Society*. Vol. 1 of *The Information Age: Economy, Society and Culture*. Cambridge, MA: Blackwell, 1996.

———. *The Power of Identity*. Vol. 2 of *The Information Age: Economy, Society and Culture*. Cambridge, MA: Blackwell, 1997.

———. *End of Millennium*. Vol. 3 of *The Information Age: Economy, Society and Culture*. Cambridge, MA: Blackwell, 1998.

Chossudovsky, Michel. *The Globalisation of Poverty and the New World Order: Impacts of IMF and World Bank Reforms*. London: Zed Books, 1997.

Clifford, James. *The Predicament of Culture: Twentieth Century Ethnography, Literature, and Art*. Cambridge, MA: Harvard University Press, 1988.

Cole, Helena, and Mark D. Griffiths. "Social Interactions in Massively Multiplayer Online Role-Playing Gamers." *CyberPsychology & Behavior* 10, no. 4 (2007): 575–83.

Collins, Randall. *Macrohistory: Essays in the Sociology of the Long Run*. Stanford, CA: Stanford University Press, 1999.

Cook, Francis. *Hua-yen Buddhism: The Jewel Net of Indra*. University Park, PA: Pennsylvania State University Press, 1977.

Davis, Mike. *Planet of Slums*. London: Verso, 2006

Deleuze, Gilles. *Bergsonism*. Translated by Hugh Tomlinson and Barbara Habberjam. New York: Zone Books, 1991.

———. *Difference and Repetition*. Translated by Paul Patton. New York: Columbia University Press, 1995.

Deleuze, Gilles, and Felix Guattari. *Anti-Oedipus: Capitalism and Schizophrenia*. Translated by Robert Hurley, Mark Seem, and Helen R. Lane. Minneapolis, MN: University of Minnesota Press, 1983.

———. *A Thousand Plateaus: Capitalism and Schizophrenia*. Translated by Brian Massumi. Minneapolis, MN: University of Minnesota Press, 1987.

———. *What is Philosophy?* Translated by Hugh Tomlinson and Graham Burchell. New York: Columbia University Press, 1994.

Derrida, Jacques. *Writing and Difference*. Translated by Alan Bass. Chicago: University of Chicago Press, 1978.

Diamond, Jared. *Collapse: How Societies Choose to Fail or Succeed*. New York: Penguin Books, 2006.

Digha Nikāya. Translated by Maurice Walshe. Boston: Wisdom Publications, 1995.

Dorfman, Ben. "Thinking the World: A Comment on Philosophy of History and Globalization Studies." *International Social Science Review* 80 (Fall–Winter 2005): 103–18.

Dworkin, Ronald. "What Is Equality? Part 1: Equality of Welfare." *Philosophy and Public Affairs* 10 (Summer 1981(a)): 185–246.

———. "What Is Equality? Part 2: Equality of Resources." *Philosophy and Public Affairs* 10 (Autumn 1981(b)): 283–345.

Edel, May and Abraham Edel. Anthropology and Ethics: The Quest for Moral Understanding. Cleveland, OH: Press of Case Western University, 1968.

Farias, Victor. *Heidegger and Nazism*. Philadelphia, PA: Temple University Press, 1991.

Ferreira, Francisco H. G., and Michael Walton. *Equity and Development* (A World Bank Report). New York: Oxford University Press, 2005.

Fischlin, Daniel. "Improvisation and the Unnameable: On Being Instrumental." *Critical Studies in Improvisation* 5, no. 1 (Winter 2009). http://www.criticalimprov.com/issue/view/97 (accessed November 10, 2011).

Fischlin, Daniel, and Ajay Heble, eds. *The Other Side of Nowhere: Jazz, Improvisation and Communities in Dialogue*. Middletown, CT: Wesleyan University Press, 2004.

Flynn, Dennis O. *World Silver and Monetary History in the 16th and 17th Centuries*. Aldershot, UK: Variorum, 1996.

Foucault, Michel. *Discipline and Punish: The Birth of the Prison*. Translated by Alan Sheridan. New York: Vintage, 1997.

Franck, Georg. (1999a) "The Economy of Attention." *Telepolis*, July 12, 1999. http://www.heise.de/tp/artikel/5/5567/1.html (accessed October 1, 2011).

————. (1999b) "Scientific Communication—A Vanity Fair?" *Science* 286, no. 5437 (October 1, 1999): 53–55.

Fraser, Nancy. "From Redistribution to Recognition? Dilemmas of Justice in a 'Postsocialist' Age." *New Left Review* I/212 (July–August 1995): 68–93.

Fraser, Nancy, and Axel Honneth. *Redistribution or Recognition? A Political-Philosophical Exchange.* Translated by Joel Golb, James Ingram, and Christiane Wilke. New York: Verso, 2003.

Friedman, Thomas L. *The Lexus and the Olive Tree: Understanding Globalization.* New York: Farrar, Straus and Giroux, 2000.

————. *The World is Flat: A Brief History of the 21st Century.* New York: Farrar, Straus and Giroux, 2005.

Fukuyama, Francis. *The End of History and the Last Man.* New York: Avon Books, 1992.

Galbraith, John Kenneth. *The Affluent Society.* 4th ed. Boston: Houghton Mifflin, 1984.

Garfield, Jay L. *The Fundamental Wisdom of the Middle Way: Nagarjuna's Mulamadhyamakakarika.* Oxford: Oxford University Press, 1995.

Georgescu-Roegen, Nicholas. *The Entropy Law and the Economic Process.* Cambridge, MA: Harvard University Press, 1971

Gergen, Kenneth J. "The Self in the Age of Information." *Washington Quarterly* 23 (Winter 2000): 201–214.

Giddens, Anthony. *The Transformation of Intimacy.* London: Polity, 1992.

Goldstone, Jack A. "The Rise of the West—or Not? A Revision to Socio-Economic History." World History Archives, February 2001. http://www.hartford-hwp.com/archives/10/114.html (accessed May 6, 2008).

Gray, John. *Berlin.* Princeton, NJ: Princeton University Press, 1996.

Gregory, Peter N. *Inquiry into the Origin of Humanity: An Annotated Translation of Tsung-mi's Yuan jen lun with a Modern Commentary.* Honolulu: Kuroda Institute Book, University of Hawaii Press, 1995.

Guerloc, Suzanne. *Thinking in Time: An Introduction to Henri Bergson.* Cornell University Press, 2006.

Guptan, Ashin Das. *Merchants of Maritime India, 1500–1800.* Aldershot, UK: Variorum, 1994.

Gutmann, Amy, and Dennis Thompson. *Democracy and Disagreement.* Cambridge, MA: Belknap Press of Harvard University Press, 1996.

Habermas, Jurgen. *The Philosophical Discourse of Modernity.* Translated by Frederick Lawrence. Cambridge, MA: MIT Press, 1987.

————. *The Theory of Communicative Action.* Translated by Thomas McCarthy. Boston: Beacon Press, 1981.

Hall, David L. *The Uncertain Phoenix.* New York: Fordham University Press, 1982.

Hall, David L., and Roger T. Ames. *Anticipating China: Thinking through the Narratives of Chinese and Western Culture.* Albany, NY: State University of New York Press, 1995.

Hardin, Garret. "The Tragedy of the Commons." *Science* 162, no. 3859 (December 13, 1968): 1243–48.

Harrison, Ann, ed. *Globalization and Poverty.* Chicago: University of Chicago Press, 2006. (A National Bureau of Economic Research Conference Report).

Harvey, David. *The Condition of Postmodernity: An Enquiry into the Origins of Cultural Change.* Cambridge, UK: Blackwell, 1990.

———. *Justice, Nature and the Geography of Difference.* Oxford: Blackwell, 1996.

———. *Spaces of Hope.* Berkeley: University of California Press, 2000.

———. *Spaces of Global Capitalism: Towards a Theory of Uneven Geographical Development.* London: Verso, 2006.

———. *A Brief History of Neo-Liberalism.* New York: Oxford University Press, 2005

Heidegger, Martin. *Poetry, Language, Thought.* Translated by Alfred Hofstadter. New York: Harper and Row, 1971.

———. *Being and Time: A Translation of Sein und Zeit.* Translated by Joan Stambaugh. Albany, NY: State University of New York Press, 1996.

Hershock, Peter D. *Liberating Intimacy: Enlightenment and Social Virtuosity in Chan Buddhism.* Albany, NY: State University of New York Press, 1996.

———. *Reinventing the Wheel: A Buddhist Response to the Information Age.* Albany, NY: State University of New York Press, 1999.

———. "Dramatic Intervention: Human Rights from a Buddhist Perspective." *Philosophy East and West* 50, no. 1 (January 2000): 9–33.

———. "Media, Attention and the Colonization of Consciousness: A Buddhist Perspective." In *Reason and Insight: Western and Eastern Perspectives on the Pursuit of Moral Wisdom*, edited by Timothy Shanahan and Robin Wang, 412–19. Florence, KY: Wadsworth Publishing, 2002

———. "Buddhist Philosophy as Buddhist Practice." In *From Africa to Zen: An Invitation to World Philosophy*, 2nd ed., edited by Robert C. Solomon and Kathleen M. Higgins, 239–54. Lantham, MD: Rowman and Littlefield Publishers, 2003.

———. "Turning Away from Technotopia: Critical Precedents for Refusing the Colonization of Consciousness." In *Technology and Cultural Values: On the Edge of the Third Millennium*, edited by Peter D. Hershock, Marietta Stepaniants, and Roger T. Ames, 587–600. Honolulu: University of Hawaii Press, 2003.

———. *Chan Buddhism.* Honolulu: University of Hawaii Press, 2005.

———. *Buddhism in the Public Sphere: Reorienting Global Interdependence.* London: Routledge, 2006.

———. "Valuing Karma: A Critical Concept for Orienting Interdependence toward Personal and Public Good." In *Revisioning Karma—The eBook*, edited by Charles Prebish, Damien Keown, and Dale S. Wright. JBE Online Books, 2008.

———. "Diversity Matters: Buddhist Reflections on the Meaning of Difference." In *A Companion to Buddhist Philosophy*, edited by Steven Emmanuel. New York: Wiley-Blackwell (forthcoming).

Heyne, Paul. "Economics and Ethics: The Problem of Dialogue." In *Belief and Ethics*, edited by W. W. Schroeder and G. Winter, 183–98. . Chicago: Center for the Scientific Study of Religion, 1978.

Honneth, Axel. *The Struggle for Recognition: The Moral Grammar of Social Conflicts.* Translated by Joel Anderson. Cambridge, MA: MIT Press, 1996.

Hornborg, Alf. 2001. *The Power of the Machine: Global Inequalities of Economy, Technology and Environment*, Walnut Creek, CA: AltaMira Press

Hutcheon, Pat Duffy. "Value Theory: Toward Conceptual Clarification." *The British Journal of Sociology* 23 (June 1972): 172–87.

Illich, Ivan. *Tools for Conviviality.* New York: Harper and Row, 1973.

Jameson, Fredric. *Postmodernity, or, The Cultural Logic of Late Capitalism.* Durham, NC: Duke University Press, 1991.

Johnson, Paul. *The Birth of the Modern: World Society 1815–1830.* New York: Harper and Row, 1991.

Jullien, Francois. *Detour and Access: Strategies of Meaning in China and Greece.* Translated by Sophie Hawkes. New York: Zone Books, 2000.

Kaul, Inge, Pedro Conceical, Katell Le Goulven, and Ronald U. Mendoza, eds. *Global Public Goods: International Cooperation in the 21st Century.* Oxford: Oxford University Press, 1999.

Kaul, Inge. "Public Goods: Taking the Concept to the 21st Century." In *The Market of the Public Domain: Global Governance and the Asymmetry of Power,* edited by Daniel Drache, 255–73. . London: Routledge, 2001.

Kaul, Inge, and Ronald U. Mendoza. "Advancing the Concept of Public Goods." In *Providing Global Public Goods: Managing Globalization,* edited by Inge Kaul, Pedro Conceical, Katell Le Goulven, and Ronald U. Mendoza, 78–111. Oxford: Oxford University Press, 2003.

Kennedy, Robert F., Jr. *Crimes against Nature: How George W. Bush and His Corporate Pals Are Plundering the Country and Hijacking Our Democracy.* New York: HarperCollins, 2004.

Keohane, Robert O., and Elinor Ostrom, eds. *Local Commons and Global Interdependence: Heterogeneity and Cooperation in Two Domains.* London: Sage Publications, 1995.

Koggel, Christine. *Perspectives on Equality: Constructing a Relational Theory.* New York; Rowman and Littlefield, 1998.

Kompridis, Nikolas. "Normativizing Hybridity/Neutralizing Culture." *Political Theory* 33, no. 3 (June 2005): 318–43.

Korten, David C. *When Corporations Rule the World.* Bloomfield, CT, and San Francisco: Kumarian Press and Berrett-Koehler Publishers, 2001.

Kruks, Sonja. *Retrieving Experience: Subjectivity and Recognition in Feminist Politics.* Ithaca, NY: Cornell University Press, 2001.

Kymlicka, Will. *Multicultural Citizenship.* Oxford: Oxford University Press, 1995.

LaFleur, William R., Gernot Bohme, and Shimazono Susumu, eds. *Dark Medicine: Rationalizing Unethical Medical Research.* Bloomington, IN: Indiana University Press, 2007.

Lakoff, George, and Mark Johnson. *Metaphors We Live By.* Chicago: University of Chicago Press, 1980.

Lanham, Richard A. . *The Economics of Attention: Style and Substance in the Age of Information.* Chicago: University of Chicago Press, 2006.

Lash, Scott. "Reflexivity and its Doubles: Structure, Aesthetics, Community." In *Reflexive Modernization: Politics, Tradition and Aesthetics in the Modern Social Order,* edited by Beck, Giddens, and Lash. Stanford, CA: Stanford University Press, 1994.

———. *Critique of Information.* London: Sage Publications, 2002

Lemert, Charles, and Anthony Elliott. *Deadly Worlds: The Emotional Costs of Globalization*. New York: Rowman and Littlefield, 2006.

Lemke, J. L. "Discourse, Dynamics and Social Change." *Cultural Dynamics* 6, no. 1 (1994): 243–75.

Levinas, Emmanuel. *Totality and Infinity: A Treatise on Exteriority*. Translated by Alphonso Lingis. Pittsburg, PA: Duquesne University Press, 1961.

———. *Otherwise than Being or Beyond Essence*. Translated by Alphonso Lingis. Boston: Martinus Nijhoff, 1981.

———. *Difficult Freedom: Essay on Judaism*. Translated by Sean Hand. Baltimore, MD: Johns Hopkins University Press, 1990.

———. "Meaning and Sense." 1972. In *Collected Philosophical Papers*, translated by Alphonso Lingis. Boston: Martinus Nijhoff Publishers, 1987.

Linji. *Zhenzhou Linji Huizhao chanshi yulu*. Taishō shinshū daizōkyō, Volume 47, Number 1985.

Lipset, Seymour Martin, and Gary Marks. *It Didn't Happen Here: Why Socialism Failed in the United States*. New York: W. W. Norton, 2001.

Lowe, Donald M. . *The Body in Late-Capitalist USA*. Durham, NC: Duke University Press, 1995.

Löwith, Karl. *Nietzsche's Philosophy of the Eternal Recurrence of the Same*. Translated by J. Harvey Lomax. Berkeley: University of California Press, 1997.

Luhmann, Niklas. *The Reality of the Mass Media*. Translated by Kathleen Cross. Stanford, CA: Stanford University Press, 2000.

Luke, Allan. "Curriculum, Ethics, Metanarrative: Teaching and Learning beyond the Nation." In *Struggles over Difference: Curriculum, Texts and Pedagogy in the Asia-Pacific*, edited by Yoshiko Nozaki, Roger Openshaw, and Allan Luke, 11–24. . Albany, NY: State University of New York Press, 2005.

Lyotard, Jean-François. *The Postmodern Condition: A Report on Knowledge*. Translated by Geoff Bennington and Brian Massumi. Minneapolis, MN: University of Minnesota Press, 1984.

Mason, John Hope. *The Value of Creativity: The Origins and Emergence of a Modern Belief*. Aldershot, Hampshire, UK: Ashgate, 2003.

May, Todd. *Reconsidering Difference: Nancy, Derrida, Levinas and Deleuze*. University Park, PA: Pennsylvania University Press, 1997.

McBride, Cillian. "Deliberative Democracy and the Politics of Recognition." *Political Studies* 53, no. 3 (September 2005): 497–515.

MacIntyre, Alasdair. *After Virtue*. Notre Dame: Notre Dame University Press, 1984.

Mead, George Herbert. *Mind, Self and Society: From the Standpoint of a Social Behaviorist*. Chicago: University of Chicago Press, 1934.

Mookherjee, Monica. "Affective Citizenship: Feminism, Postcolonialism and the Politics of Recognition." *Critical Review of International Social and Political Philosophy* 8, no. 1 (Winter 2005): 31–50.

Nakayama, Wataru, William Boulton, and Micheal G. Pecht. *The Japanese Electronics Industry*. Boca Raton, FL: CRC Press, 1999.

Nancy, Jean Luc. *The Inoperative Community*. Translated by Simona Sawhney. Minneapolis, MN: Minnesota University Press, 1991.

————. *Being Singular Plural*. Translated by Robert Richardson and Anne O'Byrne. Stanford, CA: Stanford University Press, 2000.

Noë, Alva. "Experience and the Active Mind." *Synthese* 129 (2001): 41–69.

Olson, Mancur. *The Logic of Collective Action: Public Goods and the Theory of Groups*. Cambridge, MA: Harvard University Press, 1965.

O'Shaughnessy, John, and Nicholas Jackson O'Shaughnessy. *The Marketing Power of Emotion*. New York: Oxford University Press, 2003

Ostrom, Elinor. *Governing the Commons: The Evolution of Institutions for Collective Action*. Cambridge, UK: Cambridge University Press, 1990.

Page, Scott. *The Difference: How the Power of Diversity Creates Better Groups, Firms, Schools and Societies*. Princeton, NJ: Princeton University Press, 2007.

Parekh, Bhikhu. *Rethinking Multiculturalism: Cultural Diversity and Political Theory*. Cambridge, MA: Harvard University Press, 2000.

Paxton, Robert O. *The Anatomy of Fascism*. New York: Knopf, 2004.

Peters, Gary. *The Philosophy of Improvisation*. Chicago: University of Chicago Press, 2009.

Polanyi, Karl. *The Great Transformation: The Political and Economic Origins of our Time*. Boston: Beacon Press, 2001.

Pomeranz, Kenneth. *The Great Divergence: China, Europe, and the Making of the Modern World Economy*. Princeton, NJ: Princeton University Press, 2000.

Powers, Richard. *Gain*. New York: Farrar, Straus and Giroux, 1998.

Qvortrup, Lars. *The Hypercomplex Society*. New York: Peter Lang, 2003.

Rao, J. Mohan. "Equity in a Public Goods Framework." In *Global Public Goods: International Cooperation in the 21st Century*, edited by Inge Kaul, Pedro Conceical, Katell Le Goulven, and Ronald U. Mendoza, 68–87. . Oxford: Oxford University Press, 1999.

Rawls, John. *A Theory of Justice*. Cambridge, MA: Belknap Press, 1971.

————. *Justice as Fairness: A Restatement*. Cambridge, MA: Belknap Press, 2001.

Reich, Robert. *After-Shock: The Next Economy and America's Future*. New York: Alfred Knopf Publishing, 2010.

Rheingold, Howard. *The Virtual Community: Homesteading on the Electronic Frontier*. Reading, MA: Addison-Wesley Press, 1993.

————. *Tools for Thought: The History and Future of Mind-Expanding Technologies*. Cambridge, MA: MIT Press, 2000.

Rifkin, Jeremy. *The End of Work: The Decline of the Global Labor Force and the Dawn of the Post-Market Era*. New York: G. P. Putnam's Sons, 1995.

Robinson, Richard H., and Willard L. Johnson, eds. *The Buddhist Religion: A Historical Introduction*. Belmont, CA: Wadsworth Publishing, 1997.

Robinson, William I. *A Theory of Global Capitalism: Production, Class, and State in a Transnational World*. Baltimore, MD: Johns Hopkins University Press, 2004.

Roemer, John. *Equality of Opportunity*. Cambridge, MA: Harvard University Press, 1998.

Rosenau, James. *Distant Proximities: Dynamics beyond Globalization*. Princeton, NJ: Princeton University Press, 2003.

Sacks, Jonathan. *The Dignity of Difference: How to Avoid the Clash of Civilizations*. London: Continuum, 2002.

Samuelson, Paul A. "The Pure Theory of Public Expenditure." *Review of Economics and Statistics* 36, no. 4 (1954): 387–89.

Sandel, Michael. *Liberalism and the Limits of Justice*. New York: Cambridge University Press, 1982.

Sandler, Todd. *Global Challenges: An Approach to Environmental, Political and Economic Problems*. Cambridge: Cambridge University Press, 1997.

Schutz, Alfred. "Making Music Together: A Study in Social Relationship." In *Collected Papers*, Vol. 2, edited by Maurice Natanson, 159–78. The Hague: Martinus Nijhoff, 1976.

Sen, Amartya. *Commodities and Capabilities*. Amsterdam: North-Holland Press, 1985.

———. *Inequality Reexamined*. Cambridge, MA: Harvard University Press, 1992.

———. *Development as Freedom*. New York: Anchor Books, 1999.

———. (1999a) "Global Justice: Beyond International Equity." In *Global Public Goods: International Cooperation in the 21st Century*, edited by Inge Kaul, Pedro Conceical, Katell Le Goulven, and Ronald U. Mendoza, 116–25. Oxford: Oxford University Press, 1999.

———. "Globalizing What? History, Economics, Equity and Efficiency." *Harvard Asia Pacific Review* 6, no. 2 (Fall 2002): 79–82.

Sharf, Robert H. *Coming to Terms with Chinese Buddhism: A Reading of the Treasure Store Treatise*. Honolulu: University of Hawaii Press, 2002.

Shenk, David. *Data Smog: Surviving the Information Glut*. San Francisco, HarperOne, 1997.

Simon, Herbert A. "Designing Organizations for an Information-Rich World." In *Computers, Communication, and the Public Interest*, edited by Martin Greenberger, 37–72. . Baltimore, MD: Johns Hopkins University Press, 1971.

Singer, Peter. *One World: The Ethics of Globalization*. New Haven, CT: Yale University Press, 2002.

Smith, Adam. *An Enquiry into the Nature and Causes of the Wealth of Nations*. New York: Modern Library, 1994.

Sternhell, Zeev, Mario Sznajder, and Maia Asheri. *The Birth of Fascist Ideology*. Translated by David Maisel. New York: Vintage, 2005.

Stiglitz, Joseph. *Globalization and its Discontents*. New York. W. W. Norton and Co., 2002.

Stivers, Richard. *The Illusion of Freedom and Equality*. Albany, NY: State University of New York Press, 2008.

Sutta Nipāta. Translated by H. Saddhatissa. London: Curzon Press, 1985.

Swanson, Paul L. *Foundations of T'ien-t'ai Philosophy: The Flowering of the Two Truths Theory in Chinese Buddhism*. Berkeley, CA: Asian Humanities Press, 1989.

Tan, Sor-Hoon, and John Whalen-Bridge, eds. *Democracy as Culture: Deweyan Pragmatism in a Globalizing World*. Albany, NY: State University of New York Press, 2008.

Taylor, Charles. *Sources of the Self: The Making of the Modern Identity*. Cambridge, MA: Harvard University Press, 1989.

———. *The Ethics of Authenticity*. Cambridge, MA: Harvard University Press, 1992.

———. *Multiculturalism: Examining the Politics of Recognition*. Edited and introduced by Amy Gutmann. Princeton, NJ: Princeton University Press, 1994.

———. *Modern Social Imaginaries*. Durham, NC: Duke University Press, 2004.

Taylor, Mark C. *The Moment of Complexity: Emerging Network Culture*. Chicago: University of Chicago Press, 2001.

———. *Confidence Games: Money and Markets in a World without Redemption*. Chicago: University of Chicago Press, 2004.

Thomas, William I., and Florian Znaniecki. *The Polish Peasant in Europe and America*. Chicago: University of Chicago Press, 1918–1920.

Thompson, Simon. *The Political Theory of Recognition: A Critical Introduction*. Cambridge, UK: Polity Press, 2006.

Toulmin, Stephen. *Cosmopolis: The Hidden Agenda of Modernity*. Chicago: University of Chicago Press, 1990.

United Nations Development Program, *Human Development Report 1999*, Principal Coordinator Richard Jolly. New York: Oxford University Press, 1999. Available online: http://hdr.undp.org/en/media/HDR_1999_EN.pdf (accessed March 11, 2012)

Vickers, Douglas. *Economics and Ethics: An Introduction to Theory, Institutions, and Policy*. Westport, CT: Praeger, 1997.

Wagner, Peter. *A Sociology of Modernity, Liberty and Discipline*, London: Routledge, 1994.

Williams, Raymond. *Marxism and Literature*. Oxford, UK: Oxford University Press, 1977.

Willson, Michelle A. *Technically Together: Rethinking Community within Techno-Society*. New York: Peter Lang Publishing, 2006.

Wynne, Brian with Scott Lash, and Bronislaw Szersynski, eds. *Risk, Environment and Modernity: Towards a New Ecology*. London: Sage Publications, 1996.

Young, Iris Marion. *Justice and the Politics of Difference*. Princeton, NJ: Princeton University Press, 1990.

———. *Inclusion and Democracy*. Oxford: Oxford University Press, 2000.

Young, H. Peyton. *Equity in Theory and Practice*. Princeton, NJ: Princeton University Press, 1994.

Zengotita, Thomas de. *Mediated: How the Media Shapes Your World and the Way You Live in It*. Bloomsbury: New York, 2005.

Zinn, Howard. *A People's History of the United States: 1492 to Present*. New York: Harper Perennial, 2001.

Ziporyn, Brook. *Being and Ambiguity: Philosophical Experiments with Tiantai Buddhism*. Chicago and LaSalle, IL: Open Court, 2004.

Index

Index

Made in the USA
San Bernardino, CA
18 March 2014